RENEWALS 458-4574

	DATE DUE		
GAYLORD			PRINTED IN U.S.A.

Network Management
Know It All

Sebastian Abeck

Igor Bryskin

John Evans

Adrian Farrel

Clarence Filsfils

Heinz-Gerd Hegering

James D. McCabe

Monique Morrow

Thomas P. Nadeau

Bernhard Neumair

Rajiv Ramaswami

Kumar N. Sivarajan

John Strassner

Kateel Vijayananda

ELSEVIER

AMSTERDAM • BOSTON • HEIDELBERG • LONDON
NEW YORK • OXFORD • PARIS • SAN DIEGO
SAN FRANCISCO • SINGAPORE • SYDNEY • TOKYO

Morgan Kaufmann is an imprint of Elsevier

MORGAN KAUFMANN PUBLISHERS

Morgan Kaufmann Publishers is an imprint of Elsevier.
30 Corporate Drive, Suite 400,
Burlington, MA 01803

This book is printed on acid-free paper. ∞

Library of Congress Cataloging-in-Publication Data
Network management : know it all / Adrian Farrel . . . [et al.].
    p.   cm. — (Morgan Kaufmann know it all series)
    Includes bibliographical references and index.
    ISBN 978-0-12-374598-9 (alk. paper)
    1. Computer networks—Management.   I. Farrel, Adrian.
TK5105.5.N4661855 2009
004.6068—dc22   2008039610

For information on all Morgan Kaufmann publications,
visit our Website at *www.mkp.com or www.books.elsevier.com*

Printed in the United States
08 09 10 11 12   10 9 8 7 6 5 4 3 2 1

Working together to grow
libraries in developing countries

www.elsevier.com | www.bookaid.org | www.sabre.org

ELSEVIER   BOOK AID International   Sabre Foundation

Contents

Preface

Introduction

Network management is the poor cousin of network design and implementation. All too often it is treated as an inconvenience by equipment manufacturers, or forgotten entirely. But the ability to manage network devices is fundamental to their utility, and a successful and functional network can only be built from equipment that can be easily managed and operated.

Management refers to the ability to configure, control, operate, and diagnose equipment. Of course, no vendor ships devices that cannot be managed, but typically each is operated and controlled in a different way. This is not a problem for the vendor, and might not be a problem for a network operator if all equipment in the network is located at the same site and purchased from the same vendor. Obviously, however, networks are dispersed across large distances, have components in unattended sites, and are constructed from switches and routers supplied by various companies (often with different versions and releases of the devices that come from the same firm). This makes diverse network management approaches a significant hurdle to efficient and effective network operation.

The resultant mélange of control mechanisms leaves the operator with a wide array of tools that must be used for each day-to-day management task. A lot of money has been spent attempting to develop unified provisioning systems, operations support systems, and network management systems that can present a single interface to users while managing a range of equipment. These have been partially successful, but are chronically difficult to maintain and must be updated for every new release from a vendor and for each new piece of equipment installed in the network.

Over the years, various attempts have been made to standardize the way in which networks and network equipment are managed. Many standards bodies— the International Standards Organization, the International Telecommunications Union, the TeleManagement Forum, the Internet Engineering Task Force, the Object Management Group, and the Multiservice Switching Forum, to name just six—have devoted considerable time and effort to specifying architectures, data schemas, and management communication protocols.

One general view is that the subject of network management should be separated into five distinct subtopics known by the acronym FCAPS: fault management, configuration management, accounting management, performance management, and security management. Note that these relate to the management aspects in each case and not to the underlying principles. Thus, for example, security management relates to how security is configured, enabled, and operated within a network, but does not relate directly to the security procedures themselves. Another approach that has strong support is to manage the network through a set of policies that are configured by the operator and distributed to the devices that act within the network according to the instructions they have been given.

However, the solutions proposed by these different standards bodies compete among themselves, and each vendor must select which one(s) to support. Even then, vendors may continue to prefer their own, in-house management techniques and only pay lip-service to the standardized approaches. The nightmare continues!

This Book's Content

This book contains eleven chapters arranged in order to introduce the material starting with the basics, leading on through the application of network management to different areas of networking technology from Internet Protocol (IP) and Multiprotocol Label Switching (MPLS) to optical networking and Generalized MPLS (GMPLS), and culminating in a discussion of policy-based management.

Chapter 1 sets the scene for the rest of the book by presenting sample scenarios from a variety of different application areas with completely different levels of abstraction to outline some of the requirements for the management of networked systems. The chapter shows that the requirements vary considerably. It appears, therefore, that it is sensible to consider whether the management functions should be structured as a whole to give a consistency across application types and deployment scenarios. The discussion in the chapter considers this possibility and looks at the complexity of "management" from the standpoint of functional areas, life cycles, and organizational consequences.

Chapter 2 gives an overview of centralized and standardized techniques for remote management of the devices that make up a network. It begins with a brief description of the benefits of network management and then discusses some common techniques for the collection of operational statistics and the motivation for doing so. The chapter moves on to compare the benefits of proprietary configuration methods with standardized approaches. Then individual sections introduce some of the standardized management models, including Management Information Bases (MIBs), the Simple Network Management Protocol (SNMP), the eXtensible Markup Language (XML), and the Common Object Request Broker Architecture (CORBA). After a discussion of the differences between the models, the chapter concludes with a section describing the use of *policy* within modern networks.

Chapter 3 discusses the implementation and delivery of IP-based services. While technology plays an important role in developing services, it is also important that the services be provisioned and delivered in an easy and profitable manner. *Easy and profitable* here refers to the scalability of the solution in terms of the staffing and skills required to implement the solution for a mass market. Technical implementation in the lab is an academic exercise to show the feasibility of a solution. This solution may not be profitable for a service provider if provisioning the service for a large number of customers is too expensive or time consuming.

Chapter 4 examines the component architecture for network management. Proper management is critical to the success of any network, and this chapter shows the many factors to consider in providing network management. It discusses the various functions of network management and the mechanisms used to achieve these functions. In addition, the chapter discusses and compares a number of variations for network management architecture, as well as the internal and external network management relationships.

Chapter 5 describes the technologies and techniques available for service level agreement (SLA) and network monitoring in QoS-enabled IP networks. Two main approaches are generally used in concert to monitor performance of a QoS-enabled network service to determine whether SLAs have been or can be met: passive network monitoring and active network monitoring. The chapter examines the implications of using each of these approaches and contrasts them to help you understand when to use each one.

Chapter 6 looks at the origins of MPLS and introduces some of its basic concepts, including the separation of the control and forwarding planes of MPLS, the Forward Equivalence Class, and the MPLS label, as well as some of the new applications of MPLS networks such as traffic engineering and virtual private networks. After this introduction to MPLS, the chapter explains the basic premise behind why MPLS-enabled networks need to be managed to provide scalable; usable; and, most important, *profitable* MPLS networks. Given this motivation, the author describes how MPLS networks can be managed effectively using both standards-based and nonstandard tools, many of which are described in this book.

Chapter 7 introduces several different types of management interfaces that may be used to manage MPLS deployments. In particular, it presents an introduction to XML, CORBA, SNMP, and the command-line interface (CLI). There is an investigation and explanation of why operators might or might not wish to use one, none, or all of these interfaces to manage their MPLS networks, as well as to hopefully provide device vendors with reasons why they should or should not implement them on their MPLS devices. The end of the chapter focuses particularly on the SNMP interface by introducing it in such a way that it may be understood for use in managing MPLS networks.

Chapter 8 starts with a brief introduction to network management concepts in general and how they apply to managing optical networks. This is followed with a discussion of optical layer services and how the different aspects of the optical network are managed. The chapter notes that however attractive a specific technology might be, it can be deployed in a network only if it can be managed and interoperates with existing management systems. The cost of operating and managing a large network is a recurring expense and in many cases dominates the cost of the equipment deployed in the network. As a result, carriers are now paying a lot of attention to minimizing *life cycle* costs, as opposed to worrying just about up-front equipment costs.

Chapter 9 introduces some of the ways GMPLS networks and devices can be provisioned and managed. GMPLS reduces the management burden in transport networks by offloading functions from the operator and management plane to the control plane. From the perspective of operators at their consoles in the Network Operations Center, there may be very little visible difference between the tools used to manage a traditional transport network and a GMPLS-enabled network; however, it would be a mistake to assume that the efficiency or mode of operation of the underlying transport plane is unchanged. The GMPLS control plane ensures that operators are always working with the most up-to-date information and also makes sure that the services are managed efficiently by the management plane. Nevertheless, the management plane is an essential component of the GMPLS-enabled network. The chapter also examines the structure that is applied to the management framework for GMPLS networks.

Chapter 10 provides a brief retrospective about how Policy-Based Network Management (PBNM) has been conceived in the past. Policy management means many things to many people, and this chapter presents the fundamentals. This material is used to point out two basic problems of previous solutions: the lack of use of an information model and the inability to use business rules to drive configuration of devices, services, and networks. A path forward, and benefits resulting from this improved approach, are described.

Chapter 11 introduces the basic terms and definitions used in the study of policy management, as well as a simplified conceptual policy model. This is followed by a description of the high-level system requirements of a policy-based network management system. Key among these requirements is the notion that business rules drive the construction and deployment of device and network configuration. This approach enables the network to be operated as a profit center instead of a cost center. The chapter describes where policy-based management systems fit in to the overall scheme of management systems and provides an introduction to their operating context.

A final section of this book provides a list of references for further reading extracted from all of the chapters that make up this book.

Source Material

Of course, many of the topics covered here have already been described at length in other books. The Morgan Kaufmann Series in Networking includes a comprehensive range of titles that deal with many aspects of network management.

However, each book in the series has as its main focus a particular function or technology. In some cases source texts are entirely devoted to the subject, while other chapters are included from more general works in which network management is presented as one aspect of some specific technology such as MPLS or optical networking.

Therefore, what we have done in this book is to bring together material from nine sources to provide you with a thorough grounding in network management. When necessary we have edited the source material; however, on the whole, the original text provides a rounded view of a particular author's thoughts on the subject and is simply reproduced here. This results in a single reference that introduces network management and explains the basics. Readers wanting to know more about a particular topic are encouraged to go to the sources and read more.

There is some intentional overlap in the subject matter presented in this book, and this is. All of the contributing authors have their own specific take on how to present the problems of network management, and their own views on how issues should be solved. By providing readers with the full text from the selected chapters, we hope that we will give you a broad view of the problem space and allow you to make up your own mind about the challenges that must be addressed.

In producing *Network Management: Know It All* we have drawn on material from the following Morgan Kaufmann books.

Integrated Management of Networked Systems: Concepts, Architectures, and Their Operational Application by Hegering, Abeck, and Neumair—This comprehensive book covers the architecture, implementation, and operational use of all the major approaches to management currently in favor. It is a must-have for any network or management system architect, and anybody else in need of a thorough understanding of network management technologies, tools, and practices.

The Internet and Its Protocols: A Comparative Approach by Farrel—This book covers all the common IP-based protocols and shows how they combine to create the Internet in its totality. Each protocol, including the various MPLS and GMPLS ones, is described completely, with an examination of the requirements that the protocols address and the exact means by which they do the job.

Developing IP-Based Services by Morrow and Vijayananda—This book meets the challenge of uniting business and technical perspectives to provide a cohesive view of the MPLS development and deployment process that enables networking organizations to leverage IP and MPLS to drive traffic and boost revenue.

Network Analysis, Architecture, and Design, Third Edition, by McCabe—In this book, James McCabe provides readers with design methods they can use to avoid the common pitfalls of poorly functioning networks caused by network designer's' temptation to jump straight into implementation without first understanding the scope of the problem. The book covers the step-by-step progression through proven processes that will result in designs that are not only viable, but designs that will also stand up to the scrutiny of technical and financial reviews.

Deploying IP and MPLS QoS for Multiservice Networks: Theory and Practice by Evans and Filsfils—The authors of this book have provided a comprehensive treatise on the subject of QoS in IP and MPLS networks. They have included topics such as traffic engineering, capacity planning, and admission control. It provides real- world case studies about multiservice networks to help remove the mystery behind QoS by illustrating the how, what, and why of implementing QoS within networks.

MPLS Network Management by Nadeau—Practical information on managing MPLS networks remains scarce, but this book, written by the coauthor of most of the MPLS management standards, provides a comprehensive view of the relevant techniques and tools.

Optical Networks, Second Edition, by Ramaswami and Sivarajan—Fiber-optic networks are established as a crucial part of the core of today's telecommunications and data networking infrastructures. Second-generation, all-optical networks that fully exploit the enormous bandwidth capacity of fiber are just beginning to emerge. This book is an indispensable and practical guide, written by two of the principal architects of wavelength division multiplexing, that explores the driving need for all-optical networks, the economic trade-offs involved, and their fundamental capabilities and design.

GMPLS: Architecture and Applications by Farrel and Bryskin—The relatively new area of GMPLS is not covered in detail by many books; however, this one, written by two leading engineers who have been involved in the design of the GMPLS protocols from the very start, presents a deep and broad view of GMPLS from the protocol essentials, through the early deployment functions, to advanced and future topics.

Policy-Based Network Management by Strassner—PBNM systems enable business rules and procedures to be translated into policies that configure and control the network and its services. This book cuts through the hype surrounding PBNM and makes it approachable for those who really need to understand what it has to offer. It discusses system requirements, information models, and system components for policy-based management.

Adrian Farrel

Contributing Authors

Sebastian Abeck (Chapter 1) received the diploma and doctorate degrees in computer science from the Technical University of Munich in 1987 and 1991, respectively. Until 1996, he worked as a senior researcher with the Munich Network Management Team. During that time he designed and implemented management solutions for large-scale IT service providers. He is now a professor at the University of Karlsruhe, where he teaches networking and distributed systems.

Igor Bryskin (Chapter 9) is Chief Protocol Architect at ADVA Optical, Inc., where he is responsible for high-level and detailed architecture of the Generalized Multiprotocol Label Switching (GMPLS) control plane software running on ADVA's optical cross-connects. He has been involved in data communications since the 1980s, and since the 1990s he has worked primarily in the areas of IP/MPLS and ATM. Igor has served as principal author or coauthor of several Internet drafts and RFCs in the area of MPLS and GMPLS.

John Evans (Chapter 5) is a Distinguished Consulting Engineer with Cisco Systems, where he has been instrumental in the engineering and deployment of QoS and policy control. His current areas of focus include policy/resource control, admission control, QoS, and traffic management, with associated work in the DSL Forum, the Multiservice Forum, and ETSI/TISPAN. Prior to joining Cisco in 1998, John worked for BT, where was responsible for the design and development of large-scale networks for the financial community. Prior to BT, he worked on the design and deployment of battlefield communications networks for the military. He received a B.Eng. degree in electronic engineering with honors from the University of Manchester Institute of Science and Technology (UMIST now part of the University of Manchester), UK, in 1991 and an M.Sc. in communications engineering from UMIST in 1996. He is a Chartered Engineer (CEng) and Cisco Certified Internetworking Expert (CCIE).

Adrian Farrel (Chapters 2 and 9) has more than two decades of experience designing and developing portable communications software. At Old Dog Consulting, he is an industry-leading freelance consultant on MPLS, GMPLS, and Internet routing. Formerly he worked as MPLS Architect for Data Connection Ltd. and as Director of Protocol Development for Movaz Networks Inc. He is active within the Internet Engineering Task Force, where he is co-chair of the CCAMP working group responsible for GMPLS, the Path Computation Element (PCE) working group, and the Layer One VPN (L1VPN) working group. Adrian has co-authored and contributed to numerous Internet Drafts and RFCs on MPLS, GMPLS, and related technologies.

Clarence Filsfils (Chapter 5) is a Cisco Distinguished System Engineer and a recognized expert in Routing and QoS. He has been playing a key role in engineering, marketing, and deploying the QoS and Fast Routing Convergence technology at Cisco Systems. Clarence is a regular speaker at conferences, has published several journal articles, and holds more than 30 patents on QoS and routing mechanisms.

Heinz-Gerd Hegering (Chapter 1) is a professor of Informatics at Ludwig Maximillians Universität. Since 1989, he has been the chairman of the Board of Directors of Leibniz Computing Centre (LRZ) of the Bavarian Academy of Sciences and Humanities. He is also a member of various organizations including the National Coordination Board for Supercomputing of the Wissenschaftsrat, the Steering Committee of the German eScience Initiative D-Grid, and numerous governmental IT planning committees and the External Committee of the Bavarian Minister-President's Office.

James D. McCabe (Chapter 4), Network Architect for BeamReach Networks, is the recipient of multiple NASA awards and holds patents in supercomputer network research. He has been architecting, designing, and deploying high-performance networks for more than 20 years. He also consults, teaches, and writes about network analysis, architecture, and design. McCabe holds degrees in chemical engineering and pPhysics from the Georgia Institute of Technology and Georgia State University.

Monique Morrow (Chapter 3) is currently CTO Consulting Engineer at Cisco Systems. She has 20 years of experience in IP internetworking, including design implementation of complex customer projects and service deployment. Morrow has been involved in developing managed network services such as remote access and LAN switching in a service provider environment. She has worked for both enterprise companies and service providers in the United States and in Europe, and led the Engineering Project team for one of the first European MPLS-VPN deployments in 1999. She has an M.S. in telecommunications management and an M.B.A. in marketing and is a CCIE.

Thomas P. Nadeau (Chapters 6 and 7). Tom works at BT Group, where he is a Senior Network Architect responsible for the end-to-end network architecture of

BT's 21C Network. Prior to BT, Tom worked at Cisco Systems, where he was a technical leader responsible for the leadership and architecture of operations and management for MPLS-related components of Cisco ISO and IOS-XR. This included the areas of pseudowires, common optical control plane (GMPLS), bidirectional forwarding detection (BFD), NetFlow, Service Assurance Agent, layer-2 and layer-3 VPN, traffic engineering, COPS, DiffServ, and SNMP in general.

Bernhard Neumair (Chapter 1) received his diploma and his Ph.D. in computer science from the Munich University of Technology. From 1993 to 1998, he was a senior researcher at the Ludwig-Maximilians University in Munich. In 1998, he joined German Telekom as a group manager for communication solutions.

Rajiv Ramaswami (Chapter 8) leads a group planning and designing photonic switching products at Nortel Networks. He has worked on optical networks since 1988, from early research to product development, including several years at IBM Research, Tellabs, and Xros (now part of Nortel). He is an IEEE Fellow and a recipient of the IEEE W. R. G. Baker and W. R. Bennett prize paper awards, as well as an Outstanding Innovation award from IBM.

Kumar N. Sivarajan (Chapter 8) is cofounder and CTO at Tejas Networks, an optical networking start-up in Bangalore, India. He has worked on optical, wireless, ATM, and Internet networking technologies for more than a decade, first at IBM Research and then at the Indian Institute of Science–Bangalore. He is a recipient of the IEEE W. R. G. Baker and W. R. Bennett prize paper awards.

John Strassner (Chapters 10 and 11), Chief Security Officer of Intelliden Corporation, has occupied high-level roles for a number of prominent IT companies. At Cisco, where he held the distinguished title of Cisco Fellow, he was responsible for defining the overall direction and strategy for creating and deploying intelligent networks and policy-driven networked applications. Strassner has led or served on several standards committees, currently including the DMTF working group. He is frequently an invited speaker at conferences and regularly teaches tutorials on Policy-Based Network Management.

Kateel Vijayananda (Chapter 3) is currently a design consultant at Cisco Systems, has 10 years of experience in data networking, featuring design, implementation, management of IP networks, and software development devoted to OSI protocol stack implementation. He has also been involved in developing managed network service such as LAN switching and LAN interconnect in a service provider environment. Vijayananda has worked as a network engineer/architect for a European service provider, where he was part of teams that designed and implemented an MPLS network and that developed and managed IP-based services on top of an MPLS network. He holds an M.S. and a Ph.D. in computer science and is a CCIE.

Requirements for the Management of Networked Systems

To set the scene for this book, we will start by presenting sample scenarios from a variety of different application areas with completely different levels of abstraction to outline some of the requirements for the management of networked systems. This material is taken from Chapter 3 of *Integrated Management of Networked Systems: Concepts, Architectures, and Their Operational Application* by Hegering, Abeck, and Neumair.

What we find is that the requirements vary. It therefore appears sensible to consider whether the management functions as a whole could be structured in some way. The discussion that follows considers this possibility and looks at the complexity of "management" from the standpoint of functional areas, life cycles, and organizational consequences.

1.1 MANAGEMENT SCENARIOS

The scenarios presented in this section comprise customer network management requirements, management requirements of distributed data storage, central graphics archive, as well as shared document systems. Another scenario deals with help desk support systems and related management problems. Nomadic systems and domain name services make quite different demands on management. Finally, management requirements of backup and archiving systems are discussed.

1.1.1 Scenario 1: Customer Network Management

Figure 1.1 presents the national communications infrastructure (B-WIN) of German scientific institutions around the year 2000. In other words, the public corporate network for the universities and research institutes.

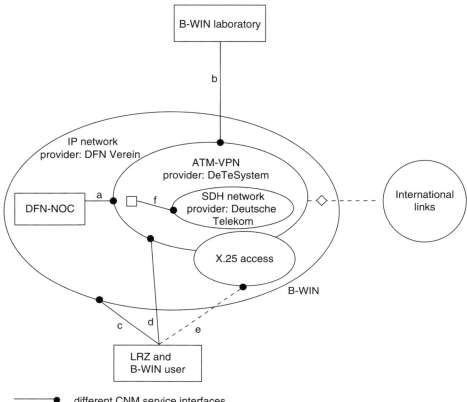

FIGURE 1.1

A German scientific network.

The example shows four customer–provider relationships, which also typify other corporate networks. The following notes apply to the four service providers, their relationships, and the services they provide:

1. *Provider, Deutsche Telekom; Customer, DeTeSystem; Service:* Provision of physical line capacity (SDH hierarchy).

2. *Provider, DeTeSystem; Customer, DFN Verein; Service:* Provision of a virtual network (ATM-VPN) with access capacities of 34 Mbps and 155 Mbps as individual or group access rates with the following types of service: available bit rate, PVC constant bit rate, SVC being planned.

3. *Provider, DFN Verein; Customer, a scientific facility (the one in the example is the Leibniz Supercomputer Center LCC); Service:* IP service (Internet access) and ATM-PVC. DFN Verein provides the mentioned services with the aid of three physically separate groups—the DFN business office, the DFN-NOC (network center), and the DFN laboratory (performance and quality-of-service monitoring).

4. *Provider, LRZ; Customer, universities in Munich, technical departments (each having its own local networks) with a total of more than 100,000 end users; Service:* IP service, directory services, Web hosting, access to diverse special-purpose computers (including supercomputers), and databases; operation from access servers (several hundred telephone-dialed access points, analog/ISDN).

As the example shows, an entire customer–provider hierarchy exists in which the contractual hierarchy and the service hierarchy with its associated technical implementation have different interfaces. The IP service as well as the ATM-PVC service are therefore available to the university end user or LRZ. Contractually, both are provided by DFN Verein; technically, the first one is provided by DFN, the second by DeTeSystem. Management information from a number of lower sources is required for use of a service, the generation of fault reports, performance supervision, and management of the services that are made available to the next highest "level" in the customer–provider chain.

Customer network management stands for the transition from a component-oriented management to a service-related management. Customer and service-relevant criteria are provided.

The scenario given is a complex one, but it provides an insight into a whole range of different management requirements:

- First of all, each provider must manage its own network. An integral part of this task is component management, which concerns the supervision of the availability, capacity utilization, security, and fault-free operation of the individual components. Added to this is the functioning of the network as a whole. This requires management tasks such as routing and switching, multiplexing datastreams, and monitoring logical paths and channels.

- At the access to a network, all providers offer their customers services with a certain quality of service (QoS) based on a service level agreement (SLA). The constant monitoring of service quality is a management task. The management of the customer–provider interface also includes procedures for fault reporting and for service adaptation or service provisioning (e.g., ordering the establishment of an ATM-PVC).

- In a scenario like the preceding one, it is essential that customers have access to specific management information (e.g., service quality, service availability) because this is the information they need if they themselves want to develop added value and other new services based on the network services they are already using. For customers, it is the service-related information based on the customer SLA that is generally interesting rather than the "raw data" from the component management of their providers.

Customer network management (CNM) or customer service management (CSM) is first and foremost a controlled transfer of information by the provider of a communications service to its customers. CNM enables a customer to see the relevant part of a usually public network (i.e., the customer's virtual private network (VPN) represented through management information) as a part of their own network structure. This makes the public network more transparent to customers so that they no longer perceive it as a "black box." Ideally, customers are informed immediately of any problems in the network and can be saved the time of making long and difficult phone calls to find out what is causing a failure.

The management information base (MIB) used by the customer (the CNM-MIB) must reflect services and SLAs. First of all, a data model for the implementation of the CNM-MIB must be defined for the scenario described. The data comprise user and accounting information, statistics and measurement results, and fault reports, as well as breakdown messages, and are derived from many different sources. Furthermore, a process model must be defined that describes the data flow and operation processes involved in obtaining and forwarding information. Lastly, a specification of the CNM service interfaces that provide access to the CNM-MIB is required. In Figure 1.1, individual lowercase letters are used to indicate the different CNM service interfaces.

1.1.2 Scenario 2: Distributed Data Storage

A company's data are stored in many places—on PCs, workstations, servers, and special-purpose computers; in computer centers and departments; within the intranet; and externally with suppliers and dealers.

Systems that are part of a data complex should have common concepts for structuring file systems and allowing data access. One possible principle is to compartmentalize individual file systems and databases using explicit security barriers such as firewalls; another concept would be to create global virtualization with locally transparent access.

If a network consists of systems with different architectures or supplied by different vendors (see Figure 1.2), there will usually be a number of details, such as different system parameters, that the network operator will first have to settle through management. A network structure must be able to cope with many different version states of the products involved. Data confidentiality and integrity must also be considered.

If transparency is wanted, then a location-dependent global name space is required: Users always want to be able to find their data over the same access route regardless of which computers they happen to be using.

If security is wanted, then domain concepts that allow areas of accountability and security to be specified are useful. Policies that control the access filtering

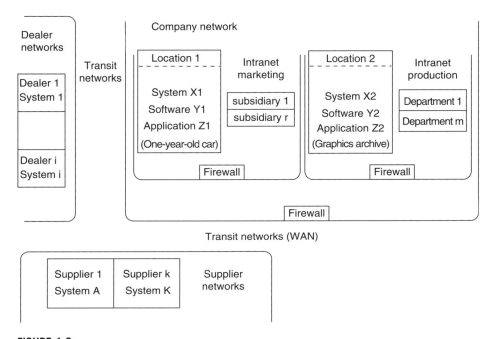

FIGURE 1.2

A corporate network.

and authentication mechanisms and initiate messages and event handling when security breaches occur must be specified for access systems.

The security aspect is also responsible for data consistency in redundant data storage with replication, for data backup to prevent short-term loss, and for long-term data storage in the form of archiving. Because some of the data are often stored in different locations at different storage hierarchy levels, policies have to be defined for migrating to these levels.

1.1.3 Scenario 3: Central Graphics Archive

Another search system provides a totally different management task. An automobile manufacturer that has operations all over the world has a central digital graphics archive for every type of design (of products as well as of production plants). Access to this archive should be available to designers, maintenance personnel, dealers, and suppliers anywhere in the world. The management task consists of the following:

- Setting up an appropriate directory structure, including directory services.
- Making available a level of fast cache servers for the central archive, which consists of several archive servers.

- Integrating cache strategies and allowing them to be changed.
- Defining and operating a platform-independent access procedure.
- Guaranteeing security through suitable authorization, authentication, and encryption procedures.
- Protecting the different intranets from one another using firewalls or other suitable privacy methods.

1.1.4 Scenario 4: Shared Document System

The patent examiners in one particular patent office use a multilevel search procedure comprising around 20 million documents in the form of image information (pixel images comprising 8 TBytes as 300-dpi documents, and 4 TBytes as 150-dpi documents); in addition, 600,000 documents are available for full-text search. Figure 1.3 illustrates a possible system for this purpose.

Based on the service level agreement, the system is to provide:

- Availability: 98 percent during main hours of work.
- Search times for 60 parallel queries and up to 100,000 hits: 3 seconds per query without trunking, 4–20 seconds per query with trunking.
- Viewing time: 0.7 second within and 1.5 seconds between documents.

The management tasks from this scenario comprise:

- Monitoring QoS parameters in accordance with SLA requirements.
- Applications management (software distribution, parameter provision and search system updates, and operation of distributed "search" applications).
- Network and system management: security of infrastructure operations (network and end systems) and data backup.

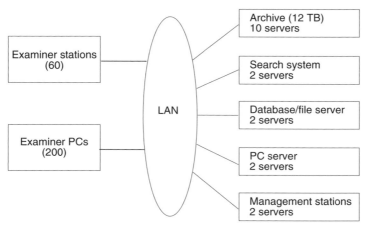

FIGURE 1.3

A search system.

- User administration and cost compilation.
- Reports and message services in regard to QoS.

1.1.5 **Scenario 5: Help Desk Support**

Fault tracking is a difficult and time-consuming process due to the increasing complexity of distributed systems and communication services. Providers of large infrastructures frequently offer their customers fault notification procedures in which a help desk, hotline, or call center serves as the central coordinating point. A variety of different tools are available to a help desk—active tools that can be used to monitor or control a distributed system, and passive tools that support a call center. These include documentation systems (inventory registers, cabling plans, system documentation, user and SLA directories) and in some cases trouble ticket systems (TTSs). A TTS is a system in which fault reports are administered as documents or trouble tickets (TTs), from the time a fault is recorded to when a diagnosis is made and the fault is then corrected.

The following case study (with numbered steps corresponding to the annotations in Figure 1.4) is a simplified example of a typical fault handling procedure and highlights the tasks of a TTS in the course of fault repair processing:

1. A user who wants to access centralized archive data in a computer center from the PC at his or her workstation is unable to make a connection. This is reported to the network operator in the computer center.

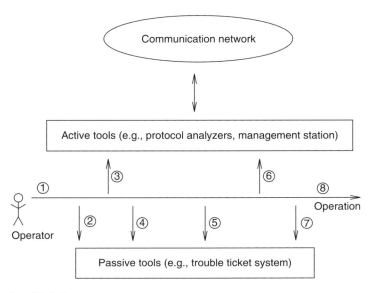

FIGURE 1.4

TTSs are used in the fault repair process.

2. The network operator searches the TTS to check whether a similar problem has already been reported. If a matching TT cannot be found, the operator records the current fault and provides the user with a fault identification number, the TT ID. This number enables the user to check at any time on the progress being made with diagnosing or repairing the fault.

3. The operator checks network component availability from a management station, but is unable to detect any faults. He or she documents actions taken, including his or her findings, in the TTS, and transfers the task of dealing with the fault to the relevant expert.

4. The expert receives the appropriate message (e.g., via email) and accesses the appropriate TT for details and any previous actions undertaken. He or she then searches the TTS for similar fault cases that have already been resolved. The results of the search query indicate that in similar cases the defective configuration of a network component was usually the cause of the fault.

5. The expert checks the network documentation system to find out about any recent modifications that have been carried out and locates an appropriate entry.

6. A configuration tool is used to verify the packet processing of a component (e.g., a router) and shows that a defective packet filter exists that is preventing access by the user to the archive. The configuration is modified, and the component is reloaded.

7. The expert documents the actions taken, including information about the source of the fault in the TTS, and completes his or her part of the process.

8. A message that is generated automatically by the TTS informs the user that the fault has been corrected.

This is, of course, only a simple scenario and omits a whole range of integrated management issues. A small number of these are:

- Direct coupling of a TTS to active management tools.
- Integration of a TTS into a workflow management system to control the overall fault handling process.
- Generation of intelligent front ends for TT creation, such as by guiding users through the process of fault localization. The basic idea is to allow users themselves—transparently using predetermined decision trees—to perform diagnostics and to query databases. Through these actions, the information needed by the experts to solve a problem is collected and formally entered into a TT.
- Accompanying support of help desks through the availability of appropriate telephone systems such as computer telephony integration (CTI), automatic call distribution (ACD), and uniform collective calling numbers.
- Intelligent use of TT databases as case study databases and analysis based on appropriate information methods (TT correlation, case-based reasoning).

Fault documentation

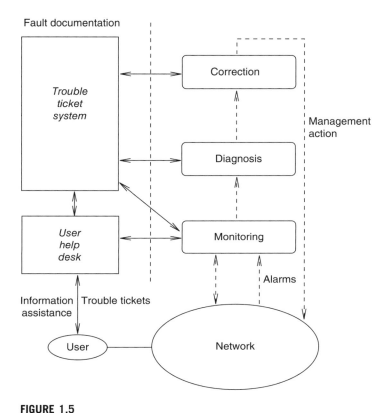

FIGURE 1.5

A TTS as a tool in the management environment.

On this basis (see Figure 1.5), TTSs can evolve into integrated tools because they are sometimes coupled with the active network and system components and with customer support systems. They may also trigger and monitor actions designed to isolate the faults, report issues, and initiate repair.

1.1.6 **Scenario 6: Nomadic Systems**

Imagine a situation involving several intranets of cooperating companies linked over a wide area network (WAN) but separated by firewalls; in other words, security components with access filter functions before a subnet. Within this framework of cooperation, employees take their mobile computers (laptops, notebooks) to the premises of one of the partner firms to work temporarily in another department. Staff, of course, want to "take along" their familiar data processing (DP) work environments. The issues that arise in this connection are:

- How do IP addresses "travel"? This is not only significant in terms of routing. There are a number of applications for which the fixed IP address of a computer is important, such as in the configuration of databases, in licensing control, and in the security area. Fixed IP addresses are also important for Internet telephony and in videoconferencing because they are treated as though they uniquely identify a user.

- How is authorization for certain resources such as printers and some servers granted on a short-term basis or transferred to the other intranet?

- How is accounting handled (e.g., how are accounts and account numbers transferred or new ones set up, how are the costs allocated)?

Addressing these issues is the challenge facing successful deployment and management of virtual private networks.

1.1.7 Scenario 7: DNS Management

Domain name service (DNS) is one of the elementary Internet services and is used to translate names to IP addresses and vice versa. For both mappings, the DNS information is divided into two independent hierarchical and worldwide unique name spaces: one for IP addresses and another for domain names. The DNS service consists of a DNS client in each terminal, a resolver, and primary and secondary DNS servers. The particularly noteworthy servers are the so-called root servers that are principally used as the first starting point for each query sent by the interconnected DNS servers. Because DNS is realized as a worldwide distributed system, the fault situations that can occur are very complex. A management solution addresses the conceptual and operational aspects, with the conceptual aspects including:

- Definition of naming conventions.
- Division of the name spaces into appropriate subspaces.
- Name server structuring.
- Mapping parts of the name space to zones (delegation).
- Definition of the resolver hierarchy.

The operational aspects include:

- Configuration of the resolvers in the terminals (hosts).
- Configuration and operation of the name server, updating the data of the zones in the name server, and caching query results obtained by each server.
- Assurance of the consistency of both address and domain name spaces.
- All measures relating to fault management.

The organizational issues arising in relation to the updating and coordination of the internal name server complex are particularly complicated when corporate-wide DNS servers are used in large firms with several hundred zones. Ultimately, the DNS relies on administration by a central authority called the InterNIC and fault-free configuration and operation of root servers.

1.1.8 **Scenario 8: Backup and Archiving System**

This example relates to a large organization with many autonomous organizational operating units (such as a university with all its departments and institutes). The basic data processing equipment for the operating units is provided on an autonomous decentralized basis. High-speed computers, overflow capacity, and certain central services, which could include a backup and archiving system, are available centrally. Because the operating units compute on all sorts of different distributed and central systems and, furthermore, are physically dispersed, a distributed file system is installed for security reasons and to provide the local transparency required. What are the management requirements of a backup and archiving system? We have listed a number of these requirements here, some of which will be familiar from the previous scenarios.

Domains: It is essential that the administration of managed data can be delegated on a hierarchical basis. The technical partitioning of an entire archive should not have a direct effect on the administration; instead, it should be possible to set up a large archive that technically is a coupling of a number of smaller archives, and vice versa, to file data in an archive independently of the areas administered. If a domain structure exists beyond the archive application, then a relationship should exist between the domain structure within and outside the archive; it could be obstructive to force a 1:1 representation in each case.

Name spaces: It must be possible to map the distributed file systems to the name spaces of the backup and archive system. In particular, a file that can be viewed on different computers cannot give the archive system the impression of being several different files.

Security techniques: If a special security technique (e.g., the use of shadow files to force consistency) exists for a file system, then the security system of the backup system should not undermine this technique.

Backup strategies: It should be possible to specify the backup strategies a user requires (e.g., frequency, life of backed-up data) as well as the operational conditions (e.g., certain times of the day for backup) to the automated system.

Allocation of resources: Control over the resources used must remain with the administrators.

Access control: Authorized users must be able to access their own files as well as those to which they have been expressly granted access rights, but not the files of other users. Administrators must be allowed to operate on behalf of the users they administer. There must be a way of controlling the extent to which users are allowed to undertake actions on their own that are normally carried out for them by the administrator (e.g., regular backups). The authorization model for archived and backed-up data should be compatible with the authorization model for online data (e.g., data accessible through the file system); under no circumstances should it undermine any of the security measures.

Integration into more global management structures: If an enterprise management tool is used in an operation, then appropriate modules must be available to control and supervise the backup and archive system using the same resources. Conversely, this process should not be contingent on the use of a specific tool.

Software distribution: A backup and archive system has client software that is distributed a hundred or a thousand times. Mechanisms are required for automating the distribution of new versions of client software.

Performance: A system must be able to cope with large quantities of files (e.g., up to a billion) and corresponding large databases for registering the archive files. With some applications in the high-speed computing area, transfer rates also play a major role. If different media are used within an archive, then there should be a way of controlling the distribution of data over this media to achieve optimal performance.

1.1.9 Importance of Management to the Business Processes

The scenarios presented serve only as examples that can be extended and expanded in any number of ways. They relate to the levels of network, system, and application management. More and more importance is being attached to distributed systems and their management because competition is increasingly being based on the processing and exchange of information—often in place of real values or things (e.g., the stock market, money transfer, ordering goods, along with simulation and virtual reality). Many companies are in the process of using "business engineering" to adapt their business processes to this information-based competition.

However, distributed systems create management barriers. These relate to system complexity, change flexibility, service availability, and cost of ownership. System complexity is a product of the variety of technologies and conceivable solutions, and the different levels of approach available. Added to this is the fact that a form of distribution can exist at every level. The complexity of the systems being managed is also reflected in the complexity of the management systems, and this in turn translates into a requirement for more highly trained staff.

Flexibility to change is essential because products and services have to adapt to a fast-changing market. Business processes and the operating processes for the information processing infrastructure derived from them are compelled to follow the market. Lastly, the management solutions must also be adaptable. However, management systems need to be flexible to deal with the consequences of change in the upper part of the management pyramid and to cope with location moves, adaptations to new hardware and software visions, adaptations to processing load changes, and so forth.

Distributed systems are not an end in themselves, but they should provide services. Services are provided by a manager in accordance with a service level agreement. But it is not enough to describe services only from the standpoint of functionality. An "operable" interface is required to allow services to be invoked and evaluated. Being evaluated means that it should be possible to assess the QoS achieved. QoS assesses the quality of a service as a whole as well as the quality of the security of the service and its customer service. Quality of service is typical interface information between a service provider and a service user. The task of monitoring it falls to performance management. We will return to this topic in the next section.

1.2 MANAGEMENT FUNCTIONS

The scenarios presented in Section 1.1 gave an indication of the variety of management tasks possible. Because the solution to a management task for distributed systems is itself a distributed application, it should also be possible to describe the modules used. In heterogeneous system environments, this even has to be an "open" (in other words, multivendor) approach. Moreover, not all management requirements will be the same in each concrete scenario. It is therefore useful to classify the total "management" task into functional areas and then to describe the management functions that are typical for each specific area.

Even this line of approach will fundamentally produce all different kinds of classifications. We will first concentrate on the five functional areas defined in the functional model of the Open Systems Interconnection (OSI) management architecture:

1. Fault management.
2. Configuration management.
3. Accounting management.
4. Performance management.
5. Security management.

The abbreviation FCAPS is often used in the literature when relating to these functional areas. We will describe typical management tasks based on these five areas. For didactic reasons, we will describe FCAPS in a different order. Later on, we will also discuss how the OSI areas could be extended.

It should be emphasized that in principle the functional areas apply to all object types; in other words, the classification of function areas is orthogonal to the classification of the objects they manage.

1.2.1 Configuration Management

The term *configuration* frequently has different meanings (depending on the immediate context). A configuration can be:

- A *description* of a distributed system based on the physical and geographical arrangement of resources (i.e., media, network components, systems or hosts, software), including how these resources are actually interconnected, and information about their logical relationships. This description of a configuration can be abstracted from the physical arrangement of the resources based on different views, such as organizational, geographical, administrative, or security-related aspects.

- The *process* of configuration as an activity or as a manipulation of the structure of distributed systems, therefore, setting and changing the parameters that control the normal operation of a system and establishing the system environment required for this normal operation.

- The *result* of a configuration process, therefore, the generated system in the sense of a set of certain parameter values that are characteristic for the normal operation of a resource.

The context will generally indicate which meaning is appropriate for the term configuration. Where necessary, we differentiate between a configuration description, which is frequently also reflected in the appropriate documentation systems, a configuration result, or generated system, and the configuration process, also known as configuration or system generation.

Configuration is an adaptation of systems to operating environments and includes installing new software, expanding old software, attaching devices, or making changes to network topology or to traffic load. Although configuration also encompasses aspects of physical installation, it is usually carried out through a software-controlled generation and setting of parameters; these include function-selection parameters; authorization parameters; protocol parameters (message lengths, windows, timers, priorities); attachment parameters (type and class of device, procedure, bit rate, parity); entries in routing tables, name servers, directories, as well as filter parameters for bridges (addresses, types of protocols, integration); spanning tree parameters for a bridge (priority of bridge or port); and parameters for the connecting paths of routers (interfaces, speed, flow-control procedures), maximum file size, computing times, and services allowed.

The following issues arise in relationship to operation and communication. There are different evaluation criteria for configuration tools:

Location of configuration: The system being configured (target system) is not always compatible with the system on which the configuration is being performed. This can be due to technical reasons such as a requirement for editors and macro processors that are not available on one of the systems. But there can also be security or organizational reasons for the problem, especially when configuration data can be loaded remotely. A configuration can take place on a component for the component itself, on each component for any other component, at a selected station for a specific component (element management system), or at a selected station (network management system) for all components.

Storage of configuration: Different solutions exist in this area also. If data are stored in NVRAM or on the hard disk in the component, a configuration can be changed easily and quickly through reloading over the network. However, this does not work when storing with EPROMs. Moreover, the scope of the configuration parameters can be lower due to capacity limitations, which can also reduce flexibility. A configuration can also be stored on a boot server and called up through appropriate load protocols.

Validity of configuration: A static configuration is one in which each reconfiguration is coupled with an interruption to operations. Dynamic configuration, on the other hand, allows changes to be made to configuration data during running operations. Thus, the events that signal the validity of new operating parameters can be the reloading of a component, the restart of a component, or the restart of one of the affected component ports.

User interface of the configurator: The quality of a user interface depends on, on one hand, to what extent individual parameters can quickly be changed and, on the other hand, to what extent the network administrator can be relieved of dealing with the individual parameters of a large number of devices. This can be addressed through the definition of different options, device profiles, or versions of configurations and the use of configuration macros to include entire groups of devices. It is also convenient to have corresponding documentation on the configuration data that at the same time lends itself to the support of network control. It should also be mentioned that the configurator and the configuration files must be protected against unauthorized use. The variations of access protection range from dispensing with passwords to breaking down the areas responsible for a configuration through a separation of network-global, component-global, and function-specific passwords. Another approach is securing the management protocols used to carry out configuration.

Tools for Configuration Management

Configuration management therefore encompasses setting parameters, defining threshold values, setting filters, allocating names to managed objects (loading configuration data, if necessary), providing documentation of configuration changes, and actively changing configurations. The tool functionality that is assigned to configuration management covers:

- Auto-topology and auto-discovery, thus the ability to extrapolate a description of a configuration from the concrete actual system environment.

- Systems for documenting descriptions of configurations, master databases.
- Tools for generating network maps for the visualization of configuration data.
- Tools for activating backup systems to detach missing components and so forth.
- Tools for setting and invoking configuration parameters and system status.
- Tools for software distribution and licensing control.
- Tools for supervising and controlling authorization.

1.2.2 Fault Management

Faults are target/performance deviations in the behavior of resources. Fault management comprises reactive and proactive measures.

Fault management deals with the detection, isolation, and elimination of abnormal system behavior. Identifying and tracking faults is a major operational problem with all data processing systems. Compared to non-networked, localized systems, fault management in computer networks and distributed systems is more difficult for a variety of reasons. These include the large number of components involved, the wide physical distribution of the resources, the heterogeneity of the hardware and software components, and the different domains components fall under (e.g., personnel of different organizational units).

A fault can be defined as a deviation from the set operating goals, system functions, or services. Messages about faults are usually conveyed by the components themselves or by the users of the system. Some of the sources of faults are data transmission paths (e.g., transceiver cable, twisted-pair cable, optical fiber, leased lines, virtual channels), network components (e.g., transceivers, repeaters, bridges, star couplers, server computers, data terminals), end systems, software for components, inadequate interface descriptions (indirectly), or even incorrect operation.

Fault Management Tasks

The function of fault management is to detect and correct faults quickly to ensure that a high level of availability of a distributed system and the services it provides is maintained. The tasks that have evolved from this objective include:

- Monitoring network and system state.
- Responding and reacting to alarms.
- Diagnosing fault causes (i.e., fault isolation and root-cause analysis).
- Establishing error propagation.
- Introducing and checking error recovery measures (i.e., testing and verification).
- Operating trouble ticket systems.
- Providing assistance to users (user help desk).

The following technical capabilities and important aids for fault management can assist in fault analysis:

- Self-identification of system components.
- Separate testability of components.
- Trace facility (i.e., keeping records of switched message traffic or labeling messages for the purpose of traceability or special compatibility reports).
- Error logs.
- Message echoes at all protocol layers (i.e., at transmission links and on an end-to-end basis), such as "heartbeat" or "keep alive" messages that detect failure.
- Retrieval possibilities for memory dumps.
- Measures for purposely generating errors in defined system environments.
- Start possibilities (which can also be initiated and monitored centrally) for self-test routines and the transmission of test texts to specific ports (loop test, remote test, problem file) as well as reachability tests such as ICMP packets for ping and trace route analysis of network reachability.
- Setting options for threshold values.
- Triggering of planned resets and restarts (directed to specific ports, port groups, and components).
- Availability of special test systems (e.g., oscilloscopes, time-domain reflectometers, interface checkers, protocol analyzers, hardware monitors for line supervision).
- Support of filter mechanisms for fault messages or alarms and event correlation for reducing the number of relevant events and for root-cause analysis.
- Interfaces of fault management tools to trouble ticket systems and help desks (e.g., for automated propagation of fault notifications and corrections).

1.2.3 Performance Management

In terms of its objectives, performance management could be seen as a systematic continuation of fault management. Whereas fault management is responsible for ensuring that a communications network or a distributed system operates, this is not enough to satisfy the objectives of performance management, which wants the overall system to perform well. It is this "performing well" that signals the first problem that has to be resolved by performance management, namely, the definition of quality of service.

The starting point for performance management is the guarantee of quality of service. Quality of service is a typical mechanism for conveying interface information between provider (i.e., the one responsible for a communications network or for the IT infrastructure) and customer, thus the service user. Its importance increases as more customer–provider relationships are involved in the implementation of corporate networks or distributed systems. The service interface is defined as follows:

- Specification of the service and service type (e.g., deterministic, statistic, best possible).
- Description of relevant QoS parameters (with quantifiable values; this includes usage value, mean value, limit value).
- Specification of the monitoring operations (information regarding measurement method, measuring points, and measurement values; specification of measurement report).
- Description of reactions to changes of the QoS parameters mentioned earlier.

It is very difficult to provide uniform guarantees in a layered and distributed system. The crux, however, is that it is very difficult and not always possible to provide a complete definition of a service interface on the basis of the aforementioned. The following problems tend to arise:

Vertical QoS mapping problems: Because communication systems are layered systems, the layer-specific QoS parameters of layer N have to be mapped onto the QoS parameters of layers $(N + 1)$ or $(N - 1)$ at the respective layer boundaries. For example, applications-oriented QoS (e.g., speech quality) needs to be mapped to network-dependent QoS (e.g., jitter). QoS hierarchies have not yet been definitively specified for all services and protocol hierarchies. This problem is exacerbated when services of different layers are provided by different carriers or providers.

Horizontal QoS mapping problems: If more than one carrier is incorporated into a corporate network, the result can be a concatenation of the different subnets or trunk sections that are used to provide services with a uniform quality of service for end user–to–end user communication. This assumes that the different carriers have implemented the same quality of service features or else are using standardized QoS negotiating protocols, resource reservation protocols, or management protocols. The more complex the service is, the less often this requirement is met. You just have to think about the voice service and the noncompatible proprietary signaling protocols of telecommunications systems and the fact that quadrature signaling (QSIG) is used.

Measurement methods: The optimal way to assess quality of service would be to apply measurement methods based on visible quantities at the service interface rather than to use an analysis of the technology supplied by the provider. The latter can change quickly, and furthermore, the quantities measured are often of no interest to the customer who first has to convert them into QoS parameters.

Performance management therefore encompasses all the measures required for ensuring that the quality of service conforms to the service level agreement. It includes:

- Establishing QoS parameters and metrics.
- Monitoring all resources for performance bottlenecks and threshold crossings.
- Carrying out measurements and trend analysis to predict failure before it occurs.
- Evaluating history logs (i.e., records on system activity, error files).
- Processing measurement data and compiling performance reports.
- Carrying out performance and capacity planning. This entails providing analytical or simulative prediction models that are used to check the results of new applications, tuning measures, and configuration changes.

Monitors, protocol analyzers, statistics packets, report generators, and modeling tools are some of the typical tool functionalities in this area.

1.2.4 Accounting Management, User Administration

User administration comprises tasks such as name and address administration, including the related directory services, authorization granting the right to use resources, and finally, the accounting services.

User Administration as a Basis for Authentication, Authorization, and Customization

There are costs involved in providing communication and server services that must be allocated to the users of the respective service (e.g., access charges and utilization charges). The strategies and procedures for cost allocation cannot and should not be rigidly established by an accounting system; it is the subject of accounting policy. It is therefore important that accounting management is able to configure this following the guidelines of accounting policy.

Accounting management includes compiling usage data (resource usage or service usage accounting based on monitoring and metering), defining accountable units, keeping settlement accounts and accounting logs, allocating costs to these accounts, assigning and monitoring quotas, maintaining statistics on usage, and lastly, defining accounting policies and tariffs, which leads to billing and charging. If several providers are involved to support a service, usage reconciliation also belongs to accounting management. The settlement of the reconciliation between two providers can be done using either an accounting revenue division procedure, a flat-rate procedure, or a traffic unit–price procedure.

How an accounting system is implemented, which approach will be used in compiling accounting parameters, and how costs will be allocated are management decisions. These decisions can be influenced by company policy because of the need to balance the ratio between the cost of compiling the costs and the benefits derived.

Once the fixed and variable costs of all the components (e.g., cabling systems, network components, connection paths, servers, system services) to be included in the calculation have been compiled, the costs must be allocated to the appropriate user. There are all sorts of ingenious ways of compiling and then passing on these costs. The more subtle the approach, the more complicated and cost intensive is the accounting procedure. This means that usage accounting services need to be cost-justified in the same way as any other service.

The underlying usage parameters of a cost compilation include number of transmitted packets or bytes, duration and time of day/week of a connection, bandwidth and QoS of the connection, location of other communication partners (e.g., when public networks are used), conversion costs for gateway services, use of resources in the server, and use of software products (licensing control). In addition to variable costs, fixed costs are also taken into account (cost of office space, maintenance charges, depreciation).

Accounting Is Extremely Important for Telcos

To sum up, the accounting management functions comprise at least usage management functions (usage generation, usage edits and validation of call events or service requests, usage error correction, usage accumulation, usage correlation, usage aggregation, usage distribution); accounting process functions (usage testing, usage surveillance, management of usage stream, administration of usage data collection); control functions (tariff administration, tariff system change control, record generation control, data transfer control, data storage control); and charging functions (charge generation, bill production, payment processing, debt collection, external reconciliation, contract processing).

Many of the functions mentioned are especially important for public telco providers. In such environments, services are often multinetwork services (i.e., multiple network nodes, different providers, or mobile subscribers may be involved). So, accounting management must address distributed collection of usage data, improved performance requirements for usage collection and report generation (in near real time), and multiple charging strategies.

The administration data needed for user administration and accounting management include subscriber details (demographic data, contract ID, credit information, subscriber history), contract information services covered, contract validity, authorized users, quotas, service level agreements, billing and payment details, tariff information, usage information, and administration system parameters.

From this nonexhaustive list, it should become obvious that accounting management bears a very close relationship to service and business management layers.

1.2.5 Security Management

The term *security management* is not used to refer to the security of management (i.e., ensuring management is performed securely), but to the management of security in distributed systems.

Security Management Requires Threat Analysis

The starting point for the discussion is the resources of a company that are worth protecting: Information, IT infrastructures, services, and production represent values that are exposed to threats of attack or improper use. Security measures that reflect the results of threat analyses or security risk analyses are needed to prevent damage and loss. Typical threats are created by:

- Passive attacks: eavesdropping on information; producing a user profile or an undesirable traffic flow analysis or theft of information (passwords, etc.).

- Active attacks: masquerades (i.e., users pretending to be someone else, or spoofing); manipulating message sequences by changing the sequence, inadmissible repeating, giving priority to or delaying messages; modifying messages; manipulating resources through overloading, reconfiguration, reprogramming, and so forth (unauthorized access, viruses, Trojan horses, denial-of-service attacks).

- Malfunctioning of resources.

- Faulty or inappropriate behavior and incorrect response operation.

Breakdown of Security Management Tasks

Security requirements and goals are established on the basis of threat analyses and the values (resources and services) needing protection. The security policies defined ultimately identify the security requirements. Examples of security policies are: "Passwords have to be changed every three weeks"; "Only second-line managers have access to personnel data"; "All attacks on security have to be recorded and followed up." These policies serve as the framework for the security services needed and consequently implemented. Security management therefore comprises:

- Conducting threat analyses.
- Defining and enforcing security policies.
- Checking identity (authentication based on signatures, notarization, or certification).
- Carrying out and enforcing access controls.
- Guaranteeing confidentiality (encryption).
- Ensuring data integrity (message authentication).
- Monitoring systems to prevent threats to security.
- Reporting on security status and violations or attempted violations.

It can be assumed that a reliable set of recognized security procedures, which for the most part are already available as public-domain software, exists in the security management area.

The main problem is finding the right way to embed these procedures into management architectures and to control them in a uniform way within the framework of a security policy.

1.2.6 Other Approaches to Classifying Management Functions

Up to this point, we have chosen to use the OSI management functional areas as the examples in our presentation of management functions. The literature even mentions other areas such as inventory/asset management, problem management, systems administration, change management, and service level agreements.

Business and Service Management Yield Other Functional Areas

Inventory management comprises functions that have to do with inventory, archiving, backup, change services, and ordering. Activities of the directory services are also included. If we disregard the ordering area, we see that we have subsumed the other functions under configuration management. Inventory management is the updating of documentation systems (e.g., network databases, directories of all components). We have also included these management functions under configuration management. A documentation system is without doubt the heart of all management procedures.

Asset management differs from inventory management in that it also incorporates an economic assessment that helps to provide more reliable information about the "cost of ownership" of IT infrastructures.

Problem management refers to facilities provided in the environment of help desks, hotlines, and trouble ticket systems. These have been presented as components of fault management.

Service level agreements are part of performance management within our interpretation. They can also be interpreted as a component of service management from the standpoint of the management pyramid. This often happens in the telecommunications network area where a distinction is made within service management of the stages service creation, service provisioning, service subscribing, and service operation. The SLA would then particularly apply to the two last stages.

In a narrower interpretation, change management can be viewed as part of configuration management. On the other hand, it can also be seen as a process that transcends all functional areas ("management building" shown in Figure 1.6).

Administration is responsible for updating user profiles, for providing software services, including the monitoring of versions, and for distributing software. We added the first area to user administration and the last two to configuration management. Administration is sometimes described as being system management.

We could also take the tack of dissecting the complex management according to management layering to arrive at a description and classification of management functions. This approach is, however, orthogonal to the one we have selected. The functional areas we have selected break down types of tasks; the layering breaks down objects of management.

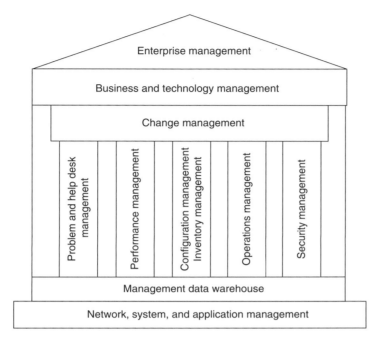

- Enterprise management (pediment/roof)
- Business and technology management
- Change management
- (Columns, read vertically) Problem and help desk management | Performance management | Configuration management / Inventory management | Operations management | Security management
- Management data warehouse
- Network, system, and application management (base)

FIGURE 1.6

The management building.

1.3 ORGANIZATIONAL ASPECTS OF MANAGEMENT

The management of IT infrastructures should not only be considered from a technical standpoint; but an integrated solution must always also be analyzed in its entirety.

1.3.1 Integrated Management Must Consider Organizational Aspects

On the one hand, an integrated approach involves slotting the solution into the layered management pyramid, but it also means adapting management to the corporate operational and organizational structure. This entails:

■ Defining the management processes that support the business processes. A definition of the different roles involved is also required.

■ Defining the *domains* to which specific management policies and procedures apply.

- Specifying interfaces between domains to enable the exchange of management information and the invocation of management actions.

- Planning and establishing a management infrastructure. This planning entails defining procedures for implementing the management processes and specifying the tool functionality required.

- Establishing an operational and organizational structure for carrying out management. This includes specifying job specifications for workplaces in areas such as operating, administration, planning, analysis, and help desks. The qualifications of required staff vary according to the assignment of duties.

The term *operating concept* is used to refer to the specification of conditions for technical management in a concrete environment. The operating concept defines the distributed application "management" as something that defines services, tasks, job allocations to organizational units, procedures, and information flows. This concept is therefore the prerequisite for the selection and operation of management systems, procedures, and tools.

IT infrastructures can also be structured into domains (logical subdomains) based on:

- Different organizations or companies that are part of the management environment (carriers, Internet service providers, outsourcers, suppliers of management tools, user organizations).
- Organizational structure of a particular company (teams, groups, departments, operating areas).
- Geographical conditions (country, location, campus, building, floor, room).
- Business areas.
- Data processing–related aspects (e.g., LAN/WAN, central/distributed DP, systems of a specific vendor).
- Types of resources (hardware, system software, applications software, data, operating materials, premises, technical infrastructure).

Establishing domains also always means forming groups of managed objects. These groups of managed objects are assigned different jobs such as planning, selection, procurement, provisioning and implementation, operation, maintenance, and adaptation.

When an organizational definition of management is provided, it also includes a distribution of responsibility, in other words, a domain-related assignment of jobs and responsibilities. This distribution of responsibility essentially plays a key role in determining the extent of management-relevant communication required as well as the complexity of the security concept needed by management. There are several basic models for the distribution of responsibility (centralized, hierarchical, distributed management). In addition to the subareas and activities mentioned earlier, the distribution of responsibility can also be oriented toward the management function areas presented in Section 1.2. It has an influence on the positioning of management systems and tools, the development of procedures, and the definition of name spaces.

1.4 TIME ASPECTS OF MANAGEMENT

Time is an issue that occurs in different places during the management operations. Similar to what happens with objects that are the subject of management, the consideration of the time factor in the implementation of management tasks leads to the life cycle phases planning, provisioning, operating, and change. This applies as much to the framework for the operating concept as it does to an individual management application or a management tool.

1.4.1 Planning as a Stage in the Life Cycle Requires a Number of Accompanying Analyses

Although the planning phase is not dealt with as a single block here, many references are made to planning aspects. Planning itself is another process that consists of different steps, including:

Application analysis: This determines which services are to be provided. The services for their part are characterized by the definitions of functionality and quality of service.

Demand priority analysis: This analysis establishes how the users and resources of a distributed system are physically distributed and serves as a basis for topology studies and an analysis of traffic relationships.

Demand size analysis: This deals with determining the distribution of transactions and exchanged data from the standpoint of time and volume.

Component analysis: Component analysis establishes the type and quantity of components to be taken into account in a distributed system, including interface characteristics and software.

Analysis of other conditions: Other conditions that can affect planning or product selection include protection of current investments (e.g., compatibility requirements for software versions, interfaces, and services); availability times of MTBF/(MTBF + MTTR) with MTBF meaning "mean time between failure" and MTTR meaning "mean time to repair"; data protection requirements; capacity reserves; expansion capabilities; cost restrictions; implementation costs; technological developments; market trends; and standardization.

Planning the introduction of a system: This includes, at the very least, checking operational procedures (operating concepts), adapting organizational charts, planning the physical installations, making plans for training, and making plans for delivery and installation.

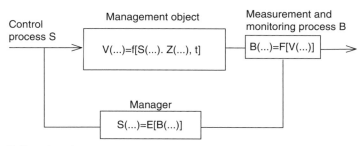

B: Control result
F: Measurement and analysis rules for monitoring
E: Decision-making for management operation
S: Control process as a management operation
Z: State of management object before intervention and change context
V: Behavior of management object due to intervention
 t: Time

FIGURE 1.7

Time behavior of managed objects as a feedback loop result.

The adaptation phase mentioned earlier generally also impinges on the planning phase. This observation of feedback applies in general and can also be applied within each phase. The time behavior of managed objects can be seen as a feedback loop result (Figure 1.7).

Resources are controlled or manipulated through parameter changes resulting from management intervention (control). The effect of this intervention is apparent later and is monitored at the appropriate location. The results of this measurement are evaluated by the manager or management system (e.g., event analysis, threshold analysis) and can sometimes initiate new management actions.

The different management activities that take place during the operating phase can in turn be assigned to different time horizons according to Figure 1.8.

Short-term horizon: Short-term management tasks comprise those measures that have to be implemented within seconds or minutes. These include a whole area of monitoring tasks that involve determining in a short time, therefore in seconds or in minutes, whether certain operating goals, such as availability and security, are being endangered. Other examples of short-term actions include executing fault messages and replacing resources that have failed with automated standbys.

Medium-term horizon: Medium-term tasks are carried out within a period of hours. Whereas short-term tasks have to be completely automated in the management system because of the short time frame allowed, medium-term tasks are usually undertaken in conjunction with a human expert. An example of a medium-term task is the diagnosis of a fault by an expert with the help of a diagnostic or trouble ticket system. Other examples include carrying out tests,

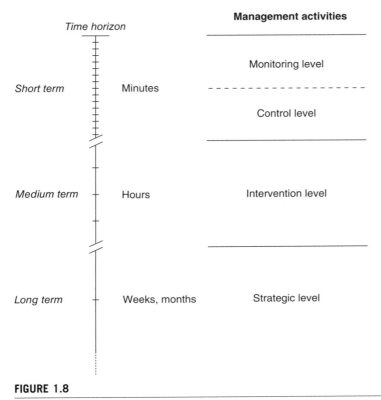

FIGURE 1.8

Time horizons and management activities.

generating configuration changes, activating and deactivating, and collecting and evaluating short-term measurement data.

Long-term horizon: In this case the time horizon relates to weeks or even months. The goal of long-term tasks is to use the experience from day-to-day network operations to improve operations for the future. Planning is therefore a key aspect here. An example of a long-term management task is the maintenance of statistics on failures to help in selecting the right vendor for the procurement of new network components in the future. Relevant terms in this context are trend analysis and capacity planning.

The services at the *monitoring level* must be able to detect all types of faults short term, and services at the *intervention level* must reproduce the required state in the medium term. However, certain kinds of faults must be corrected immediately. A *control level* is introduced between the monitoring level and the intervention level for the relevant services. As has already been mentioned, long-term services incorporate planning aspects. To delineate conceptually from the tasks of the planning phase, we refer to the level of long-term services as the *strategic level*.

1.4.2 The Time Horizon Affects How Resources Are Interpreted for Management Purposes

The time horizon does not only identify activities but is also important for the generation of tools and databases. Therefore, for many monitoring tasks, the monitoring interval must be stipulated as a frame of reference. This frame of reference determines the resolution granularity with many benchmarks and consequently has an effect on counter sizes, buffer sizes, measurement frequency, measurement accuracy, and analysis procedures. It also affects the distribution and communication aspects of relevant management information. Time aspects also affect management-relevant data storage. Thus, for example, contractual conditions require that accounting information should be kept for a minimal period; data protection laws dictate how long data have to be stored for the purposes of furnishing proof of individual charges, traffic matrices, and so forth. The storage of system history data and different versions of configurations is essential for tracking faults and resetting configurations.

IP Network Management

2

This chapter, based on Chapter 13 of *The Internet and Its Protocols: A Comparative Approach* by Farrel, gives an overview of centralized and standardized techniques for remote management of the devices that make up a network. The term *network management* is used to cover all aspects of configuration, control, and reporting that are useful to a network operator who is trying to understand how a network is functioning, commissioning new equipment, directing traffic along specific paths, or performing maintenance on parts of the network.

We begin with a brief description of the benefits of network management and then discuss some common techniques for the collection of operational statistics and the motivation for doing so. The chapter moves on to compare the benefits of proprietary configuration methods with standardized approaches, followed by the introduction of some of the standardized management models—management information bases (MIBs), the Simple Network Management Protocol (SNMP), the eXtensible Markup Language (XML), and the Common Object Request Broker Architecture (CORBA). After a discussion of the differences between the management models, the chapter concludes with a description of the use of policy within modern networks.

This chapter is not intended to present each management mechanism in detail but rather to give a working overview. Where specific protocol-related components exist they are highlighted and described.

2.1 CHOOSING TO MANAGE YOUR NETWORK

At some level all network devices require some management. Even the most simple devices have physical management needs as they are commissioned and connected to a power supply. But most devices need some form of configuration to tell them what role they are to play in the network and precisely how to behave. Even when autoconfiguration protocols like the Dynamic Host Configuration Protocol (DHCP) are used to dynamically assign IP addresses and to download basic configuration information, a network operator will still want to use management operations to inspect the devices to discover what addresses they are using.

In practice, many network devices are complex, requiring a large number of configuration parameters. Many, if not most, of these parameters can usually use default values, but fine tuning may be necessary to ensure optimal functioning of the network, and that requires some form of management access to the device.

At the same time, it is crucial to the understanding of the operation of a network to be able to inspect each node and observe how it is behaving. What resources are active and how much traffic are they carrying? Who has provisioned those connections that are causing a bottleneck for the CEO's emails? Why can't I send any packets to that host? The background information needed to answer these types of question ranges from basic state information about the devices, through detailed data concerning the inner functioning of the devices and thorough statistics recording the number of errors, packets, and bytes.

In order to get the most meaning out of management information retrieved from a device, it is usually decomposed in a logical and modular fashion. So, for example, one might be able to access data about a whole router, the line cards on the router, the interfaces on each line card, the protocol components running on the router, and so on. Conversely, configuration is most flexible when it can be applied to the same logical components of the system.

A final management requirement is the ability to provision new services. This may require commissioning resources at each node along a path through the network, or if a signaling protocol is in use, simply issuing management requests to the starting point of the new connection.

So, at many levels it is impossible to operate a network without some form of management. The remainder of this chapter introduces how to use standardized approaches to produce a coherent management strategy for the whole of the network, making it possible to debug the network more effectively and to reduce the management resources required to operate a network constructed from computers from different vendors.

Network management is an area in which most Internet service providers (ISPs) seem to struggle. The nature of their networks is constantly changing, and the market is continually driving them to provide new and different services. These changes put a strain on existing network management tools and require the ISPs to race to adapt their techniques to their customers' requirements. In previous years, managed Internet services were the highest requirement, but these days, enterprises are looking for their ISP to support intranet or extranet services. This means that the service provider needs to provide an entire "network" to an individual enterprise customer and not just a set of simple and unrelated connections to the Internet. The new network services are provided to the customer as virtual private networks (VPNs) across a common shared network infrastructure owned by the ISP. This sharing of network resources provides a new challenge to the network management capabilities of the service provider that must now be able to partition resources and share them between customers.

2.2 CHOOSING A CONFIGURATION METHOD

There are many ways to configure devices, from automatic configuration protocols such as BOOTP and DHCP, through command line interface and configuration files, to graphical user interfaces. These techniques may use a mixture of proprietary manufacturer information and techniques and standardized protocols and data formats. As will be shown in the following sections, there are benefits and disadvantages to using the vendor-specific approaches, but the standardized methods give a great benefit in providing a centralized and coherent view of the network.

2.2.1 Command Line Interfaces

The easiest management tool for a manufacturer of network equipment to write is a command line interface (CLI), sometimes known as a craft interface (CI). A CLI is a set of text-based commands issued by the operator at a terminal. The commands have specific (sometimes complex and esoteric) syntaxes specified by the manufacturer and are very specific to the hardware being managed. This means that an operator running a network of diverse nodes from different manufacturers must learn the command language for each node—no small task. Fortunately, devices from one manufacturer tend to use the same commands where there is an overlap of function, and the same syntaxes for all commands. Because devices that perform the same functions need roughly the same configuration, and because vendors recognize the difficulties of managing networks built from hardware from many different vendors, there is a tendency for CLIs to look quite similar, with convergence on the command syntaxes used by the incumbent manufacturers. This has obvious benefits, but can also be frustratingly confusing when the syntaxes are so similar as to make the differences hard to remember.

In its simplest form, the CLI requires that the operator be present at a terminal directly attached to the device being managed. This is not viable in large networks in which the routers and switches are distributed over a large geographic area and are often installed in inaccessible places. Remote console access can be achieved running a product such as a terminal server that the user connects to using Telnet and that is physically connected to the device as though it were a local terminal.

Alternatively, if the device supports TCP and runs a Telnet server, the operator can log in using Telnet and run the CLI. In either case, the user can manage the device remotely and must visit the location in which the equipment is installed only in the event of a catastrophic failure.

It is a considerable inconvenience to an operator to have to reconfigure a device each time it is restarted (that is, power cycled), so most devices store their configuration data in some form. It is not really important whether this information is on a local hard disk, in flash memory, or in a file held on a remote server and accessed through some means such as the Trivial File Transfer Protocol

(TFTP). The effect is the same: The device is able to recover its configuration by reading a file and commence operation without any further management intervention. Such configuration files may be stored in any format, and could be simple binary files that are easily read into memory and have meaning only to the software that is using them, but a more sensible approach is to record the configuration commands necessary to recreate the required state and to replay the file as though it were being typed by the operator. Command-based configuration files have the advantages that they can be inspected and understood by an operator, they can be edited so that new configuration is automatically picked up on reboot, and they are more easily proofed against software version upgrades.

It should be noted that the one great benefit of a CLI is that it is easily able to give a very fine level of control over a device and allows a user to examine every last detail of the device's operation. Debug commands are rarely available in any other form.

2.2.2 Graphical User Interfaces

Graphical user interfaces (GUIs) are a more user-friendly configuration tool. The operator does not need to remember a command language, but is led through a series of screens with spaces to fill in the necessary configuration information. Default values are provided automatically and context-sensitive help is often available. Advanced GUIs support point-and-click provisioning in which an operator can achieve a high level of management using a mouse to select devices and components and to drag and drop configuration objects.

The biggest benefit to a GUI is the way in which data retrieved from devices can be displayed. Although it is possible to just show tables of data as in the CLI output, these tables can be easily enhanced to allow the user to click on any piece of information to drill down further and see more details. Better still, the GUI can provide graphical representations of information, tracking data against time or mapping resources in physical space. A GUI can, for example, build a picture of a device by learning from it what components it has that are installed and operational, and can present this to the operator as though he or she were looking at the real device. Similarly, by connecting to multiple devices in the network, the GUI can present a single, graphical view of the entire network.

This latter feature means that the GUI must be capable of operating remotely and must not be limited to direct access on the managed device. Remote GUI access can be achieved in a variety of ways, including through the X/Open remote console protocols, but this requires that the complex graphical manipulation and presentation are performed on the managed device. It is more common to place the bulk of the function at the central management site on a dedicated computer and to have the GUI-based management program contact the managed devices using some form of communications protocol.

The GUI can be implemented "over the top of" the CLI so that all commands issued at the GUI are mapped to CLI commands that are sent to the managed device using Telnet. Data that are displayed by the GUI can be collected in the same way before being massaged to make the pretty screens. Alternatively, GUIs may use their own communications protocols and data formats to "talk" to devices with the benefit of a more condensed information exchange since only the raw data are sent without the lengthy text control commands and output strings.

There is still a place for configuration files in systems that are managed using a GUI. There is, however, a less obvious way to store the data. If the GUI is implemented over the top of the CLI either locally or for remote transmission, then it is obvious to store the configuration using the CLI commands, but if the GUI is implemented using direct access to configuration data structures, it is often tempting for an implementer to build a binary configuration store. This loses the benefits of the text-based configuration file described in the previous section and makes it difficult to handle a system with a GUI and CLI, so the most common approach is to convert the GUI configuration into the equivalent CLI commands before storing the information.

It is worth noting that despite the user-friendly aspects of a GUI, an experienced network operator or field engineer will often prefer to use the CLI. The CLI gives access to a finer level of control and a greater amount of information than the GUI, even if that information is not always formatted in the most readable way. Further, many engineers claim that they can operate with the CLI much faster than they can handle a GUI.

2.2.3 **Standardized Data Representations and Access**

Network managers dream of having a single application that they can use to manage their entire network. This application must be capable of controlling all of the devices in the network, and of collecting and integrating the information and statistics stored on each device. The advantages for the operator are a coherent view and a less complex management task because he or she doesn't have to learn to speak the different command languages for the different equipment vendors and the different dialects for the different devices and models from the same vendor.

One approach to building the global network management tool is to incorporate modules designed to talk to each of the individual components and map these to a common display and control component. This is hard work for the writer of a management application since he or she has to keep up with the latest command syntaxes and products produced by each vendor. This is, however, a viable solution, especially if a modular approach is taken.

One easier way to produce a global management tool is to make the individual vendors responsible for the modules that manage all of their devices and to make those modules distinct (usually running on separate computers) with a *northbound interface* to the global application. This can be seen in Figure 2.1, in which the operator works at a network management system (NMS) or through an operations support system (OSS) such as Telcordia's TIRKS or NMA. Use of an OSS

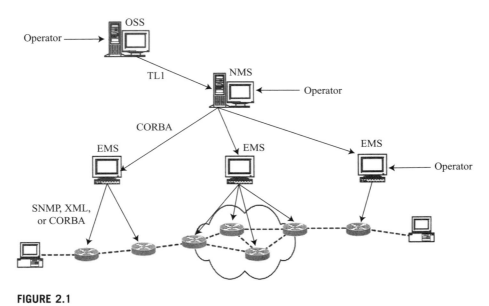

FIGURE 2.1

The management network can be built up from a series of management systems so that the operator can use a single, central management server.

allows the operator to utilize sophisticated provisioning and accounting services, and the OSS uses a scripting language such as TL1 to pass CLI-like commands on to the NMS. The NMS is the global management application that communicates to many element management systems (EMSs), each of which is responsible for managing a collection of devices of the same type. It is the EMS that the equipment vendor supplies as a distinct module for incorporation into the whole management network.

As shown in Figure 2.1, the operator may have access to the EMSs where he or she uses proprietary CLIs and GUIs to control the devices. But if the operator is working at the NMS or OSS there must be a channel of communications between the NMS and each EMS. This is popularly referred to as a *northbound interface* to the EMS. There are two requirements for this communication: (1) the messages must be understood universally (there must be a common communications protocol), and (2) the data must be comprehensible (there must be a common data format). The popular standard for NMS to EMS communications is the Common Object Request Broker Architecture described later. CORBA provides a standardized way for the NMS to access data objects managed by each EMS, and a way for the equipment vendors or EMS authors to publish a database format for the NMS to access. These formats can become standardized, making the job even simpler.

The EMS is now free to manage the devices themselves. Each equipment vendor may take a different approach to the management of its devices, as described in the previous section, but it is increasingly popular to use one of a small set of standardized protocols and data formats. There is a clear advantage for vendors because they are able to leverage lots of existing code when they produce a new device and they do not have to make substantial upgrades to their EMS to support the new product. Three popular standards-based configuration techniques have emerged: CORBA, SNMP, and XML. If CORBA is used by the EMS to manage its devices, the mapping between the NMS and a device is particularly simple for the EMS, but otherwise a conversion component must be written.

However, once the devices support a standardized configuration protocol, there is less need for an EMS. It does continue to add management features specific to the vendor's equipment, but it gets in the way of centralized management from the NMS and affects management performance if translations are required on every command. For this reason, the EMS is increasingly dropped from the picture and the NMS communicates with the devices directly using one of the standardized protocols.

2.2.4 Making the Choice

Making the choice between configuration methods may be constrained by what protocols and techniques are supported by the equipment in your network. At the worst, you will need to use the CLI on each piece of equipment, operating via Telnet and possibly with the use of a terminal server.

If standardized management protocol support is available there are many advantages to using it, but it should not be forgotten that there will often be more detail and flexibility available through proprietary configuration interfaces than are available through the standards. Nevertheless, except for the configuration of advanced features or for debugging, the benefits of a consolidated management system dictate the use of a standardized technique.

2.3 MANAGEMENT INFORMATION BASE

One problem in the management of networks is deciding how the statistics and configuration data should be represented. Each device (switch, router, host, etc.) will have different configuration requirements and internal data structures according to its implementation. Similarly, each network management tool will have different commands and management screens displaying and requiring subtly different pieces of information. Nevertheless, any two devices that perform the same function in the network (e.g., two OSPF routers) require substantially the same configuration to enable them to operate their IP-based protocols. This means all that is required is a common, standardized way to represent the data while they are moved between management station and device. The management tools are free to collect and display the information in whatever way they choose, and the devices can store the information and use it (or discard it) as they see fit.

For each protocol that it develops, the IETF produces a standard set of operational configuration and statistics information necessary for successful configuration and management of a device that runs the protocol. This information is published in separate RFCs for each protocol and constitutes a module from the global network MIB.

The MIB is an ordered, structured view of all of the information in all networks, all at the same time. This is a pretty ambitious claim that is, in fact, true only within the global uniqueness of identifiers such as IP addresses and router identifiers. The secret to meeting this aim lies in the way that data values (or *objects*) are given unique *object identifiers* (OIDs) in a hierarchical and somewhat long-winded way.

To illustrate this, consider the part of the *OID tree* shown in Figure 2.2. This shows the root of the tree and the branches down as far as some individual *MIB modules*. As can be seen, the MIB is broken into branches according to the standards-making body. Within the ISO branch, the American Department of Defense is responsible for the Internet. So all Internet OIDs begin with the value 1.3.6.1 using dot notation to represent the OID. Standardized IETF MIB modules are assigned from the MIB-2 branch of the Management branch, but those that are still under development usually come from the Experimental branch. Another

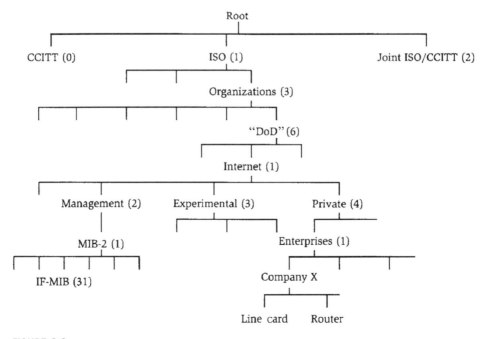

FIGURE 2.2

The OID tree from its root shown at the top of the example.

branch is designated for private use and allows enterprises (companies, network operators, research establishments, etc.) to develop their own MIB modules. So, for example, OIDs in proprietary Cisco MIB modules begin 1.3.6.1.4.1.9, where 9 has been assigned to denote Cisco.

Below these points in the OID tree come the individual MIB modules. An MIB module contains all of the configuration and reporting information for a single type of logical component. This may be a line card or router, as shown for Company X in Figure 2.2, or may be a component of a protocol such as an interface as managed by the Interfaces MIB (IF-MIB) module. In other words, MIB modules are defined to manage all instances of a single type of manageable entity.

MIB modules comprise individual *scalar objects* and *MIB tables*. On a managed object (e.g., a router) the scalar objects can be thought of as global variables, and a MIB table can be thought of as an array of control blocks. Just as an implementation might need several types of control blocks, so a MIB module may include more than one table.

The scalar objects are each assigned a single object identifier within the MIB module. Thus, in the IF-MIB module documented in RFC 2863, there is an object called ifTableLastChange that records the time at which the Interface table was last changed. This object is assigned the OID 5 from within the MIB module, giving it the full OID of 1.3.6.1.2.1.31.1.5, where the penultimate 1 indicates that this is an object in the MIB.

Each table is also assigned an OID within the MIB module. So, for example, the Interfaces Receive Addresses table (ifRcvAddressTable) in the IF-MIB module that is used to list all of the addresses that can be used on an interface has the value 4. Each table is made up of a series of *MIB rows* or *entries*. An entry is the equivalent of a single instantiation of a control block and is made up of a sequence of objects, each with its own object identifier. The ifRcvAddressTable contains three objects: the address itself, the current status of the address (available for use or not), and the volatility of the address on the interface assigned the OIDs 1, 2, and 3, respectively, so that the address object (ifRcvAddressAddress) has the full OID of 11.3.6.1.2.1.31.1.1.4.11, where the penultimate 1 indicates that this is an entry in the table. Thus, all of the addresses in this table form a conceptual column in the table with the same OID.

Rows in MIB tables are distinguished by indexes. Indexes are object values within the table or within some other MIB table on which this one depends. In our example of the Interfaces Receive Addresses table, there are two indexes. The *primary index* is the interface identifier itself, a value stored in a separate table, and the secondary index is the interface receive address in the ifRcv-AddressAddress object. Using these two indexes it is possible to select an individual row in the table and find out about a specific address on a specific interface. Alternatively, using just the primary index, and a "get next" operation, it is possible to read each of the addresses in use on a given interface. The table format is shown in Figure 2.3.

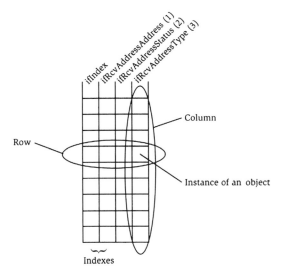

FIGURE 2.3

MIB tables are built from rows with conceptual columns.

2.3.1 **Representing Managed Objects**

The Structure of Management Information (SMI) is specified in RFC 2578. It describes a subset of the Abstract Syntax Notation One (ASN.1) that may be used to define MIB modules and to encode MIB objects when they are passed from one node to another in management requests. ASN.1 was devised by the Open Standards Organization (OSI) and provides a text-based, macro language that may be used to define data structures in a form that is both intelligible to humans and machine readable. At the same time, ASN.1 also provides a set of rules for encoding data when they are passed on the wire between network nodes called the Basic Encoding Rules (BER). These rules provide for a very efficient (that is, requiring the smallest number of bytes) way to pass data along with their data types, but are somewhat complicated by flexibility of ASN.1 to handle complex and nested data structures—a feature not required for MIB modules.

The SMI lays out a minimal subset of data types and constructs from ASN.1 and extends these concepts to support the specific requirements of MIB modules. Table 2.1 shows these data types. They form the basis of more complex data types or *textual conventions* that can be defined within MIB modules. Textual conventions usually define interpretations to place on an object of a specific type. For example, the MPLS Textual Conventions MIB module defines `MplsBitRate` as an integer number of thousands of bits per second with a special meaning assigned to zero (see Figure 2.4). Any other MIB module may *import* this textual convention and is thereby saved the effort of redefining it and also benefits from a consistent definition of bit rates. The SMI also defines some

Table 2.1 The Eleven Basic Data Types Defined in the SMI

Data Type	Meaning
INTEGER	Signed 32-bit integer.
OCTET STRING	A series of bytes, each greater than or equal to 0 and less than or equal to 255.
OBJECT IDENTIFIER	An OID that can be displayed in dot notation.
Integer32	The same as INTEGER except that it is guaranteed to never need more than 32 bits for a two's complement representation.
Unsigned32	Unsigned 32-bit integer.
Counter32	A 32-bit integer used to count events (such as the number of packets received). When the value of an object of this type reaches 4,294,967,295, it wraps to 0.
Gauge32	A counter that can go up or down to register the number of instances of some object. Unlike Counter32 it cannot increment beyond 4,294,967,295, and does not wrap to 0. Similarly, it does not increment below 0.
Counter64	A 64-bit version of Counter32. This is particularly useful when counting things that are very fast (e.g., bytes on a high-capacity link), and the SMI mandates that Counter64 be used for any counter that may wrap more frequently than once an hour.
TimeTicks	An unsigned 32-bit integer counting hundredths of seconds and wrapping to 0.
Opaque	An OCTET STRING wrapper of any arbitrary ASN.1 construct.
IpAddress	A sequence of 4 bytes containing an IPv4 address. Note: This data type is deprecated and new MIB modules use Unsigned32 for the same purpose.

important macros used to embed useful information (e.g., status of the object, a description, and display hints) and to define common concepts such as MIB objects and modules.

2.4 SIMPLE NETWORK MANAGEMENT PROTOCOL

Once the management station and the managed devices have a common view of the management data (that is, MIB objects) all that remains is to provide a mechanism for the management station to create, write, read, and delete those objects. This is achieved using the Simple Network Management Protocol (SNMP), which, like anything that calls itself "simple," should be taken with a pinch of salt.

```
MplsBitRate::=TEXTUAL-CONVENTION
DISPLAY-HINT "d"
STATUS current
DESCRIPTION
   "If the value of this object is greater
   than zero, then this represents the
   bandwidth of this MPLS interface (or Label
   Switched Path) in units of '1000 bits per
   second.'
   The value, when greater than zero,
   represents the bandwidth of this MPLS
   interface (rounded to the nearest 1000)
   in units of 1000 bits per second.
   If the bandwidth of the MPLS interface
   is between ((n * 1000) − 500) and
   ((n * 1000) + 499), the value of this
   object is n, such that n > 0.
   If the value of this object is 0 (zero),
   this means that the traffic over this MPLS
   interface is considered to be best effort."
SYNTAX Unsigned32 (0|1..4294967295)
```

FIGURE 2.4

A textual convention allows multiple MIB modules to import the same construct and meaning without having to redefine it.

SNMP is an application-level protocol that can use any transport mechanism. In practice, it is most often used with UDP using port 161 since that is mandatory for conformance with SNMP standards. Other transport protocols are sometimes used in a misguided attempt to handle some of the security issues covered in Section 2.4.2. TCP is occasionally chosen when a management application does not handle lost messages.

2.4.1 Requests, Responses, and Notifications

SNMP is a client-server protocol. Management agents connect to the managed devices and issue requests. Managed devices return responses.

The basic requests are very simple. They are GET and SET to read and write to an individual MIB object identified by its OID and, if the object is in a table, by the appropriate index values. Index objects are read and write protected—there is no need to specifically read an index because it is always supplied in a GET request and returned in a GET response to give context to the read request, and clearly it would be a bad idea to allow the index of a row to be changed dynamically. Some MIB modules also make some of their objects read-only so that the device may report information (such as statistics) without it being modifiable by an external component. Other than these restrictions, however, GET and SET are quite straightforward in their operation.

However, it would be hugely inefficient to manage the configuration of a remote device one object at a time, so SNMP allows multiple objects within a single MIB row to be read or written in a single request. That is, a single GET or SET command can operate on multiple objects within a single row. Further, the GET-BULK command allows a management station to read multiple rows from a table, improving the retrieval time when an entire table is being read. Similarly, the GET-NEXT request allows a management agent to "walk" the OID tree to find the next object in a MIB row, or more usually to navigate a MIB table (which may be sparsely populated) reading one row at a time.

Row creation and deletion are special functions that are handled using the SET command and not through their own special messages. MIB rows contain a special writable object called the *row status* that is used to control the creation and deletion of the row. When a management station creates a row for the first time, it writes the value create to the row status object—if the row already exists, the operation will be failed by the managed device. If the row creation was successful, the management status goes on to write the other objects, and when the row is ready for use, it sets the row status to active. At this point, the configuration information is available and the device or component can be activated.

At any time the management station can move the row back into the not ready state by writing that value into the row status object. This effectively takes the row back into the state it was in as it was being created. To delete the row, the row status is set to the value deleted and the managed device must stop the corresponding process or device and delete the corresponding information.

A final SNMP message called a TRAP (sometimes known as a notification) may be issued by the managed device to report a specific event (e.g., the crossing of a threshold).

2.4.2 **SNMP Versions and Security**

MIB data are encoded for transmission using the Basic Encoding Rules (BER) from the ASN.1 specification in the international standard ISO 8825. This is a compact way of representing data and data types on the wire. For consistency, BER is also used for encoding SNMP messages, with the added advantage that the messages can be specified using the ASN.1 text notation.

SNMP messages are built from an SNMP header and an SNMP protocol data unit (PDU). The header is quite short and contains a protocol version number. The PDU contains the request and any data.

There are three versions of SNMP. The original version of SNMP was produced at the end of the 1980s. SNMPv1 turned out to be too simple in many respects, not having sufficiently powerful requests and using the limited SMIv1 to build its PDUs. After several abortive attempts, the IETF produced SNMPv2 and documented it in RFC 1901 as an experimental protocol. At the same time, work began on SMIv2, which was finally documented as RFC 2578, and SNMPv2 messages may carry only PDUs built using SMIv2.

SNMPv1 and SNMPv2 have considerable security concerns. Even on networks in which the data exchange is secured (e.g., by using the facilities of IPsec) there is no control within these versions of SNMP as to who on the secure network is allowed to perform SNMP operations and access the objects in a MIB module. That is, any user on the network who can exchange UDP packets with the managed device will be able to examine and modify the MIB objects. This is clearly undesirable, so SNMPv3 includes application-level cryptographic authentication to enable individual users to be authenticated. SNMPv3 differs from SNMPv2 in the message header only—the PDUs are the same and both use SMIv2.

The IETF recommends strongly that deployment of SNMPv1 and SNMPv2 should be avoided, and that SNMPv3 be used instead. Further, they recommend that cryptographic authentication be implemented and enabled so that it is a matter for the network operator to manage the legitimacy of access to the management information on each device.

2.4.3 Choosing an SNMP Version

As explained in the preceding section, the IETF has some strong views about which version of SNMP should be deployed. In practice, however, although SNMPv1 is pretty well deprecated except in a relatively small number of older devices, SNMPv2 saw significant deployment and new devices are still being shipped that support only SNMPv2.

Therefore, although SNMPv3 is the ideal, management stations need to be able to support both SNMPv2 and SNMPv3 for the foreseeable future. All new devices should, however, be produced with support for SNMPv3, and it is reasonable to assume that management software will support SNMPv3 so that it is no longer necessary for a device to include SNMPv2 support.

2.5 EXTENSIBLE MARKUP LANGUAGE

The eXtensible Markup Language is a subset of the Standard Generalized Markup Language (SGML) specified in ISO 8879. XML defines data objects known as *XML documents* and the rules by which applications access these objects. XML documents look very much like Hypertext Markup Language (HTML) documents (e.g., Web pages), but XML document specifications include strict definitions of the data type in each field of an object. This makes XML documents applicable to database formats, whereas HTML documents are more suited for text management. Thus, while presentation instructions (such as "center this text and print it in Arial 12 point") are part of SGML, they are not relevant to XML but are very important in HTML.

In effect, XML provides encoding rules for commands that are used to transfer and update data objects. The syntax of these commands can be precisely specified and can be automatically parsed by a simple text-based application. Just as in HTML, formatting and control are managed using text *tags* that delimit the data, but unlike in HTML, the semantics of a tag is not global, but is specific to a given XML document. The data themselves are presented as strings of bytes with each string enclosed by a pair of tags known as a single *XML element*. ISO 8879 defines how tags are used to enclose XML elements and what the meaning of the tags is (i.e., how the tags cause the receiving application to operate on the data in the XML element).

The collection of tags in an XML document is referred to as the *markup data.* The markup data not only give instructions on the interpretation of individual data elements, but define how the elements are associated, and also describe the purpose of the entire document and its applicability.

XML is developed by the World Wide Web Consortium (W3C) based on SGML. SGML was standardized in the mid-1980s and work on XML started in 1996, reaching its first standard (or Recommendation) in 1998. As such, XML is neither a communications protocol, nor tied to use within the Internet, but its applicability and increasing popularity as a configuration and management tool for Internet devices makes it worthy of further examination.

2.5.1 Extensibility and Domains of Applicability

Key to the nature of XML is its extensibility. XML elements can be defined as they are needed to fulfill the needs of specific document uses. Network management is one such area of use or *domain,* and subdomains might be defined for the management of a type of network element (e.g., a router) or even for a specific make and model of a network element.

It is important to note that the definition of new XML elements is not the same as the definition of new tags or syntaxes within XML. Tags and syntaxes are standardized, meaning that all XML documents can be successfully parsed by any correctly implemented XML engine regardless of the domain to which the document applies. The semantics of an XML element may, however, only be understood within its domain of applicability.

The documents used within a specific domain will use a well-known set of XML elements, tags, and markup data. Knowledge of this information is useful to implementers since it governs the amount of code they have to write to construct and parse XML and to interpret XML elements. XML documents for a domain are described in a *document type definition* (DTD) and, conversely, a document identifies the domain to which it belongs by indicating the DTD. Note that DTDs may be nested as subsets of other DTDs so that a document that conforms to a child DTD will also conform to the parent.

2.5.2 XML Remote Procedure Calls

XML is a data encoding technique that can be used to represent data and data requests that are transmitted between components on a single node or across a network. It does not define what data should be transferred (that is the responsibility of the application developer, and any data including ASN.1-encoded SNMP data can be encapsulated in XML), nor does it define how the XML documents should be exchanged.

XML documents may be transferred using any data or file transfer process. Various processes have been applied, from UDP or TCP, through the File Transfer Protocol (FTP) and the Hypertext Transfer Protocol (HTTP). The early uses of XML utilized a remote procedure call (RPC) mechanism based on HTTP—this made good sense because XML is closely related to HTML, which HTTP is designed to carry, and because HTTP contains basic get and put operations.

XML-RPC is still in use and has been successful, but it is considered by some to have too much overhead. A more object-oriented approach was desired, and so the Simple Object Access Protocol (SOAP) was devised.

2.5.3 Simple Object Access Protocol

SOAP was originally named as the Simple Object Access Protocol. It was designed as a lightweight protocol for exchange of XML documents over an underlying transport protocol. It supports transactions on distributed objects in a Web-based environment by defining how remote procedure calls and responses may be represented within messages that may be sent between participating network elements. As SOAP has developed and been extended, its longer name was considered to be somewhat misleading, and so the protocol is now simply known as SOAP.

SOAP messages are encoded in XML, which makes them reasonably easy for a user to read. The whole message is contained in an *envelope* and comprises an optional header and a mandatory body. The header contains control information about the message (things like priority and destination) and is not always required because in most cases the default behavior can be applied and the assumed destination is the receiver of the message. SOAP does allow messages to be relayed, however. That is, a SOAP message from node A to node C may be sent on a transport connection from node A to node B and relayed by the SOAP component on node B, which sends the message onward on a connection to node C. This feature requires that the header includes the target node for the message. The SOAP body contains the XML operations and data being transferred, as shown in Figure 2.5.

The SOAP envelope may alternatively contain a SOAP fault construct. This is used to report errors and has several mandatory components, including an error code for the fault, a text string describing the fault, and the identifier of the reporting node. Figure 2.6 shows a sample fault message copied from the SOAP specification.

2.5.4 XML Applicability to Network Management

XML is a useful management tool, and some network equipment vendors support only XML and their proprietary CLI. XML lends itself to the easy development of

```
<env:Envelope xmlns:env="http://www.w3.org/2003/05/
  soap-envelope">
  <env:Header>
    <t:transaction xmlns:n="http://elsevier.com/
      example-msg" env:mustUnderstand="true">
    <n:priority>Low</n:priority>
    <n:expires>2005-10-15T23:59:59-05:00</n:expires>
    display
  </t:transaction>
</env:Header>
<env:Body>
  <dsp:text>This message is displayed.</dsp:text>
</env:Body>
</env:Envelope>
```

FIGURE 2.5

Example SOAP message carrying a message to be displayed.

```
<env:Envelope xmlns:env="http://www.w3.org/2003/05/soap-envelope"
            xmlns:m="http://www.example.org/timeouts"
            xmlns:xml="http://www.w3.org/XML/1998/namespace">
  <env:Body>
  <env:Fault>
  <env:Code>
      <env:Value>env:Sender</env:Value>
      <env:Subcode>
          <env:Value>m:MessageTimeout</env:Value>
      </env:Subcode>
  </env:Code>
  <env:Reason>
      <env:Text xml:lang="en">Sender Timeout</env:Text>
  </env:Reason>
  <env:Detail>
      <m:MaxTime>P5M</m:MaxTime>
  </env:Detail>
  </env:Fault>
  </env:Body>
</env:Envelope>
```

FIGURE 2.6

Example SOAP fault message.

Web-based management applications that can read and write network configuration information from and to remote devices.

It is relatively simple to use a DTD to generate the screens that an application will display, and this is an important point since each vendor's device managed through XML is likely to have a different DTD even if the function of the devices is similar.

XML is, however, a comparatively verbose way of encoding data. The tags are usually descriptive, meaning that several text words may be used to encapsulate a single piece of data. This is a large overhead compared with a binary encoding of a known structure, but it is also a great strength because the format and meaning are encoded in XML in a way that can be simply parsed by the recipient. The overhead of XML encoding is overcome to some extent by compression algorithms built into the protocols used to transfer XML documents.

2.6 COMMON OBJECT REQUEST BROKER ARCHITECTURE

The Common Object Request Broker Architecture is a distributed management architecture that takes an object-oriented approach to management. CORBA includes the specification of the managed objects; the communications and requests that are exchanged between management applications and the managed objects; and the requests, access control, security, and relationships between the objects.

CORBA is developed by the Object Management Group (OMG), which was founded in 1989 and is currently developing version 3.0 of the CORBA specification.

2.6.1 Interface Definition Language

Each managed object (e.g., a device, a line card, or a connection) is represented in CORBA by a CORBA object. The object is defined by an *object interface,* which (much as in an object-oriented programming language) indicates the accessible fields within an object, the operations that can be performed on the object, and the relationship between the object and other objects. Relationships with other objects are defined through inheritance.

The Interface Definition Language (IDL) is an object-oriented language specified by the OMG to describe object interfaces. IDL uses a subset of the C^{++} programming language, but extends it with a small set of additional constructs to support the type of object management that is needed in the context of network management. The most notable extension is the `any` data type, which can be used to represent an unknown or unspecified data type.

2.6.2 The Architecture

CORBA is a client–server architecture. The client is a management agent that performs operations on objects that are controlled by the server. The client and

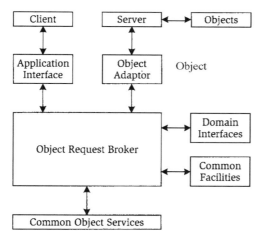

FIGURE 2.7

OMA reference model as defined by the Object Management Group.

server are connected by the Object Request Broker (ORB), which is responsible for correlating the location of the client and server and managing the communications between them. This architecture protects the client from knowledge of the location of the server for each object and allows local and remote objects to be managed in a uniform way.

The Object Management Architecture (OMA) is illustrated in Figure 2.7. Central to the architecture is the ORB that is responsible for relaying the client's requests to the correct component at the correct location. Client requests are typically passed to the ORB through an application interface developed for the specific management application. Application interfaces are usually developed for specific purposes or management applications, although because these purposes are sometimes common, they may be standardized by the OMG. The ORB delivers the requests to the appropriate components, which may be local or remote. Common facilities are utilities or operations oriented toward applications, and they may be common across multiple applications such as system and task management, operations on distributed document handling, and information management such as the embedding of an object from one application within a document from another application. Common object services (COS) are the underlying common functions used by the ORB to answer the requests issued by the client. COS include the necessary components to ensure end-to-end delivery of object transactions, and also common services that range from object location and naming, through the management of object relationships, persistence and life cycles to timing, security, and event notifications.

The domain interfaces are a collection of components that serve purposes similar to those of the common facilities and COS, but have scope limited to a particular application (that is, to a specific domain). These components are specified as part of the object definition, but if any of them is discovered to be common across multiple domains, it may be standardized and moved into the set of common components.

Finally, the ORB delivers object operations to the server for application to the objects themselves through the object adaptor. Like the application interface, the object adaptor is domain specific (that is, it is developed for managing a specific set of objects) and implementation specific, converting between the standard ORB requests and the local server implementation. In particular, the object adaptor may convert between the public and standard form of an object and the local storage format.

Figure 2.8 shows the interaction between the ORB and the client and server in more detail. It also shows the information repositories that are held at the client and server. The interface repository is held on the client and contains information about how the objects are handled, such as the interfaces and data attributes. The implementation repository is held on the server and contains the information that allows the ORB to locate and manage the objects; it also contains the active values of the fields within the object.

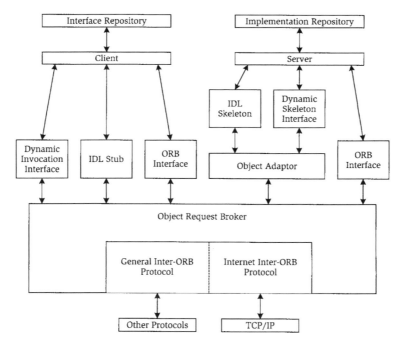

FIGURE 2.8

Interaction between client, server, and an ORB is handled by a set of components that provide abstraction and mapping functions. Communication between ORBs is provided by a general protocol with a specific adaptation to bridge the gap to TCP/IP.

There are three components that provide the application interface from client to ORB. The ORB interface is a standard abstract interface to the ORB defined by the CORBA specification to allow application implementations to be decoupled from the ORB with an abstract representation of the objects. The IDL stub provides a mapping of object formats between the local application and the ORB. This mapping is important when the local application has not been coded using an IDL programming language—ORB development kits typically support mappings to standard languages (e.g., C, C⁺⁺, and Java) and provide IDL compilers to allow new objects to be defined in IDL and converted to the local programming language. The third application interface component is the dynamic invocation interface (DII), which provides direct access to the request–response mechanism of the ORB, including an IDL stub but with full awareness of the format of the objects.

Similarly, at the server, there are three components that provide access to the implementation repository. The ORB interface supplies the same level of standard abstract interaction on the server that it does on the client. The other two components interact with the ORB through the object adaptor described earlier. The IDL skeleton fulfills the same role on the server that the IDL stub does on the client: It provides a mapping between the standard object formats and the local formats stored in the implementation repository. The dynamic skeleton interface (DSI) provides direct access to the request–response mechanism of the ORB, including an IDL skeleton, but with full awareness of the format of the objects.

Figure 2.8 also shows how the ORB communicates with other client or server ORBs. The ORBs talk to each other using the General Inter-ORB Protocol (GIOP) that defines a set of application-level messages and data representations for transactions between ORBs. GIOP may be carried over a variety of transport protocols, but we are interested only in transport over the Internet. For this purpose, CORBA requires that an additional adaptation layer be used to bring the level of function of TCP/IP up to the requirements of GIOP and to make visible the IP addresses of the nodes on which objects reside. The combination of GIOP and this adaptation layer is known as the Internet Inter-ORB Protocol (IIOP). GIOP and IIOP are described further in the next section.

2.6.3 CORBA Communications

CORBA's GIOP is defined along with CORBA by the OMG. GIOP is a generic object exchange protocol designed to be mapped onto any connection-oriented transport protocol. The OMG lists the objectives of GIOP as simplicity, scalability, low cost, generality, and architectural neutrality. GIOP attempts to achieve these goals by defining a set of assumptions about the underlying transport mechanism, messages to carry the data and data manipulation requests across the transport mechanism, and a list of syntaxes for the representation of IDL data types within the messages.

The GIOP common data representation (CDR) defines how objects and data are encoded within messages. There are several key points to note:

- All data types are aligned on their natural boundaries to make it easier for applications to read and write data to messages. This has the obvious consequence that messages may be larger than strictly required, but makes application implementation more simple. Note that as data objects are placed in a message, they may need to be prepadded to bring the message up to the correct byte offset.

- Integers are supplied in messages in the sender's native format. This differs from the normal process in which all integers are transferred in "wire format" with the most significant byte first. Again, this allows for a simpler implementation—a sender never has to manipulate data before placing it in a message. A flag in each GIOP message indicates the sender's integer format and the receiver need only manipulate the data from a message if its own integer format is different.

- Other encodings (such as ASN.1 for SNMP requests) may be encapsulated as octet strings (that is, transparent streams of bytes) within the CDR.

- The CDR includes a construct called an *indirection* that allows one part of a message to point to data in another part of the message. This enables a degree of compression so that repeated data need only be present in the message once.

GIOP is a client-server protocol. The client is responsible for initiating a connection (using the underlying transport mechanism) with the server, and initiating the communications. In early versions of GIOP the server was not allowed to send request messages—it could only respond to requests from the client so that if two nodes wished to operate on each other's data objects it was necessary to maintain two connections between them. Although this added some simplicity to implementations in which only a unidirectional service was needed, the limitation has been relaxed in later versions of GIOP to allow bidirectional request exchanges on a single connection with the distinction of client and server diminished to connection management.

All GIOP messages begin with a common header. The first 4 bytes contain the magic cookie "GIOP" encoded in ASCII. The next two fields give the version number—the current version is 1.3, but any implementation supporting version 1.x must also support version 1.y for each $y < x$. The F-bit indicates whether this is the last or only fragment of a message (zero) or whether further fragments will follow (one). The B-bit shows how the integers in this message (including the subsequent Message Length field) are encoded—zero means the integers are Big-Endian and one means Little-Endian. The Message Type field indicates what the message is for, using values from Table 2.2. The Message Length gives the length of the remaining message, excluding the common header in bytes.

Each GIOP message starts with the common message header and continues with some message-specific fields, including a 4-byte request identifier to help

Table 2.2 GIOP Messages	
Message Type	**Message**
0	Request. Sent by client (or server if bidirectional GIOP is in use) to invoke a CORBA object that is to read, write, or otherwise operate on an object. Request messages carry unique identifiers used to correlate replies and fragments.
1	Reply. Sent in response to a Request to return data that are read or to return the result of the operation in the request. A flag in the Request indicates whether a Response should be sent.
2	CancelRequest. Sent by the sender of a Request to attempt to cancel it before the receiver acts on it and sends a Reply.
3	LocateRequest. Sent to determine whether the receiver is capable of performing the requested operation on the specified object. The LocateReply can affirm or deny the request and can also redirect the request to another location. Note that these results are identical to the response to a Request message carried by a Reply, but that the LocateRequest does not carry the full data, which are useful if redirection is likely.
4	LocateReply. Sent in response to a LocateRequest.
5	CloseConnection. Sent by either end of a connection to indicate that the sender intends to close the connection and that any outstanding Request messages sent to it will not receive a Reply and will not be acted on.
6	MessageError. Reports a general, high-level parsing error such as an unsupported version number or an unknown message type. More detailed message-specific errors are handled in Reply messages.
7	Fragment. This message is used to continue and complete a sequence of fragments started by a Request or Reply that has the F-bit in the common header set to 1 to indicate that the data have been fragmented between multiple messages.

```
<value>::=      <value_tag> [<codebase_URL>][<type_info>] <state> |
                <indirection_tag> <indirection> |
                <null_tag>
```

FIGURE 2.9

Basic encoding of values in GIOP messages.

correlate responses and fragments. The data are presented as a series of data values. On a Request message the data values are the input parameters to the object operation, and on a Reply they are the output parameters. Data values in a GIOP message can be represented by the BNF encoding shown in Figure 2.9. Each value begins with an integer value tag to identify the data type. The value

```
<state>::=              <octets>|
                        <value_chunk> [<end_tag>]|
                        <value> [<end_tag>]
<value_chunk>::=        <chunk_size_tag><octets>
<octets>::=             octet[<octets>]
```

FIGURE 2.10

Encoding of data values within a GIOP message may be a series of bytes, chunks of data, or nested data types.

tag may optionally (according to the value of the value tag) be followed by strings giving a codebase universal resource locator (URL) and type information to help locate the data in a repository. Then comes the data (called the *state*). Alternatively, the value tag may be replaced by an indirection to the data, or a special tag to show that no data are present.

The state may be a sequence of one or more bytes (called *octets*) or may be a nested sequence of values, allowing data structures to be represented as shown in Figure 2.10. Note that there is support for splitting large (that is, of many bytes) data values across messages by chunking them. The end tag is used to indicate the end of a series of data chunks or the end of a nesting of values.

Connections are initiated in GIOP by a client. It uses the transport mechanism to open a connection to the server. In early versions of GIOP only the client was able to send `Request`, `LocateRequest`, and `CancelRequest` messages, and only the server could send a `CloseConnection` message. In more recent versions the distinction between client and server is limited to connection establishment. The connection gives context to the request identifiers used in the messages and (obviously) transports the messages.

TCP/IP provides reliable connection-oriented transport and so should be suitable for use by GIOP, but TCP/IP is limited by the failure or closure of connections. In particular, TCP does not provide a graceful shutdown whereby data "in the pipe" are flushed before the connection is torn down. This is a requirement of GIOP because the server may send a `CloseConnection` message and then shut down the connection; if this operation is attempted in TCP, the `CloseConnection` message may be lost, leaving the client unsure whether a new invocation is required because the previous connection failed or whether the old connection was closed under the control of an application. To bridge this gap, an additional adaptation layer is added to GIOP to make the IIOP. Since IIOP is a minimum requirement of a conformant CORBA implementation, and since TCP/IP is almost ubiquitous, the term IIOP is used interchangeably with GIOP. IIOP is also defined by the OMG in the base CORBA specification along with GIOP.

The first requirement of IIOP is to extend the object profiles to contain the host on which the object is located and the port through which it can be accessed. The host is presented as a string that may contain a partially or fully specified host name (that is, a name such as "enterprise," or a fully qualified domain name for the host such as "enterprise.accounts.mycompany.com"), or the IP address of the host presented in dotted notation (e.g., "192.231.79.52"). The port number identifies the TCP port on which the server (that is, the identified host) will be listening.

IIOP modifies the procedure for closing a connection by stipulating that the receiver of a `CloseConnection` message must close the connection. This takes the responsibility for connection closure away from the sender of the message and allows the process to complete successfully.

2.7 CHOOSING A CONFIGURATION PROTOCOL

Choosing between CORBA, XML, and SNMP is not simple even if you have decided to use a standardized technique rather than one of the proprietary configuration mechanisms built into your equipment. SNMP is well established, with MIB modules designed within the IETF, often by the people who wrote the protocols that are being managed. The MIB modules offer a great deal of detail and fine control, but to some extent this is a downfall since the level of detail increases the apparent complexity of a MIB module for the reader or the implementer. The argument is often made that MIB modules are too complex and are consequently hard to understand. In the end, the amount of information that needs to be managed is static regardless of the protocol used to manage it; there is a constant amount of information needed to control and operate a device no matter how that information is transferred to the device. This means that discussions about the quantity of managed data are bogus and all that remains to be considered are the encodings and protocols.

XML provides an encoding technique that is at once easy to extend, readable by a human, and easy for a program to parse. Its downside is that its very readability makes it verbose, although compression techniques in the transport protocol may help to ameliorate this. XML is unquestionably easy and quick to develop and for this reason it is beginning to gain considerable popularity.

CORBA has an established foothold, especially with the larger service providers where the structured management network shown in Figure 2.1 is popular. Since CORBA is so often a requirement as a northbound interface from EMSs, it may make sense to offer CORBA support on the managed devices. Note that CORBA is also popular with object-oriented programmers because of its inherent object-oriented nature and the ready availability of ORB components in C^{++} and Java.

SNMP remains the most-deployed network management protocol. Despite fears about security, SNMPv2 is widely used and MIB modules give a well-known and detailed breakdown of the configuration data. Although ASN.1 is initially hard to get into, with familiarity the text representation is easy to read and can be automatically parsed to generate management applications and source code for clients and servers.

Note that it is possible to mix and match. One option that is sometimes used is to maintain the configuration data in MIB format, but to transfer them as bulk data using CORBA or XML. This can avoid some of the security concerns of the earlier SNMP versions while continuing to use the detailed MIB modules.

2.8 CHOOSING TO COLLECT STATISTICS

Successful network operation is not just about configuring devices, but also requires constant monitoring of the status of the links and nodes that make up the network to detect faults, congestion, and network "hot spots." For ISPs to achieve contracted levels of service, they must be continuously aware of the load within their network and must discover node and link failures as quickly as possible.

SNMP provides notifications through trap messages to alert the management station when key events occur, although it is of the nature of networking failures that they may themselves prevent the delivery of any notification messages. SNMP also gives access to counters that provide basic statistical information about the traffic flows through a specific interface or device, and a management station may read these counters repeatedly to get a view of the change in network usage.

It should be borne in mind that the process of collecting network statistics in real time may have a detrimental effect on the operation of the network. This is not quite Heisenberg's Uncertainty Principle, but repeated requests to read data at many nodes can cause a lot of additional traffic and may congest the network around the central location at which the data are accumulated. For this reason, network statistics should be collected in a very structured way for day-to-day operation, focusing on entry and exit points to networks rather than on every link and node within the entire network. This has the benefit of policing Internet work agreements as well as checking to see which external links are close to their limits. Figure 2.11 shows how only certain links in a network might be monitored.

At the same time, multiple collection points can be used within the network to share the load of statistics collection. These intermediate collection points serve to coalesce the data sets into a single useful group of statistics before forwarding the information to the central collection point. In particular, since some statistics are used for billing, some for fault detection, some for long-term planning, and some for service maintenance, the intermediate collection points can filter the statistics and send information to the appropriate consumer while still providing just a single point of contact for each device. This hierarchy is shown in Figure 2.12.

Although SNMP may provide access to the necessary statistical information, it is not the best choice for network monitoring because it is request–response based. The client (or collection point) must issue read requests to the server (the device being monitored) in order to read the information. Further, the MIB modules are structured for wide configuration reporting rather than pure statistics gathering. These two factors mean that SNMP introduces a considerable overhead if it is used for this purpose.

As an alternative, the NetFlow architecture was devised by Cisco and is now being considered for standardization by the IETF. NetFlow is based on a series of

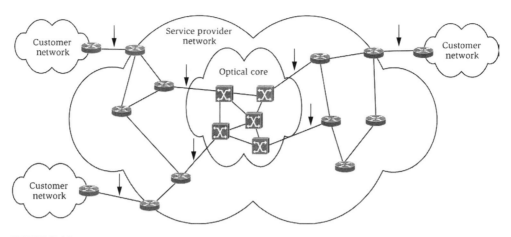

FIGURE 2.11

Network statistics can be monitored at specific points in a network (shown by the arrows) to gain a good view of overall operations without overloading the network.

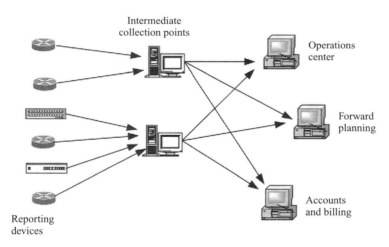

FIGURE 2.12

Hierarchy of collection points for network statistics reduces the associated traffic and offloads some of the processing requirements.

record formats specifically designed to contain statistical information and to allow devices to report bulk data to their collection points. An important consideration is that the maintenance and dispatch of the NetFlow records should have the smallest possible impact on the ability of the device to forward data.

The NetFlow records can be collected by the device and sent periodically (based on a timer or a threshold) to the collection point, generally using a transfer protocol such as FTP. An intermediate collection point can operate on the data and then send them onward. Since NetFlow is not an IP protocol, we will not discuss it further.

2.9 POLICY CONTROL

Policy control is a variation of network management. It recognizes that when configuration requests arrive through signaling protocols rather than through management protocols, each network node is responsible for applying some policy to decide how to treat the requests. This policy may be local (specific to the node making the decision) or applicable across a wider domain, and the decision can be made at each node or devolved to centralized policy servers.

Note that when devices are managed through a management protocol there is still a policy that governs what resources can be provisioned in support of which services, but that policy is usually applied by the network operator in consultation with a management application.

The IETF defined a framework for policy control in RFC 2753 and the Common Open Policy Service (COPS) protocol to convey policy requests between clients and servers in RFC 2748. Since then, it has been recognized that policy requests and responses, and also policy pushes, are simple client/server data transfers similar to file transfers, and the rather complicated COPS protocol has been largely abandoned in favor of transferring XML-encoded policy information using SOAP (see previous discussion) or the Blocks Extensible Exchange Protocol (BEEP).

2.9.1 Choosing to Apply Policy

When resources in a network are reserved to support service management for integrated services or the Resource Reservation Protocol (RSVP) they are removed from general availability and are held for exclusive use by a specific datastream. This happens solely on the say-so of the requesting node—usually the node that will be sending or receiving the data. This requesting node knows the characteristics of the data being transferred and what network resources will be required to support them, so the reservation request asks for what is needed.

A node in the network receives many such requests but has only limited resources available. It must decide which requests should be satisfied and which rejected. These decisions obviously take into account the available bandwidth, and may consider authentication data (e.g., whether or not the request is from a valid neighbor or not) and request priority (as in RSVP-TE for MPLS). However, in a large network additional policy-based decisions need to be made to determine whether precious resources should be tied up for use by data flows between particular applications at the source and destination nodes.

It is not necessary to make these policy decisions at each node in the network. It is sufficient to consider the requests as they pass into and out of policy admin-

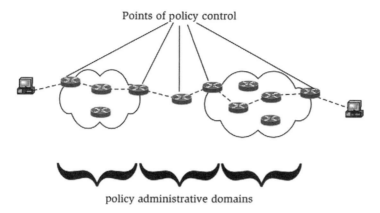

Points of policy control

policy administrative domains

FIGURE 2.13

Policy is enforced at the boundaries of administrative domains.

istrative domains. Once a request has entered such a domain, the nodes within the network may consider that the local domain policy has been satisfied and can reserve the resources as requested. This is shown in Figure 2.13. Policy checking on departure from an administrative domain may not be necessary, but network operators may want to distinguish between reservation requests that are satisfied entirely within their network and the financial cost of resources reserved outside their network.

The points of policy control shown in Figure 2.13 may be configured with sufficient information to make policy decisions on their own. This would certainly be the case for simple policies, but for more complex decisions based on detailed information about the topology and players in the network—and possibly a frequently changing network-wide policy—the points of policy control must consult an external policy server.

Figure 2.14 shows how a router that makes policy decisions might be constructed. When a reservation request is received by the signaling component of the router (step 1) it consults the local policy component (step 2). If the policy control component on the router cannot make a decision, it consults a remote policy server (step 3). The policy decision (step 4) is relayed by the local policy component to the signaling component (step 5), which is able to make the required resource reservations (step 6) before signaling to the next node in the network (step 7). Finally, the data can flow, making use of the reserved resources (steps 8 and 9).

Figure 2.15 shows the full architecture for policy-based decision making. The IETF has named a point of policy control a policy enforcement point (PEP). The PEP receives a policy request and consults its local policy decision point (LPDP), which may involve examination of a cache of locally stored policy information. If

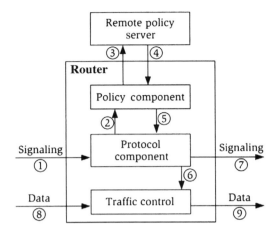

FIGURE 2.14

Policy is the responsibility of a distinct component within a network node and may require the assistance of a remote policy server.

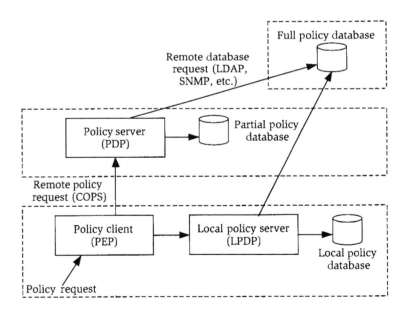

FIGURE 2.15

Policy architecture allows for local decisions and the consultation of a remote policy database.

the LPDP is unable to make a decision, the PEP consults a remote policy decision point (PDP) on another node in the network. Since the PDP is remote from the PEP, the two nodes must use a protocol to communicate; although the IETF specified the COPS protocol for this purpose, this protocol never gained much momentum and has been replaced by other mechanisms such as the exchange of XML-encoded policy information using SOAP (see Section 2.5.3) or Blocks Extensible Exchange Protocol (BEEP). The PEP fills the role of a client, making policy inquiries or requests to the PDP server.

The PDP has much more information available to it and can apply the full policy rules to produce an answer for the PEP. However, as the size of networks grows it may be infeasible for a single PDP server to retain all of the information necessary to make proper policy decisions about all possible traffic flows. The architecture handles this by allowing both the LDPD and PDP to read additional policy data from a full (and probably distributed) policy database using whatever protocol is suitable (perhaps LDAP, the Lightweight Directory Access Protocol, or maybe SNMP).

2.9.2 Policy Information Base

The policy information that is exchanged between the PDP server and PEP and stored in policy databases needs some structure and format. Initial policy uses were specified using text (see RFC 2749 that describes the use of COPS in support of RSVP), but this is neither sufficiently precise to be safe, nor easily extensible as more client types are produced. In particular, there may be common concepts such as interfaces that are shared between policy data for different clients— it would be helpful if this information could be configured and managed coherently.

The IETF recognized that the information to be managed was not dissimilar to that for device configuration and management and that the MIB described in Section 2.3 already had an infrastructure suitable for specifying and encoding such data. So the policy information base (PIB) was born.

The PIB is in many ways very similar to the MIB. It has tables and rows to contain the information about instances of specific devices and managed entities. These may range from the capabilities and restrictions of devices and interfaces, through the resources and bandwidth, to the specific data flows and policy request. PIBs are specified using the ASN.1 BER just as MIBs are and they use the same basic data types defined in the Structure of Management Information (SMIv2 in RFC 2578). RFC 3318 defines a framework PIB in the context of policy decision points and defines some basic textual conventions for use by other PIB modules.

IP-Based Service Implementation and Network Management

This chapter, taken from Chapter 6 of *Developing IP-Based Services* by Morrow and Vijayananda, discusses the implementation and delivery of those services. While technology plays an important role in developing services, it is also important that the services be provisioned and delivered in an easy and profitable manner. "Easy and profitable" here refers to the scalability of a solution in terms of the staffing and skills required to implement the solution for a mass market. Technical implementation in the lab is an academic exercise to show the feasibility of a solution. This solution may not be profitable for a service provider if provisioning the service for a large number of customers is too expensive or time consuming.

It is important that the provisioning of the service be (1) simple, meaning that it can be done easily and does not require skilled staff; and (2) scalable, meaning that a significant number of customers can be provisioned in a reasonable period of time. The terms *significant number* and *reasonable period of time* have to be defined by the service provider with reference to profitability. The choice of network devices and provisioning tools plays an important role in making the service provision simple and scalable.

Another significant factor in provisioning services is *service upgrades.* A service upgrade may require changes in the configuration of existing devices or a software/hardware upgrade of the network devices. The ease and speed at which a service upgrade can be done for a large number of customers also play an important role in making a service profitable for the service provider.

Another important aspect of delivering IP-based services is network management. It is not enough if the service is implemented correctly. It must also be monitored on a regular basis to ensure that it is functioning properly. This requires an investment in equipment, staffing, and intelligence in the network devices. There is a trade-off between the cost of monitoring and the benefits provided by monitoring. Proactive monitoring is useful and helps to prevent service outages and network downtime. The cost of repairing a fault after its manifestation can be much higher than the cost of monitoring the network and preventing the occurrence of the fault in the first place.

Consider the situation in which a network device starts malfunctioning as the memory usage and load on it reaches a certain threshold. This device is in a remote location, so it takes a few hours for the maintenance crew to physically reach it. The load and memory usage are directly proportional to the number of customer connections terminating on the device. When the load reaches the threshold, the device stops functioning and must be reset. The maintenance crew must go to the site where it is located in order to reset it. Proactive monitoring of the load and memory usage of the device can help to prevent this situation. In order to keep a good balance between the cost and benefits of monitoring, it is necessary to have a good network management infrastructure.

This chapter focuses on the implementation of IP-based services, monitoring the network to ensure correct delivery of the services, and reporting the status of the devices to customers as part of the *service level agreement* (SLA). Simple Network Management Protocol (SNMP) plays an important role in implementing IP-based services, therefore, a brief discussion on SNMP is presented in Section 3.1.

Several aspects related to the implementation of IP-based services are presented in this chapter, such as security and management. The *operations support system* (OSS) is the system responsible for implementing IP-based services. A discussion on the importance of OSS, its architecture, and its requirements is presented in Section 3.5.

3.1 SIMPLE NETWORK MANAGEMENT PROTOCOL

SNMP is an application-layer protocol that facilitates the exchange of management information between network devices. It is part of the *Transmission Control Protocol/Internet Protocol* (TCP/IP) suite. SNMP enables network administrators to manage network performance, find and solve network problems, and plan for network growth. Three versions of SNMP exist: SNMP version 1 (SNMPv1), SNMP version 2 (SNMPv2), and SNMP version 3 (SNMPv3). All three versions have a number of features in common, but SNMPv2 offers enhancements, such as additional protocol operations, and SNMPv3 offers security features.

SNMP plays an important role in managing networks. It helps provide a uniform interface to access and manage all network devices.

3.1.1 Description

SNMP defines a client–server relationship. The client program (called the *network management system,* or NMS) makes virtual connections to a server program (called the *SNMP agent*) that executes on a remote network device, and serves information to the NMS regarding the device's status. The database, controlled by the SNMP agent, is referred to as the SNMP *management information base* (MIB) and is a standard set of statistical and control values. SNMP additionally allows the extension of these standard values with values specific to a particular agent through the use of private MIBs.

Directives, issued by the NMS client to an SNMP agent, consist of the identifiers of SNMP variables (referred to as *MIB object identifiers* or *MIB variables*) along with instructions to either get the value for the identifier or set the identifier to a new value. Through the use of private MIB variables, SNMP agents can be tailored for myriad specific devices, such as network bridges, gateways, and routers. The definitions of MIB variables supported by a particular agent are incorporated in descriptor files, written in *Abstract Syntax Notation* (ASN.1) format, made available to network management client programs so that they can become aware of MIB variables and their usage.

3.1.2 Components

As shown in Figure 3.1, an SNMP managed network consists of four key components: managed devices, agents, MIBs, and an NMS.

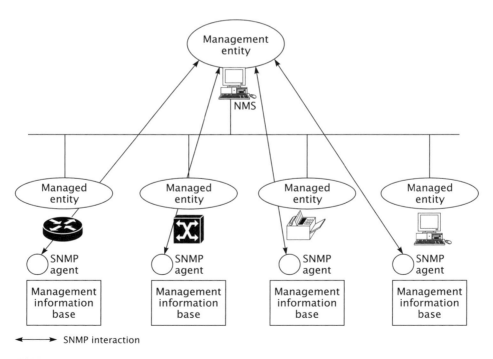

FIGURE 3.1

SNMP components.

Managed device: A network node that contains an SNMP agent and resides on a managed network. Managed devices collect and store management information and make this information available to the NMS using SNMP. Managed devices, sometimes called *network elements,* can be routers and access servers, switches and bridges, hubs, computer hosts, and printers.

Agent: A network management software module that resides in a managed device. An agent has local knowledge of management information and translates that information into a form compatible with SNMP.

MIB: Consists of the management information that resides in the managed device. The agent provides a standard access to the MIB.

NMS: Executes applications that monitor and control managed devices. The NMS provides the bulk of the processing and memory resources required for network management. One or more NMSs must exist on any managed network.

3.1.3 Operations

Managed devices are monitored and controlled using four basic SNMP commands: read, write, trap, and traversal operations.

Read command: Used by an NMS to monitor managed devices. The NMS examines different variables that are maintained by managed devices.

Write command: Used by an NMS to control managed devices. The NMS changes the values of variables stored within managed devices.

Trap command: Used by managed devices to asynchronously report events to the NMS. When certain types of events occur, a managed device sends a trap to the NMS.

Traversal operations: Used by the NMS to determine which variables a managed device supports and to sequentially gather information in variable tables, such as a routing table.

3.1.4 Management Information Base

A MIB is a collection of information that is organized hierarchically. MIBs are accessed using a network management protocol such as SNMP. They are composed of managed objects and are identified by object identifiers. A managed object (sometimes called a *MIB object,* an *object,* or a *MIB*) is one of any number of specific characteristics of a managed device. Managed objects are composed of one or more object instances, which are essentially variables. Two types of managed objects exist: *scalar* and *tabular.* Scalar objects define a single object instance. Tabular objects define multiple related object instances that are grouped together in MIB tables.

Figure 3.2 shows a sample MIB tree and examples of scalar and tabular managed objects. An example of a scalar managed object is ifNumber, which is a scalar

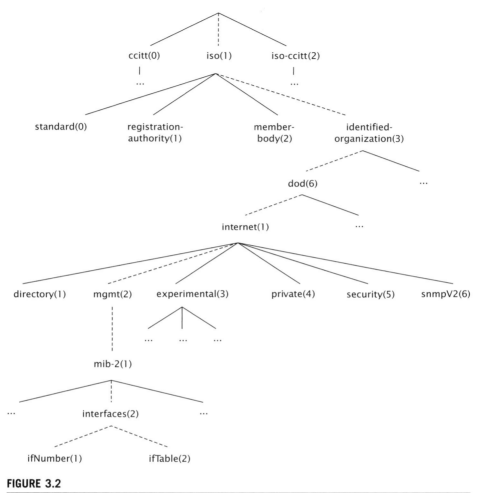

FIGURE 3.2

Sample MIB tree.

object that contains a single object instance, the integer value that indicates the total number of interfaces in the router. An example of a tabular managed object is ifTable, which is a tabular object that contains a multiple object instance. Each instance contains detailed information about the interfaces in the router. The top-level MIB object IDs belong to different standards organizations, while lower-level object IDs are allocated by associated organizations. Vendors can define private branches that include managed objects for their own products. MIBs that have not been standardized typically are positioned in the experimental branch. The managed object ifNumber can be uniquely identified either by the object name—

"iso.org.dod.internet.mxmt.mib-2.interfaces.ifNumber"—or by the equivalent object descriptor—1.3.6.1.2.1.2.1.

3.1.5 SNMP Version 1

SNMPvl is the initial implementation of the SNMP protocol. It is described in RFC 1157 and functions within the specifications of the *structure of management information* (SMI). SNMPvl operates over protocols such as the User Datagram Protocol (UDP), IP, OSI Connectionless Network Service (CLNS), AppleTalk's Datagram Delivery Protocol (DDP), and Novell's Internet Packet Exchange (IPX). SNMPvl is widely used and is the de facto network management protocol in the Internet community.

SNMPvl and the Structure of Management Information
The structure of management information (SMI) defines the rules for describing management information, using ASN.1. The SNMPvl SMI is defined in RFC 1155. It makes three key specifications: ASN.1 data types, SMI-specific data types, and SNMP MIB tables.

SNMPvl and ASN.1 Data Types
The SNMPvl SMI specifies that all managed objects have a certain subset of ASN.1 data types associated with them. Three ASN.1 data types are required: name, syntax, and encoding. The name serves as the object identifier (OID). The syntax defines the data type of the object (e.g., integer or string). The SMI uses a subset of the ASN.1 syntax definitions. The encoding data describe how information associated with a managed object is formatted as a series of data items for transmission over the network.

SNMPvl and SMI-Specific Data Types
The SNMPvl SMI specifies the use of a number of SMI-specific data types, which are divided into two categories: simple data types and application-wide data types. Three simple data types are defined in the SNMPvl SMI, all of which are unique values: integers, octet strings, and oids.

> *Integer data type:* A signed integer in the range of –2,147,483,648 to 2,147,483,647.
> *Octet strings:* Ordered sequences of 0 to 65,535 octets.
> *Object identifiers:* Come from the set of all oids allocated according to the rules specified in ASN.1.

Seven application-wide data types exist in the SNMPvl SMI: network addresses, counters, gauges, time ticks, opaques, integers, and unsigned integers.

> *Network addresses:* Represent an address from a particular protocol family. SNMPvl supports only 32-bit IP addresses.

Counters: Nonnegative integers that increase until they reach a maximum value and then return to zero. In SNMPvl, a 32-bit counter size is specified.

Gauges: Nonnegative integers that can increase or decrease but retain the maximum value reached.

Time tick: Represents a hundredth of a second since some event.

Opaque: Represents an arbitrary encoding that is used to pass arbitrary information strings that do not conform to the strict data typing used by the SMI.

Integer: Represents signed integer–valued information. This data type redefines the integer data type, which has arbitrary precision in ASN.1, but bounded precision in the SMI.

Unsigned integer: Represents unsigned integer–valued information and is useful when values are always nonnegative. This data type redefines the integer data type, which has arbitrary precision in ASN.1, but bounded precision in the SMI.

SNMP MIB Tables

The SNMPvl SMI defines highly structured tables that are used to group the instances of a tabular object (i.e., an object that contains multiple variables). Tables are composed of zero or more rows, which are indexed in a way that allows SNMP to retrieve or alter an entire row with one Get, GetNext, or Set command.

SNMPvl Protocol Operations

SNMP is a simple request-response protocol. The network management system issues a request, and managed devices return responses. This behavior is implemented by using one of four protocol operations: Get, GetNext, Set, and Trap.

Get *operation:* Used by the NMS to retrieve the value of one or more object instances from an agent. If the agent responding to the Get operation cannot provide values for all the object instances in a list, it does not provide any values.

GetNext *operation:* Used by the NMS to retrieve the value of the next object instance in a table or list within an agent.

Set *operation:* Used by the NMS to set the values of object instances within an agent.

Trap *operation:* Used by agents to asynchronously inform the NMS of a significant event.

3.1.6 SNMP Version 2

SNMPv2 is an evolution of the initial version, SNMPvl. Originally, SNMPv2 was published as a set of proposed Internet standards in 1993. Currently, it is a draft standard. As with SNMPvl, SNMPv2 functions within the specifications of the SMI.

In theory, SNMPv2 offers a number of improvements to SNMPv1, including additional protocol operations.

SNMPv2 and the SMI

The SMI defines the rules for describing management information, using ASN.1. The SNMPv2 SMI is described in RFC 2578. It makes certain additions and enhancements to the SNMPv1 SMI-specific data types, such as including bit strings, network addresses, and counters.

Bit strings: Defined only in SNMPv2 and comprise zero or more named bits that specify a value.

Network addresses: Represent an address from a particular protocol family. SNMPv1 supports only 32-bit IP addresses, but SNMPv2 can support other types of addresses as well.

Counters: Nonnegative integers that increase until they reach a maximum value and then return to zero. In SNMPv1, a 32-bit counter size is specified. In SNMPv2, 32-bit and 64-bit counters are defined.

SMI Information Modules

The SNMPv2 SMI also specifies information modules, which specify a group of related definitions. Three types of SMI information modules exist: MIB modules, compliance statements, and capability statements.

MIB modules: Contain definitions of interrelated managed objects.

Compliance statements: Provide a systematic way to describe a group of managed objects that must be implemented for conformance to a standard.

Capability statements: Used to indicate the precise level of support that an agent claims with respect to a MIB group. An NMS can adjust its behavior toward agents according to the capability statements associated with each agent.

SNMPv2 Protocol Operations

The Get, GetNext, and Set operations used in SNMPv1 are also used in SNMPv2. SNMPv2 adds and enhances some protocol operations. The SNMPv2 trap operation, for example, serves the same function as that used in SNMPv1, but it uses a different message format and is designed to replace the SNMPv1 trap. SNMPv2 also defines two new protocol operations: GetBulk and Inform.

GetBulk operation: Used by the NMS to efficiently retrieve large blocks of data, such as multiple rows in a table. GetBulk fills a response message with as much of the requested data as will fit.

Inform operation: Allows one NMS to send trap information to another NMS and receive a response. In SNMPv2, if the agent responding to the

`GetBulk` operation cannot provide values for all of the variables in a list, it will provide partial results.

3.1.7 **Security Issues**

SNMP lacks any authentication capabilities, which results in vulnerability to a variety of security threats. These include masquerading, modification of information, message sequence and timing modifications, and disclosure.

> *Masquerading:* Consists of an unauthorized entity attempting to perform management operations by assuming the identity of an authorized management entity.
>
> *Modification of information:* Involves an unauthorized entity attempting to alter a message generated by an authorized entity so that the message results in unauthorized accounting management or configuration management operations.
>
> *Message sequence and timing modifications:* These occur when an unauthorized entity reorders, delays, or copies and later replays a message generated by an authorized entity.
>
> *Disclosure:* Results when an unauthorized entity extracts values stored in managed objects, or learns of notified events by monitoring exchanges between managers and agents.

The security issues related to SNMP are addressed in the latest version of SNMP, SNMPv3.

3.1.8 **SNMP Version 3**

SNMPv3 uses the framework provided by SNMPv2 and provides some additional features. The new features of SNMPv3 (in addition to those of SNMPv2 listed above) include:

- Security features:
  - Authentication.
  - Privacy.
  - Authorization and access control.
- Administrative framework features:
  - Naming of entities.
  - People and policies.
  - User names and key management.
  - Notification destinations.
  - Proxy relationships.
  - Remotely configurable via SNMP operations.

SNMPv3 includes three important services: authentication, privacy, and access control. To deliver these services in a flexible and efficient manner, SNMPv3

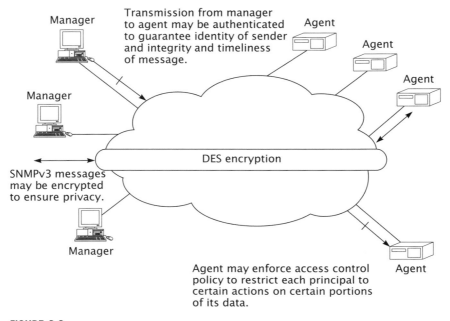

Manager

Transmission from manager to agent may be authenticated to guarantee identity of sender and integrity and timeliness of message.

Agent

Agent

Agent

Manager

DES encryption

SNMPv3 messages may be encrypted to ensure privacy.

Manager

Agent may enforce access control policy to restrict each principal to certain actions on certain portions of its data.

Agent

FIGURE 3.3

SNMPv3 security options.

introduces the concept of a *principal,* which is the entity on whose behalf services are provided or processing takes place. A principal can be an individual acting in a particular role. It can also be a set of individuals with every individual acting in a particular role. In essence, a principal operates from a management station and issues SNMP commands to agent systems. The identity of the principal and the target agent together determine the security features that will be invoked, including authentication, privacy, and access control. The use of principals allows security policies to be tailored to the specific principal, agent, and information exchange, and gives human security managers considerable flexibility in assigning network authorization to users. SNMPv3 security options are shown in Figure 3.3.

3.2 IP-BASED SERVICE IMPLEMENTATION—OSS

IP-based service implementation plays an important role in delivering services to customers. It is also critical for service providers, because it helps them to roll out their services in a timely manner, ensure that the services are implemented correctly, win the confidence of the customers, and thereby gain and maintain a large share of the customer base. A good service implementation model is the key to implementing services. The term *implementation* in regards to an IP-based service for a customer refers to several aspects of the service. It starts when the customer is sold the idea of the service, and the end result is when the customer can make use of the service.

3.2.1 Selling the Services

To begin with, the customer is sold the idea of the service by the service provider. Once the service is sold, it has to be realized before the customer can actually use it. In some cases, the customer has to provide essential details for implementing the service—for example, information about the IP addressing plan of the customer network, the number of customer sites that require the service, the network infrastructure available at each site, and so on. Once all of the information is available, new network devices have to be installed as required on the customer sites and connected to the nearest POP. The service provider's network devices have to be configured to provision all of the new connections; after the configurations are complete, the service is ready to be made available to the customer.

3.2.2 Integration within and among Key Business Departments

The devices have to be integrated into the network monitoring system of the service provider. SLA reporting for the customer (if relevant for the service) has to be activated so that reports can be generated and made available. The billing department has to be informed about the new service so that the customer can be charged for it.

The following key departments are involved in implementing IP-based services:

Business marketing: Responsible for defining the business aspect of the services like pricing, service options, time to market, and so on.

Sales: Responsible for selling the IP-based services to the customer, maintaining the customer contact, and getting the requirements and information from the customer that are required for implementing the IP-based services.

Engineering: Responsible for developing and testing the technical solution for implementing the IP-based services.

NMS: Responsible for developing the NMS tools required for mass deployment of the services, service upgrades, billing, and SLA reports.

NOC: Responsible for deploying the services, monitoring the network, and ensuring that SLAs are reported to the customer.

Billing: Responsible for billing the customer for their IP-based services.

Each department has information that is critical for the correct implementation of the services to each individual customer. Oftentimes, the information provided by one department is crucial input for another department in order to implement the service. For example, the NOC is responsible for deploying the services. The billing department needs to know when the services have been implemented in order to start billing the customer. If the customer is charged based on the bandwidth of each link from the customer site to the nearest PoP, then the NOC must also inform the billing department about the bandwidth of each installed link.

It is essential that information flow properly, accurately, and promptly from one department to another. The service implementation model must meet the requirements of all the departments and must also ensure that the services can be correctly implemented. This system responsible for the integration of all the requirements is often referred to as the *operation support system* (OSS). (More details about the OSS are presented in Section 3.5.)

3.3 PROVISIONING ISSUES

This section presents the issues related to provisioning the services for the customer. Details about the various tasks are also sketched out, giving you an insight into the complexity of provisioning.

3.3.1 What Is Provisioning?

First of all, it is important to define the term *provisioning* before discussing anything about the issues related to this subject. When an IP-based service is offered to a customer, it has to be implemented for that customer. This implementation can involve the following tasks:

1. Installing new devices (customer-premises equipment, or CPE) at customer sites.
2. Connecting the CPE device to the service provider network.
3. Configuring the CPE devices for the new service.
4. Updating the configuration of the relevant network devices in the service provider network to activate the service.
5. Updating the network management systems with the information about the new customer and the network devices that have been installed.
6. Activating the service.
7. Activating the monitoring of the devices that are relevant for service delivery.

All of these tasks may not be necessary for every new customer. The term *provisioning* loosely refers to all of these tasks. The following section discusses these activities in detail.

Installation and Configuration of CPE Devices

Most services require a CPE device to be installed at the customer site. After the installation, they must be physically connected to the service provider network.

The next step is the logical connection between the CPE device and the service provider network: CPE devices have to be configured, or programmed, to deliver the correct service for the customer. It is important that the configuration be correct in order for the service to be delivered correctly. In most cases, the configuration on the CPE device has several parts: a part that is responsible for the normal operation of the CPE device and other parts that are responsible for specialized functions specific to the service in question.

For example, consider a router that is responsible for providing Internet connectivity to a corporation. A part of the router is responsible for sending and receiving IP packets. This can be considered as a basic configuration on the router. Another part of the router is responsible for ensuring that the IP address space of the corporation is correctly advertised to the Internet using a routing protocol such as the Border Gateway Protocol (BGP). This is the specialized configuration that is responsible for implementing the service (Internet access).

Another aspect of the configuration on the CPE devices is the parameters necessary to generate the configuration. Some of these parameters may be the same for all devices, while others are variable and depend on the service being offered or on the customer location. For example, consider the same router providing Internet access. The IP address on the router interface connected to the customer network is related to the IP addressing plan of the customer. The link capacity to the Internet also depends on the customer requirements. All of this information must be correctly configured on all of the CPE devices in order for the service to function properly.

Configuration of Network Devices

Before the CPE devices can communicate with the service provider network, the devices in the service provider network have to programmed, or configured. It may be necessary to program a single device or several devices before establishing communication between the CPE device and the service provider network. It is necessary that the configuration on all the intermediate devices be correct before the communication can be established.

For example, when ATM is used as the access technology, the VPI/VCI must be configured correctly on all of the ATM switches between the CPE and the PE in the access network. In addition, if bandwidth guarantee (quality of service, or QoS) is a requirement, then the ATM *class of service* (CoS) must also match on all of the ATM switches between the CPE and PE devices in order for the ATM network to meet the bandwidth requirements of the CPE device.

It is also important that the configurations of the CPE device and the service provider network match in order for them to communicate. Mismatch in configurations can result in no communication or incorrect delivery of the service. For example, the IP address on the CPE device and the PE in the service provider PoP must be in the same network in order for them to be able to exchange IP packets and routing information. If the IP addresses do not match, then there will be no communication between these devices. In the case of guaranteed bandwidth services using ATM technology, mismatch in the ATM CoS parameters can result in loss of packets and hence a degradation in the service.

Service Activation

When all of the relevant devices have been correctly configured, the next step is to activate the service. This step may involve several activities, such as:

1. Activating the Layer 2 connectivity on the CPE device.
2. Introducing all of the new CPE devices into the monitoring system.
3. Activating the monitoring of all CPE devices.

When all of these steps are completed, the service has been activated.

3.3.2 Device Configuration

Every IP-based service requires configuration of the CPE and service provider network devices. Some of this configuration is specific to a service and may not affect all the devices. Several solutions may be available to implement the same service, and each solution will have its advantages and disadvantages.

Consider the following scenario, in which a service provider wants to implement guaranteed bandwidth services in the access network. The access technology is ATM, and the service provider has an ATM access network. The service provider manages the CPE device. In order to implement guaranteed IP bandwidth service, it is enough to implement ATM traffic shaping on the CPE device. In order to ensure that traffic shaping functions properly on the CPE device (after all, this is done in software and it is practically impossible to write bug-free software), ATM traffic policing can be implemented on the first ATM switch (Figure 3.4).

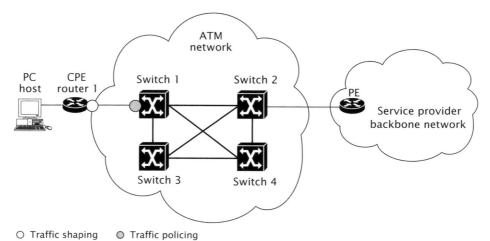

○ Traffic shaping   ◉ Traffic policing

FIGURE 3.4

Implementing guaranteed bandwidth service—solution 1.

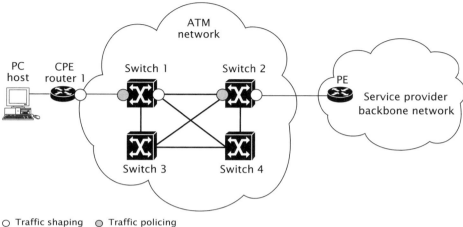

FIGURE 3.5

Implementing guaranteed bandwidth service—solution 2.

Another possible variation is to implement traffic shaping on all of the outbound interfaces and traffic policing on the inbound interfaces (Figure 3.5). The second solution requires more resources to configure all of the devices and also makes the configuration more complicated.

Another major issue in the configuration of network devices is the chance of misconfiguration. The potential risk of misconfiguration is always there and cannot be avoided. Modifications to the configuration of network devices to provision new service requests may not be done correctly and may disrupt service for other customers if the changes to the configurations are incorrect and are not implemented in the correct order. By keeping configuration changes to a minimum number of devices, the overall chance of misconfiguration can be reduced.

Consider again the scenario described in Figure 3.4. The link between the CPE device and the PE device is supposed to deliver 2 Mbps. In the case of solution 2, due to a mismatch in configuration if the traffic policing on Switch 2 is set for 512 Kbps instead of 2 Mbps, then the effective bandwidth between the PC and the file server is only 512 Kbps. This problem could have been avoided if the policing were restricted to Switch 1.

To summarize, to keep a service simple and easy to implement, it is necessary to make the service-specific configuration as simple as possible and restrict it to a minimum number of devices. In doing so, one can reduce (1) the staffing and time required to provision a service request, (2) the risks of misconfiguration, and (3) disruption in service for other customers.

3.3.3 **How to Configure the Devices**

Most network devices have software installed on them that allows the configuration of the device in order to support several functions. Modification to relevant parameters in the device activates the corresponding functions on the device. Depending on the device and the manufacturer, several methods are available for modifying configurations of network devices. Some common methods include:

- *Text-based command line interface* (CLI) to modify values of parameters or activate functions.
- *Menu-driven CLI* to modify values of parameters or activate functions.
- *Web-based CLI* to modify values of parameters or activate functions.
- *SNMP-based interface* to set value of variables.

Most of these methods provide the operator with an interface to modify the configuration. In order to prevent unauthorized access to the device, some form of authentication (user name/password) is implemented on all of the devices. Operators are allowed to modify the configuration only when they have correctly identified themselves to the device.

Text-Based CLI
Text-based CLI provides the operator with the possibility of viewing and modifying the configuration of the device. This requires the operator to log onto the device. Devices normally have a console monitor that provides the interface to the device. The operator then has the possibility of typing the commands that are then executed by the device. A text-based interface requires the operator to have a good understanding of the syntax and semantics of CLI. The operator must also have a good knowledge about the semantics of the parameters that can be modified and also how to modify the value of parameters. The CLI, the syntax of the commands, and the semantics of the variables may all vary from device to device. Operators need to have a good understanding of all of these and must be well trained in order to reduce the risks of misconfiguration.

Menu-Driven CLI
Like text-based CLI, menu-driven CLI helps the operator; unlike text-based CLI, however, the operator does not need to know the syntax of all the commands. The operator is prompted to choose from a list of commands—the menu-driven CLI may have several choices—and is required to know the significance of each command. All of the commands may not be presented to the operator at the same time.

The menu-driven CLI may be organized in a hierarchical manner, and the commands may be grouped based on functionality. In this case, the operator needs to have knowledge about the groups of commands and how to navigate through the set of menus before executing the necessary commands in order to make configuration changes.

Web-Based CLI

Today, Web-based interfaces are very popular in all domains. Most of the network devices from vendors also support Web-based interfaces. Web-based CLI helps provide a standard access method. Most workstations support some form of Web browsers and hence can be used to access the network device. Depending on the support available on the network device, the Web-based CLI may have either a menu-driven or a text-based CLI.

SNMP-Based Interface

The most popular method is the SNMP-based interface. SNMP is a standard protocol that is widely used in the industry. Its simplicity makes it a popular choice for configuring network devices. SNMP provides an operation known as Set, with which it is possible to modify the value of parameters on the device. The MIB includes definitions for parameters, or variables, that are a part of the device configuration. By modifying the value of these parameters using SNMP, it is possible to change the configuration of a network device.

Each device has its own MIB. In order to provide a common interface independent of the network device and the manufacturer, standard MIB variables have been defined for IP networks. This standardization has helped to provide a common interface for accessing network devices independent of the manufacturer. The MIB also contains device-specific variables and vendor-specific features on each network device. These variables are defined as a private MIB specific to each device.

In order to use SNMP to configure a network device, the MIB on the network device must contain all of the variables that are required to modify the configuration. The SNMP agent residing in the network device must be capable of reading and modifying the value of these variables.

The use of SNMP helps to develop standard tools to configure devices, which in turn helps to automate the tasks of configuring new network devices and modifying the configuration of existing network devices in the service provider network. General-purpose tools reduce the staff required to configure network devices and help to fasten the process to provision new service requests. Automation also helps to reduce the chances of misconfiguration. Even if there is a misconfiguration due to software bugs in the configuration tools, it is easy to fix the bugs and ensure that all of the devices are correctly configured.

3.3.4 Service Modification

A typical service offered by a service provider will have several features. Over a period of time, the customer will want to modify the service to include additional features or to upgrade the quality of the service. This may require a change in the configuration of the devices or the installation of new devices. Consider the example shown in Figure 3.4. The customer is offered a guaranteed bandwidth service. Initially, the customer was offered a 512-Kbps ATM connection to the service provider network. Over a period of time, the volume of traffic from the customer has grown steadily, so the requirements have increased to 2 Mbps. This requires a change in the configuration of all of the ATM switches and the CPE device.

In the next phase, due to rapid expansion, the number of users in that customer site increased dramatically. The volume of traffic from this customer site has outgrown the maximum link capacity on the CPE interface. Now it is necessary to install new interfaces on the CPE device or install a new CPE device. This upgrade in service requires installation of new equipment and also modifications to the configuration of the new devices.

3.3.5 Database Information

Information about all of the devices in the network is necessary to manage the network. This information should be maintained in a database and must be accessible to all of the systems that require them. It must be correct and consistent. This is critical for the operation of the network, to guarantee the services to the customer, and to meet the SLA requirements of the customer. When new service requests are provisioned, it is necessary to update the database information as part of the provisioning process.

3.4 NETWORK MANAGEMENT ISSUES

Network management is an integral part of any service offered by a service provider. It encompasses several issues and is important for the service provider to manage their network in order to ensure the correct operation of all of the devices and services that are offered using the network. A typical service provider network has a wide geographic spread, covering several cities. The network devices are installed in several locations and can be far apart. It is necessary to have a good infrastructure to access and manage these devices from a central location to reduce the cost of the network management infrastructure. Security is another important aspect that must also be taken into account when managing a network. The network management system and the network devices must be shielded from illegal access by intruders and hackers. Most service providers invest a lot of time and money in building a solid and secure network management infrastructure.

3.4.1 Network Management System

The *network management system* (NMS) is the crux of the network management of a service provider network, providing the necessary infrastructure to manage the network. It consists of both hardware and software that are necessary to perform the network management activities (see Section 3.4.2). Several off-the-shelf NMSs are available today that provide a framework to perform network management activities. The service provider must modify or adapt them to meet their requirements. Considering the fact that all service providers buy network devices and NMS solutions from vendors, the competitive edge lies in adapting the network devices and the NMS solutions to efficiently implement the services and deliver SLAs to customers. Since the NMS plays a crucial role, it is important that they have redundancy in case of failure. The design of the NMS infrastructure must take into account failure of components and must provide redundancy for critical components.

3.4.2 Network Management Activities

Managing a service provider network involves several activities, including:

- Verifying the status of all devices.
- Recording and analyzing the error messages from all devices in order to monitor the health of all devices.
- Recording and analyzing statistical information in order to monitor the health of the devices.
- Recording and analyzing statistical information for SLA reporting.
- Maintaining and periodically verifying all the configurations on all devices.
- Upgrading software and hardware to accommodate more customers or to remove bugs.

Monitoring Devices

Network devices must be up and functioning correctly in order to deliver services to customers, so they must be monitored periodically. Monitoring can be a proactive or a reactive activity, depending on the nature of the devices. Proactive monitoring is important for critical devices. Reactive monitoring can be done for devices whose failure can be anticipated based on information received from other devices that do not affect the services offered to the customer.

Proactive monitoring is not free. It requires bandwidth to send requests and receive responses from devices, and it requires a good management system to handle the volume of traffic. The interval between each request to monitor the status of devices is also an important factor: If the interval is too high, then faulty devices may not be detected for a long time, and this increases the downtime of the device and the service offered by the device. Shorter intervals can help to overcome this problem, but they result in a lot of load on the device, the NMS system, and the network. A good balance has to be maintained between the two choices. The optimum interval for monitoring devices must be determined by the service provider when designing the monitoring system.

The monitoring system must be designed to take into account service windows during which devices may not be functioning (e.g., for software or hardware upgrades). It must be capable of selectively turning off the monitoring of devices that are being upgraded. The system must inform the operator when devices do not respond to monitoring requests. It must also be designed with the topology of the network and the physical and logical relationship between devices in mind.

Sometimes the failure of a single device may result in several other devices (connected to this device) not being reached by the monitoring system. In this case, the monitoring system must filter all of the alarms and forward a single alarm to the operator.

Error Logs

Most network devices are capable of detecting failure of hardware or software components. They can also anticipate such failures, depending on the situation. For example, temperature sensors can be used to detect high temperatures, and transmission errors on an interface can be used to detect loss of connectivity. Network devices can be configured to send this information (as alarms or error messages) to the NMS, which maintains it in a log. This log information is then used by other systems to detect the failure of components of devices or devices themselves, or even to anticipate failure and take corrective actions.

Error logs provide valuable information to the network operator in detecting and troubleshooting problems in the network. For example, increasing transmission errors on an ATM interface can be used to anticipate degradation in the QoS offered to the customer, and investigations can be initiated to determine the cause of this problem before complete loss of connectivity on that interface.

Network management systems must be properly designed to ensure that the network devices are configured to send critical error messages and to verify that these error messages are logged and analyzed. Similar to the problems associated with the monitoring interval, this must be designed properly to ensure that critical errors are logged and detected and also that the NMS is not flooded with too many alarms or error messages.

Statistical Information

Network statistics play an important role in managing a network, delivering IP-based services, and reporting SLAs to customers. Most network devices collect and locally store statistical information in the device itself. This information can be retrieved by the NMS and stored in a database to be used at a later stage. (Section 3.4.3 provides more details about how the statistical information is collected from network devices.) Statistical information can be used for several purposes, including error detection and troubleshooting, SLA reporting, and capacity planning.

Statistical information about errors observed by a network device can be useful in detecting and even anticipating faults. Errors can also provide useful information for troubleshooting. For example, the number of IP packets received on an interface can help to detect if the interface is properly receiving and forwarding IP packets. During troubleshooting, this information can be very useful in isolating faulty interfaces.

Statistical information is also useful in reporting link utilization to customers. It can be used to generate SLAs indicating the availability of the service—for example, the availability of a service may be computed in terms of the *uptime* of all the devices involved in delivering the service. (Uptime can be considered the time the device has been up, or active, since it was last reset.)

Statistical information like link utilization or the number of interfaces on a device can be useful in capacity planning. When these values reach a certain threshold, it is time to install more interfaces for a new device with additional interfaces.

Hardware and Software Upgrades

Technology grows at a very rapid rate, so it is necessary to upgrade the hardware and software of network devices to keep up. Sometimes it is also necessary to upgrade the software on devices in order to fix problems. A hardware upgrade may be required to meet the growing demand for a service and to provision more customers.

Upgrading hardware and software is an important activity associated with network management. Procedures must be defined to do it so as to reduce the downtime associated with the services and the downtime for customers affected by the upgrade. Normally, an SLA has a provision for downtime specifying a fixed time. This is sometimes referred to as a *service window.* As far as possible, hardware and software upgrades must be done during the service window in order to minimize the service downtime.

3.4.3 Carrying Out Network Management

As seen in this section, communication between the NMS and the network devices is critical for managing the network. Without this communication, it is almost impossible to configure and monitor the devices, generate SLAs for customers, or predict the growth of the network and do capacity planning. There are two aspects of the communication that are of interest: (1) the communication protocol and the access method between the NMS and the network device, and (2) the network that supports this communication.

Communication Protocols and Access Methods

For an IP-based network, it is logical to use a communication protocol based on IP for communication between the NMS and the network devices. Most of the network devices from vendors support some form of IP-based protocol to communicate with the network device. Depending on the communication protocol, the access method can also vary. Some of these methods have been standardized, and some of the most popular access methods and the communication protocols used by these methods are discussed in this section. Of course, there are also vendor-specific access methods and communication protocols. Each method has its advantages and disadvantages. Good NMS systems must incorporate all of these methods and help the operator in efficiently performing the tasks of network management.

SNMP

SNMP is the industry standard for communication between the NMS and network devices. The operations supported by SNMP make it practical for network monitoring and for the devices to report alarms to the NMS system.

`snmptrap` is an operation supported by SNMP that makes it very useful for devices to report unusual activities to the NMS. The SNMP agent on the network device can be configured to report several types of alarms, `snmptrap` provides information about the severity of the trap, and additional information can be included in the trap to indicate the nature of the fault and the possible cause of the problem. Some of these traps have been standardized, and there are also device-specific and vendor-specific traps.

`snmpget` is an SNMP operation that can be used to access and extract statistical information from a network device by the NMS.

`snmpset` is an SNMP operation that can be used to modify the value of variables in the MIB of the network device. By using private MIB variables, this operation can be used to modify the configuration of the network device.

All of these operations make it possible to perform most of the activities of network management discussed in Section 3.4.2. SNMP requires IP connectivity between network devices and the NMS.

Text-Based CLI

Text-based CLI is another method to access network devices and get the required information to do some of the tasks associated with network management. It can be used to get the status of a device, to get statistical information, to modify the configuration of devices, and so on. It can use TCP-based protocols like Telnet if the network device supports this protocol.

Text-based CLI is a popular method for getting small amounts of information—for example, interface status, configuration details, and so on for short-term activities like troubleshooting or quickly modifying the configuration of a device. An operator can use this method during troubleshooting to determine and isolate the cause of problems.

Text-based CLI may not scale for a network with a large number of devices to perform certain activities of network management like collecting statistical information. It can cause an unnecessary load on the devices when trying to extract information on a periodic basis. It also requires additional programs to process this information and save it in formats that can be used by other systems (e.g., SLA reporting). Most of the off-shelf NMSs use SNMP and provide some limited support for text-based CLI.

Depending on the vendor and their implementation, text-based CLI may be able to provide more information than SNMP. Proprietary implementations of new technologies may not have the necessary MIBs to provide an SNMP interface. Under these circumstances, it may be necessary to develop tools that can help to automate network management activities. Tools that can process and extract information from text-based responses are required to enable an operator to efficiently perform tasks.

Other Methods

Several other methods are available for getting information status about network devices and also performing basic troubleshooting activities like device reachability. These tools use some IP-based protocols to achieve their tasks. For example, tools like *ping* use ICMP to determine the reachability of devices, and tools like *traceroute* use ICMP to trace the path to destination networks and network devices. These tools have to be adapted to meet the requirements of the network management activity.

Communication Network

A network is required for communication between the NMS and the network devices. It must support the protocol that is used for such communication. Two possible solutions are *in-band network management* and *out-of-band network management.*

In-Band Network Management

"In-band" refers to using the service provider network to communicate with all network devices. The links that forward customer traffic are used for communication between the NMS and the network devices. In-band network management is a simple solution (Figure 3.6). All it requires is IP connectivity between the NMS and the service provider network. Once this is established, then IP communication between the NMS and network devices is very simple and straightforward.

The disadvantage of this approach is that failure in certain parts of the service provider network may result in loss of connectivity between the network device and the NMS. This may be critical at times when it is necessary to have direct access to network devices. Moreover, this approach requires additional bandwidth in the service provider network to accommodate the network management traffic.

Out-of-Band Network Management

Out-of-band network management implements a separate network to provide communication between the NMS and the network devices (Figure 3.7). This network is implemented separately from the service provider network (which is used for transporting customer traffic) and is used only for communication between the NMS and the network devices. The advantage of this approach is that customer traffic will not affect the reachability between the NMS and the network devices. Bandwidth need not be reserved in the service provider network for the purpose of network management.

3.4.4 Security Issues: Managing an IP Network

Security is an important issue that must be addressed when discussing the management of IP networks. Networks are prone to attack by hackers, so network devices

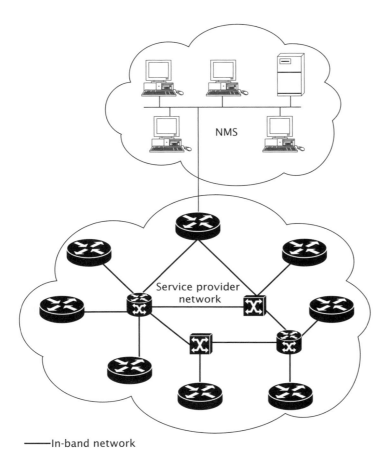

—————In-band network

FIGURE 3.6

In-band network management.

and the NMS must be secured against intentional (or unintentional) intrusions. The NMS devices must be protected from external intrusion. This can be achieved by using firewalls between the service provider network and the NMS system.

3.5 OSS ARCHITECTURE

The OSS architecture plays an important role in implementing IP-based services. Several key departments of both service providers and customers use this system in order to implement services. The OSS maintains information that is critical to service implementation and has the responsibility of ensuring that this information is made available promptly to the various departments.

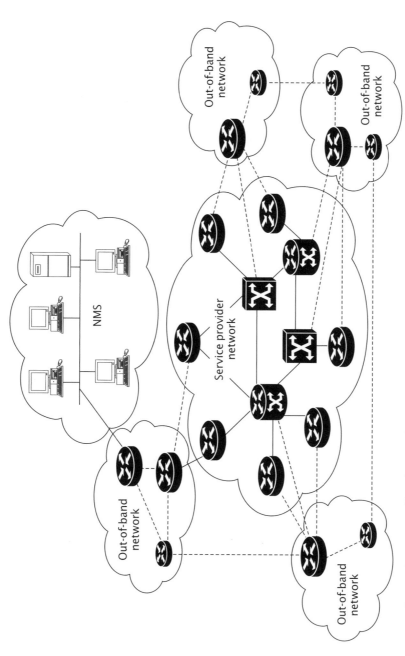

----- Connection to out-of-band network

FIGURE 3.7

Out-of-band network management.

3.5.1 **OSS Components**

Some of the key components of this system are as described in the following subsections.

Database System

A good database system is the key to OSS architecture. The OSS has a lot of information that is relevant to service implementation and is also related to the customer. The OSS must be capable of maintaining all of this information and making it easily available to the different departments and to various other components of the OSS that are responsible for service implementation.

Network Provisioning and Monitoring Tools

Network provisioning and monitoring tools are also essential components of the OSS architecture. They can be vendor-specific, standard tools that are openly available, or even developed in-house. These tools interact with the network devices and are responsible for configuring the network devices, monitoring the status of these devices, and extracting information (e.g., link utilization) that is essential for SLA reporting and billing. The OSS architecture must have the capability of seamlessly integrating all of these tools and ensuring that they can interact with other components in order to get the correct information that is essential for provisioning and monitoring the network devices.

SLA Reporting and Billing

SLA reporting and billing are important parts of service implementation. They use the information related to customer requirements, services requested by the customer, and the actual status of network elements responsible for delivering the services to the customer to generate periodic reports to the customer. It is essential that SLA reporting and the billing system have access to correct information.

3.5.2 **Requirements of the OSS**

Some of the requirements of the OSS architecture are that it be open, scalable, automated, and easy to interface between network operators in the network operations center (NOC) and customers.

Open Architecture

The OSS has several components that must communicate with one another in order to ease the task of service implementation. These components may be purchased from several different software vendors. It is essential that the OSS architecture allow the integration of all of these components into one system and ensure that the information required by a component for its proper functioning is readily made available to it.

Scalability

Scalability of the OSS refers to the ability to support a large number of services and customers, to implement service requests from multiple customers within a short period of time, and to maintain information related to several thousands of customers in order to implement the services. Service providers typically have a large customer base (hundreds of thousands of customers) and offer several services. It is essential that the OSS be capable of supporting the implementation of services for all of the customers.

When there is a surge in demand for a new service, several customers may request this new service in a single day. This places a huge burden on the OSS to implement all of the service requests. Scalability in this context refers to the ability of the OSS to implement several service requests within a short period of time.

As the number of customers using a service offered by the provider increases, the OSS system must be capable of maintaining the information about all of the customers. The time required to access the customer information must not increase as the number of customers increases. This is essential when online SLA reports are made available to customers. SLA reporting must have access to customer information (e.g., number of links and the bandwidth for each customer link) and to the status of network devices (e.g., link utilization) in order to make reports available to the customer online.

Another aspect of scalability is related to the network provisioning and monitoring tools. These tools must be capable of managing several network devices. As the network grows, the number of network devices will increase. The time taken to manage the network devices must be independent of the number of devices managed by the OSS.

Automation

It is essential that the activities of implementing services are automated to the maximum possible extent and that the intervention by human operators is minimized as much as possible. This is a key requirement because it helps to minimize both the mistakes due to manual intervention and the time taken to implement the services.

As discussed in the beginning of Section 3.3, provisioning involves updating the configuration of various network devices before the service can be activated for a customer. Depending on the type of service and the SLA offered to the customer, the amount of information required to provision a service can be considerable. In order to ensure that all of this information is correctly configured on the relevant devices, it is better to have software tools that can automate this process. The software tools can extract this information from a database and consistently configure all relevant devices in the correct order. The advantage of software tools is that if they can correctly do a task once, they can do the same task correctly several times. This is what is required in order to provision several customer service requests in a short period of time and in a correct manner.

SNMP provides the basic means for communication between the NMS and the network devices. The operations provided for by SNMP help to extract information from network devices and allow the network devices to report problems or events to the NMS. Software tools based on SNMP can be used to automate the task of configuring network devices.

As seen in Section 3.4.2, network management involves many activities, most of which are repetitive tasks that have to be performed periodically. Some of these tasks involve correlating large volumes of data in order to verify the proper functioning of the network devices and also to generate reports. Software tools are best suited for such tasks, as they can do this much faster than human operators. Tools to periodically monitor the devices are a must when the number of devices in the network is large.

Intelligent systems based on rules or models (e.g., finite-state machines) can be easily built to scan through event logs from all of the devices. The rules or models can vary based on the service offered by the provider. Once these rules or models are defined, they can be easily used to verify that the service offered to the customer is functioning properly.

SLA reporting is another activity that can be automated. The information required for generating the SLA reports must be made available to the reporting system in order to automate this task. Once this is done, the reports can be automatically generated, either periodically or on demand (e.g., upon customer request).

Using Web-Based Tools

Web-based interfaces to applications are becoming more and more popular. Web applications are based on HTML and use IP-based application-layer protocols like HTTP for communication with servers. Web-based tools can help standardize the interface to configure and manage network devices. With a few mouse clicks or keystrokes, an operator can easily modify the configuration of network devices and get information about their status. The tools also make it easy to present SLA reports to customers or provide customers with online information about the status of their service or other information (e.g., link utilization).

Web-based tools can help the service provider to allow online access to SLA reports. This will make it easy for customers to get information about their network. Information related to link utilization can help customers in doing capacity planning and ordering more bandwidth for sites that have very high link utilization.

3.6 SUMMARY

This chapter has stressed the need for simple and efficient provisioning and network management systems as a differentiator for the service provider. Good tools are required to simplify the task of provisioning new customers, to manage services, and to deliver the SLA reports promised to customers. A good OSS architecture is the key to rapid deployment of IP-based services and to making it scalable.

SNMP plays a key role in managing IP networks. The features provided by SNMP make the task of provisioning IP-based services and managing IP networks easier for service providers. However, SNMP only provides the basic means to communicate with the network device for the purpose of network management. SNMP-based tools must be developed by the service provider to perform network management activities in an efficient manner.

Network Management Architecture

4

This chapter, taken from Chapter 7 of *Network Analysis Architecture and Design* by McCabe, examines the component architecture for network management. Proper network management is critical to the success of any network, and, as you will see, there are many factors to consider in providing network management.

In this chapter you will learn about network management and the network management architecture. We discuss the various functions of network management and the mechanisms used to achieve these functions. We discuss and compare a number of variations for the network management architecture, as well as the internal and external relationships for network management.

To be able to understand and apply the concepts in this chapter, you should be familiar with network management protocols (SNMP and optionally CMIP/CMOT); the utilities ping, traceroute, and tcpdump; management information base (MIB) structures and parameters; and operations support system (OSS) functions.

4.1 BACKGROUND

Network management (NM) consists of the set of functions to control, plan, allocate, deploy, coordinate, and monitor network resources. Network management used to be an afterthought in many network architectures. For example, most network architectures and designs were developed without a thought about users being malicious, which was generally true up until a few years ago. Consider the changes that have recently been made in SNMP security. Today, and in the future, networks are a resource whose integrity must be measurable and verifiable.

The network management architecture, as with the other component architectures, begins with the requirements and flow analyses. Areas that should be addressed during the analysis process include:

- Choosing a network management protocol.
- Implementing high-level asset management as part of the network management architecture.
- Reconfiguring the network often to meet changing requirements.
- Monitoring the entire system from a single location or device.
- Testing service provider compliance with service level agreements (SLAs) and policies.
- Monitoring for performance to avoid problems.
- Out-of-band access requirements.

We begin this chapter by defining and characterizing management for a network architecture, and how to plan for monitoring, configuring, and troubleshooting the planned network. We then examine network management protocols and instrumentation requirements. This will lead to considerations for developing the network management architecture.

4.2 DEFINING NETWORK MANAGEMENT

Network management can be viewed as a structure consisting of multiple layers:

Business management: The management of the business aspects of a network—for example, the management of budgets/resources, planning, and agreements.

Service management: The management of delivery of services to users—for example, for service providers this would include the management of access bandwidth, data storage, and application delivery.

Network management: The management of all network devices across the entire network.

Element management: The management of a collection of similar network devices—for example, access routers or subscriber management systems.

Network-element management: The management of individual network devices—for example, a single router, switch, or hub.

This structure is a top-down approach, with the most abstract component (business management) at the top of the hierarchy, and the most specified, concrete component (network–element management) at the bottom of the hierarchy. This is shown in Figure 4.1.

Correspondingly, as the components become more abstract, the ways that they are applied and measured (their information elements) change. Thus, at the bottom of this hierarchy (network-element, element, network), management is applied with variables and parameters, while at the top of this hierarchy (service, business), management is applied in more abstract terms, using policies. This is

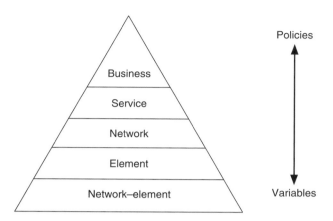

Policies

Business

Service

Network

Element

Network–element

Variables

FIGURE 4.1

Network management hierarchy.

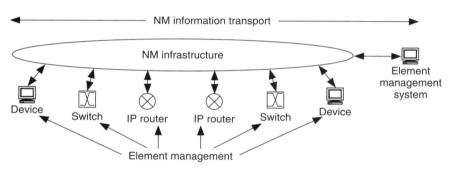

FIGURE 4.2

Network management is composed of managing elements and transporting management data.

common to all architectural components, and we will find that policies can be used for each component.

Network management can be divided into two basic functions: the transport of management information across the system, and the management of NM information elements (Figure 4.2).

These functions, as shown in Figure 4.2, consist of a variety of tasks—monitoring, configuring, troubleshooting, and planning—that are performed by users, administrators, and network personnel. One of the first challenges in developing a network management architecture is to define what network management really means to the organizations that will be performing the tasks and receiving the end services—namely, the users, or customers, of the system.

There are four categories of network management tasks that we consider here, corresponding to the four tasks mentioned above:

1. Monitoring for event notification.
2. Monitoring for trend analysis and planning.
3. Configuration of network parameters.
4. Troubleshooting the network.

4.2.1 Network Devices and Characteristics

A *network device* is an individual component of the network that participates at one or more of the protocol layers. This includes end devices, routers, switches, data service units (DSUs), hubs, and network interface cards (NICs). Network devices have characteristics that can be measured. They are grouped into end-to-end, per-link, per-network, or per-element characteristics, as shown in Figure 4.3.

End-to-end characteristics are those that can be measured across multiple network devices in the path of one or more traffic flows, and may be extended across the entire network or between devices. Examples of end-to-end characteristics for network devices are availability, capacity, delay, delay variation (jitter), throughput, error rates, and network utilization. These characteristics may be modified or added to, depending on the types of traffic on the network.

Per-link, per-network, and *per-element characteristics* are those that are specific to the type of element or connection between elements being monitored. These characteristics may be used individually, or may be combined to form an end-to-end characteristic. Examples of per-link characteristics are propagation delay and link utilization, while examples of per-element characteristics include (for an IP router) IP forwarding rates (e.g., packets/second), buffer utilization, and any logs of authentication failures.

Management of network devices and networks includes network planning (e.g., cell site planning for wireless), initial resource allocation (e.g., frequency or bandwidth allocations), and FCAPS from the telecommunication network management model: fault, configuration, accounting, performance, and security management.

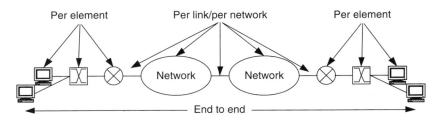

FIGURE 4.3

Network characteristics can be per-element, per-link, per-network, or end-to-end.

4.3 NETWORK MANAGEMENT MECHANISMS

We now take a look at some of the popular management mechanisms, including network management protocols. There are currently two major network management protocols: the Simple Network Management Protocol (SNMP) and the Common Management Information Protocol (CMIP). CMIP includes CMIP over TCP/IP (CMOT). These network management protocols provide the mechanism for retrieving, changing, and transporting network management data across a network.

SNMP has seen widespread use and forms the basis for many popular commercial and public network management systems. It provides facilities for collecting and configuring parameters from network devices. These are done through the SNMP commands Get (to collect the value of a parameter), GetNext (to collect the value of the next parameter in the list), and Set (to change the value of a parameter). There are also provisions for the unsolicited notification of events, through the use of traps. A *trap* is a user-configurable threshold for a parameter. When this threshold is crossed, the values for one or more parameters are sent to a specified location. A benefit of trap generation is that polling for certain parameters can be stopped or the polling interval lengthened, and instead an automatic notice is sent to the management system when an event occurs.

Parameters that are accessible via SNMP are grouped into MIBs. Parameters can be part of *the* standard MIB (MIB-II), other standard MIBs (typically based on a type of network device, technology, or protocol), remote-monitoring MIBs, or enterprise-specific MIBs, which have parameters specific to a particular vendor's product.

SNMP version 3 (SNMPv3) builds on the previous versions of SNMP, providing more secure authentication, the ability to retrieve blocks of parameters, and trap generation for most parameters. When SNMP is mentioned in this chapter, it refers to SNMPv3 unless otherwise noted.

CMIP/CMOT provides for parameter collection and setting, as with SNMP, but also allows for more types of operations. Many CMIP/CMOT features, such as globally unique object naming, object classification, alarm reporting, audit trails, and test management, can also be provided by SNMP by creating new MIBs and tools to support such abstractions.

In general, SNMP is simpler to configure and use than CMIP/CMOT, helping to make it widely accepted. It is usually easier to instrument network devices with SNMP. SNMP is used in monitoring, instrumentation, and configuration mechanisms, all of which are discussed below.

4.3.1 Monitoring Mechanisms

Monitoring is obtaining values for end-to-end, per-link, and per-element characteristics. The monitoring process involves collecting data about the desired characteristics, processing some or all of these data, displaying the (processed) data, and archiving a subset of these data.

Data are usually collected through a polling (actively probing network devices for management data) or monitoring process involving a network management protocol (e.g., SNMP) or proxy service. As we see later in this chapter, several techniques may be used to get this data as well as to ensure that the data are current and valid. When the data are gathered, they may or may not reflect the characteristics we wish to monitor. Values for some characteristics may have to be derived from the gathered data, while other values may be modified (e.g., added, subtracted, time-averaged). This is processing of the data.

Sets of raw (unprocessed) and processed data will need to be displayed. There are different types of displays you may use, including standard monitor displays, field-of-view or widescreen displays, and special-purpose displays. Along with choosing displays you will also want to consider how the data will be shown to the user, administrator, or manager. There are several techniques to display data, such as logs and textual displays, graphs and charts (both static and moving), and alarms. Some data may be abstracted by symbols, such as showing parts of the network as a cloud.

At some time during this process some or all of the data are saved to a (semi-)permanent media or system. This part of the process may have multiple steps, including *primary storage,* the staging of data for short periods of time, which could be at the network management server; *secondary storage,* the aggregation of data from multiple primary storage sites, at a storage server for the network; and *tertiary storage,* which is usually the most permanent—and slowest—storage within the network. Secondary and tertiary storage are often termed *storage archives.* Figure 4.4 shows each part of this process occurring on a separate device, but they may all be combined on a single device.

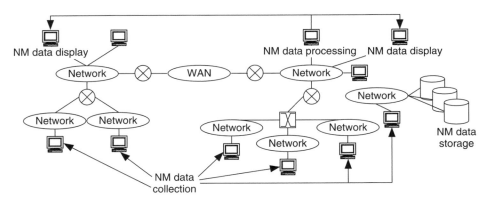

FIGURE 4.4

Elements of the monitoring process.

Monitoring for Event Notification

An *event* is something that occurs in the network that is noteworthy. This may be a problem or failure in a network device, across the network, or when a characteristic crosses a threshold value. It may only be something that is informational to the user, administrator, or manager, such as notification of an upgrade. Events may be noted in a log file, on a display, or by issuing an alarm, depending on the priority level of the event. Events are similar to transients, which are short-lived changes in the behavior of the network. Thresholds or boundaries may be set on end-to-end, per-link, or per-element characteristics for short-term or immediate notification of events and transients; this is termed *real-time analysis*.

Figure 4.5 shows an example of such monitoring. *Ping* is used to gather round-trip delay information, which is presented as a chart on the monitoring system. A threshold of 100 ms has been chosen for this display. When this threshold is crossed, it triggers an alarm to notify the network manager that a problem may exist in the network.

Real-time analysis usually requires short *polling intervals* (time periods between active probing of the network and network devices for management data), and there is a trade-off between the number of characteristics and network devices polled for real-time analysis versus the amount of resources (capacity, computer processing unit, memory, storage) needed to support such analysis.

In some cases the amount of network data generated (and the resulting traffic) by the periodic polling of multiple characteristics on many network devices can impact the overall performance of the network. For example, consider a network that has 100 network devices, where each element has an average of

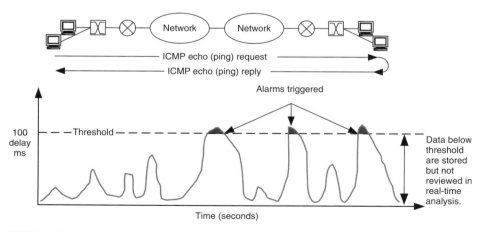

FIGURE 4.5

Monitoring for event notification.

four interfaces and each interface is monitored for eight characteristics. This would add up to

$$(100 \text{ network devices}) \times (4 \text{ interfaces/network device}) \times$$
$$(8 \text{ characteristics/interface}) = 3200 \text{ characteristics}$$

If each of the 3200 characteristics generates an average of 8 bytes of data and an estimated 60 bytes of protocol overhead, the amount of data generated per polling session would be

$$(3200 \text{ characteristics}) \times (8 \text{ bytes} + 60 \text{ bytes}) = 217.6 \text{ KB, or } 1.74 \text{ Mb, of traffic}$$

If we plan to poll with a polling interval of five seconds, at best this 1.74 Mb of traffic would be spread out over the five seconds, or 384 Kbps. It is more likely, however, that most of the data will arrive shortly after the polls are generated, so the traffic may be more like a spike of 1.74 Mb for the second after the polls occur. For a period of one day, the total amount of traffic will be

$$(1.75 \text{ Mb/polling interval}) \times (720 \text{ polling intervals/hour}) \times (24 \text{ hours/day})$$
$$= 30.2 \text{ Gb of traffic}$$

The amount of data stored will be

$$(3200 \text{ characteristics/polling interval}) \times (8 \text{ bytes}) \times (720 \text{ polling intervals/day}) \times$$
$$(24 \text{ hours/day}) = 442 \text{ MB data stored/day}$$

Over the course of a year, this would add up to over 161 GB of data. And this is a conservative estimate for a mid-range enterprise environment.

Monitoring for Trend Analysis and Planning

The same end-to-end, per-link, and per-element characteristics used for event monitoring can also be put to work in trend analysis. *Trend analysis* utilizes network management data to determine long-term network behaviors or trends. This is helpful in planning for future network growth.

In doing continuous, uninterrupted data collection, usually with long polling intervals (minutes or hours instead of seconds), we can begin by establishing baselines for trends, and then use these baselines to plot trend behavior. This is shown in Figure 4.6. This figure shows long-term trends for availability, delay, and percent of utilization. Polls for each characteristic are saved to network management on a regular basis, and over a long period of time (usually weeks or months, but sometimes up to years) trends in these characteristics begin to emerge. In Figure 4.6, upward trends are clearly visible for delay and percent of utilization.

4.3.2 Instrumentation Mechanisms

Instrumentation is the set of tools and utilities needed to monitor and probe the network for management data. Instrumentation mechanisms include access to

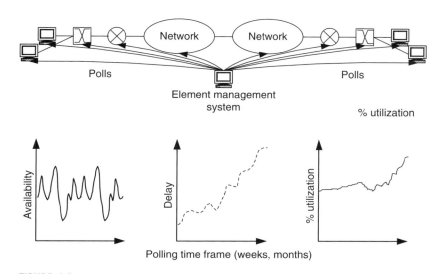

FIGURE 4.6

Monitoring for metrics and planning.

network management data via SNMP, monitoring tools, and direct access. Instrumentation can be coupled with monitoring, display, processing, and storage to form a complete management system.

SNMP (currently in version 3) provides access to MIB variables, including those in MIB-II, other standard MIBs (e.g., DS1 MIB), enterprise-specific MIBs, and other monitoring MIBs (remote monitoring (RMON) and switch monitoring (SMON)). SNMP is the most common method for accessing network management data. There are several commercially available and publicly available monitoring software packages available that use SNMP for data access.

Monitoring tools include utilities such as ping, traceroute, and tcpdump, while direct-access mechanisms include Telnet, FTP, TFTP, and connections via a console port. An example of a base set of parameters to monitor can be developed from the standard MIB-II. The following parameters can be collected on a per-interface basis:

- ifInOctets: Number of bytes received
- ifOutOctets: Number of bytes sent
- ifInUcastPkts: Number of unicast packets received
- ifOutUcastPkts: Number of unicast packets sent
- ifInNUcastPkts: Number of multicast/broadcast packets received
- ifOutNUcastPkts: Number of multicast/broadcast packets sent
- ifInErrors: Number of errored packets received
- ifOutErrors: Number of packets that could not be sent

These parameters can be used for both short-term event monitoring and long-term trend analysis of throughput and error rates. In addition, the following parameter may be collected to determine availability. It could be used in conjunction with monitoring tools such as ping to verify availability.

- `ifOperStatus`: State of an interface (up, down, testing)

In developing the network management architecture, the instrumentation requirements for each type or class of network device, such as forwarding elements (e.g., routers, switches, hubs), pass-through elements (e.g., DSUs, simple concentrators, simple bridges), and passive devices such as those that use RMON, should be collected.

A consideration for the network management architecture is to ensure that the instrumentation is accurate, dependable, and simple. There are a couple of ways to ensure accuracy in the instrumentation: testing and taking alternate measurements. If a lab environment is available, some limited network conditions can be replicated and tested. For example, generating known quantities of traffic by devices and/or traffic generators and comparing the results in the routers with those from the devices/traffic generators can test packet-forwarding rates in routers.

Sometimes parameters can be verified from the current network. Taking alternate measurements of the same parameter at different points in the network is one way to verify parameters. We may be able to get link-layer data from DSUs, routers, and switches in the path of a flow, and, by comparing the various sources of data, determine if and where there are discrepancies in parameter measurements.

For a network management system to work properly, the instrumentation needs to be dependable. A network management system is useless if it is the first thing to crash when network problems occur. This may seem obvious, but few current management systems are truly robust and dependable. Ways that dependability can be enhanced in the architecture include physically separating and replicating the management components. By having multiple systems collecting, processing, displaying, and storing management data for different parts of the network, and by building hierarchy in the management data flows, the loss of any single component of the management system will have less impact on the network's manageability. This is covered in more detail later in this chapter.

4.3.3 Configuration Mechanisms

Configuration is setting parameters in a network device for operation and control of that element. Configuration mechanisms include direct access to devices, remote access to devices, and downloading configuration files (Figure 4.7):

- SNMP `Set` commands.
- Telnet and command line interface (CLI) access.
- Access via HTTP.

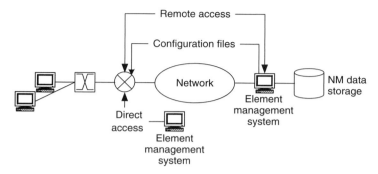

FIGURE 4.7

Configuration mechanisms for network management.

- Access via Common Object Request Broker Architecture (CORBA).
- Use of FTP/TFTP to download configuration files.

As part of this process, we want to generate a working set of end-to-end, per-link, and per-element characteristics, and plan for the architecture and design to have the facilities to monitor these characteristics at short- and long-term polling intervals. Later in this chapter we develop some guidelines on where monitoring facilities should be placed in the network.

Many network devices require some degree of configuration by network personnel. For each type or class of network device (e.g., Brand X router, Ethernet switch, etc.), we want to generate a table of configuration parameters, establish the methods for configuring these parameters, and understand the effects of changing each parameter (when possible). In order to properly manage a network, it is important to understand how configuration parameters affect each network device.

We also need to understand the effects of problems with network devices and how to correct such problems. Troubleshooting, which consists of problem notification, isolation, identification, and resolution, can be aided by knowing likely failure modes in the network, their effects, and any possible steps to correct them.

It should be noted that, in generating a set of working characteristics, configuration parameters, and failure modes, we are going through a detailed review of how the network will operate. The result is that you will better understand what will happen in the network.

4.4 ARCHITECTURAL CONSIDERATIONS

The network management process consists of choosing which characteristics of each type of network device to monitor/manage; instrumenting the network devices (or adding collection devices) to collect all necessary data; processing these data for viewing, storage, and/or reporting; displaying a subset of the results; and storing or archiving some subset of the data.

Network management touches all other aspects of the network. This is captured in the FCAPS model:

Fault management: processing events and alarms (where an *alarm* is an event that triggers a real-time notification to network personnel); problem identification, isolation, troubleshooting, and resolution; and returning the network to an operational state.

Configuration management: setting system parameters for turn-up; provisioning the network; configuration, system backups, and restores; and developing and operating system databases.

Accounting management: monitoring and managing subscriber service usage and service billing.

Performance management: implementing performance controls, based on the IP services architecture; collecting network and system performance data; analyzing these performance data; generating short- and long-term reports from these data; and controlling network and system performance parameters.

Security management: implementing security controls, based on the security architecture; collecting and analyzing security data; and generating security reports and logs from these data.

The network management process and management model both provide input to the network management architecture. With the knowledge of what network management means for our network, we can consider the following in the architecture:

- In-band and out-of-band management.
- Centralized, distributed, and hierarchical management.
- Scaling network management traffic.
- Checks and balances.
- Managing network management data.
- MIB selection.
- Integration into OSS.

4.4.1 In-Band and Out-of-Band Management

In-band management occurs when the traffic flows for network management follow the same network paths as the traffic flows for users and their applications. This simplifies the network management architecture, in that the same network paths can be used for both types of data, and a separate path (and possibly network) is not required (Figure 4.8).

A trade-off with in-band management is that management data flows can be impacted by the same problems that impact user traffic flows. Since part of

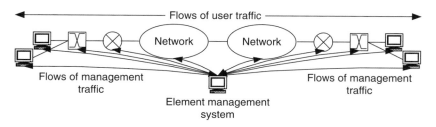

Flows of user traffic

Flows of management traffic

Flows of management traffic

Element management system

FIGURE 4.8

Traffic flows for in-band management.

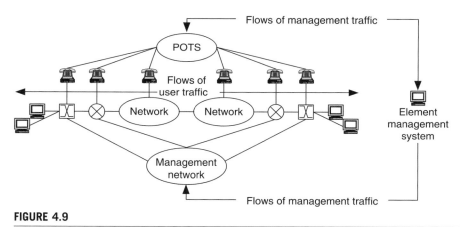

FIGURE 4.9

Traffic flows for out-of-band management.

network management is troubleshooting problems in the network, this function is negatively impacted if the management data flows are delayed or blocked. So when network management is most needed, it may not be available. Also, a primary objective of the network management architecture is to be able to do event monitoring when the network is under stress—for example, when congested with traffic, suffering from network hardware/software configuration problems, or under a security attack.

Out-of-band management occurs when different paths are provided for network management data flows and user traffic flows. This type of management has the distinct advantage of allowing the management system to continue to monitor the network during most network events, even when such events disable the network. This allows you to effectively see into portions of the network that are unreachable through normal paths (i.e., user data-flow paths).

Out-of-band management is usually provided via a separate network, such as frame relay or plain old telephone service (POTS) connections. Figure 4.9

illustrates this point. An advantage of having a separate network is that additional security features can be integrated into this (network management) network. Since this network provides access to most or all network devices, having additional security here is important. Another advantage is that the out-of-band connection can be used to troubleshoot and configure network devices that are in remote locations. This saves time and resources when the user data network is down and remote network devices need to be accessed.

Whenever out-of-band management is planned, a method to check and verify its availability is needed. This can be as simple as planning to use out-of-band management on a regular basis, regardless of need. This will help to ensure that problems with out-of-band management are detected and solved while the network is still healthy.

A trade-off with out-of-band management is the added expense and complexity of a separate network for network management. One way to reduce the expense is to provide out-of-band monitoring at a low level of performance, relative to the user data network. For example, out-of-band monitoring may be achieved using phone lines. While this may be less expensive than providing dedicated network connections, it does require time to set up (e.g., call) the out-of-band connections, and the capacity of each connection may be limited.

For some networks a combination of in-band and out-of-band management is optimal (Figure 4.10). Usually this is done when the performance of the user data network is needed to support network management data flows (for monitoring the operational network), but the separate, out-of-band network is needed when the user data network is down.

Some trade-offs of combining in-band and out-of-band management are that the expense of a separate network is still incurred, and security issues on the user data network still need to be addressed.

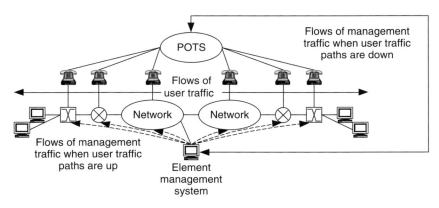

FIGURE 4.10

A combination of in-band and out-of-band management traffic flows.

4.4.2 **Centralized, Distributed, and Hierarchical Management**

Centralized management occurs when all management data (e.g., pings, SNMP polls/responses, traceroute, etc.) radiate from a single (typically large) management system. The flows of management data then behave like the client–server flows shown in Figure 4.8.

The obvious advantage to centralized management is that only one management system is needed, simplifying the architecture and reducing costs (depending on the choice of management system). In centralized management the management system often has a variety of management tools associated with it. The trade-offs to centralized management are that the management system is a single point of failure, and that all management flows converge at the network interface of the management system, potentially causing congestion or failure.

Distributed management occurs when there are multiple separate components to the management system, and these components are strategically placed across the network, localizing network management traffic and distributing management domains. In Figure 4.11 multiple local element management systems (EMSs) are used to distribute management functions across several domains.

In distributed management the components either provide all management functions (monitoring, display, storage, and processing) or the distributed components are the monitoring devices. For example, distributed management may take the form of having multiple management systems on the network (e.g., one management system per campus or per management domain, as shown in Figure 4.11), or a single management system with several monitoring nodes, as in Figure 4.12.

Advantages to distributed management are that the monitoring devices act to localize the data collection, reducing the amounts of management data that transit

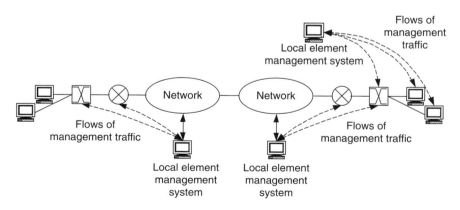

FIGURE 4.11

Distributed management where each local EMS has its own management domain.

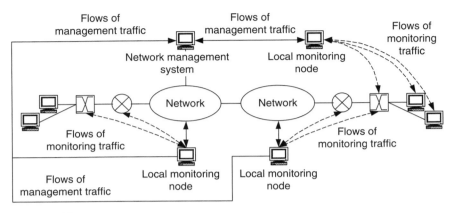

FIGURE 4.12

Distributed management where monitoring is distributed.

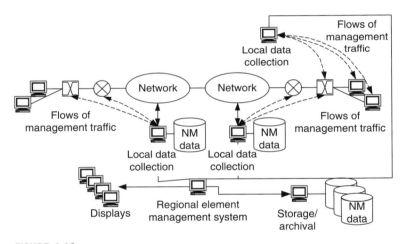

FIGURE 4.13

Hierarchical management separates management into distinct functions that are distributed across multiple platforms.

the network. They may also provide redundant monitoring, so that other monitoring devices on that network can cover the loss of any single monitoring device. A trade-off with distributed management is that costs increase with the number of monitoring devices or management systems needed.

Hierarchical management occurs when the management functions (monitoring, display, storage, and processing) are separated and placed on separate devices. Management is hierarchical in that, when the functions are separated, they can be considered layers that communicate in a hierarchical client–server fashion. Figure 4.13 shows the structure of a hierarchical management system.

In hierarchical management, localized monitoring devices collect management data and pass these data either directly to display and storage devices or to monitoring devices to be processed. When the management data are passed on to display and storage devices without processing, the monitoring devices act as they did in distributed management, localizing the data collection and reducing the amounts of management data that transit the network.

When the management data are processed before being sent to display and storage devices, then the monitoring devices act as local filters, sending only the relevant data (such as deltas on the values of counters or updates on events). This can substantially reduce the amount of management data in the network, which is especially important if the monitoring is in-band. Thus, we can have monitoring devices at strategic locations throughout the network, polling local devices and network devices, collecting and processing the management data, and forwarding some or all of these data to display and storage devices. The numbers and locations of each type of device will depend on the size of the network, the amount of management data expected to be collected (discussed later in this chapter), and where the displays and storage devices are to be located in the network management architecture.

An advantage to hierarchical management is that every component can be made redundant, independent of the other components. Thus, it can be tailored to the specific needs of your network. In some networks it may be preferable to have several display devices, while in other networks, several processing devices or storage devices are better. Since these components are separate, the numbers of each can be individually determined. A trade-off in hierarchical management is the cost, complexity, and overhead of having several management components on the network.

4.4.3 Scaling Network Management Traffic

Some recommendations are presented here to help determine and optimize the capacity requirements of network management traffic.

Recommendation 1: One Monitoring Device per IP Subnet

For a local area network (LAN) environment, start with one monitoring device per Internet Protocol subnet. For each subnet, estimate values for the following traffic variables:

- The number of devices and network devices to be polled.
- An average number of interfaces per device.
- The number of parameters to be collected.
- The frequency of polling (polling interval).

Combining these variables gives you an estimate of the average data rate for management traffic per subnet. If this rate is greater than approximately 10 percent of the capacity (line rate) of the LAN, you may want to consider reducing the

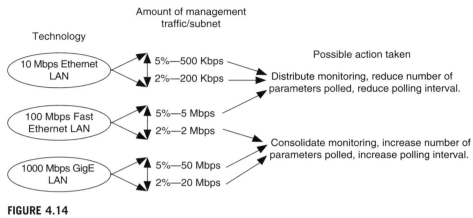

FIGURE 4.14

Scaling network management traffic.

amount of management traffic generated, by reducing one or more of the above variables. When the estimated average rate is less than 1 percent of LAN capacity, this indicates that it may be possible to increase one or more of the above variables.

For most of the standard LAN technologies (Ethernet, Fast Ethernet, Gigabit Ethernet, Token Ring, FDDI), the management traffic rate should be targeted at 2 to 5 percent of the LAN capacity. As LAN capacity increases, you will have more available capacity for network management traffic and may choose to increase one or more traffic variables (Figure 4.14).

Recommendation 2: One Monitoring Device per WAN

For a wide area network (WAN) environment, start with one monitoring device per each WAN–LAN interface. This is in addition to any monitoring devices indicated in Recommendation 1. However, if a monitoring device is on a LAN subnet that is also the WAN–LAN interface, that device may be used to collect data for both the LAN and WAN. Placing a monitoring device at each WAN–LAN interface allows us to monitor the network at each location, as well as to measure, verify, and possibly guarantee services and performance requirements across the WAN.

4.4.4 Checks and Balances

Checks and balances are methods to duplicate measurements in order to verify and validate network management data. Although implementing checks and balances adds effort to the network management process, it is advisable to have more than one method for collection network management data, particularly for data considered vital to the proper operation of the network. SNMP agent and MIB implementations are vendor-implementation specific and are not guaranteed to provide data that are consistent across all vendors.

Objectives of performing checks and balances are to locate and identify:

- Errors in recording or presenting network management data.
- Rollovers of counters (e.g., returning a counter value to zero without proper notification).
- Changes in MIB variables from one software version to another.

In addition, checks and balances help to normalize network management data across multiple vendors, by verifying data through measurements from multiple sources.

Collected management data should be verified for accuracy. For example, when polling for SNMP variables for an interface, consider RMON polling as well to verify these data. Consider using a traffic analyzer to verify data for various random periods of time. You may also run independent tests with traffic generators, the vendors' network devices, and data collection devices to verify the accuracy of collected data.

4.4.5 Managing Network Management Data

Flows of network management data typically consist of SNMP parameter names and values, and the results of queries from utilities such as ping or traceroute. These data are generated by network devices and other devices on the network, transported via SNMP to monitoring devices, and possibly forwarded to display and storage devices. It is important to the network management architecture that we understand where and how the data are generated, transported, and processed, as this will help us to determine where network management components may be placed in the network.

Management data may be generated either in a query/response (stateless) method, as with SNMP or ping queries, or in response to a prearranged set of conditions (stateful), as with SNMP traps. Large numbers of SNMP queries should be spread out over a time interval (e.g., polling interval), not only to avoid network congestion, but also to avoid overburdening network devices and monitoring devices with the processing required to generate management data.

Management data consist of frequently generated parameters for real-time event notification and less frequently generated (or needed) parameters for trend analysis and planning. It may be that the same parameters are used for both purposes. Since frequent polling can generate large amounts of data, storage of these data can become a problem. Some recommendations for managing these data are presented in the following subsections.

Recommendation 1: Local versus Archival Storage

Determine which management data are necessary to keep stored locally and which data may be archived. Management data are usually kept locally, cached

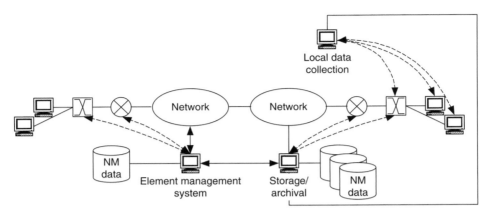

FIGURE 4.15

Local and archival storage for management data.

where they can be easily and quickly retrieved, for event analysis and short-term (on the order of hours or days) trend analysis. Management data that are not being used for these purposes should be archived to secondary or tertiary storage, such as tape archives or off-site storage (Figure 4.15).

Recommendation 2: Selective Copying of Data

When a management parameter is being used for both event notification and trend analysis, consider copying every Nth iteration of that parameter to a separate database location, where the iteration size N is large enough to keep the size of these data relatively small, yet is small enough so that the data are useful in trend analysis. In Figure 4.16 SLA variables are polled regularly (each variable polled per second), while every Nth poll is saved in long-term storage (archival). Depending on the bandwidth and storage available for network management traffic, N can range from 10^2 to 10^5.

A trade-off in selective copying of data is that whenever data are copied, there is a risk that some data may be lost. To help protect against this you can use TCP for data transmission or send copies of data to multiple archival systems (e.g., one primary and one redundant).

If there are indications that more immediate analysis needs to be done, then either a short-term trend analysis can be performed on the locally stored data (from recommendation 1), or the iteration size N can be temporarily shortened.

Recommendation 3: Data Migration

When collecting management data for trend analysis, data can be stored local to the management device and then downloaded to storage/archival when traffic is expected to be low (e.g., at night). In Figure 4.17 polls of network management data are made in five-minute intervals and stored locally. These data are then

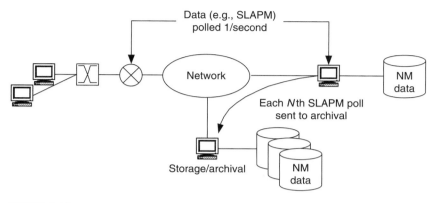

FIGURE 4.16

Selective copying to a separate database.

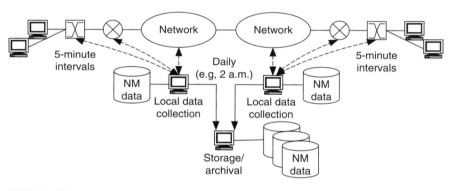

FIGURE 4.17

Data migration.

downloaded to archival storage once or twice daily, usually when there is little user traffic on the network (e.g., at 2 a.m.).

Recommendation 4: Metadata

Metadata is additional information about the collected data, such as references to the data types, timestamps of when the data were generated, and any indications that these data reference any other data. A management data-archival system should provide such additional information regarding the data that have been collected.

4.4.6 MIB Selection

MIB selection means determining which SNMP MIBs to use and apply, as well as which variables in each MIB are appropriate for your network. This may, for example, be a full MIB (e.g., MIB-II is commonly used in its entirety), a subset of each MIB required for conformance to that MIB's specification (also known as *a conformance subset* of the MIB where conformance subsets of MIBs are usually listed at the end of each MIB's specification RFC), enterprise-specific MIBs (the parameters available from each vendor-element or network-element type), or possibly a subset of MIB parameters that you define to apply to your network.

For example, a subset of performance-monitoring parameters can be used from the interfaces MIB (RFC 2863): `ifInOctets`, `ifInErrors`, `ifInUcastPkts`, `ifOutOctets`, `ifOutErrors`, and `ifOutUcastPkts`. This set of six parameters is a common starting point for MIB parameters. These parameters can usually be measured on all interfaces for most network devices.

One can consider MIB variables falling into the following sets: a common set that pertains to network health, and a set that is necessary to monitor and manage those things that the network needs to support, including:

- Server, user device, and network parameters.
- Network parameters that are part of SLAs, policies, and network reconfiguration.

4.4.7 Integration into OSS

When the network includes an interface to an operations support system, the network management architecture must consider how management is to be integrated with the OSS. The interface from network management to OSS is often termed the *northbound interface,* as it is in the direction of service and business management (see Section 4.2). This northbound interface is typically CORBA or SNMP (Figure 4.18).

4.4.8 Internal Relationships

Internal relationships for the network management architecture comprise the interactions, dependencies, trade-offs, and constraints between network management mechanisms. It is important to understand these relationships, as they are part of a complex, nonlinear system and they define and describe the behavior of this architecture.

Interactions

Interactions within network management may include interactions among components of the management system; between the network management system and network devices; and between the network management system and the OSS. If there are multiple network management systems, or if the network management

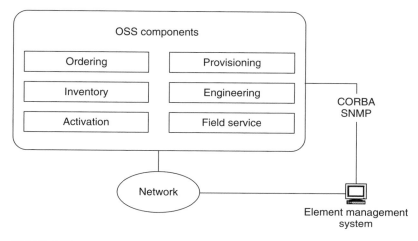

FIGURE 4.18

The integration of network management with OSS.

system is distributed or hierarchical, then there will be multiple components to the management system. The network architecture should include the potential locations for each component and/or management system, as well as the management data flows between components and/or management systems. The interactions here may be in the form of SNMP or CMIP/CMOT queries/responses, CORBA, HTTP, file transfers, or a proprietary protocol.

Part of network management inheres in each managed network device, in the form of management data (e.g., MIB variables) and software that allows access and transport of management data to and from the management system (e.g., SNMP agent software). Therefore, interactions between network management components (particularly monitoring devices) and managed network devices can also be considered here. We may choose to consider all of the managed network devices, depending on how many of them are expected in the network; however, we usually do not consider all managed devices in the network, as there can be quite a large number of them. The devices that are most likely to be considered are those that interact with several users, such as servers and specialized equipment. Interactions here are likely to be in the form of SNMP or CMIP/CMOT queries/ responses.

If your environment includes an OSS, there will likely be some interactions between network management and the OSS, for flow-through provisioning, service management, and inventory control. The network management architecture should note where the OSS would be located, which components of the network management system will interact with the OSS, and where they will be located in the network. Interactions here are likely to use CORBA, but may use SNMP or HTTP (see Dependencies subsection).

Dependencies

Dependencies within network management may include dependencies on capacity and reliability of the network for management data flows, dependence on the amount of data storage available for management data, and dependence on the OSS for the northbound interface requirement.

Network management may be dependent on the performance of the underlying network for support of management data flows. In its most basic sense, the network must provide sufficient capacity for the estimated amount of management data. This estimate can be derived using information on network layout. This is particularly important when network management is centralized and all management data will be aggregated at the network management system interface. This may also be a dependency on IP services, discussed later in this section.

The amount of management data that can be stored is partly a function of how much storage will be available; thus, network management can be dependent on data storage availability.

While network management may interface with an OSS, it may also be dependent on that OSS to determine the northbound interface. For example, some OSSs require CORBA for their interface, which will have to be supported by network management. This may also be considered a constraint on network management.

Trade-Offs

Trade-offs within network management may include trade-offs between in-band and out-of-band management, and trade-offs among centralized, distributed, and hierarchical management. Trade-offs between in-band and out-of-band management include:

- In-band management is cheaper and simpler to implement than out-of-band management; however, when management data flows are in-band, they can be impacted by the same problems that impact user traffic flows.

- Out-of-band management is more expensive and complex to implement than in-band management (since it requires separate network connections); however, it can allow the management system to continue to monitor the network during most network events, even when such events disable the network. In addition, out-of-band management allows access to remote network devices for troubleshooting and configuration, saving the time and effort of having to be physically present at the remote location.

- Out-of-band management, by definition, requires separate network connections. This may be a benefit, in that security for the separate network can be focused on the requirements of management data flows, or it may be a liability, in that additional security (with its associated expense and overhead) is required for this network.

- When in-band and out-of-band management are combined, there is still the expense and complexity of out-of-band management, as well as the additional security requirements. However, the combination allows (typically) higher-performance in-band management to be used for monitoring (which is the high-capacity portion of network management), yet still allows out-of-band management to be used at critical times (e.g., when the user data network, including in-band paths, is down).

The following are trade-offs among centralized, distributed, and hierarchical management:

- In centralized management only one management system is needed (all management components, as well as other tools, are on one hardware platform), simplifying the architecture and reducing costs (depending on the choice of management system) over distributed or hierarchical management systems, which may have several separate components. However, centralized management can act as a single point of failure; all management data flows are aggregated at the management system's network interface, potentially causing congestion or failure. Distributed or hierarchical management can avoid central points of failure and reduce congestion points.

- The degrees of distribution or hierarchy in management are a function of how complex and costly you are willing to allow the management system to become, and how important it is to isolate management domains and provide redundant monitoring. Costs for distributed or hierarchical management increase with the number of monitoring devices or management systems needed. However, if you are willing to accept high management costs, you can provide a fully redundant, highly flexible hierarchical management system for your network.

Constraints

Constraints include the northbound interface from network management to the OSS. This interface may be constrained by the interface requirement of the OSS. Since the OSS potentially ties together several service and business components, its interface requirements may be forced onto network management. CORBA is often required for this northbound interface.

4.4.9 External Relationships

External relationships comprise trade-offs, dependencies, and constraints between the network management architecture and each of the other component architectures (addressing/routing, performance, security, and any other component architectures you may develop). Network management should be a part of all the other architectural components as they will need some or all of the monitoring, control, and configuration capabilities that network management provides. As such, each of the other components will interact at some level with network management.

There are common external relationships between network management and each of the other component architectures, some of which are presented in the following subsections.

Interactions between Network Management and Addressing/Routing

Network management depends on the addressing/routing architecture for the proper routing of management data flows through the network. If the management is in-band, then the routing of management data flows should be handled in the same fashion as the user traffic flows and does not require any special treatment in the architecture. However, if the management is out-of-band, then the routing of management data flows may need to be considered in the architecture.

Network management is often bounded by the network or networks that are under common management. A *management domain* is used to describe a set of networks under common management; *autonomous system* is another term often used. Thus, the routing and addressing architecture may define the management domain for the network, setting the boundaries for network management.

If the management is out-of-band, the separate management network may require routing and addressing as part of the architecture.

Interactions between Network Management and Performance

Network management interacts with the performance architecture through the collection of network performance data as it seeks to verify the proper operation of performance mechanisms. This may occur through a northbound interface (described earlier) to OSS or to a policy database for performance. Performance also depends on network management to provide data on the performance and function of the network.

A trade-off between network management and performance comes in how much network resources (e.g., capacity) network management requires, as this may impact the network's ability to support various performance levels. This is particularly true when management is centralized, as management data flows in centralized management are aggregated at the management system's network interface.

Network management can depend on performance in two ways: First, when performance mechanisms support best-effort traffic (as determined in the flow specification), part of this best-effort traffic can be allocated to network management data flows; second, if a higher-priority service is desired for network management data flows, then network management will be dependent on performance mechanisms to provide the necessary support for such services. When network management data flows require high-priority service, network management may be dependent on performance mechanisms to function properly.

Interactions between Network Management and Security

Network management is dependent on some level of security in order to be used in most operational environments. This may be security at the protocol level (e.g., SNMP security) and/or for securing access to network devices. If the management is out-of-band, the separate network that supports this management must be secured. Network management may be constrained by security, if the security mechanisms used do not permit network management data or access across the security perimeter. This may also be considered a trade-off, when it is possible to reduce the level of security in order to support access or management data transport across the security perimeter. For example, consider the use of POTS for out-of-band access. Such dial-in access is unacceptable to many organizations, unless extra security measures are taken on each access line (e.g., dial-back, security keys, etc.).

4.5 SUMMARY

While network management can appear to be a simple function, it is actually a complex set of functions with interesting architectural features. In this chapter we decomposed network management into monitoring, instrumentation, and management, and explored how each of these can be achieved within the network management architecture.

The essence of the network management architecture is in understanding what you want to monitor and manage, determining where you want to locate each network management function, and managing the flows of network management traffic. Depending on the characteristics of the network you are developing, you have a wide range of architectural solutions, from a simple, single-platform system with preconfigured monitoring and management capabilities, to a distributed, hierarchical system where you determine and configure its monitoring and management capabilities.

Based on the information in this chapter, you have the flexibility to create a network management architecture tailored to the requirements of your customer.

SLA and Network Monitoring

This chapter is drawn from Chapter 5 of *Deploying IP and MPLS QoS for Multi-service Networks* by Evans and Filsfils. Many of the concepts referred to in this chapter can be found explained in more detail in other chapters in the source text. This chapter discusses the technologies and techniques available for service level agreements (SLAs) and network monitoring in quality-of-service (QoS)-enabled IP networks.

5.1 APPROACHES FOR NETWORK MONITORING

There are two main approaches that are generally used in concert to monitor the performance of a QoS-enabled network service in order to determine whether SLAs have been or can be met:

Passive network monitoring: With passive network monitoring, network devices record statistics on network traffic, which can provide an indication of the status at a particular network element. Periodic polling is typically used to gather these data for reporting and analysis. This is a micro measure that looks at each device in isolation; by looking at multiple network elements, an aggregate view of the status of a network service may be deduced. Passive network monitoring does not require any additional traffic to be used for measurement purposes.

Active network monitoring: Unlike passive monitoring, active monitoring involves sending additional traffic into the network. Synthetic test streams comprising "probe" packets are sent across the network solely for the purpose of characterizing the network performance; analysis of the received streams is used for this characterization. Active monitoring provides a macro measure of network SLAs in that it reports the measured performance across a number of network elements as a system.

Passive and active network monitoring systems may be deployed for a number of reasons:

■ For monitoring and reporting, so that the network service offered is achieving the committed SLA targets; this may include:
  – Proactive network and SLA monitoring.
  – Long-term trending of the relative changes in network SLA performance over time.
■ For monitoring, so that network performance is sufficient to meet the required application quality of experience (QoE) targets.
■ As a feedback loop to network capacity planning processes, results from passive and active monitoring may provide heuristics, allowing capacity planning thresholds to be tuned based on correlation between network or per-class load and SLA probing reports of delay, jitter, and loss.

For network service providers, active and passive network monitoring provide potential value-added service opportunities as end customers look to outsource their end-to-end wide area network (WAN)–related capacity management. Hence, the service provider may report enough information to customers to let them assess their network usage and how well their SLAs were met.

5.2 PASSIVE NETWORK MONITORING

From a QoS perspective, passive network monitoring involves polling the network devices for statistics that they maintain for QoS functions they perform, such as packet and byte counts or queue depths. This is typically performed using the Simple Network Management Protocol (SNMP—RFC 1157) to poll for information contained in management information bases (MIBs). The considerations on polling and the types of statistics polled are described in the following sections.

5.2.1 How Often to Poll?

Any polling of network devices for statistics raises the question of how frequently to poll? In practice, this represents a balance between the polling capacity of the network management system (NMS), the number of devices that need to be polled, the load incurred on the polled devices, and the impact of the polling traffic on the network.

Many of the retrieved statistics will be in the form of packet and byte counts; these can be used to determine the average traffic demands over the previous sampling interval. Longer polling intervals implicitly have a larger sample size and may be acceptable for trending purposes; however, the polled data will implicitly be averaged over a longer time and therefore issues may be hidden. Therefore, shorter intervals are preferred where measurements that are more granular are required, although this has to be balanced against the increased polling load.

For troubleshooting, proactive measurement, and SLA reporting, within the bounds of the NMS and network constraints and capabilities, QoS statistics should be polled as often as possible to prevent visibility of SLA-affecting network issues being lost due to the effects of averaging. If the polling is frequent, the data can always be averaged over longer timeframes. For trending, it may be more appropriate to poll every hour. Longer-duration measurements make the comparison between days, months, and years easier and more statistically relevant.

5.2.2 Per-Link Statistics

Per-link QoS statistics can be used for different purposes, depending on from where in the network they are recorded:

Access links: Network access links can be both the boundary of a DiffServ (differentiated services) domain and a customer/provider boundary. Hence, access link QoS statistics are used both for fault finding and reporting statistics to customers of end services such that they can provision their edge QoS classes adequately.

Core links: On core links, per-link QoS statistics are used both for fault finding and as an input to the core network capacity planning processes.

Most vendors implement proprietary MIBs, which can be used to retrieve the relevant per-link statistics. They could also be retrieved from the DiffServ MIB defined by RFC 3289, although this is not widely implemented by network equipment vendors. Where it is supported, the DiffServ MIB may be used for both monitoring and configuration of a router or switch that is capable of differentiated services functionality. As the DiffServ MIB is designed to be generic across vendors, vendor proprietary MIBs may provide information on QoS statistics that are specific to their implementation, and therefore that are not available in RFC 3289.

The following subsections describe the most important per-link QoS statistics for monitoring DiffServ deployments in terms of the QoS functions and mechanisms that are applied. Consideration is also provided on how these statistics should be interpreted to assure the performance of a QoS-enabled network service. In some cases, it may not be necessary to monitor all of the statistics that are described; some of the statistics are interrelated and therefore may be deduced from others without requiring explicit monitoring. This duplication can be useful in providing a means for cross-verifying the retrieved statistics.

Monitoring Classification

The main use for classification statistics is to verify that traffic is being correctly classified in the appropriate class. Classification statistics can also be used to verify or deduce other statistics; for example, the total number of packets dropped and transmitted by the other functions applied to a particular class after classification must equal the total number of packets classified into that class.

A router may classify a number of traffic streams into a single traffic class, to which actions may subsequently be applied. The following classification statistics are useful in understanding the offered traffic load in each class, and the constituents of that traffic class.

Per-Classification Rule

If multiple rules are used to classify traffic streams into a single class, it may be useful to know the total number of packets and their cumulative byte count that have been classified per rule. For example, if traffic marked DSCP 18 (i.e., AF21) and DCSP 20 (i.e., AF22) is to be classified into the same class, which is serviced with an AF per-hop behavior (PHB), then it may be useful to know how much AF21 traffic (which could, for example, represent the in-contract traffic) and how much AF22 traffic (which could represent the out-of-contract traffic) there is within the class.

Further, by knowing both the number of packets and bytes classified into a class, it is possible to estimate the average packet size for the class. This information can be useful for ensuring that, for example, only small voice over Internet Protocol (VoIP) packets are being classified into a voice class. Therefore, in general, for most QoS statistics polled, the results retrieved include both a packet and a byte count.

On Aggregate

For the per-traffic class, it is also important to know the total number of packets and bytes that have been classified on aggregate (i.e., across all classification rules) into that particular class.

Monitoring Policing

Policers may be applied for a number of reasons. Which statistics are relevant when monitoring policers depends on the way in which they are used.

Enforcing a Maximum Rate for a Voice Class

The single-rate, three-color marker (SR-TCM) defined in RFC 2697 is commonly applied to police the maximum rate of a voice class. This may be used both on core and access links. On core links policers are commonly applied to voice classes to ensure the voice class cannot starve other classes of bandwidth. On access links policers are used both to prevent starvation of other classes and to enforce a DiffServ edge traffic conditioning agreement (TCA), ensuring that only voice traffic that conforms to the voice class TCA is admitted into the DiffServ network.

In either case when the SR-TCM is used to police a voice class it would typically have a defined common information rate (CIR) and committed burst size (CBS), with excess burst size (EBS) set to zero; a violate (i.e., red) action of transmit; and a conform (i.e., green) action of drop. Applied in this way, the SR-TCM would enforce a maximum rate of CIR and a burst of CBS on the voice class and any traffic in violation of this would be dropped.

Wherever a policer is applied to a voice class, the following statistics should be monitored per policer:

Number of packets and bytes conforming (i.e., green): This is the number of packets and bytes transmitted by the policer.

Number of packets and bytes violating (i.e., red): This is the number of packets and bytes dropped by the policer. Wherever a policer is used to enforce a maximum rate for a voice class, the policer is meant as a protective measure. If the policer actually drops voice packets there is an issue somewhere that is affecting the service (that is, assuming that the policer has been correctly configured) and voice call quality will be affected. Therefore, ideally there should be no packets violating the SR-TCM policer definition. If there are, the resulting actions will depend on where the policer is being used:

- *Access links:* To resolve drops by a voice class policer on an access link, either the bandwidth provisioned for the voice class (and therefore the policer rate) needs to be increased, or controls need to be put in place to limit the offered voice traffic load (e.g., using admission control).
- *Core links:* Drops by a voice class policer are an indication of either a capacity planning failure or a major network failure or a network attack. In either case, the occurrence of such drops should trigger further investigation to determine the cause of the drops and to prevent a reoccurrence.

Marking In-Contract and Out-of-Contract

Either the SR-TCM or the two-rate, three-color marker (TR-TCM) defined in RFC 2698 are commonly applied to AF classes to mark certain amounts of traffic in-contract and out-of-contract. When deployed in this way, which statistics are important depends on whether the SR-TCM or TR-TCM is used.

The *SR-TCM* is commonly used for in-contract or out-of-contract marking with EBS = 0, a green action of {transmit + mark in-contract} and a red action of {transmit + mark out-of-contract}. Applied in this way, the SR-TCM would enforce a maximum rate of CIR and a burst of CBS on the traffic stream. Conforming traffic would be marked in-contract and any traffic in violation of this would be marked out-of-contract. When deployed in this way the important statistics are:

- *Number of packets and bytes conforming (i.e., green):* This is the number of packets marked in-contract by the policer, and their respective byte count.
- *Number of packets and bytes violating (i.e., red):* This is the number of packets marked out-of-contract by the policer, and their respective byte count.

The purpose of marking certain amounts of traffic in-contract or out-of-contract is to be able to offer a committed SLA for a defined in-contract rate, and to allow traffic in excess of this rate to be transmitted, but to mark it differently to indicate that it is out-of-contract such that it may potentially be given a less-stringent SLA. Therefore, when the SR-TCM is applied in this way, the main use for statistics of packets and bytes conforming and violating is for reporting to customers of end services such that they can provision their edge QoS classes adequately, rather than for fault finding.

The *TR-TCM* can be used to mark a certain amount of a traffic class as in-contract, and everything above that as out-of-contract, up to a maximum rate above which all traffic is dropped, by applying a green action of transmit, yellow action of {transmit + mark out-of-contract}, and red action of drop. Applied in this way the TR-TCM would enforce a maximum rate of CIR and a burst of CBS on the traffic stream; any traffic in excess would then be marked out-of-contract up to a maximum rate of peak information rate (PIR) and a burst of peak burst size (PBS). When deployed in this way the important statistics are:

- *Number of packets and bytes conforming (i.e., green):* This is the number of packets marked in-contract by the policer, and their respective byte count.
- *Number of packets and bytes exceeding (i.e., yellow):* This is the number of packets marked out-of-contract by the policer, and their respective byte count.
- *Number of packets and bytes violating (i.e., red):* This is the number of packets and bytes dropped by the policer.

Similarly to where the SR-TCM is used for in-contract or out-of-contract marking, where the TR-TCM is used for this purpose, the main use for statistics of packets and bytes conforming and exceeding is for reporting to customers of end services. However, if there are a significant number of packets that are violating (i.e., dropped) relative to the number of packets transmitted (i.e., conforming + exceeding), this is an indication that the class load is exceeding the available capacity and the performance of all applications within that class may be affected. Therefore, consideration should be given to increasing the PIR configured for that class or to reducing the traffic load within the class.

Monitoring Queuing and Dropping

For all queuing classes, it is normal to monitor the following statistics:

- *Number of packets and bytes transmitted:* This is the number of packets successfully transmitted from the queue by the scheduler, and their respective byte count.
- *Number of packets and bytes dropped:* This is the number of packets dropped by queue management functions acting on that queue, and their respective byte count. The statistics that matter with respect to

dropping mechanisms depend on the particular dropping mechanisms that are used.

Monitoring Tail Drop

If simple tail drop is used to enforce a queue limit then a count of the number of packets and bytes dropped per queue should be monitored.

If a queue limit is applied to a voice or video class queue, it is normal practice for the queue limit to be at least as great as the burst size for the policer configured for the class. In this case, the policer burst should constrain the class burst and there should be no tail drops experienced for that queue; if tail drops are experienced, this would be an indication of an issue. If the queue limit were set less than the policer burst and tail drops were experienced, then the same actions should be taken as if policer drops had occurred.

If a queue limit is applied to a data class queue and the measured drop rate—that is, the ratio of packets and bytes dropped to packets and bytes transmitted—is high (where high is dependent on the impact on application performance), then this indicates one of the following:

- The queue is operating in significant congestion and therefore consideration should be given both to increasing the bandwidth assurance offered to that queue and to reducing the traffic load within the queue.
- The queue limit is set too low to accommodate the burst profile of the offered traffic load and therefore the queue limit may need retuning.

Monitoring Weighted Tail Drop

Weighted tail drop is sometimes applied to AF class queues to discard a subset of the traffic within the queue preferentially if congestion is experienced within the queue. This can be used to differentiate between traffic that has been differentially marked as in-contract and out-of-contract. Traffic that is marked out-of-contract is subjected to a lower queue limit and therefore is discarded in preference to traffic that is marked in-contract and that is subject to a higher queue limit.

If weighted tail drop is used, then statistics of the number of packets and bytes dropped and transmitted per weighted tail drop profile should be monitored. If the intent of deploying weighted tail drop in this way is to ensure that in-contract traffic has a low loss rate, then the drop rate for the in-contract (i.e., higher) queue limit should be very low, where low is defined by the in-contract SLA for loss. If this is not the case, then the indications and rectifying actions that should be taken with respect to the in-contract traffic are the same as for simple tail drop as described in the previous discussion of monitoring tail drop.

When weighted tail drop is used, it would be expected that the drop rate for out-of-contract traffic would be higher than for in-contract traffic. It should be noted, however, that individual flows might have some packets marked as in-contract and others as out-of-contract. Therefore, if the drop rate for out-of-contract packets is too high, the performance of all applications using that queue may be affected and the indications and rectifying actions that should be taken with respect to the in-contract traffic are the same as for simple tail drop, as previously described.

Monitoring RED

Random early detection, or RED, is an active queue management mechanism that was designed to improve overall throughput for TCP-based applications. If RED is applied to a data class queue, then the following statistics should be monitored:

The number of packets and bytes enqueued is the number of packets subjected to this RED profile that were successfully enqueued, and their respective byte count. Where only a single RED profile is active on the queue, this should be the same as the number of packets and bytes transmitted from the queue.

The number of packets and bytes randomly dropped, or "random drops," comprise the RED drops that occur when the measured average queue depth is between the configured minimum threshold and maximum threshold for that particular RED profile. If RED is configured and working correctly, then the majority of dropped packets should be random drops. If the drop rate for all RED drops is high relative to the number of packets transmitted, then this indicates one of the following:
- The queue is operating in significant congestion and therefore consideration should be given to increasing the bandwidth assurance offered to that queue, or to reducing the traffic load within the queue.
- The configured minimum and maximum thresholds or exponential weighting constant for that queue are set too aggressively (i.e., too low) to accommodate the burst profile of the offered traffic load and therefore may need retuning.
- There are applications in that queue that are not responding to random drops and consideration should be given to whether these applications may be better serviced from a different class queue.

The number of packets and bytes force dropped make up the drops that occur when the measured average queue depth is above the configured maximum threshold; these are referred to as "forced drops." If RED is configured and operating correctly, then random drops should ensure that the average queue limit is below the configured maximum threshold and therefore there should be very few forced drops. If there are a significant number of forced drops relative to the total number of RED drops, then the possible causes and rectifying actions that should be taken are as described previously for high RED drops.

Polling for the measured RED *average queue depth* is not essential but provides additional data, which can be used to supplement the RED other statistics. If the measured average queue depth is frequently close to or above the configured RED maximum threshold, then this is also an indication that either the queue is operating in significant congestion or the RED configuration is set too aggressively and rectifying actions that should be taken are as previously described for high RED drops.

Monitoring WRED

Weighted RED (WRED) is commonly applied to AF queues to differentiate between in-contract and out-of-contract traffic. To achieve this, two RED profiles are applied to the same queue and traffic marked out-of-contract is subjected to the more aggressive RED profile (i.e., with lower minimum threshold and maximum threshold), and therefore "in" congestion is discarded in preference to traffic that is marked in-contract and that is subject to a RED profile with higher minimum and maximum thresholds.

Where WRED is used, the number of packets and bytes dropped and transmitted per RED profile is required. The sum of the packets successfully enqueued across all RED profiles should be the same as the number of packets and bytes transmitted from the queue.

As for weighted tail drop, the intent of deploying WRED in this way is to ensure that in-contract traffic has a low loss rate, then the drop rate for the in-contract RED profile should be very low, where low is determined by the in-contract SLA for loss. If this is not the case then the indications and rectifying actions that should be taken with respect to the in-contract traffic are the same as for RED as described previously.

As for weighted tail drop, if the drop rate for out-of-contract packets is too high the performance of all applications using that queue may be affected and the indications and rectifying actions that should be taken with respect to the in-contract traffic are the same as for RED, as described previously.

5.2.3 System Monitoring

Ideally, all packet drops within a router are handled intelligently by the QoS functions configured on that router, which may be applied outbound on each interface, for example. In practice, however, depending on how a particular router is architected and implemented, there may be cases where drops can occur on other parts of the system, due to system constraints. If, in the part of the system where these drops occur, there is no understanding of the class of the traffic being dropped, then traffic may be dropped indiscriminately of traffic class.

Clearly, systems should be designed to try to minimize the occurrence of such indiscriminate traffic drops; however, in cases where they can occur it is essential to monitor them, because they can provide an indication of serious system issues that can potentially affect the SLAs across all traffic classes.

The system drops that can occur will depend on the implementation of a particular device; however, some of the most common types of system drops are:

No-buffer drops: Where buffer memory is shared between queues in a system, there may be cases where a packet arrives and there is insufficient packet buffer memory available to store the packet, in which case there is no alternative but to drop the packet. Such "no-buffer drops" should be an exception in any well-designed system, rather than the norm; however, the occurrence of no-buffer drops can be exacerbated in a heavily congested system if RED and queue-limit settings are excessively high.

Input drops/ignores: Input drops, which are also known as ignores, occur when there are insufficient packet buffers to store a packet even before a routing or switching decision can be made. Input drops are a symptom of an oversubscribed system, for example, where the packets-per-second forwarding performance of the system or component is being exceeded.

System drops such as no-buffer drops and input drops will generally need to be monitored using vendor-specific MIBs, as system-specific statistics are not available from the DiffServ MIB. Due to the impact they can have on the SLAs of all traffic classes, the occurrence of any such system drops should trigger further investigation to determine the cause of the drops and to prevent a reoccurrence.

5.2.4 Core Traffic Matrix

The core traffic demand matrix is the matrix of ingress to egress traffic demands across the core network. Traffic matrices can be measured or estimated from statistics gathered using passive monitoring techniques. The main benefit of the core traffic matrix is for core network capacity planning, in that it can be used to predict the impact that demand growths can have, and in the simulation of "what-if" scenarios, to predict the impact that the failure of core network elements can have on the utilization of the rest of the network.

5.3 ACTIVE NETWORK MONITORING

Ideally, it would be possible to measure the delay, jitter, loss, and throughput that actual traffic experiences as it traverses a network. In some cases, it may be possible to retrieve this information from the application end systems. Where the real-time protocol (RTP—RFC 3550) is used, for example, the timestamp and sequence number information in the RTP header could be used to determine the delay, jitter, and loss of the received stream at the receiving end system. This is not generally possible in practice, however, due to the following reasons: many applications do not use RTP; retrieving such statistics from all application end systems would be unscalable; or the end systems may not be under the same administrative responsibility as the network elements. Further, to provide this information at the network level would require the network elements to uniquely identify a packet at every single hop and to timestamp it very accurately, which is not possible in practice.

Network-level active network monitoring is an alternative approach, which is more generally applicable. Active monitoring uses specially tailored synthetic traffic test streams comprising "probe" packets—that aim to emulate actual network traffic—which are sent between active monitoring devices in order to characterize network performance and thereby infer the performance experienced by the emulated traffic. In DiffServ deployments, active monitoring can be used to measure the performance of all classes of traffic.

Active network monitoring requires the deployment of an active SLA probing system, supporting capabilities such as those defined by the IP performance metrics (IPPM) working group within the IETF. In such a system, active monitoring agents are deployed (potentially on existing network elements) and test streams are sent between the agents. The agents measure the received streams and typically keep a statistical analysis of the measured results, which can then be retrieved periodically from the active measuring devices, via SNMP for example. In addition, the active monitoring devices may proactively issue traps, if defined thresholds for the measured performance of the test streams are exceeded.

In deploying an active monitoring system, consideration should be given to the following questions, which are addressed in the proceeding sections:

- Which test streams should be used?
- How often should testing be undertaken and for how long?
- Which metrics should be measured for the received streams?
- Where should active monitoring devices be deployed and what paths should the active monitoring streams monitor?

To avoid confusion, we differentiate between the active monitoring traffic (i.e., the active measurement probes) and the monitored traffic, the performance of which the active monitoring traffic is trying to estimate.

5.3.1 Test Stream Parameters

The characteristics of the test stream will affect the characteristics of the network that the test stream will measure. These measured test stream results are only useful if they are in some way representative of the performance experienced by the monitored application or traffic class. This gives rise to the question of what test stream parameters are required to ensure that the measured characteristics of the active measurement stream accurately reflect the characteristics (e.g., delay, jitter, loss, packet reordering, and availability) of the traffic from the monitored application or traffic class.

The answer to this question is still the subject of further study; however, the following sections consider the key parameters to define for an active measurement stream. It is noted that the term *accurately* in this context does not mean that the difference between measured test stream characteristics and the characteristics of the traffic must be small, but is does mean that the two results must be highly correlated, such that it is possible to predict the measured traffic performance from test stream measurements with high fidelity.

Packet Size

There are two general approaches to the setting of packet sizes for active monitoring probes. One is to use probe packets that are the same size as the packets of the monitored traffic. There are two justifications for this approach:

1. Packet size has a more significant impact on serialization delay with lower-speed links, therefore, using packets the same size as the packets of the monitored traffic will potentially provide a more accurate measurement of delay. It is noted, however, that if the link speeds on the path are known, adjustments can be made to take differences in serialization delay between monitoring and monitored traffic into account.

2. Packets larger or smaller than the packets of the monitored traffic may experience a different loss than the monitored traffic itself; if congestion occurs in part of the network, as the queue depth increases a smaller packet is more likely to be enqueued than a larger one.

An alternative is to use small-size packets, for two reasons:

1. In environments where there are very low-speed links, such as in some mobile environments where the bandwidth is scarce and expensive, the smallest possible–size packets are used for bandwidth economy.

2. Where a high rate of test packets is needed to achieve measurement accuracy, the use of larger packets may have a significant impact on the traffic being measured. In this case, small-size packets are used to minimize the potential impact.

There is no industry consensus on which approach is best. However, Hill, in his M.Sc. thesis *Assessing the Accuracy of Active Probes for Determining Network Delay, Jitter, and Loss*, concludes from simulations studying the effectiveness of active SLA monitoring on a 2-Mb link that, "The accuracy of the probes is not really affected by probe size. Both sizes (41 bytes and 850 bytes) show equally good correlation coefficients for delay and loss." He also concludes that larger-size probes have significantly greater impact on the delay and jitter of the traffic whose performance the test stream is trying to estimate. Therefore, he recommends that probes should be small such that the active monitoring traffic has less impact on the other traffic. Lima et al. also found no evidence that packet size affected the measurements of packet loss, as described in *Measuring QoS in Class-Based IP Networks Using Multipurpose Colored Probing Patterns*, in the *Proceedings of SPIE*.

In practice, however, most deployments use the same packet size for test streams that are used by the applications they are emulating. It is further noted that on higher-speed links, where the impact of serialization delay is less, and the traffic is more highly aggregated, the impact of probe packet sizing is likely to be less significant.

Sampling Strategy

The probe sampling strategy determines the distribution of the delay separating consecutive test packets. There are three general probe sampling strategies that may be used: periodic, random, and batch.

Periodic sampling consists of sending probes at equally spaced intervals (i.e., every *n* seconds). Opponents of this approach argue that one cannot fully characterize the network behavior by "sampling" at regular intervals. There might be some cases where unforeseen synchronization between the sending of probe packets, or possibly other network events, could potentially lead to inaccuracies. This kind of phenomenon, although theoretically possible, is rarely seen in practice. RFC 3432 describes a methodology for network performance measurement with periodic streams.

Random sampling consists of sending a probe at random intervals, where the interval is regulated by a probability density function. Most commonly, a Poisson process is used to distribute the probe packets, meaning that the interarrivals between probing packets should be independent and exponentially distributed with the same mean. This approach provides an unbiased estimate of the desired time average, which is a property referred to as *Poisson Arrivals See Time Average,* or PASTA. This approach is suggested by the IETF, where RFC 2679 and RFC 2680 standardize metrics based on Poisson sampling processes. Consequently, the IPPM working group has made the support of Poisson streams mandatory for their One-Way Active Measurement Protocol (OWAMP) described in RFC 4656.

    The counterpoint to the use of a variable interpacket delay is based on the fact that most of the real-world applications, which require tightly bounded delay and jitter and therefore are often a focus of active monitoring, do not have a Poisson distributed interpacket delay. Voice and video applications, for instance, commonly have streams with a constant interpacket delay; so why attempt to measure the performance of these applications on the network with something other than a stream that emulates the application?

    A variation on random sampling is to divide the total sampling period into fixed time intervals and then to send a probe within each interval with a random offset from the start of the interval, where the offset is regulated by a probability density function. The benefit of this approach is that the sample size within a defined number of intervals is known. This approach is referred to as stratified random sampling, where each interval represents a stratum.

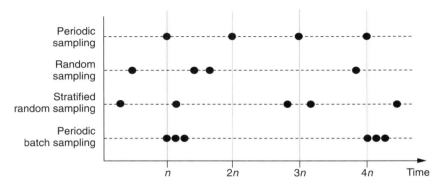

FIGURE 5.1

Active monitoring sampling strategies.

In *batch sampling*, rather than sending individual probe packets, probes are sent in bursts, where the spacing between bursts may be periodic or random.

The different sampling regimes are illustrated in Figure 5.1.

Several works have attempted to compare both approaches to find if there is a tangible difference between the methods. The conclusions are that there may not be a significant difference between Poisson and periodic probing, but that a periodic pattern may lead to a slightly better match than a Poisson pattern. At the same time, while both random and periodic sampling provide acceptable accuracy for measuring delay and loss for VoIP and TCP, neither approach seems to provide acceptable accuracy for measuring jitter.

In practice, however, periodic test streams with a constant interpacket delay are most commonly used because this approach is easier to implement and interpret and because it most closely emulates the applications that the active monitoring is targeting. In recognition of this, RFC 3432 states:

> Poisson sampling produces an unbiased sample for the various IP performance metrics, yet there are situations where alternative sampling methods are advantageous. . . . Predictability and some forms of synchronization can be mitigated through the use of random start times and limited stream duration over a test interval.

Test Rate

The test rate determines the amount of packets sent within the test duration, and consequently, it affects the perturbation introduced by the measurement stream on the actual network traffic. For instance, sending a large amount of test traffic over a path with small bandwidth may potentially interfere with the delivery of the actual measured traffic stream that the active monitoring is trying to monitor.

Such an effect would clearly invalidate the measured results. Conversely, if the test rate is too low, the measured characteristics of the test stream may not reflect the characteristics of the measured traffic stream itself.

Determining an appropriate test rate is a balance between testing with a high enough rate that the measured result is an accurate reflection of the measured traffic stream, while ensuring that the measuring stream does not interfere with the measured traffic stream significantly, such that it affects the very characteristics it is trying to measure. There is no general answer to the question of what test rate to use, but rather it depends on the characteristics of the application or class being monitored.

Test Duration and Frequency

The test duration defines how long an active measurement test case will run. The test frequency determines how many times the test will repeat within a specified time window. Assuming a given test traffic rate, the test duration and frequency need to be high enough that the measured result is an accurate reflection of the measured traffic stream. The lower the (*duration* × *frequency*) in any given time window, the greater the probability that significant events will be missed, as illustrated in Figure 5.2.

If the active monitoring devices do not keep the raw data of the individual probes, but rather keep a statistical representation of the results over the test duration, as is commonly the case, then assuming a given test traffic rate the test duration will implicitly impact the measured statistics, as shown in Figure 5.3.

Similarly to the discussion on the passive monitoring polling interval in Section 5.2.1, longer active monitoring test durations may be acceptable for trending purposes; however, shorter durations are preferred where more granular measure-

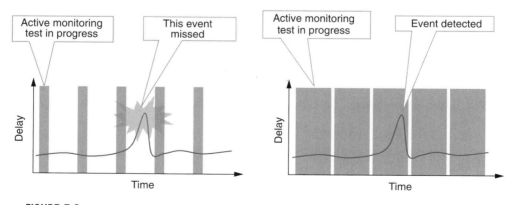

FIGURE 5.2

Impact of test (*frequency* × *duration*).

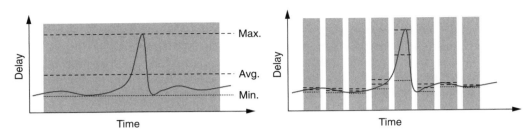

FIGURE 5.3

Impact of test duration.

ments are required, although this has to be balanced against the increased polling load. A possible polling scheme could be as follows:

- For troubleshooting, proactive measurement, and service level agreement reporting, a network segment could be measured constantly with a test duration of two minutes.

- For trending, it may be more appropriate to measure for one hour every day, during the peak hour previously determined by the more granular measurements. Longer-duration measurements make the comparison between days, months, and years easier and more statistically relevant.

Protocols, Ports, and Applications

In order to ensure that the network characteristics determined by a measuring traffic stream are representative of the traffic stream they are measuring, it is important that the measuring stream is classified the same as the target stream along the end-to-end network path. If DiffServ is deployed the network performance experienced by applications will depend on how the traffic is classified within the network; if measurement probes are classified differently than the emulated stream in any part of the network, they may experience different delay, jitter, and loss, and therefore will not provide representative results.

Where simple classification is used, the probe packets should share the same marking (be it DSCP, IP precedence, or even 802.1p based) as the target stream, but need not necessarily share the same IP addressing or protocol as the target stream.

Where complex classification is used, the criteria used for complex classification should produce the same results for the measuring test stream as for the measured application. If, for example, Voice over IP traffic is classified by a combination of identifying UDP packets, with even UDP port numbers (e.g., representing RTP data) and from a specific source IP address, then headers of the probe packets should be such that they also match these criteria. If the target traffic stream is TCP based and complex classification is used, the IP protocol number of the probe packets may also need to be set to 6 to indicate that the packets are TCP.

Where DiffServ is deployed with AF classes supporting the concept of in-contract and out-of-contract, the in-contract traffic has a lower probability of packet loss than the out-of-contract traffic. Hence, if monitoring of the in-contract SLA is required, it is important that any policers used to mark traffic as in-contract or out-of-contract do not remark the in-contract probes, else they may be wrongly classified and may not correctly report the in-contract SLA.

Some probing systems may attempt to characterize application as well as network performance. For example, a probe may record the response time of a domain name server (DNS) query to a particular DNS server or an HTTP Get query of a specific Web page. In these cases, the results will capture multiple components such as session establishment, end-system processing, sending, and receiving multiple packets between the client and the server, and closing the connection. This kind of application-oriented operation may be useful to measure the user experience, but gives no visibility of the performance of the individual components that make up the measured response.

5.3.2 Active Measurement Metrics

Certain SLA metrics are important for defining IP service performance. Once the appropriate test stream for your particular application has been identified, consideration needs to be given to which metrics to measure, how they are measured, and how the resultant measurements should be interpreted. Multiple metrics can be determined from a single test stream.

Delay

Delay can be quantified either as one-way delay or as round-trip delay (round-trip time, or RTT). Measurement of RTT requires that probes are sent from a sending active monitoring agent to a responder and then back to the sender. In this case, the RTT can be determined if the sender timestamps the probes when it sends them (the timestamp is carried in the data of the probe packet) and subtracts this value from the corresponding timestamp when it receives the probe response. Measurement of one-way delay requires that the sender and receiver's local time clocks are synchronized such that the one-way delay can be determined by the receiver, if the receiver also timestamps the probe packets on receipt; the difference between the sending timestamp and receiving timestamp is the one-way delay.

Ensuring synchronization between sender and receiver with acceptable accuracy poses challenges; this is discussed later in more detail in the section on clock synchronization. RTT is easier to implement and measure than one-way delay, and may provide sufficient measurement utility for many applications.

For applications such as VoIP or interactive video conferencing, the important delay metric when considering the engineering of the network is the one-way end-to-end delay in each direction from end system to end system. From a monitoring perspective, however, it may be acceptable to monitor the RTT between the end systems, because from a service perspective, it may not matter in which direction excess delay is experienced; if excess is experienced at all, then the service will be impacted. If SLA violations for delay occur, however, RTT hides the detail of which direction the issue causing the violation occurred. Therefore, measurement of one-way delay may be more useful for network troubleshooting.

Delay can provide a number of important indicators of network performance. Most active monitoring end systems will analyze the received probes and present statistics on the resulting data set, but which statistics are important with respect to delay measurement?

Minimum delay: The minimum network delay is the network delay "baseline," providing an indication of the delay that traffic will experience when the path from source to destination is lightly loaded. This will largely be composed of propagation delay, switching delay, and serialization delay. Delay values above the minimum provide an indication of the congestion experienced along the path. Considering the percentile delay for a low percentile (e.g., 0.1 percentile) will provide an indication of the minimum delay experienced while discounting outliers (i.e, spuriously low results due to measurement system glitches).

High-percentile delay: The maximum delay across a network may not be interesting if it is caused by a very small percentage of outliers. Considering the percentile delay for a high percentile (e.g., 99.9 percentile) will provide an indication of the maximum delay experienced while discounting outliers.

Threshold-exceeded count: For applications that have a stringent requirement on delay, it may be useful to count the number of probe packets out of the total that experienced a delay in excess of a defined threshold, set to indicate when a packet arrived too late to be useful.

Average delay: The average delay may be interesting for trending purposes, but for purposes of comparison, it should be recorded together with the standard deviation of the sample; higher-than-normal standard deviations may be indicative of spurious issues rather than of a trend.

Delay-Jitter

Delay-jitter, also known as jitter, is generally considered to be the variation of the one-way delay for two consecutive packets. Measurement of one-way delay requires timestamping at both sending and receiving devices, which requires synchronization between sender and receiver; this is difficult for the reasons discussed later, in the section on clock synchronization. Fortunately, to calculate jitter there is no need to know the individual one-way delays: instead, this can be calculated from the difference between timestamps taken on single devices. No operation need be performed between timestamps on two different devices, which makes measurement of one-way delay-jitter simpler than measurement of one-way delay.

Consider that $T_s[n]$ is the time when packet n was sent, and $T_r[n]$ is the time when packet n was received; the one-way delay of this packet is denoted as $D[n]$. Then, the jitter J between packets n and $n + 1$ can therefore be calculated as:

$$J[n, n + 1] = D[n + 1] - D[n]$$
$$= (T_r[n + 1] - T_s[n + 1]) - (T_r[n] - T_s[n])$$
$$= (T_r[n + 1] - T_r[n]) - (T_s[n + 1] - T_s[n])$$

The most important statistics to report with respect to jitter are high-percentile jitter, threshold-exceeded count, and average jitter. It is noted that the higher the rate of the traffic stream, the lower the measured jitter will be, as illustrated in Figures 5.4 and 5.5, which show the variation in queuing delay within a queue, and the resulting jitter measured by probes within that queue, for different probe rates.

Therefore, measurement streams at rates below that of the measured traffic will likely report higher jitter than that actually experienced by the traffic itself. A batch sampling strategy may be used to overcome this problem.

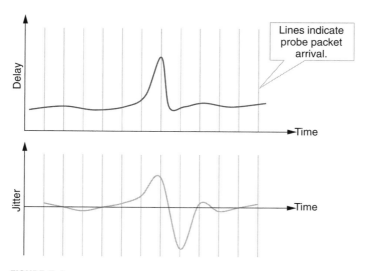

FIGURE 5.4

Lower rate, higher measured jitter.

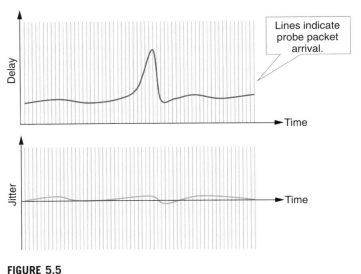

FIGURE 5.5

Higher rate, lower measured jitter.

Packet Loss

In order to determine packet loss there needs to be a way to distinguish between a lost packet and a packet with a large but finite delay. In practice, depending on application and end-system implementations, packets delayed beyond a certain threshold will be of no use and therefore can be considered lost; acceptable delay thresholds may be set for different applications. The loss of an individual packet is a binary measure, however, SLAs for loss are generally defined statistically and therefore loss commitments need to be provided over a defined time interval.

The measure of the percentage of packets dropped may be useful for trending purposes; however, it does not say anything about how those packets were dropped. Therefore, it is not possible to understand the potential impact on applications from this measure alone. RFC 3357 introduces some additional metrics that describe loss patterns and can be used to analyze the possible impact on applications:

Loss period: The loss period defines the frequency and length (loss burst) of loss once it starts.

Loss distance: The loss distance defines the spacing between the loss periods. It is therefore recommended that the loss period and loss distance are measured and compared against application-specific thresholds indicating where the measured loss will unacceptably affect application performance. The impact of packet loss may be significantly different for different applications.

Bandwidth and Throughput

Application throughput is dependent on many factors, which can vary widely depending on end-system implementations and traffic profiles. Hence, active monitoring systems generally do not attempt to characterize application throughput explicitly. Rather, application throughput is generally inferred. Considering TCP for example, TCP performance can be inferred from the measured network RTT and packet loss rate. Active monitoring systems may send packets that appear to be TCP packets (i.e., use the IP protocol number 6), but they need not, and commonly do not, implement a TCP stack (i.e., the transmission of the packets is not controlled by TCP's flow and congestion control mechanisms).

Reordering

IP does not guarantee that packets are delivered in the order in which they were sent, and packet reordering can have an adverse impact on the performance of many applications. Within an active monitoring test stream, reordering is determined by adding sequence numbers to the packets transmitted in the stream and then comparing the sequence numbers of the received packets with the order in which they are received. If a packet arrives with a sequence number smaller than its predecessor's then that packet would be defined as out of order, or reordered.

The simplest metric by which to measure the magnitude of reordering is as a reordering ratio, which is the ratio of reordered packets that arrived, relative to the total number of packets received. A number of other metrics for quantifying the magnitude of reordering are defined in RFC 4737.

Availability

Availability for IP services is generally defined either as network availability or as service availability.

Network availability: Bidirectional network availability or connectivity between two active monitoring devices can be determined using probes sent from a sender to a responder and then back to the sender. For each response successfully received the network is considered available and for each not received the network is considered unavailable. As with packet loss, a delay threshold needs to be defined after which a response is considered "lost."

Service availability: Service availability is a compound metric defining when a service is available between a specified ingress point and a specified egress point within the bounds of the committed SLA metrics for the service (e.g., delay, jitter, and loss).

Quality of Experience

Active monitoring end systems do not normally implement the full end-system behavior for the applications they are trying to measure. Some active monitoring devices, however, will interpret the metrics of a received stream in order to provide an objective measure of the quality of the application performance that will be experienced from the perspective of the end users, which is also known as the user quality of experience, or QoE. The most common QoE measure is the mean opinion score (MOS), which provides a subjective numeric measure of the QoE of a voice call. ITU standard G.107 uses a number of measured network parameters to determine a "rating factor," which can be transformed to give estimates of the MOS for calls that use that network service.

5.3.3 Deployment Considerations

The following subsections detail the issues that should be considered in the deployment of an active network monitoring system.

External versus Embedded Agents

An active measurement system uses active monitoring agents to send and receive probe packets. These agents may be implemented in dedicated active monitoring devices or alternatively may be embedded into existing network devices.

External Agents

External agents are implemented in dedicated active monitoring devices, which may either use specialized hardware or dedicated but off-the-shelf computers running active monitoring software. This approach decouples the forwarding path (routers and switches) from the measurement devices; the dedicated active monitoring devices appear as customers connected to the network and therefore this approach may provide the closest view to the end-customer experience.

However, the use of dedicated devices requires additional network equipment, which incurs additional cost in terms of capital expenditure, accommodation, power, management, and maintenance. Therefore, for individual end users or small branch office locations the use of dedicated active monitoring devices is generally not viable.

Embedded Agents

Some network hardware vendors implement software active monitoring agents embedded in products, which may be network devices such as routers or switches or could be end systems such as IP phones. The use of embedded agents in devices that are already on the data-switching path allows the installed base of network equipment to be leveraged, enabling the rapid rollout of an active SLA monitoring system without requiring the deployment of new network equipment.

Active Monitoring Topologies

When deploying an active monitoring system, a key question is where to deploy the active monitoring devices, be they external or embedded agents. In general, the measurements from active monitoring should represent the application's experience, and therefore the active monitoring devices should be as close to the application end system as possible. In all deployments, however, there are constraints that limit the location of such devices; there may be parts of the network that are not under the control of the measuring organization, for example. In large deployments, scalability of the active monitoring system is an additional consideration.

The selection of the active monitoring topology depends on these constraints. Consider the example physical network topology shown in Figure 5.6. A number of different active SLA monitoring topologies, where the active SLA monitoring topology is defined by the sources and destinations of the active monitoring test streams, can be overlaid on this physical topology.

Full Mesh

A full mesh requires probes from every active monitoring location to every other active monitoring location, as shown in Figure 5.7. This approach is the most accurate because it measures end-to-end paths between all locations and gives full

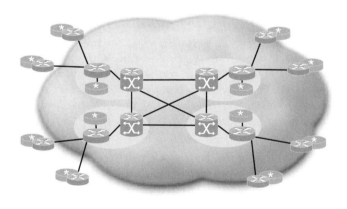

- Distribution or access routers
- Core router
- Active monitoring agent
- POP

FIGURE 5.6

Example physical network topology.

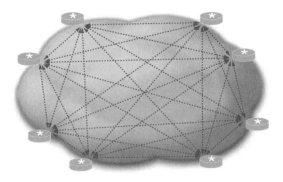

⬭🟋 Active monitoring agent

◄····► Active monitoring test streams

FIGURE 5.7

Full-mesh active monitoring topology.

network coverage. In practice, however, it does not scale well as the number of active monitoring nodes (n) increases; the number of bidirectional active monitoring test streams required to interconnect them is $n \times (n - 1)/2$, which increases more than linearly with the number of nodes. Beyond a few nodes, this approach may result in a configuration burden, the test streams may use a significant amount of bandwidth, and the retrieval of the measurement data from all nodes may incur significant management system overhead. For these reasons, it is only used where there are a limited number of sites to be monitored.

Partial Mesh

A partial mesh involves running a mesh of test streams on a subset of the topology. For example, this could be a hub-and-spoke active monitoring topology in networks where remote sites (the spokes) only communicate with the head offices (the hubs), as shown in Figure 5.8. This approach reduces the number of test streams required and provides end-to-end monitoring between a subset of locations. In a hub-and-spoke topology, if round-trip active monitoring is used, the hub sites may be configured as the active monitoring probe senders, with the spoke sites acting as responders; in this case, the active monitoring measurement data need only be retrieved from the hub sites.

Hierarchical Mesh

In networks with any-to-any communication between sites, a full mesh may be unscalable, while a partial mesh may not provide sufficient network coverage. In

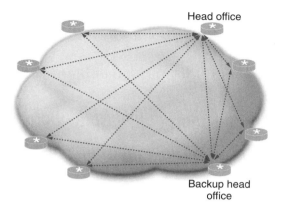

Head office

Backup head
office

 Active monitoring agent

◄┄┄► Active monitoring test streams

FIGURE 5.8

Partial mesh active monitoring topology.

these cases, a hierarchical mesh may be used. With a hierarchical mesh, the active monitoring is segmented. In a typical deployment, centralized active measurement devices are located in each point of presence (POP) and test streams are run from each POP to their connected remote sites in a hub-and-spoke active monitoring topology. Test streams are then run in a full mesh from each POP to every other POP, as shown in Figure 5.9.

A partial mesh facilitates the scaling of a network-wide active monitoring system and therefore it is commonly used in practice. It significantly reduces the number of test streams required compared to a full mesh, while providing full network coverage and being relatively easy to manage. If the POP active monitoring devices are configured as senders for round-trip probes, with their respective remote sites monitoring devices acting as responders, then the active monitoring measurement data need only be retrieved from the central sites and there is no need to access the remote sites.

This approach gives segmented measurements for the access links and across the core network and maps well to the concept of a segmented SLA. The disadvantage of this approach is that it does not provide end-to-end monitoring. Therefore, if measurements between two sites A1 and B1 were required, they would need to be statistically estimated by combining, where possible, the measured results for each segment in the end-to-end path (i.e., from site A1 to POP A, from POP A to POP B, and from POP B to site B1).

For example, it is possible to estimate the average (or a specific percentile) end-to-end delay by summing the average (or specific percentile) measured delay for each segment. To estimate the end-to-end packet loss probability, if the prob-

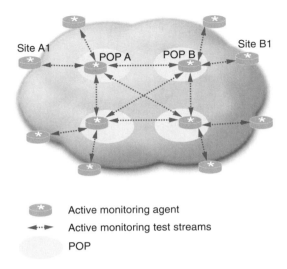

 Active monitoring agent

← ··► Active monitoring test streams

  POP

FIGURE 5.9

Hierarchical-mesh active monitoring topology.

ability of packet loss on segment x is given by P_x, then the end-to-end packet loss probability (P) across n segments is:

$$P = 1 - [(1 - P_1) + (1 - P_2) + \ldots + (1 - P_n)]$$

It is not, however, possible to estimate end-to-end jitter from the measured jitter of the segments on the end-to-end path because the measured jitter in IP networks is not statistically additive in practice. Where a measure of end-to-end jitter is required, end-to-end monitoring should be selectively deployed.

Measuring Equal-Cost Multiple Paths

Many networks have multiple paths between different parts of the network, for reasons of both resilience and capacity provision. Interior Gateway routing Protocols (IGPs) such as OSPF and IS–IS determine which paths will be used between any two points in the network by choosing whichever path has the least total cost, where the path cost is calculated by summing the individual metrics (which express the preference of a link) of the links along the path. If there is more than one least cost path, then the routing protocol will potentially distribute the traffic between the two points across all of those paths.

The algorithms that balance the load across the paths are generally referred to as equal-cost multipath (ECMP) algorithms. ECMP algorithms are generally proprietary to each vendor. Different vendors will use different criteria to determine which path will be used for a particular packet, although a common implementation is to perform a hash function using inputs including fields within the packet header, such as source IP address, destination IP address, protocol number, source UDP/TCP port, and destination UDP/TCP port.

ECMP poses a significant issue for active monitoring for which there is no ideal answer; a single measurement can only use one of the many possible paths and not all of them. There are a number of potential resolutions to this issue; however, none of them is a remedy that will provide a solution in all circumstances. It may be possible to vary the source and destination IP addresses and UDP/TCP port numbers of sent probes in order to try to use more than one of the paths. In practice, however, ECMP algorithms can be difficult to predict (some also use a random seed as an input to the hash), therefore, it may not be possible to guarantee that all paths are being tested. Alternatively, if the test is run from the load-balancing router itself, then it may be possible to force probe packets via each of the load-balancing interfaces in turn; however, this will not guarantee that response probe packets use all return paths also.

Clock Synchronization

To achieve highly accurate one-way delay measurements, the clocks on all the network elements participating in the test must be synchronized; any synchronization error will result in an error in the measured one-way delay. Network devices maintain local time using on-board clocks, which provide time to the device operating system. There are a number of potential ways that the local clocks on network devices can be synchronized.

The most accurate way to synchronize clocks on network devices is to synchronize each device with an accurate "stratum-1" external clock source such as a global positioning system clock or radio clock. This is, however, an expensive approach, and while it may be viable for devices within the core of the network, it would not be viable for individual end users or small branch office locations.

An alternative approach is to distribute stratum-1 time using a protocol, such as the Network Time Protocol (NTP). NTP synchronizes clocks between network devices by exchanging timestamped messages between a server and its clients. NTP seeks long-term accuracy at the expense of short-term accuracy; it will, for instance, slow or accelerate the internal clock (or add/subtract time quanta) to adjust the local clock progressively to what it believes is the true time. If measurements are taking place during those adjustments, strange results like negative delay might be observed. NTP can usually maintain time to within 10 ms in WANs; this does not generally provide a sufficient level of accuracy for those applications with tight delay bound requirements, which require one-way delay monitoring such as VoIP and video streaming. In local area networks (LANs), under good conditions, NTP can usually maintain time to 1 ms or better, which may be sufficient for active monitoring purposes.

Due to the constraints and costs of interdevice clock synchronization, a common deployment model is to distribute time from a stratum-1 clock source to all the devices within a POP using a separate network (commonly the management network) to ensure synchronization via NTP to within 1 ms or better. This enables the measurement of one-way delay between POPs. Synchronization of access routers via NTP is generally not accurate enough and the use of stratum-1 clock sources in these locations is generally not viable, therefore, SLA reporting of the access links from POP to access router is commonly reported as RTT rather than one-way delay.

Acknowledgment

This chapter benefited enormously from the input of Emmanuel Tychon, technical marketing engineer for Cisco IOS IP Service Level Agreement (IP SLAS), whose contribution formed the basis of the active monitoring section.

MPLS Network Management: An Introduction

In this chapter, taken from chapter 1 of *MPLS Network Management* by Nadeau, we look at the origins of Multi-Protocol Label Switching (MPLS) and introduce some of its basic concepts, including the separation of the control and forwarding planes of MPLS, the forward equivalence class, and the MPLS label. After this introduction, we then introduce and discuss some of the new applications of MPLS networks such as traffic engineering and virtual private networks.

After an introduction to MPLS, we explain the basic premise behind why MPLS-enabled networks need to be managed to provide scalable, usable, and most importantly *profitable* MPLS networks. Given this motivation, we introduce how MPLS networks can be managed effectively using both standards-based and non-standard tools.

It is not our goal for this discussion to be an in-depth introduction to MPLS. We assume you have a good level of understanding of MPLS already and that the introduction given in this chapter can be used as a refresher.

6.1 A BRIEF INTRODUCTION TO MPLS

In the past, routing devices were designed with the control and forwarding components commingled, which led to many shortcomings including low performance and scalability issues. In particular, routing lookups, especially those involving so-called longest-prefix match lookups, were quite complex and expensive in nature—in fact, quite a deal more complex than any layer-2 switching or bridging operation.

Further complicating this process was the fact that many routers were required to forward packets from many different routing protocols. By accepting packets from different protocols, the positions of fields in packet headers could potentially be different for nearly every packet received, potentially further degrading forwarding performance. In contrast, nonrouting devices such as layer-2 bridges and switches were able to forward traffic at relatively high speeds because they based their forwarding decisions not on variable-length packet headers and network addresses of varying lengths, but on a short, fixed-length field.

For example, all asynchronous transfer mode (ATM) cells have a fixed length and well-defined format. Devices switching ATM cells only need to examine a short identifier and can immediately forward the cells based on this simple piece of information. There is no question as to the position of the forwarding information in a cell. However, layer-2 devices suffered from the lack of routing information, which ultimately limited their scope and effectiveness. Let us now examine the control and forwarding planes in more detail, and then investigate how they can form the basis of an efficient and scalable MPLS label switching router (LSR).

The control component of a router is responsible for the exchange of routing information between other network nodes. It is this information that is used to form the router's routing database. This database paints a picture of the network from which a router can discern what it considers to be the most optimal path to any given destination in the network. Once stabilized, this database of best paths can be used to program the router's forwarding table. In contrast, the forwarding function of a router focuses exclusively on the actual decision of moving packets between ports on a network node.

Each packet contains a header with source, destination, and other information. When a node receives a packet on a port, it needs to decide which port (or ports) it needs to forward that packet to. The forwarding process is quite mechanical by nature. When a node receives a packet, the forwarding component in that node will first examine the destination address contained in the incoming packet as well as perhaps other fields in the header. This information is then compared with entries in its forwarding database. It is this simple process that allows the forwarding component to make quick and simple decisions as to where the packet needs to be forwarded.

In some devices, the forwarding component is tightly coupled with the routing component. This approach sometimes results in limited portability of that technology to other types of forwarding planes. It also sometimes results in difficulties in extending the protocol with additional functions. MPLS is built on both the premise of a clean separation of the control and forwarding functions to take advantage of their individual advantages, as well as using them together in concert to provide additional advantages not possible with other technologies.

The control and routing functions of MPLS are based on the Internet Protocol (IP) suite of protocols, which includes IP, RSVP, BGP, OSPF, and so on. The basic device in an MPLS-enabled network is the LSR. This device implements both the MPLS control and forwarding planes. The control function of an MPLS LSR is responsible for distributing routing information to other LSRs, as well as the information required to convert this information into forwarding tables that can then be used by the forwarding function. The MPLS forwarding function is based on the use of a short, fixed-length label. This concept comes from the use of the same concept in layer-2 technologies such as ATM and frame relay, which base forwarding actions on a short, fixed-length identifier.

6.1.1 Forward Equivalency Classes

The forwarding function of a router is responsible for forwarding traffic toward its ultimate destination. The information in the forwarding table is programmed based on information from the control plane. If a packet is not delivered via a local interface directly to the destination, the router must forward the packet toward the ultimate destination using a port that will steer that traffic on a path considered most optimal by the routing function.

For this reason, a router must forward traffic toward its destination via a next-hop router. This next-hop router may be the next-hop along the most optimal path for more than one destination subnetwork, so many packets with different network layer headers may be forwarded to the same next-hop router via the same output port. The packets traversing that router can then be organized into sets based on equivalent next-hop network nodes.

We call such a set a *forward equivalency class* (FEC). Thus, any packet that is forwarded to a particular next-hop is considered part of the FEC and can be forwarded to the same next-hop. One important feature of the FEC is the granularity of the classification of traffic it can encompass. Since the FEC is based on a next-hop router, it can include different classifications of packets. For example, since the routing information for a particular next-hop classification can be based on a destination prefix, it might include every packet traveling toward that destination. In this way, the granularity of packets classified by that FEC is quite coarse. However, if the routing database has programmed some next-hops for some traffic based on an application layer, for example, the traffic granularity might be much finer.

6.1.2 MPLS Shim Header

MPLS packets are encapsulated using an MPLS shim header. The header has this name because it defines an additional header that is placed—or shimmed—between existing layer-2 and layer-3 headers. Figure 6.1 shows the MPLS shim header format. The shim header comprises a sequence of one or more label stack entries.

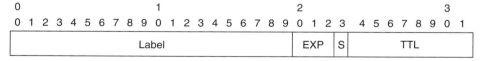

FIGURE 6.1

MPLS shim header format.

Layer-2 header	Label L(2)	EXP	S-0	TTL	Label L(1)	EXP	S-0	TTL	Label L(0)	EXP	S-1	TTL	Layer-3 header

FIGURE 6.2

The MPLS label stack as it appears within the MPLS shim header.

The entries in the sequence can be viewed together as a conceptual stack. A label stack entry comprises several components: label, EXP bits, the bottom of the stack bit, and TTL.

The first element is the MPLS label. The label is a fixed-length, 20-bit quantity that represents the label used to switch a packet. This label has local significance on a given interface between two neighboring LSRs only. That is, a label taken out of the context of a specific interface between two LSRs may or may not be found to be useful, or may be assigned to a different segment of a label switched path (LSP). The second portion of the header is 3 bits, called the experimental (EXP) bits. These bits are reserved for experimental use, such as for the purposes of classifying LSPs using differentiated services (DiffServ) code points. The next element of the shim header is a single bit used to indicate the "bottom of the stack." This bit is set to 1 for the last entry in the label stack (i.e., for the bottom of the stack) and 0 for all other label stack entries. The fourth and final element in the stack is an 8-bit quantity called the time-to-live (TTL) field. The format of a label stack entry is detailed in Figure 6.2.

Label Stack Entries

MPLS packets may contain more than one label. Depending on the application, it may be desirable to nest LSPs. For example, some traffic engineering (TE) and virtual private network (VPN) operations find it useful to nest LSPs. When labels are nested, they are represented in the MPLS shim header as a stack structure, that is, a last-in, first-out (LIFO) queue. The label stack is represented as a sequence of label stack entries in this stack. The topmost label appears closest to the layer-2 header, and the bottommost closest to the layer-3 header. Figure 6.2 demonstrates the label stack as a sequence of label stack entries. Each label stack entry is represented by 4 octets, or 32 bits, of data. Only the topmost label stack entry is used for any single lookup in the MPLS label forwarding information base (LFIB).

6.1.3 MPLS Label Switching

The MPLS forwarding plane is responsible for forwarding traffic based on an MPLS label. An MPLS label is a short, fixed-length, 20-bit value (see Figure 6.1) that has no structure. The MPLS label only has local significance between any two LSRs; therefore, the same label can be reused simultaneously within an MPLS-enabled network. In order for an MPLS LSR to be able to switch an MPLS packet, the label used in that packet's header must represent an entry in the MPLS LFIB of that LSR.

The LFIB is essentially the label-to-label switching database used to program the LSR's forwarding plane. Once a packet is received, its label will be used by the forwarding plane to make a decision on where to forward the packet. At the edges of an MPLS-enabled network, LSRs will map IP packets into FECs based on information provided by the MPLS control plane. Once classified into a FEC, the forwarding plane will be able to encapsulate any packet it receives that matches that FEC using the next-hop MPLS label assigned to that FEC.

Although assigned to a particular packet, the MPLS label does not necessarily encode the packet's network layer address, just its next-hop that will allow the packet to be forwarded to its destination, because many packets that are in the same FEC will be assigned the same label. This means that the next-hop choice may span multiple packets to many destinations. Thus, an MPLS label really encodes a FEC identifier. For example, if a FEC has classified all packets destined for the same next-hop based on multiple layer-3 destination network prefixes, all of the packets matching that FEC will be assigned the same label (and next-hop). Once a packet is assigned a label, it will be switched based on this label until it reaches its ultimate destination. At that point, the MPLS header is removed and the packet forwarded using its original encapsulation. When an MPLS packet is received, the LSR attempts to find a matching forwarding entry in its LFIB based on the packet's label and the interface on which the packet was received.

There are three operations—*pop, push,* or *swap*—that may be executed on the label stack when an MPLS packet is received and an entry matching this label is found in the LFIB. All operations are executed on the top entry of the stack. When the topmost label is "popped" from the label stack, its label stack entry is completely removed from the MPLS shim header. When a label is "pushed" onto the stack, it moves all of the existing labels down by one relative index in the stack and inserts itself at the top of the stack. When a swap operation is executed, the topmost label entry is replaced with a different label, but the size of the stack remains the same. The S bit is set to indicate the last or bottommost entry in the label stack. All other entries in the label stack must set the S bit to zero.

The example shown in Table 6.1 demonstrates what an MPLS LFIB might look like. In the example, labels that are received on this LSR's MPLS interface, "MPLS-

Table 6.1 Simplified LFIB

Incoming Interface	Incoming Label	Outgoing Label	Next-Hop	Outgoing Interface
MPLSEthI/2	1000	1050	10.20.0.1	MPLSEthI/3
MPLSEthI/2	1002	1070	10.30.0.1	MPLSEthI/6
MPLSEthI/2	1006	"pop"	—	—
MPLSEthI/2	1005	1080	10.40.0.1	MPLSEthI/7

Ethl/2," are switched to various other interfaces based on the incoming label. For example, when a packet containing label "1000" is received on interface "MPLS-Ethl/2," it is swapped for label "1050" and is forwarded on interface "MPLSEthl/3" to next-hop address 10.20.0.1. Note that this happens in all but the second-to-last row. The outgoing label in this case is noted as "pop." This refers to the removal of the MPLS shim header from the packet. Packets that have their MPLS headers stripped or "popped" are then forwarded on using their layer-3 encapsulation.

MPLS Domain

An MPLS domain is composed of one or more MPLS LSRs. An LSR is any router or switch that supports the forwarding of MPLS-encapsulated packets based solely on the incoming interface and the information in the shim header. An LSR that sits at the edges of an MPLS domain and forwards traffic into and out of the MPLS domain is called a label edge router (LER). An LER maintains at least one interface into and out of the MPLS domain and acts as the point where the MPLS shim header is first *imposed* onto the incoming packet, and where the header is ultimately stripped and the packet forwarded using its original layer-3 encapsulation. The LER must connect between the incoming technology and MPLS or vice versa. This process, in effect, tunnels the incoming technology through the MPLS network by encapsulating it within the MPLS packets.

From this point on, we will assume that the layer-3 payload is always IP. Other protocols are equally supported and handled by routing, switching, or forwarding engines specific to their characteristics. However, to avoid confusion in the text we will limit our view to the most common payload, which is IP.

Figure 6.3 shows a simple MPLS domain as well as the basic components of an MPLS-enabled network. The figure shows how MPLS LERs connect to external IP networks that may or may not contain customer sites. LERs are interconnected with other LERs within an MPLS-enabled domain. Other MPLS LSRs are interconnected in various ways within the MPLS domain.

Label Switched Path

An LSP is the path taken through the MPLS domain by a packet. The path taken may not be understood or completely stored by any one LSR within the MPLS domain, although in some cases it is. For example, traffic engineering allows the complete path to be stored at all LSRs along the path. This is because the labels swapped at each LSR have only local significance with regard to any two adjacently connected LSRs. Each LSR simply makes a local forwarding decision based on the incoming label of a packet, and switches the packet to a known outgoing label on a different interface. We should note that once the LFIBs have been established on all LSRs along the path of an LSP, the LSP is uniquely associated with the label and interface it is associated with, and therefore it is uniquely associated with a FEC.

An example of a label switched path is demonstrated in Figure 6.4. IP traffic to a destination reachable via the second LSR from the left is bound to a FEC at

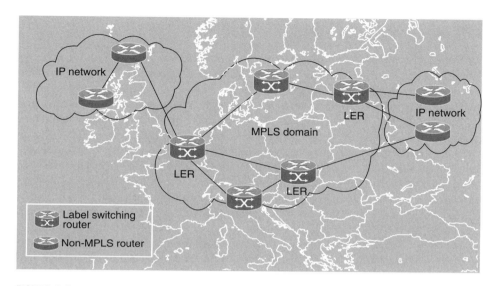

FIGURE 6.3

Components of an MPLS network.

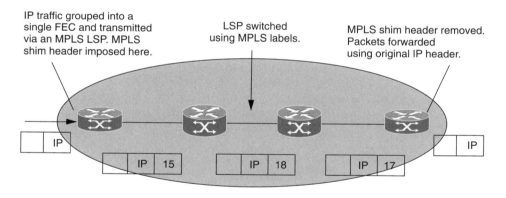

FIGURE 6.4

Example of an MPLS label switched path.

the leftmost LSR. All traffic entering the leftmost LSR will be classified using this FEC and will subsequently have MPLS shim headers imposed with a specific label associated with this FEC—in this case 15. The MPLS-encapsulated packet will leave the leftmost LSR and will have its label swapped with the one indicated on the link as it traverses the LSP. When it arrives at the rightmost LSR, the shim header is removed and the packet forwarded out the rightmost interface using its original encapsulation.

6.2 MPLS APPLICATIONS

Currently, the two most important applications of MPLS are TE and VPNs. However, other new applications are taking shape such as DiffServ-aware TE that will enable voice over IP (VoIP) applications over MPLS, as well as virtual circuit emulation and virtual private local area network (LAN) services over MPLS networks that will allow existing MPLS networks to be leveraged to offer additional emulated services. Although some of the applications of MPLS such as TE and VPNs technically can and are, in fact, currently being implemented and deployed using existing non-MPLS-based protocols, MPLS makes these applications simpler and more scalable. The reason that MPLS is able to achieve these goals is that it takes advantage of the separation of the routing and forwarding functions, and because of its integrated signaling mechanisms. This has the advantage of reducing or eliminating many of the limitations of traditional routing and provisioning. For example, in the use of VPNs, MPLS simplifies the act of configuring a VPN by only requiring that the operator configure the edge devices connecting the customer edge networks into the VPN. MPLS signaling takes care of the actual connection to other pieces of the VPN. MPLS further improves the scalability by obviating the need for state information about the VPN to be stored anywhere within the core of the network.

An example of an MPLS network that supports VPN is depicted in Figure 6.5. In this example two VPNs are supported: VPN A and VPN B. In order to support each VPN, the provider edge (PE) devices that connect the VPN sites must be configured. The core of the network is composed of provider core LSRs, or P routers. For example, P1 denotes a core P router in the figure. The core P routers do not have their configurations modified to support new sites of VPNs.

Another example of an important application of MPLS is in TE, where through the use of MPLS it is possible to specify explicit routes during the process of setting

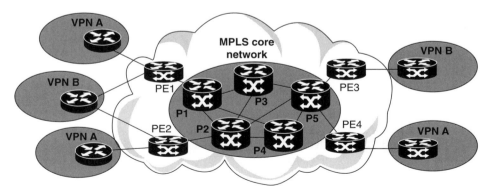

FIGURE 6.5

Example of an MPLS VPN.

up a path such that some specific data may be routed around network hot spots. Current technologies use routing protocols that tend to converge on a single, least-cost path to each possible (aggregate) destination. This occurs even if there are multiple least-cost paths to the same destination.

There are several problems with this approach. First, in many cases, parallel equal-cost paths exist to the same destinations, but all but one is preferred by the routing protocol. Second, since protocols generally prefer a single path that is considered most optimal, the routing protocols will direct all of the traffic destined to that destination onto that path. This often results in network hot spots at points in the network where many paths cross a single node.

It is possible to overcome these shortcomings with MPLS TE, since it allows an operator to specify an explicit route to direct some fraction of traffic through other parts of the network that are not selected by the routing process. These alternate paths may or may not be parallel least-cost paths. The important point is that the operator has the ability to override the routing protocol and choose which path certain flows of traffic take. Furthermore, TE allows an operator to create alternate backup paths, which bypass network trouble spots (i.e., disabled nodes or links). Given this mechanism, it is also straightforward to establish MPLS TE tunnels that transport packets that would not otherwise be correctly routed across a backbone network. For example, this is sometimes necessary in order to support VPNs across a backbone network between VPN end points, thereby making address translation and more cozily tunneling approaches unnecessary.

An example of MPLS TE is depicted in Figure 6.6. Assume that each link carries an equal cost that is given to the routing protocol. Notice that given this assumption, two equal-cost paths that traverse the same number of network nodes exist. The thick dotted line represents the path through the network that the routing protocol has chosen as most optimal. The thin dotted line represents an MPLS TE tunnel that has been configured to override the path chosen by the routing protocol. This allows some of the traffic that would have taken the default path to be steered across the alternate path. In this example, the TE tunnel has been configured to use an alternative, unused path through the network in an effort to better utilize network resources.

6.3 KEY ASPECTS OF MPLS NETWORK MANAGEMENT

Networks need to be managed for several reasons. First, from an entirely practical perspective, devices need to be monitored to ensure that they are functioning properly. Devices may also alert the operator to fault conditions, but if no corrective action is taken by the operator, then the device may continue to malfunction. For example, if a router's routing table has grown to a size that will soon exceed its available memory, it may be beneficial for the device to inform the operator of this condition.

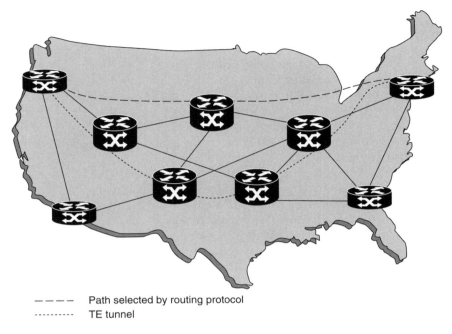

- – – –   Path selected by routing protocol
- ·········   TE tunnel

FIGURE 6.6

Example of an MPLS traffic-engineered tunnel.

Services that are offered by a network also need to be managed, particularly when they are provisioned. In these cases, devices are contacted and configured. Managed services also require monitoring and maintenance. For example, if a service provider offers a VPN service to a client, it may be necessary to monitor the health and performance of the network paths that carry that client's traffic to ensure that they are getting the network services they paid for. In fact, this monitoring arrangement is sometimes a contractual necessity.

In all of these scenarios, it is either extremely difficult or nearly impossible for operators of medium to large networks to monitor every device in their networks by hand; instead, most prefer to do this in an automated manner. Some accomplish their management using a centralized approach, as is demonstrated by the sophisticated operations center shown in Figure 6.7. However, others may choose to have several smaller operations centers that are distributed. In either case, it is extremely time consuming, and hence costly, for an operator to manually connect to each device's console in order to monitor its status, isolate faults, or configure the device. This becomes more obvious when you consider those provider networks where the network devices are located over a wide range of geographic areas. In this case, it becomes even more costly to travel to a remote location or hire additional staff to be on site where those additional devices are located.

FIGURE 6.7

A network management operations center.

Second, to make a sound business case for deploying MPLS, it must be made fully manageable so that the operational aspects of the network can scale up to numbers of devices, services, and customers that will make the network profitable. For example, the money spent debugging a problem by sending an operator into the field or by having the same operator go from router/switch to router/switch scratching his or her head might be better spent in building an automated system that can listen for alarms (see Section 7.6.6) that the router/switch can emit when in distress. These alarms can then be used to pinpoint and isolate the scope of the problem.

Once isolated, a management system can take automated actions to correct the situation or simply alert an operator. An automated system can even be smart enough to not bother an operator if it deems a problem insignificant. Furthermore, management of the MPLS network becomes paramount when placed within the context of service level agreements (SLAs) and MPLS virtual private network services. When SLAs are made between customers and providers, the service provider will not earn any money from that customer unless the services provided meet the SLA. The monitoring of the agreed-on terms such as bandwidth, latency, delay, or service availability can be best accomplished using a network management system (NMS).

6.3.1 Origins of Network Management for MPLS

Once MPLS began to become mature and operational experience began to be gained by service providers deploying the technology, it was clear that MPLS was not very manageable given the lack of standard tools and management interfaces available at the time. In particular, the majority of MPLS vendors including Juniper and Cisco had only provided proprietary command-line interface extensions for the configuration and monitoring of MPLS features. When MPLS deployments were in early stages, it was acceptable for these and other vendors to provide minimal management capabilities for the MPLS features since operators were largely interested in simply having the protocol function up to specifications.

However, as deployments became more mature and providers were more comfortable with the notion of using this protocol, it was clear that management of the protocol and its many features was now a priority. Furthermore, in heterogeneous networks where devices from multiple vendors had to coexist, an even larger problem existed. Since vendors had only deployed proprietary command-line interfaces, providers deploying devices from more than one vendor had to contend with more than one management interface for MPLS. This approach is expensive because it requires duplication of effort to manage the configuration and monitoring of the same features. The duplication of resources often ultimately translates into lost revenues for service providers. It was these requirements that began the push for standard interfaces for MPLS. In particular, the work on the IETF MIBs began in earnest during this time.

6.3.2 Configuration

One sore point for many operators is how to configure each one of the potentially hundreds of devices in their network. Further complicating the picture of configuration is the fact that many, if not most, provider networks are not comprised of devices made by a single vendor. This results in the service provider having to learn at least one different configuration language for each vendor from which it purchases equipment. Even further compounding this situation is that, through the magic of mergers and acquisitions, many vendors actually supply devices that have different configuration languages depending on which product line of theirs you choose to deploy.

It should be obvious from this description of the problems inherent in configuring a network of devices that it is a difficult situation at best. What would alleviate this situation would be the use of a common language and associated interfaces that can be used for the configuration of devices. There are many such languages available, yet no single one is used ubiquitously. Perhaps the closest contenders are the Simple Network Management Protocol (SNMP)—that is, SNMPvl (RFCs 1155, 1157, and 1213), SNMPv2c (RFCs 1901–1906), and SNMPv3 (RFCs 3411–3415)—the Common Object Request Broker Architecture (CORBA), and the eXtensible Markup Language (XML). Unfortunately, today the clear winner, at least for configuration, is the proprietary command-line interface (CLI), although SNMP is generally regarded as the best option for monitoring.

The difficulty with a proprietary CLI is that it is generally accessible only via Telnet or hardwired connections and generally has no standards-based schema. This results in every vendor implementation having a different management interface, which is clearly not something that excites a provider deploying a multivendor network. Although the CLI represents a majority of management interfaces, at least in the configuration area, the tide is turning toward standardized interfaces as networks grow ever more complex. These interfaces are commonly used for monitoring, and in many cases for provisioning as well. We will delve into the details of these various standard mechanisms for configuration in the pages to come.

6.3.3 Service Level Agreements

Typically, when a user signs up for access service (e.g., DSL, cable modem, dial-up), the service provider only agrees to provide that user with access to their network, and sometimes eventual access to the Internet. This agreement typically only specifies a minimum amount of bandwidth and provides no specifics about the average delay between access points and any other point in the network, or generally any other guarantees of service. Furthermore, there is typically no minimum response time during which outages in the network will be corrected by the service provider. This generally means that users of a service are out of luck if their service does not function as advertised.

Some operators take their level of service a step further. These operators choose to monitor and maintain what some refer to as the "user experience." Although many operators strive to have networks simply function (i.e., route and switch a lot of traffic), others wish to ensure that their network is performing at levels acceptable to its customers. For example, this can mean that if user access to the Internet is unacceptably slow, the service provider will take some action to correct the situation—sometimes automatically. This approach is in direct contrast to other providers who would be content with end users just having access to the Internet at any speed.

The notion of service assurance and verification can be taken a step further beyond a provider assuring that they will monitor the health of user services. Frequently, end users and service providers will enter a formal contract called a *service level guarantee* or *agreement*. This agreement is an official agreement or contract between the service provider and a customer that specifies that the provider will sell a certain service to an end user for a certain price.

If a service is provided as agreed on, the end user must pay a certain fee for the service. However, if the service is not provided, typical recourses for the user are a reduction or refund of the fee they pay for the service during that period. Often the amount of additional work that a provider must perform to ensure that a service is functioning according to the SLA is significant. This elevated cost is precisely why SLAs are typically only signed between service providers and higher-paying customers such as large corporations or other service providers.

For example, in the United States the service provider market is largely focused on selling bandwidth. This bandwidth is sometimes sold with guarantees of quality such as minimum delay and jitter. In other parts of the world, service providers concentrate instead on selling VPN services where site-to-site access quality is most important. All of these deployments typically contain SLA agreements with guarantees on the components of the service that the customers find most important, as well as the things a provider is willing to assure.

Given the motivation and elevated revenues from SLA agreements, providers are motivated to offer these premium services. However, these services do not come without additional effort on their part to verify the service quality and take corrective action when it does not meet the specified quality. In this regard, manual verification of SLAs is highly undesirable from a provider's perspective. This is simply because of its repetitive and frequent nature, especially when performed on a large scale. SLA agreements may also require that the operator take corrective action within some short period of time after a fault is detected. It is for these reasons that SLA monitoring and verification can be cumbersome or impossible if done manually, and therefore is a driver for the task to be performed by a fully or semi-automated network management system.

In order to realize a management system that can verify SLAs in an automated fashion, network management functions must be integrated into devices that must be monitored. In particular, common management interfaces allow a provider to effectively monitor the data points of a service. This is especially important for heterogeneous networks and is also important in cases where customers insist on having independent third parties verify the SLA, since these companies often prefer not to build SLA verification software that is customized to a particular provider's network. Instead, they prefer to build software that is able to talk to a large set of devices in order to service many different service provider networks.

Service Level Agreement Verification

One often overlooked aspect of SLAs is called *service level agreement verification*. The agreement of services between the end user and provider can be verified in several ways. The simplest form might be to issue Internet Protocol (IP) pings that emanate from the customer access points to other points in their networks or to locations within the Internet. This simulates user traffic traveling along the data path that all traffic takes through the network. If this traffic takes too long to traverse the network—or worse, is not getting to certain points within or external to the service provider's network—then the user experience suffers. Monitoring of the user experience might also be as sophisticated as monitoring the performance of many key network devices, collecting this information at a central location, and then making dynamic adjustments to the network using this information.

More sophisticated SLA verification is typically accomplished using network management tools that are specifically designed for the task. These tools include remote monitoring (RMON) or simply monitoring various counters on the network devices. Figure 6.8 illustrates how SLA monitoring and verification might be accomplished within an MPLS VPN deployment. An NMS is positioned at key

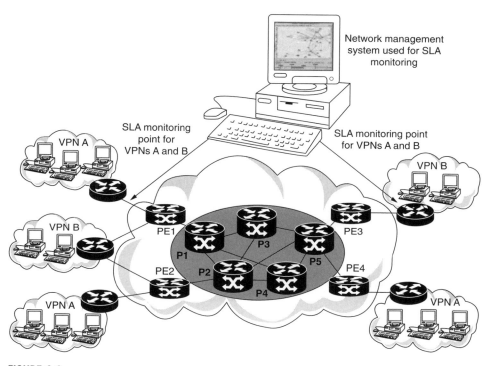

FIGURE 6.8

Example of a network of VPNs where SLAs are monitored by gathering information at certain key points within the network.

points, monitors certain traffic and quality of service (QoS) statistics, and reports them to the operator and customer. SLA verification can be done by the service provider, the customer, or by an unbiased third party.

Use of standard network management interfaces to expose variables within the often diverse population of network devices present in service provider networks is critical, especially when a third party is contracted to do the verification. The reason for this is simple: interoperability. SLA verification becomes quite cumbersome and costly if the party performing the verification is required to customize the verification suite for every device in a network. This is important if a third-party SLA verification company either sells software/hardware to service providers or performs the SLA verification service directly.

6.3.4 Fault Isolation

Fault isolation and detection are simply means by which operators can detect, isolate, and report on defects discovered within their networks. The operator can use the information to repair the defect(s) found manually or automatically. When a device detects a problem, it will emit one or more messages as an alarm to alert the operator of the fault condition. These messages can be emitted under many conditions, including loss of service, device in distress (e.g., low on memory), or when the device has rebooted. Fault isolation is usually accomplished in modern networks in a three-part process that includes devices emitting asynchronous alarms, operators receiving those alarms, and then operators taking possible action because of those alarms.

When a network device such as a router or switch discovers that an event of interest has occurred, it may issue an alarm. This alarm can be of the form of a system console message or an SNMP notification, which can be transmitted to the operators as an inform or notification. The reason for raising the alarms can include a configured threshold being exceeded, an internal fault condition such as low memory, or a system reboot. Although other forms of alarms do exist, including audible buzzers or flashing notifications on the command terminal, SNMP notifications are used in the majority of deployments.

Depending on the size and structure of the service provider's network, the operator may place one or more listening probes (i.e., workstations) around their network to listen for and collect these messages. Figure 6.9 demonstrates such a configuration where an NMS is deployed within an MPLS network. One of its purposes is to listen for notifications emitted from the LSRs in that network. The figure shows one of the links in the sample network breaking and the LSRs on either side of that link emitting an SNMP notification. The NMS would catch this

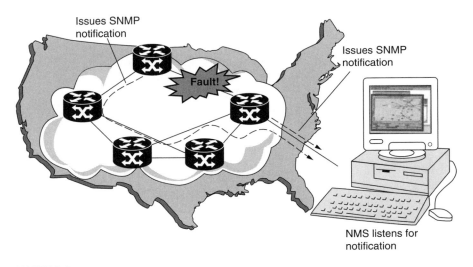

FIGURE 6.9

MPLS fault isolation using SNMP.

notification and possibly alert the operator to the situation or trigger an automated procedure for possible corrective action.

Sometimes, when the networks are large and/or multitiered, the operator will even have notifications aggregated and perhaps even summarized if processing power permits, and then relayed to a central alarm-processing center. This center will then decide whether or not to issue a trouble ticket for an alarm and dispatch personnel to address the situation. It should be obvious that the activities just described would be next to impossible to achieve if done manually in any practical network deployed today. For MPLS to be deployed successfully on a large scale, network nodes must be capable of issuing the necessary alarms (i.e., SNMP notifications) that are specific not only to MPLS functions, but also to the other functions in the devices being deployed.

6.4 MANAGEMENT INFORMATION BASE MODULES FOR MPLS

The IETF, ITU, ATM Forum, and other standards bodies define documents called management information base (MIB) modules that provide an external management interface for protocols and other features that are standardized within those organizations. Each MIB module can be thought of as a form of a data model used to manage the protocol or feature. The MIB module also defines the syntax, maximum access levels, and object interactions between those objects defined in that and other MIBs. The collection of MIB modules comprises the conceptual MIB that defines the entirety of MIB modules. We should also note that a MIB module is sometimes referred to as "a MIB" within certain contexts; thus, care should be taken to discern when you mean a single MIB module or a collection of MIB modules that comprise a MIB.

The MPLS Traffic Engineering MIB (MPLS-TE MIB) module and the MPLS Label Distribution Protocol MIB (MPLS-LDP MIB) were the first MIBs proposed at the IETF in 1998. As standards-related work on these MIBs continued within the working group, and implementation and operational deployment by both device vendors and service providers continued, the MPLS-TE MIB had grown significantly in both size and scope. The primary reason for this was due to feedback and requirements from those deploying the MIB.

In essence, the MIB has grown to encompass the functionality of both general LSR functions as well as TE functions. It was at this point that the MPLS working group decided that the MPLS-TE MIB needed to be split into two MIBs: one to encompass general LSR switching functions, and one to encompass the general MPLS TE capabilities. So the MPLS Label-Switching Router MIB (MPLS-LSR MIB) was split from the MPLS-TE MIB and chartered as a separate working group item.

As time went on, the feedback process from service providers continued. The MPLS FEC-to-Next-Hop Label-Forwarding Entry MIB (MPLS-FTN MIB) was proposed to expose the FEC-to-NHLFE mapping within LERs. In addition, MPLS BGP/

Table 6.2 MPLS MIB Module Drafts

MIB Title	Date Started	Date Published	Description
RFC 3815	August 1998	June 2004	LDP protocol
RFC 3812	November 1998	June 2004	Traffic engineering
RFC 3813	June 1999	June 2004	Active TFIB of an LSR
RFC 3814	November 2000	June 2004	FEC-to-NHLFE mapping
RFC 4265	August 2001	November 2005	Common textual conventions for MPLS VPNs
RFC 4382	August 2001	February 2006	MPLS/BGP layer-3 VPNs
RFC 3811	June 2001	June 2004	Common textual conventions for MPLS MIBs
RFC 4802	March 2002	February 2007	GMPLS TE
RFC 4801	March 2002	February 2007	Common textual conventions for GMPLS MIBs
RFC 4803	March 2002	February 2007	GMPLS

VPNs were proposed, and implementation of this new application of MPLS had begun as well. Not long after this, the Provider-Provisioned MPLS Virtual Private Network MIB (PPVPN-MPLS-VPN MIB) was proposed to the IETF and was adopted. It is likely that there will be many other standard MIBs provided by the Internet Engineering Task Force that cover all of the essential and common MPLS functionality, thereby making the manageability of MPLS networks far easier and straightforward for those who choose to utilize this technology.

Table 6.2 enumerates many of the MIB modules that were available at the time this chapter was written. More will surely become available as time goes on. However, we provide this table to illustrate those that are currently available so that you might see the progression from essentially no standard management interfaces for MPLS, to the near dozen available today.

The remainder of this text will focus on SNMP MIB-based solutions for managing MPLS networks. Figure 6.10 illustrates how each MIB fits in with the others as well as how each one depends on the others. The MIBs are organized as follows:

MPLS-TC MIB describes textual conventions that are used by all MPLS-related MIBs. The remaining four MIBs are shown as having dependencies on the MPLS-TC MIB, as well as the IF-MIB (RFC 2863). Since nearly all of the MIBs are related to the IF-MIB, a specific icon has not been included for it in the figure; instead, a gray triangle in the corner of each MIB indicates this dependency.

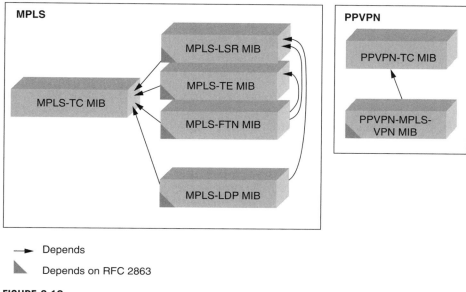

→ Depends

▸ Depends on RFC 2863

FIGURE 6.10

MIBs for MPLS network management discussed in this text.

MPLS-LSR MIB describes the basic label-forwarding operations of an LSR. The MPLS-LSR MIB also exposes which interfaces the LSR has MPLS enabled on by cross-referencing each MPLS-enabled interface that appears in the IF-MIB. This MIB presents a foundation of actual objects (as opposed to TCs in the MPLS-TC MIB) that are used in many other MIBs; thus, it is viewed as the base MPLS MIB by many.

MPLS-TE MIB provides the operator with a view of which TE tunnels are configured, signaled, or presignaled (for backup). If a tunnel is also represented as an interface in the IF-MIB, an entry will exist there as well. The MPLS-TE MIB depends on the MPLS-LSR MIB in that the system software in a device can be programmed to associate the active LSP with a tunnel when such a relationship exists.

MPLS-LDP MIB provides insight into what the LDP protocol is doing on an LSR, assuming that LDP is enabled and in use. The MPLS-LDP MIB depends on the MPLS-LSR MIB for its mapping tables that are used to associate LDP sessions with active LSPs. The MPLS-LDP MIB also depends on the IF-MIB in that it exposes which label ranges are configured on an MPLS-enabled interface. Finally, the MPLS-FTN MIB presents the operator with a view of how IP traffic is entering the MPLS network and how that IP traffic is being mapped onto MPLS LSPs or TE tunnel interfaces.

MPLS-FTN MIB depends on the MPLS-LSR and MPLS-TE MIBs because the way that it associates incoming IP traffic is to point at the associated LSP or TE tunnel head as represented in the MPLS-LSR and MPLS-TE MIBs, respectively. The MPLS-FTN MIB depends on the IF-MIB because it allows an operator to configure FEC-to-NHLFE mapping rules on a per-interface basis.

PPVPN-MPLS-VPN MIB is shown to possess only dependencies on the PPVPN-TC MIB. This MIB contains common textual conventions used by the PPVPN-MPLS-VPN MIB as well as other MIBs defined by the IETF PPVPN working group. The PPVPN-MPLS-VPN MIB provides an operator with a view of which VPN instances are configured on a specific PE, as well as related statistics, BGP, and interface information. The interface information extends those interfaces that are already represented in the IF-MIB; thus, yet another dependency on the IFMIB exists.

6.5 SUMMARY

This chapter covered the basic components of MPLS. At the heart of MPLS is the separation of the control and forwarding planes. There are distinct advantages to this approach, as we have seen. The forwarding plane is composed of various IP-based protocols such as BGP and RSVP. The forwarding plane is based on switching a short, fixed-length label. This method is based on the forwarding mechanisms of several layer-2 forwarding technologies such as ATM and Frame Relay.

The remainder of the chapter introduced some of the reasons why it is crucial for world-class MPLS deployments to provide robust and comprehensive network management capabilities. We discussed fault and configuration management and how these two components of a management solution alone were critical if the network was to be deployed effectively, especially on a large scale. We then discussed performance measurement within the context of SLAs. Monitoring and verifying the quality of a network connection is especially important when required by a service level agreement.

Finally, we presented an overview of how the MPLS MIBs fit together to provide the reader with a pictorial "30,000 foot view" of the MIBs that will be discussed later in the book.

MPLS Management Interfaces

7

This chapter, taken from Chapter 2 of *MPLS Network Management* by Nadeau, introduces several different types of management interface that may be used to manage Multi-Protocol Label Switching (MPLS) deployments. In particular, we will introduce you to XML, CORBA, SNMP, and the command-line interface. We will investigate and explain why operators might or might not wish to utilize one, none, or all of these interfaces to manage their MPLS networks, as well as to hope-fully provide device vendors with reasons for why they should or should not implement them on their MPLS devices. The end of the chapter will focus par-ticularly on the SNMP interface by introducing it in such a way that it may be understood for use in managing MPLS networks.

7.1 THE BASICS OF MANAGEMENT INTERFACES

Management interfaces allow network operators to manage the devices in their networks by providing access to each device's control, configuration, and status information. Many different types of management interfaces exist, but in general, a management interface is composed of two parts: a protocol describing the com-munication rules between the operator and the device, and the format of the information that will be exchanged using that protocol.

The basic features of a management interface are depicted in Figure 7.1. Notice how the management interface provides a unified external view of the managed device. It should be noted that devices might support more than one management interface, but all typically support at least one. Some management interfaces provide additional functions such as secure authentication, control of transactions, reliable or unreliable network transport options, and even functions that allow for the translation between other management interfaces. This collection of features, functions, and protocol comprise what is generally referred to as a management interface.

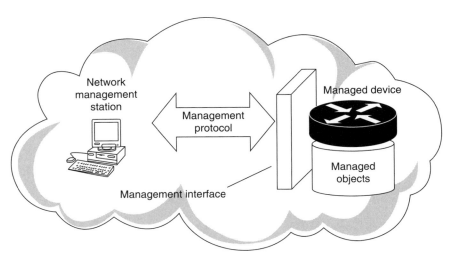

FIGURE 7.1

In general, a management interface provides two things: a protocol between the manager and the device and a consistent external representation of the managed device.

The management interface provides a consistent external view of the manageable objects in a device. This view ideally remains consistent across all devices supporting the management interface, thus providing the same interface for the operator or the operational software used to manage these devices. To be more specific, the format of manageable objects is consistent. For example, the management interface may specify that the total time that the system has been running since it was last initialized be represented as a 64-bit integer. However, some devices may only be able to maintain 32-bit integers natively depending on the specific hardware used. Therefore, devices that are unable to support the wider data type natively must simulate it in order to support the management interface. Another example is objects that are stored in tables. A device may store the objects internally as an array of objects or as a linked list; however, the external representation will always be that of a table.

Figure 7.2 demonstrates two models of Acme Corporation's routers; both support the same management interface but implement it differently internally. The management interface in the figure specifies that table A be viewed as a table of objects indexed in a certain manner to the external manager. While maintaining an external view consistent with this management interface, Acme model 7200 represents the table internally as a linked list. On the other hand, Acme model 7500 is still able to maintain a consistent external view of the same data, but represents the table internally as an array.

Some management interfaces define a data model that can be used as a map of the collection of information that the operator will have access to. This model

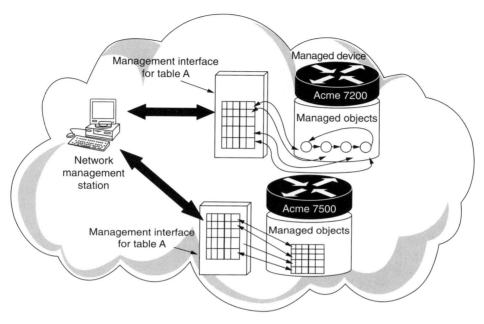

FIGURE 7.2

Two models of Acme's routers, both supporting the same management interface. The management interface specifies that table A be viewed as a table externally. While preserving the consistent external view, Acme model 7500 represents the table internally as an array. Acme model 7200 represents the table internally as a linked list, while preserving the same external representation.

can then be used to easily build applications that can be used to manage this information, while at the same time, devices implementing this model can use the model as a basis for their implementations. Still others simply define a format or syntax that operators can expect to view the managed information in, or will be required to use when configuring that same data. It is important to make a clear distinction between a data model and a management interface.

As was just described, a data model describes the relationship between managed objects in a system. It may also define the syntax for accessing these objects. This model may also describe the actions that a manager can take on these objects, as well as the actions the objects themselves may take. For example, a data model may describe how an object may trigger an event to be generated by a managed device when it reaches a certain value. Another example might be the result of a manager triggering a particular action on a managed object, such as to start a routing protocol. For those familiar with object-oriented programming methodologies, a data model used for management purposes has the same meaning as one defined for a program.

As crude as some may regard them, the Simple Network Management Protocol (SNMP) management interface defines documents called a management information base (MIB). Each document can be thought of as a form of a data model. These documents define the syntax, maximum access rights to the objects defined therein, and object interactions between those objects defined in that and other MIBs. On the other hand, more sophisticated data models can be constructed using other management interfaces such as CORBA Interface Definition Languages (IDLs). Not only can these other data models be used to describe what the MIBs can describe, but they can also be used to model the objects running inside a network management application.

The most common form of a management interface is a proprietary command-line interface (CLI). This interface typically allows an operator to connect to a device using a remote Telnet session. The format of the data viewed over this Telnet session is specified as being in ASCII format and must be entered in the command-line syntax defined by the vendor. However, the format of the output can (and sometimes does) vary depending on the version of software running on the device. Other management interfaces, such as SNMP, define stricter rules for how the managed information will both be accessed and offered to the manager.

In addition to the raw tools and protocols provided by management interfaces, the actual use of the management interface can be arranged and deployed in many different ways depending on the network or the operational philosophy of those running the network. There are far too many different approaches to investigate in this chapter. Instead, we will focus on showing you the tools that management interfaces provide.

There are at least a dozen management interfaces in use today, some useful to those managing MPLS networks, others that are less so. In general, all of the well-known management interfaces can be applied at least in some ways to MPLS networks. In addition to using a single management interface, many operators have chosen to use a combination of two or more interfaces for their networks. In the following sections, we will focus on and describe some of the management interfaces that are most prevalent in large operational MPLS networks today. Furthermore, the remainder of the chapter will focus on the specific tools that are made available within these more widely used management interfaces. While we recognize that management interfaces other than the ones we will discuss exist, and that they may be useful for the management of some MPLS networks, we will not focus on these at this time either because they are too proprietary, or because these management interfaces are simply not in enough use to interest a wide audience.

7.2 COMMAND-LINE INTERFACE

Most, if not all, network devices since the early days of networks have provided the operator with some sort of character-based command-line interface. The CLI typically provides the user with screens of information for viewing specific device functions or configuration, as well as a structured syntax for interacting with it. The CLI provided a console screen similar to that of early mainframe computers. Early implementations of the CLI were as simple as a paper-based teletype that was wired directly to the device via a serial cable. Since then, the prevalent method of connecting to a network device is to use a Telnet network connection, although other means exist that are still popular, including the good-old hardwired serial connection; however, the sophistication of the input and output of this interface has not changed substantially. Figure 7.3 shows an example of a CLI from a well-known label switching router (LSR) vendor.

In general, a vendor will specify a CLI syntax that governs how an operator may interact with it. This syntax is typically broken into two areas: display screens and configuration entry. Display screens are used by the operator to view the information stored within the device. The information shown on these screens is typically status or configuration information. The display of information on the screen can either be triggered as the result of an operator query or may be the result of an asynchronous display made by the device. Configuration information can contain all or part of the device's configuration.

For example, the commands `show router version` and `show mpls forwarding` were used to generate the output shown in Figure 7.3. The `show` command displays general system configuration information such as the version of software image that is currently executing the device, how much memory is installed in the device, or the version of the ROM code present. Notice that the command used to trigger the output has a certain form or syntax. Every time the operator enters the command `show router version`, the screen shown will appear with the same syntax. Variables in the fields may be different, however. Furthermore, if `show router version` were entered as `show routerbbb version`, it would have resulted in an error being reported to the operator, since this constitutes an illegal command.

Unfortunately, the command-line syntax specified by any two vendors is typically different even though they are used to manage identical abstract objects. In fact, sometimes it is even the case that different products from the same vendor use different screen formats and syntax to manage the same feature. Some newer vendors have tried to copy the syntax of older vendors, but even this inevitably results in some discrepancies when the vendor being copied decides to change their CLI without the other noticing. Unfortunately, no standard CLI syntax is defined by any standards body that might better help the situation. This is a large disadvantage for service providers who have to manage networks with disparate devices and corresponding CLIs, since it means that managing these types of networks will probably be much more difficult and expensive than a homogeneous network.

One important feature of a CLI is the ability to display asynchronous notifications without any operator intervention. Some devices even provide a separate CLI session that allows an operator to more easily capture and recognize these

```
Cisco Internetwork Operating System Software
IOS (tm) 7200 Software (C7200-JS-M), Experimental Version 12.2 (20011220:212756) [tnadeau-
ldp_mib_122s_pi 101]
Copyright (c) 1986–2001 by cisco Systems, Inc.
Compiled Fri 21-Dec-Ol 10:43 by tnadeau
Image text-base: 0x60008960, data-base: 0x61738000

ROM: System Bootstrap, Version 11.1(13)CA, EARLY DEPLOYMENT RELEASE SOFTWARE ( f c l )
BOOTLDR: 7200 Software (C7200-BOOT-M), Version 12.0(2)XE2, EARLY DEPLOYMENT RELEASE
SOFTWARE (fcl)

tagsw7200-43 uptime is 2 weeks, 5 days, 11 hours, 19 minutes
System returned to ROM by reload at 07:04:33 UTC Fri Dec 21 2001
System image file is "tftp://UNKNOWN/tnadeau/c7200-js-mz"

cisco 7206 (NPE200) processor (revision B) with 114688 K/16384 K bytes of memory.
Processor board ID 16065231
R5000 CPU at 200 Mhz, Implementation 35, Rev 2.1, 512 KB L2 Cache
6 slot midplane, Version 1.3

Last reset from power-on
Bridging software.
X.25 software, Version 3.0.0.

SuperLAT software (copyright 1990 by Meridian Technology Corp).
TN3270 Emulation software.
8 Ethernet/IEEE 802.3 interface(s)
2 ATM network interface(s)
125 K bytes of non-volatile configuration memory.
4096 K bytes of packet SRAM memory.

20480 K bytes of Flash PCMCIA card at slot 1 (Sector size 128 K).
4096 K bytes of Flash internal SIMM (Sector size 256 K).
Configuration register is OxO

tagsw7200-43# show mpls forwarding

Local   Outgoing    Prefix         Bytes tag   Outgoing    Next Hop
tag     tag or VC   or Tunnel Id   switched    interface
1000    Pop tag     10.0.0.5 12 [72]   0        Et1/1       10.1.2.1
1001    Untagged[T] 55.55.0.0/32    0          Tu43003     point2point
1002    Pop tag     10.0.0.1/32     0          Et1/5       10.21.22.21
1003    Untagged[T] 10.3.5.0/24     0          Tu43003     point2point
1004    Pop tag [T] 10.0.0.3/32     0          Tu43003     point2point
1005    Pop tag [T] 10.0.0.5/32     0          Tu13        point2point
1006    26          10.0.0.1 1 [77]    0        Et1/2       10.2.3.3
1007    27          10.0.0.1 2 [76]    0        Et1/2       10.2.3.3
1008    28          10.0.0.1 3 [76]    0        Et1/2       10.2.3.3
1009    29          10.0.0.1 11 [76]   0        Et1/2       10.2.3.3
Local   Outgoing    Prefix         Bytes tag   Outgoing    Next Hop
tag     tag or VC   or Tunnel Id   switched    interface

[T]     Forwarding through a TSP tunnel.
        View additional tagging info with the 'detail' option
```

FIGURE 7.3

Sample CLI output from a popular LSR vendor.

messages. Notifications, or "alarms" as some call them, can be used to alert the operator to critical or fault situations. As with the syntax of the CLI, the format of the on-screen alarms will vary from vendor to vendor. Some vendors have chosen to specify a format for what is displayed on the screen, while others will allow the software to display a freeform string that may change from version to version of the system's software.

7.2.1 CLI Security

Other features of CLIs include security functions such as authentication to verify the identity of the operator accessing the CLI, or encryption of the actual datastream over which the CLI data flows. Operators have options in terms of authentication, ranging from the simplest clear-text password authentication, whereby the operator must specify a user name and a password that are checked for authenticity within the system, to a complete RADIUS system for managing encrypted passwords. Different vendors will offer different security features with their CLIs.

One very common security option used by operators is the secure shell (SSH). Operators will run an SSH session between their operation station or network management system (NMS) and the network device rather than traditional clear-text Telnet. SSH provides the user with transparent, strong encryption, as well as reliable public-key authentication that is quite easy to configure. Implementations are freely available, so vendors have little excuse not to offer this solution to operators. Furthermore, since SSH is a popular and rather robust TCP/IP-based solution that solves many network security and privacy concerns for operators, vendors are encouraged to implement this as an option for accessing their CLI.

In addition to securing the CLI session, SSH also supports secure file transfer between management stations and network devices, so those vendors offering bulk file transfer of management information or configuration files can easily integrate this into their device software as well. Further, SSH provides the capability of "tunneling," which can be used to easily add additional encryption to otherwise insecure network applications. As has been mentioned, there are many feature-filled freeware versions of SSH available; therefore, operators will find that many device vendors have already adopted SSH in their devices.

We recommend strongly that operators who have access to secure CLI implementations use them whenever possible. This added level of security aids in completely locking intruders out of devices, or at least making it much more difficult for them to access the devices. This is important not only in preventing the viewing of such sensitive information as a device's active configuration and the activity of a device, but also in preventing unwanted and unauthorized changes to a device's configuration.

7.2.2 Using Scripts with the CLI

One common means by which operators have effectively utilized the CLI is to use UNIX shell scripts or Perl scripts to interact with the various devices in their networks. Scripts are programmed to connect to remote devices using Telnet or other means, authenticate, and then read data from what would be displayed on the user's screen, or send commands to the device to alter its configuration. Another terminology for scripts reading information from the CLI is called "screen scraping," which implies that the scripts are culling data from the characters they "scrape" off the screen.

Using scripts to scrape the CLI and configure devices can be a simple and effective means of managing a device and, in some cases, can approximate the efficiencies and ease of use provided by other management interfaces such as SNMP; however, with simplicity comes several problems. First, the syntax of the management interface that scripts are programmed to understand may change between versions of the vendor's software. Therefore, the operator needs to be keen on the changes made. This can be compounded by the fact that an operator may have to manage more than one vendor's equipment. Second, the volume of the data that are read back to the script over the network is relatively large as compared to that of other management interfaces.

The amount of fixed information printed on a screen versus the characters that are used to display variable fields is generally significant, and therefore results in superfluous network traffic, since the entire screen is read back to the script via its Telnet session. Other management interfaces provide a much more compact representation of variable data because they do not have to transmit the entire meaning of the fields being retrieved or modified. However, some of these fields may not be available via another management interface, so having the information in albeit a not-so-compact way may be better than not having it at all. This is again why the CLI is considered the lowest common denominator by many.

7.3 CORBA

The Common Object Request Broker Architecture (CORBA) defines a distributed object computing infrastructure that has several uses. In particular, CORBA provides for an architecture that automates many common network programming tasks such as object registration, location, and activation of network objects. Network objects can reside anywhere in the network, including on a traditional management station or even in embedded networking devices such as routers and switches. In addition to locality control, CORBA facilitates parameter marshalling and demarshalling, and operation dispatching among objects, as well as request demultiplexing and multiplexing for specific objects.

The CORBA standard is maintained by the Object Management Group (OMG). The primary components of the OMG CORBA reference model architecture are listed in Table 7.1.

The OMG reference model is composed of three general layers, each of which is assigned a variety of specific responsibilities. The bottommost layer in this model is called the *object services layer* and is composed of object services that

Table 7.1 OMG Reference Model Architecture Components

Component	Description
Application interfaces	Application-specific interfaces are generally not standardized; rather, they are developed specifically for a type of application and used as such. However, if over time the service becomes widely applicable, it is possible that the OMG will standardize the proprietary application interface.
Domain interfaces	These interfaces have roles similar to the object services and common facilities, but have specific application with a particular application domain such as telecommunications, medical, and finance.
Common facilities	These interfaces are oriented toward end-user applications. An example of such an application may be for the exchange of embedded objects within electronic documents. For example, objects originate within a spreadsheet application, but then can be linked into a word processor document.
Object services	Object services are domain-independent interfaces used by many distributed object programs. Two examples of object services that fulfill this role are a naming service that allows clients to find objects based on globally unique names or based on their properties. Another example of such a service might be life cycle management, security, transactions, and event notification, as well as many others.

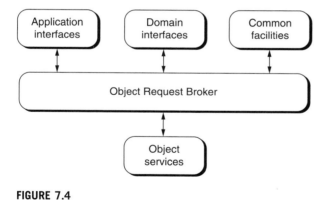

FIGURE 7.4

OMG reference model architecture.

are domain independent. The functions and responsibilities provided in this layer can be applied to many differing types of objects. An example of such a service is a generic object location service. This service can be applied across most if not all objects within a system. The topmost layer in the model provides domain-specific services, which are outlined in the following Table 7.2. The architecture is also illustrated in Figure 7.4.

Table 7.2 Description of OMG CORBA Reference Model ORB Elements

Component Name	Description
Object	This is a CORBA programming entity. Each object has an identity, interface, and implementation. An implementation is also known as a servant.
Servant	A servant is an implementation programming language entity. Servants define operations that support a CORBA IDL interface.
Client	This is a CORBA programming entity that is capable of triggering operations on an object. When services are accessed, the specifics of the service should remain transparent to the client. Invocation of services is typically performed in the same way that an object method is invoked in order to keep the operation as simple as possible for the caller.
Object Request Broker (ORB)	The CORBA ORB provides a mechanism for transparently communicating client requests to target object implementations. The ORB decouples the client from the details of the method invocations, which results in client requests appearing to be local function calls. When a client triggers an operation, the ORB must find the correct object implementation to invoke the action, and then transparently activate it if necessary. The ORB is also responsible for delivering the request to the object and returning a response (if any) to the caller.
ORB interface	The CORBA specification defines an abstract interface for an ORB that decouples applications from the details of their implementation. This interface achieves transparency by providing various functions that help hide the internal details of the interface.
CORBA IDL stubs and skeletons	CORBA IDL stubs serve as a layer between the client and server applications, and the ORB. Transformation from CORBA IDL definitions into the target programming language such as C or C++ is typically performed by a CORBA IDL compiler.
Dynamic Invocation Interface (DII)	The DII allows a client to directly access the underlying request mechanisms provided by an ORB. Applications utilize the DII interface in order to dynamically issue requests to objects without requiring an IDL interface-specific stub to be linked with its code. This is in contrast to IDL stubs that function as RPC-style requests. The DII interface also allows clients to invoke nonblocking, deferred, and synchronous (separate send and receive operations), which may be necessary for certain operations to function correctly. This interface also provides for one-way calls that are made to objects that act as events (they are sent only, and no response is sent).
Dynamic Skeleton Interface (DSI)	This interface is similar to the client DII interface except that it runs on the server side. The DSI interface allows an ORB to deliver requests to an object implementation that does not have compile-time knowledge of the type of object it is implementing. Specifically, it allows the client issuing the operation request to have no specific knowledge of whether the implementation is using type-specific IDL skeletons, or if it has employed dynamic skeletons.
Object adapter	The purpose of the object adapter is to assist the ORB in delivering request objects. It also assists the ORB with activating the specific object. An object adapter can be used to associate a specific object implementation with the ORB by smoothing out differences between the two. Furthermore, object adapters can provide support for certain *types* of object implementations. For example, object adapters for object-oriented databases can be provided to support persistent library objects.

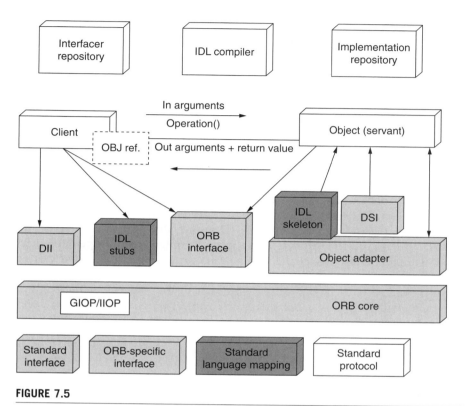

FIGURE 7.5

ORB elements from OMG CORBA reference architecture.

The middle layer of the OMG reference model is referred to as the Object Request Broker (ORB). In essence, the ORB provides the middle layer of abstraction that "glues" the object services layer to the upper application interface, domain interface, and common facilities functions.

Figure 7.5 illustrates the primary components in the CORBA ORB architecture. The ORB architecture is comprised of several components. The object (servant) is a programming language implementation component that defines the operations used to support a CORBA IDL interface. IDL interfaces can be implemented in several programming languages including C, C++, and Java. The client component is a program construct that invokes an operation on an object. This operation will potentially access the services of a remote object. When this occurs, this action should be transparent to the caller. The ORB provides a mechanism for transparently communicating client requests to other object implementations. The architecture of the ORB greatly simplifies distributed programming in that it removes the client from the specific details of method invocation. This allows the client requests to appear to be local procedure calls, when in fact they may be remote calls.

The ORB is responsible for locating the appropriate object implementation when a client invokes an operation on that object. The ORB must also deliver the request to the possibly remote object and return a response, if one is given, to the calling client. To decouple applications from their specific implementation details, the abstract interface for an ORB is called the ORB interface. This provides various functions and routines that convert between internal implementation specifics and those provided in the standard CORBA application programming interface (API). The CORBA IDL provides various stubs and skeletons that "glue" the client and server applications together with the ORB. The conversion between the CORBA IDL definitions and the programming language used to implement the objects is usually automated using a CORBA IDL compiler. The object adapter associates object implementation specifics with the ORB. In doing so, an object adapter can be specialized to provide support for implementation-specific object styles. This function also assists the ORB in delivering requests to and activating a remote object.

Finally, the DSI is the server-side counterpart to the client-side DII. The DSI enables an ORB to deliver requests to a specific object implementation that might not have compile-time knowledge of the specific internal type of the object it is implementing.

7.3.1 CORBA and SNMP Usage Description

Although we will cover SNMP in detail in Section 7.6, we will touch on one variation on the use of CORBA that works in conjunction with SNMP to leverage existing MIB module deployments without having to convert the code on each device to support CORBA. Instead, SNMP MIB modules can be translated into CORBA IDLs using some well-defined rules. These new IDLs can then be translated into DSI or DII functions that can be used to build CORBA applications containing data models supporting those defined in the MIBs. A further modification is to allow these new objects to be queried regardless of whether they are implemented within an SNMP manager or agent entity.

Specifically, if an object is queried on a management station (e.g., an API asks a counter object to display itself), this object, through the ORB architecture described earlier, can locate the value of its corresponding embedded side instance, which is located within an agent running on a network device. Once it locates the object, it can convert the request from CORBA into SNMP and send the managed device a request for its value using SNMP. This is illustrated in Figure 7.6 as the SNMP-aware CORBA management station.

One variation on this theme is to build applications that act as SNMP *proxy agents,* which are sometimes known as *midlevel managers.* These entities are responsible for translating SNMP requests and responses to and from CORBA. This allows existing CORBA applications to speak to SNMP devices without any modi-

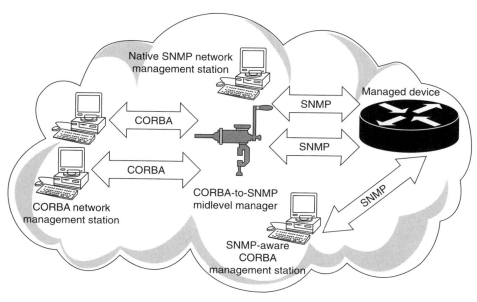

FIGURE 7.6

CORBA midlevel manager translates (SNMP protocol converter) between CORBA and SNMP for native CORBA management stations, while a native SNMP manager communicates directly with the managed device using SNMP. An SNMP-aware CORBA management station also can communicate directly with the managed device without the help of the midlevel manager.

fication. Instead, they speak to a CORBA ORB that does the translation externally. This ORB can also catch SNMP notifications and relay them to the appropriate application as CORBA events.

Figure 7.6 demonstrates how a midlevel manager translates between CORBA and SNMP for native CORBA management stations that cannot speak SNMP. At the same time, a native SNMP manager entity communicates directly with the agent entity on the managed device using SNMP. Note that both the midlevel manager and the native SNMP management station can be configured to receive SNMP notifications from the managed device. The CORBA translator will translate these notifications into CORBA object messages that will be delivered to the appropriate objects, while the native SNMP NMS will process the events directly.

As with all translation mechanisms, we have witnessed that this method too suffers from performance issues, even if implemented correctly. Those who have used CORBA implementations in the past can attest to the fact that they were not very fast to begin with, so this added layer of indirection simply adds to the time between management requests and their corresponding responses. A further difficulty with this approach is simply the implementation and maintenance. If a new SNMP object is introduced into the system, several pieces of code must be modified in a harmonious fashion.

We should note that the translation between SNMP and CORBA messages and events is not unique to these two management interfaces. Other translations are possible. For example, XML, which we discuss in the next section, can be used to translate to and from a proprietary CLI language. The same can be done between a CLI and SNMP. The important point to keep in mind about any translation mechanism is the data model mapping between management interfaces. If the mapping is not accurate and complete, inconsistencies may arise.

7.4 **XML**

The eXtensible Markup Language (XML) provides an encoding method for individual and batched management commands that allows for the creation of a command-specific syntax that can be automatically parsed and checked. It can be applied to existing management schemas such as a CLI or SNMP, or allows for the creation of a new set of commands and parameters specific to an XML client and server. XML describes a class of data objects called *XML documents* and specifies the behavior of applications that are used to process these documents. XML represents a subset of the Standard Generalized Markup Language (SGML) (ISO 8879); thus, XML documents are by nature conforming SGML documents.

To the untrained eye, the markup in an XML document may appear similar enough to an HTML document that the two may be confused with each other until some crucial differences are noticed. XML represents a meta-language to markup text documents. XML offers the reality of both a truly cross-platform and long-term data format.

Data are embedded within XML documents as strings of text and are surrounded by special markers that describe the data so that they can be parsed and displayed. Each piece of data delineated by markup markers is referred to as an XML *element*. The exact syntax of how data are delineated by markup markers is detailed in the XML specification. The XML specification includes the details of such things as how each element is delimited by tags, what the precise definition of what a valid tag is, and the valid format of document names for elements, among others. XML documents are comprised of virtual storage bins called *entities*. An entity can contain parsed or unparsed data. While the contents of unparsed data are unknown, the contents of parsed data represent characters that form either markup or character data. Markup data are used to encode instructions indicating how the document is structured and how it is stored.

The markup used in an XML document not only describes the document's structure, but also allows you to determine which elements are associated with one another. Furthermore, good XML documents also include information about the semantics of the document so that you can understand which domain the document best applies in. For example, the semantics of a document might indicate that a data element represents model numbers for computer monitors, or automobile license plate numbers. An important distinction between XML and other document formats is that XML is not a document presentation language; rather, it is used to describe the structure of the document. For example, XML documents do not contain markers that specify that a particular word is to be displayed in a blue, 12-point, Times Roman font. This information can be embedded in the document, but it is not specifically XML data.

XML is a flexible meta-markup language. Specifically, XML does not have a rigid set of tags and elements; instead, XML allows elements to be defined as they are needed. This has fostered the development of domain-specific XML element sets that allow XML to be extended and expanded to meet the unique needs of a particular domain of use. Although XML allows user-defined sets of elements, it does not allow users to modify the grammar or syntax of XML documents. The grammar defined for XML is specific about the syntax for the placement and appearance of tags, as well as other points about the syntax of elements. This grammar is then used to build XML parsers that can interpret any standard XML document. Documents that follow the syntax defined in the grammar are known as *well-formed* documents, while documents that are not are referred to as *non-well-formed* documents.

The markup style permitted in a particular XML application is typically described in a *document type definition* (DTD). The DTD is a place where all markup and other specifics about the domain where this DTD applies are included. This is loosely analogous to a common header file in C that is included by all files that use a particular library. In this case, a particular instance of a document that is being applied to a specific domain will specify that it conforms to the specific DTD of that domain. XML parsers can then compare this document to the DTD to verify that it matches the DTD. If the document matches the DTD for the domain that it specifies, it is considered a *valid* document. Bear in mind that it is possible to compare the same document to multiple DTDs and have the document be considered valid for all DTDs. This can happen, for example, if the DTDs are subsets of a common DTD.

It is important to understand that DTDs are an optional element in XML; therefore, either they may not exist or they may be inadequate to completely validate a document. Furthermore, documents that are considered invalid may still be useful under some conditions. This is simply because the syntax specified for DTDs is limited. In short, buyers beware!

It is also important to understand that XML is *not* a programming language, nor is XML a database or a network transport protocol. Many marketing departments may try to convince you that it is one or all of these things, but it is not. XML is simply a document description language. Some may be tempted to try to convince you that a configuration file for a network device contains XML programming, but it does not. In reality, this file is just formatted using XML and an XML DTD instead of a proprietary vendor's format. This configuration file cannot be written in XML; it is instead *described* in XML, which is an important distinction. It may contain configuration commands that are surrounded by XML tags, and these strings might be parsed by an XML-aware command parser. Actions such as configuration changes may even be taken as a result, but XML does not constitute a structured programming language for the file; it only describes its format (and perhaps its semantics). Similarly, the XML-formatted configuration file does not represent a database of information, even if stored within the network device in that format.

The database must be implemented using operations and structure that are outside the scope of XML. An example may be an Oracle database format. SQL operations are used to access the database, even if the data are stored in XML format. Finally, XML does not represent a network transport protocol. XML, like HTML, cannot be used to send data across a network per se. Data can be sent formatted as XML across a network using some network transport protocol such as IP/UDP, IP/TCP, or IP/TCP/HTTP. ASN.l-encoded SNMP data can even be transported after being encapsulated within XML, but it still must be transported using a real network transport protocol such as the User Datagram Protocol (UDP). In short, XML can be used to format data sent across a network, but software that is not part of the XML document must actually transmit the document.

XML documents are ASCII text files that are divided into logical pieces referred to as *records.* Therefore, any tool that is capable of reading ASCII text files can read an XML document. This is quite important, since most, if not all, document editors available today can read ASCII text. What most cannot do is read each others' proprietary formats. Several XML document fragments can comprise a single document. It is also possible for documents not to reside anywhere in particular. XML documents may reside in a device's memory after being dynamically generated, or the file fragments may be stored across multiple file systems. The temporal locality of an XML document does not have to be common among a set of document fragments that constitute its totality. XML represents a format that can be truly ubiquitous because the format is in clear ASCII text and provides all of the important information about the document's structure (and sometimes its semantics).

XML parsers are applications that interpret the contexts of XML documents and validate them. XML parsers can be contained within other parsers and be used to trigger actions that result from the successful interpretation of an XML document. The successful interpretation might include just a single line or a series of lines contained in an XML document. For example, XML-formatted CLI commands might first be transported to a command-line interface that understands XML-formatted commands. The command will first be validated by running it through the embedded XML parser. Once the command has been validated, the command is then passed to the command interpreter that reads the command and, if appropriate, triggers the appropriate action function. Similarly, the result of the command might be formatted internally and then sent to the command-line interface. The CLI might then, in turn, format the response using XML and return that to the operator. The operator's terminal or management application must then be able to interpret XML-formatted responses. This should not be difficult since the application had to send an XML-formatted command to the device in the first place.

7.4.1 XML-RPC and SOAP: XML Serialization and RPC over HTTP

Since its inception, XML has been applied in various ways. Originally, XML Remote Procedure Call (XML-RPC) was developed to provide a simple RPC mechanism using XML and HTTP as a transport protocol. XML-RPC presented an interesting application of XML in that it positioned it as the basis for standards-based transactional computing. Several implementations of XML-RPC are still in use today. These implementations demonstrate that XML-RPC is platform-neutral and language-neutral while still being very useful.

Simple Object Access Protocol (SOAP), like XML-RPC, can be thought of as a Web-based abstraction of traditional distributed object communication. SOAP represents a lightweight XML-based protocol that can be used to exchange information in a distributed environment. SOAP consists of the following three principal components:

- It defines a container framework that is used to describe what the contents of a valid message are and how a parser should process it.
- It defines a set of encoding rules that can be used to express instances of application-defined data types.
- It defines a representation for remote procedure calls and their corresponding responses.

SOAP itself does not address higher-level distributed object issues such as object activation, nor does it address object life cycle management. SOAP does not specify the messaging semantics of the XML transport encapsulation. That is, it does not define quality of service (QoS), queuing, or other related issues. On the contrary, applications that process SOAP messages must provide the transport semantics used for the connection. Finally, issues do exist regarding the use of SOAP as an RPC mechanism over HTTP. Specifically, the issues of transaction control, replay protection, and encryption are in question. Due to these limitations, some have built true messaging models using SOAP as the base and addressed these issues in the new layer.

7.4.2 Encoding Managed Information Using XML

As was mentioned, XML can be used to encapsulate or wrap managed objects from existing management interfaces such as proprietary CLI (see Section 7.2) or SNMP (see Section 7.6). When XML is used as a transport encapsulation, managed information can be encoded for display or storage at a network management station in several different ways. First, SNMP can be encoded within XML. In this way, XML tags can encode SNMP object names and values in clear text, allowing

XML parsers to understand the information and display it. The same can be done for CLI data. Although allowing for easy display, this mechanism, however, has the disadvantage that the format of the data is quite verbose as compared to the standard data encapsulations, and thus results in significantly more network traffic.

7.5 BULK FILE TRANSFER

Bulk file transfer is an option that some device vendors offer as a means of offloading large amounts of data from their devices via a File Transfer Protocol (FTP). In particular, deployments of devices that are required to maintain large configurations or large amounts of manageable information may find an advantage when exporting these data in bulk form using a file transfer mechanism. Of course, other options such as the SNMP `GetBulk` operation exist, but in some cases, even this optimized approach is still too inefficient for some networks.

Bulk file transfer generally results in one or more files containing the equivalent management data that would have been offloaded using a more traditional management interface such as SNMP or CLI. Data can be exported to or imported from a device, just as files can be transferred to and from any networked computer. The choice of exporting or importing data depends on the goals of such activities. For example, statistics or an existing configuration might be exported from a device, while a new configuration might be loaded into a device by importing a bulk file. The actual details of how this process is configured and eventually triggered vary from vendor to vendor. For example, some vendors simply allow this to be engineered from the CLI, while other vendors may even provide a MIB that can be used to both configure and instigate the file upload/download process.

In all cases, the motivation for using such a mechanism is simple: efficiency of operations and a reduction in network overhead resulting from management protocol inefficiencies. In comparison to using any other management protocol, the amount of overhead when using a bulk file transfer of the same amount of manageable objects is very low. The reason is simple: The bulk file transfer generally requires one or two operations by the manager, and then the file is either sent or received using a very efficient FTP. The data being transferred can be highly compressed. By comparison, other management interfaces require several operations to achieve the same goals, as well as additional framing for each piece of managed data to identify it.

With this efficiency comes a low amount of flexibility. Essentially bulk file transfer is used for one or two types of operations: configuration upload/download or bulk statistical data offload. In the case of bulk statistical transfer, potentially large volumes of data are offloaded to an offline server for processing. Instead of the management station querying for each managed object, they are all packed a priori into the bulk file and are transferred in one operation. This is important also for the recording of historical data that may result in large volumes of data being transferred across the network to the management station. Instead, the device can cache the data and transfer them all together as a single file. This saves on network traffic and makes it more likely that sensitive statistical data will not be lost.

In the case of configuration files, some network devices require very large configuration files. If each managed object must be transferred one at a time to the managed device, it may take several minutes (or hours!) to configure a device that has rebooted, or one that requires a large amount of reconfiguration. In these cases, it is preferable to simply transfer the configuration file to the device and allow it to read the data either from its memory or from an onboard disk drive.

Bulk files can either be "pushed" or "pulled" from a device. This describes how the manager extracts the file data. In the case of files being pushed, an operator would specify a target machine to which the machine later transfers files using the FTP or the UNIX Network File System (NFS). The machine either would then send the file at some specific time or might be triggered to send the file if some SNMP variable is set. The pull model is used when a device wishes to be the host of the files created. The operator would then use one of the aforementioned FTPs to connect to the router as if it were a host computer, and then transfer the files from it. In either case, files, such as one containing the device's configuration, can be offloaded or uploaded using the efficiency of a bulk file transfer rather than individual protocol configuration operations.

7.5.1 Encoding Bulk Data

The format of the bulk file can vary, as several encoding methods exist including XML, proprietary CLI, and SNMP. For example, the information in a file can be encoded using the SNMP SMI, type, and value. This information is then encoded using Basic Encoding Rules (BER), ASN.1, for example. Other options are to simply include ASCII text of commands or to encode these in binary. Since the specific format is typically proprietary, the shortcoming of using such an approach is that it is not an open standard used by more than one vendor. The downside to this is that it is generally only provided by the vendor and the vendor's management applications, requiring decoding of multiple formats in a heterogeneous network. Sometimes the vendor will not even provide the format to third-party application developers or operators, requiring that they use that company's device management software. This may unfortunately result in a network comprised of devices from N vendors, requiring an operator to understand and manage as many as N different bulk file export/import applications. For most vendors we have interacted with, this is an unacceptable solution. This also applies to other management interfaces that we have already discussed or that we will discuss, including XML, CLI, and CORBA. Fortunately, SNMP does solve this problem. We will discuss how in Section 7.6.

Further compounding this problem for operators is the fact that in order for commercial parsers to convert proprietary formats that may have much of their semantic information "compressed" out, they may have to be uncompressed into more verbose representations that are more easily useable by applications that are generally unavailable. To alleviate this problem, some vendors provide applications to their customers that accomplish these things, but again, these applications are proprietary and only understand the format of the devices made by that vendor. This results in higher operating costs for the operator since they are only left with the options of either writing their own parsers to decode bulk-formatted data or purchasing one from each vendor. For these reasons, some vendors are moving toward providing their customers with an XML-based representation of bulk data that can be parsed and understood by many different applications, including readily available off-the-shelf versions. Although this does not solve the problem of providing a ubiquitous format for the encoded data, it does allow an operator to build a single application using a common protocol.

An example of how you can reduce the complexity associated with interpreting SNMP data encoded into a proprietary bulk transfer format is to define a new bulk data format that is based on an XML schema. Let's call this new format `vendor-x-bulk-xml`. This format will be similar to the existing proprietary `vendor-x-bulk-snmp`, which formats SNMP data as a pair containing an SNMP object identifier (oid) that describes the object and an instance of that data, as well as the value (if any) associated with that object instance. The XML version of this formation will modify the format slightly by replacing the oids with the verbose representation of the object. Additional XML tags may also be needed to denote fields within the file, as well as an XML database template library (DTL). The tags used in this format will be relatively small, while still providing enough semantic meaning about the tagged data. By formatting data in the `vendor-x-bulk-xml` format, we lose some compression that the `vendor-x-bulk-SNMP` format provides, but the data produced in the `vendor-x-bulk-xml` format will still be sufficiently compressed.

A benefit of using the `vendor-x-bulk-xml` format is that we can provide DTD specifications that provide a well-understood format for describing well-formed XML documents. This same format is either not provided by proprietary formats, or when it is, it is almost completely different from any other vendor's format. In addition, we can provide style sheets that can be used to transform the `vendor-x-bulk-xml`-formatted data into user-friendly representations or other XML representations.

There are significant advantages to this `vendor-x-bulk-xml` format. Such data would be easy to interpret with existing XML parsers, saving customers from having to write their own parsers. The structured tagging makes for easier debugging in customer environments. Furthermore, the advantages of bulk transfer are still present: large volumes of data can be offloaded from a device in a very efficient (and now well-understood) format. This reduces the complexity of managing devices, as well as provides an efficient mechanism for doing so.

7.6 SIMPLE NETWORK MANAGEMENT PROTOCOL

SNMP was devised many years ago by the IETF to solve the problem of managing network devices remotely using a standard protocol, access methods, and a well-known format for representing managed data stored in network nodes. The standard for SNMP has been enhanced and extended over the course of its existence to include additional protocol operations, enhanced security, and additional standard management models. The first version, called SNMPvl (RFCs 1155, 1157, and 1213), has since been surpassed by SNMPv2c (RFCs 1901–1906) and, most recently, SNMPv3 (RFCs 3411–3415). With each new revision came many new features including new protocol operations, security features, and modifications to the language SNMP uses to represent managed information. In addition, during this time, the acceptance of SNMP in the marketplace grew. Today, most production networks use SNMP as at least a part of their overall network management strategy.

SNMP is composed of three basic components: structure of management information (SMI), MIB, and SNMP.

7.6.1 Structure of Management Information

Management information is viewed as a collection of managed objects, residing in a virtual information store that is referred to in SNMP as a management information base (see Section 7.6.2). The SMI is the data modeling language used to model the management data. The SMI (RFC 2578) is the language that is used to write, define, and specify a MIB module. The roots of the SMI are actually in an adapted subset of OSI's Abstract Syntax Notation One (ASN.1). This adaptation was first done in 1988. The SMI has since changed in the second version of the SMI, called SMIv2. The SMIv2 has been used for several years now as the standard language in which to define MIB modules. Furthermore, a new SMI is being worked on at the IETF, called the SMIng, that encompasses even more powerful modeling language and constructs. It is important to understand that it is much better not to call this ASN.1.

Structure information management is divided into three parts: object definitions, MIB module definitions, and notification definitions. A SMI macro called the `ModuleIdentity` is used to specify the semantics of an information module. This macro is always found at the top of the module definition. Object definitions are used to describe managed objects. The ASN.1 `ObjectType` macro is used to specify the semantics and syntax of a managed object. Finally, notification definitions are provided to describe spontaneous transmissions of management information. The ASN.1 `NotificationType` macro is used to specify the syntax and semantics of a notification.

Textual Conventions and Basic Data Types

The SMI provides a number of basic data types that are used to specify the semantics and syntax of objects defined in MIB modules. When designing a MIB module, it is sometimes beneficial to define new types that are derived from those defined in the SMI. Each of these new types has a different name and a similar syntax, but more precise semantics than the type it is derived from in the SMI. These newly defined types are termed *textual conventions* (TCs) and are defined with the `TextualConvention` data type. TCs do not add any new basic types to the SMI. This is very important because a TC is encoded within an SNMP packet—a protocol data unit (PDU)—using the same rules that define their derived type. That is, the actual underlying basic data that are transmitted in the SNMP PDUs (i.e., on the wire) remain the same as the basic data type that the TC is derived from.

Table 7.3 lists most of the basic types that are defined in the SMIv2 (RFC 2578). These objects do not, however, represent the totality of object types in SMIv2. As mentioned, these types can be and frequently are extended using SNMP textual conventions to adapt their syntax or semantics to different domains.

SMI Versions

There have been two versions of the SMI. Let's briefly discuss them, since they are often confused or incorrectly used interchangeably. Back in the late 1980s, when SNMPv1 was first specified, SMIv1 was defined to facilitate the definition of SNMP MIB modules. The first version of the SMI consisted largely of the specifications in RFC 1155, RFC 1212, and RFC 1215. SMIv1 is currently a full standard (STD 16) within the IETF, although since 1995/1996 standard MIB modules have not been typically allowed to be defined using SMIv1. It should be noted that some corporations still define their enterprise MIB modules using SMIv1, although that is more of an exception to the norm. The SMIv2 consists of RFC 2578, RFC 2579, and RFC 2580 and is currently a full standard (STD 58) within the IETF.

It is important to understand that all of the data types defined in SMIv1 can be represented in SMIv2. It was the intent of the IETF when it defined the SMIv2 not to break existing implementations that used the SMIv1. It should be noted that although the data types in SMIv2 are a superset of those defined in SMIv1, some of the data types from SMIv1 are only in SMIv2 for backward compatibility, and so should not be used in new MIB module definitions. These exceptions are noted in the definitions for those types in SMIv2. Despite this backward compatibility between SMIv1 and SMIv2, translation in the other direction, from SMIv2 to SMIv1, is a bit more problematic. For example, the new type `Counter64` is particularly difficult to convert because there is no direct mapping from this type to any other single type in SMIv1. For those readers interested in the specifics of how these conversions are performed or recommendations on this subject, RFC 2576 explains how to convert SMIv1 MIB modules into SMIv2 MIB modules and vice versa.

7.6.2 The Management Information Base

Each managed system is composed of a collection of objects that are used to model system functions, concepts, or attributes. Objects are capable of representing

Table 7.3 Basic Data Types as Defined in SMIv2 (RFC 2578)

Data Type	Description
INTEGER	A signed 32-bit integer quantity with a range that is from −2,147,483,648 to 2,147,483,647.
Integer32	This is the same as INTEGER except that it never needs more than 32 bits for a two's complement representation. The valid range is from −2,147,483,648 to 2,147,483,647.
Unsigned32	An unsigned 32-bit quantity with a range of 0 to 4,294,967,295.
OCTET STRING	A series of bytes, each ≥0 and ≤255.
Gauge32	An unsigned 32-bit quantity used for counters with a range of 0 to 4,294,967,295. This object latches onto a specific value, but does not wrap around as a normal counter would, so it should not be confused with the standard Unsigned32 or Counter32.
OBJECT IDENTIFIER	Contains a unique oid. When displayed, it is typically shown as a series of dot-separated unsigned integers.
IpAddress	Contains an IPv4 address as a sequence of 4 bytes. Note that this type is only present in the SMIv2 for backward compatibility. It is no longer used in the specification of new MIBs.
Counter32	The Counter32 type is used when a nonnegative integer that monotonically increases is necessary. The Counter32 type increases in value monotonically until it reaches the maximum value of a 32-bit integer (4,294,967,295 decimal), and then "wraps around" to 0, where it starts increasing again.
Counter64	64-bit counter used for counters that wrap in less than one hour with 32-bit counters. The valid range is from 0 to 18,446,744,073,709,551,615.
BITS	The BITS construct represents an enumeration of named bits. The collection of named bits is assigned nonnegative, contiguous values starting at 0. Only those named bits that are enumerated by the definition may be present in a value. Therefore, enumerations of bit positions must be assigned to consecutive bits (i.e., there cannot be holes in the enumeration).
Opaque	The Opaque type supports the capability to pass arbitrary ASN.1 syntax. A value is encoded using the ASN.1 BERs (RFC 2578) into a string of octets. This, in turn, is encoded as an OCTET STRING, which in effect "wraps" the original ASN.1 value twice. The Opaque type is provided for backward compatibility and is no longer used in new MIBs.
TimeTicks	Represents an unsigned integer that represents the time modulo 232 in hundredths of a second between two epochs. The DESCRIPTION clause defines both reference epochs.

many things and are only limited in power and flexibility by the data modeling language in which they are defined. For example, an object might represent a finite component within the system, such as an interface, and keep track of that interface's counters, state, or name. Another object might represent the state of a routing protocol on that same system. However, given the modeling language used, it is possible, for example, that some of the specific attributes or behaviors of these objects will not be possible.

The collection of managed objects can be thought of as a database of manageable information. This information can be used to form a data model of the system. In addition to the objects themselves, the database must also represent the type, behavior, and associated access policy for each object. It may also be necessary to represent the interaction between objects in the database. The objects in the model can be accessed using a variety of management interfaces to query or modify them. Examples of management interfaces include XML, CORBA, CLI, or SNMP, among others.

However, maintaining this information in a database alone does not guarantee that all manager entities can access this information. Unless an external representation of the managed information such as an abstract data model is agreed on by both manager and agent entities, an agent on one device may provide access to its information in a manner that is inconsistent with that of another device. This could easily happen, for example, if one manufacturer produced a representation of one variable as a string, while another represented it as an integer—perhaps because the management interface is nonstandard, as is the case with the CLI. In addition to these challenges, managed objects can be, and usually are, implemented in a variety of ways depending on the specific device, or even the software revision running on that device. Therefore, it is important for the management interface to provide a consistent view of the data model that agent entities can present to manager entities. SNMP accomplishes this using its MIB.

The MIB is the collective set of MIB modules that together make up the MIB that is being managed/monitored. The MIB is also sometimes referred to as the device's *virtual object store* because it defines the data model for a device. MIB modules are defined using the SMI, which provides a consistent data modeling language in which managed objects are defined. It also allows MIB modules to be parsed by MIB compilers can that not only check their syntax, but can also generate code that is used to implement the objects defined in that MIB module. An individual MIB module specification should not be confused with the entire collection of specifications implemented by any particular device, which is referred to as a device's MIB proper. Many use the terms *MIB* and *MIB module* interchangeably. This is sometimes problematic, since the actual meaning must be distinguished based on the context in which it is used; therefore, we will use the term *MIB module* to describe a specific subset of the MIB, and *MIB* as the entire collection of MIB modules.

MIB module specifications are generally produced by two types of organizations: standards organizations and private entities such as corporations. In the case of standards-based definitions, standards bodies such as the IETF, ITU, and ATM Forum have produced, and continue to produce, MIB module specifications that can be used to manage various protocols and network device functions. The advantage to MIB modules that are produced by standards organizations is that they provide a common data model that can be adhered to by all vendors implementing the feature being managed. For example, the OSPF MIB module defines standard managed objects that can be used to manage a standards-based OSPF implementation. All devices implementing this MIB will represent the objects defined in that MIB externally in the manner in which they are specified in the MIB module, regardless of their actual internal implementation.

Aside from standards-based MIB modules, company-specific versions called *enterprise* MIB modules are also produced by corporations. These MIB modules are typically produced to extend existing standards-based MIB specifications because they do not adequately reflect the entirety of managed information for that feature as implemented by a specific corporation's device. It is common that the standard MIB module contains a subset of managed objects required to manage a specific feature. Vendors typically augment the standard function, thereby adding value to it. These additional functions are then represented in that company's enterprise MIB module.

Each MIB module specification is composed of several components: a textual preamble, a MIB module defined using the SMI, and references to other related documents. Standards-based MIB module specifications rarely vary from this format, while proprietary MIB module specifications typically only contain the MIB module.

Each managed object in an agent's virtual object store must be modeled in a specific MIB module before it can be made available for access through the SNMP management interface. Each managed object is defined using the OBJECT-TYPE macro. This macro allows the specific syntax and semantics for an object to be defined. Two basic types of objects exist in MIB modules: *scalar* and *columnar*. If an object can only exist as a single instance, it is referred to as a scalar object. Management operations in SNMP apply exclusively to scalar objects; that is, the basic operations in SNMP always act on a scalar object.

The Get and Set operations, for example, may only act on an instance of an object such as a scalar object or columnar instance. No specific construct exists within SNMP to organize together scalar objects; however, related scalar objects can be found grouped together at least conceptually within a MIB module. For example, scalars related to the OSPF protocol may be found in the OSPF MIB module. Organizing objects together in this way sometimes enhances the MIB module's readability and usefulness. Figure 7.7 illustrates a collection of scalar objects. Notice that the scalar objects are not organized in any particular way, and that each represents a single instance of an object (i.e., no two overlap in color).

We mentioned that two basic types of objects exist in SNMP. Let us now investigate columnar (i.e., tabular) objects. It is often a necessity to group managed objects together into a conceptual tabular structure to form an ordered collection

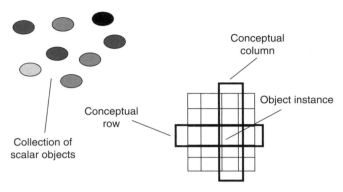

FIGURE 7.7

SMI conceptual table containing columns, rows, and object instances, and a collection of scalar objects.

of objects within the MIB module. Each conceptual table contains zero or more *rows,* each of which can contain one or more *columnar* objects. Thus, conceptual tables in SNMP contain a series of rows and columns. This conceptualization is specified using the OBJECT-TYPE macro. This macro can be used to define both an object that corresponds to a table and an object that corresponds to a row in that table. The intersection of a row and one or more columns represents a specific object *instance* and is how specific instances of objects are called out or indexed from within a conceptual table of objects.

Figure 7.7 illustrates how a conceptual table in a MIB module might be configured with several rows and columns. The table represents horizontal rows, where the specific row is identified by the indexes for the table, and the specific instances of a columnar variable. Object instances are indicated by the cell within the table where both the columnar and row rectangles intersect.

Table Indexing

Each table defined in a MIB module is indexed by one or more objects. The indexing of a table is specified using either the INDEX or AUGMENTS clauses. The INDEX clause contains objects that are either present in the table or are found elsewhere that are used to index the rows in that table. The most common approach is to include objects defined in the table as indexes for the table. When this approach is used, the objects used as indexes must not be accessible.

Two additional choices exist when a table wishes to extend the entries of an existing table without having to add additional columns to that table. This may be necessary if, for example, you wish to extend a table defined in a standard MIB module with objects that are enterprise specific. In this case, it would not make sense to add additional objects to the standard table. The choice of using one of the table extension mechanisms or another depends specifically on whether a one-to-one relationship exists at all times between the instances of the objects contained in both tables. If a row in the new table will exist for every row created in the base table, then the AUGMENTS clause can be used instead of the INDEX clause to define the indexing of this table. The AUGMENTS clause specifies the base table that the new table will augment, but does not specify any indexes. In doing so, the new table is implicitly indexed using *exactly* the same indexes as the base table.

The other method of table extension is used if a sparse relationship exists between the objects in both tables. This method is called the *extends* relationship. This approach requires the new table to define its indexes with the INDEX clause using the same indexes as are found in the base table. This method allows entries in the base table to be created that do not correspond to entries in the new table. This is an important feature of this approach since this allows entries in the new table to correspond to those in the base table only if it makes sense to do so. For example, if a new table wishes to extend the IF-MIB's ifTable to include additional objects for a new type of interface, this new table would be implemented using an *extends* relationship, because the possibility exists that the ifTable could contain interfaces that might not be related to all of the entries in this new table. However, if the new table was defined to contain counter objects that applied to *every possible type* of interface, then it would be appropriate to use the AUGMENTS clause to specify the indexing for this table.

7.6.3 Access to Objects

Each object defined in a MIB module must have a MAX-ACCESS clause associated with it. The valid values for MAX-ACCESS are ordered, from least to greatest: not-accessible, accessible-for-notify, read-only, read-write, and read-create. The MAX-ACCESS clause indicates the *maximum* access that would make what is called "protocol sense" for the object. For example, if the MAX-ACCESS is defined as read-only, then a Set operation that attempted to modify that object would fail. If that object's MAX-ACCESS is set to read-write or read-create, then the Set operation may succeed. However, there may still be many reasons why a Set might fail.

First, an implementation may not have implemented the object such that it could be modified. Therefore, the object's actual access is read-only, thus preventing modifications of the object. Similarly, the RowStatus for the conceptual row containing that object might be implemented or configured to disallow write access. Second, the Set request may be attempting to modify an object that is configured with noAuthNoPriv in the view-based access model (VACM). Third, the device's configuration may be set to not allow Sets for unsecured requests, and the Set request comes in unsecured. Fourth, the specific user requesting the modification of that object is not allowed to execute that operation on that object given the configuration in the VACM MIB (RFC 2575). Please note RFC 2576 also maps community-based (that is, SNMPv1 and SNMPv2c) access into the VACM access control. Table 7.4 enumerates the five specific access types in increasing order of permissions granted to the manager.

Table 7.4 Possible Values of the MAX-ACCESS Clause

MAX-ACCESS Type	Description
Not-accessible	Not allowed for scalar or columnar object types; only for indexes.
Accessible-for-notify	This value indicates that an object is available only via a notification. That is, this object may only be contained within a notification, but cannot be accessed using the other SNMP operations (e.g., Get, Set, etc.).
Read-only	The object type may be an operand in only retrieval and event report operations.
Read-write	The object type may be an operand in modification, retrieval, and event report operations.
Read-create	Same as read-write, except specified for columnar objects that require a value to be set before a row in that table can be created. Once created, these objects can be read or written.

It is important to understand that the MAX-ACCESS clause specifies the maximum access that is required for an object, but it does not specify the minimum access possible. It is up to the implementation to choose this, given how it has chosen to implement the object. It is permissible to implement an object using a MAX-ACCESS that is lower than the MAX-ACCESS specified in the MIB module. The implementation can specify how it has varied from the MIB module where the object is defined by noting this variation in the agent capability statement (see RFC 2580 for more information) for that MIB module. For example, an object that is specified with a MAX-ACCESS as read-write might actually be implemented as read-only. Alternatively, this can be accomplished by specifying a MIN-ACCESS clause in the conformance section of the MIB module.

7.6.4 Object Identifier

SNMP specifies a scheme by which all of the objects and instances of those objects present within a system can be uniquely identified. These items are called *object identifiers,* or more commonly, oids. Oids are specified as an ordered sequence of nonnegative integers written from left to right and separated by a period (i.e., dot). This is referred to as the *dot notation.* For example, "1.1" represents an oid. The oid space itself does not have any limitation as to how many branches (subIDs) are possible. For SNMP, however, a limit of 128 subIDs has been defined. Each consecutive integer is separated from the numbers around it by a period. The sequence must contain two integers at a minimum and does not have a maximum number (although all implementations will have a specific limit to this size).

Oids are arranged and organized in a hierarchical tree structure. The topmost levels in the oid tree are controlled by the ITU and ISO standards bodies. These

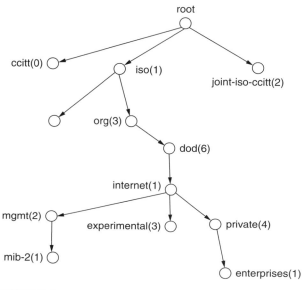

FIGURE 7.8

Sample portion of the oid tree containing IETF subtree oid assignments starting at internet(1).

organizations delineate how new assignments are given. A portion of this oid tree is managed and maintained by standards organizations or corporations. A portion of the oid tree is shown in Figure 7.8. Note that the example contains the IETF subtree. Standard MIBs typically contain oids that use the prefix 1.3.6.1.2.1.

SNMP objects and object instances—sometimes referred to as SNMP *variables*—are assigned unique oids. As was noted earlier, SNMP variables are either scalar or tabular objects. SNMP MIB modules are also typically assigned an oid within the oid tree shown in Figure 7.8. This oid often represents the root oid for all objects present in that MIB module. The point where the MIB module is rooted depends on the status of the MIB specification as well as which organization owns and maintains the document. As mentioned earlier, two general types of MIB specifications exist: enterprise (or proprietary) and standard. Documents that are produced by a standards organization are typically rooted somewhere below that organization's node in the overall oid tree. For example, MIBs that are produced by the IETF are sometimes first placed under the experimental(3) oid. These MIB modules will be assigned oids with a prefix of 1.3.6.1.3.

Once the MIB specification has been adopted for standards-track status, it is moved under a different portion of the IETF's oid subtree, typically mib-2. Similarly, private organizations maintain enterprise MIB modules. These modules are assigned oids that are rooted under the IETF organization's private(4) enterprises(1) subtree. For example, Cisco Systems maintains a subtree of oids under 1.3.6.1.4.1.9. Corporations sometimes further delineate their oid space in a manner that is consistent with the one used by the IETF. That is, corporations sometimes maintain additional subtrees that contain portions for experimental or prototype MIBs, as well as those that are officially released.

The general format of an oid is of the form `<object identifier>.<instance id>`. The first part of the identifier represents the oid of the object, as defined in the MIB module. The second portion identifies the specific object instance. In general, the oid representing a scalar object instance contains the object prefix and an instance identifier of 0. The format of a tabular object instance oid is comprised first of the table entry's oid. The second portion contains the columnar identifier. The last portion contains one or more identifiers that represent the index of the row. This is sometimes confusing, but remember that this must be the case because tables may be indexed by one or *more* object instances. Thus, the general format of an oid representing an object instance in a table is of the form:

```
<table entry suboid>.<column>.<index0> . . . <indexn>
```

We will investigate how oids are operated on in Section 7.6.9.

MIB Module Versions

Since around 1996, MIB modules have, in general, been written using SMIv2. However, a small set of MIB modules are still written in SMIvl. The most visible and important one is MIB II, which is defined in RFC 1213 as well as Standard 17 (STD 17). It is also important to understand that much of MIB II has been split off into new MIB modules that replace these functions. These new modules are written in the newer SMIv2. For example, the system group from MIB II can now be found in the SNMPv2-MIB module (RFC 1907). This can sometimes be confusing for the novice (or someone who has been doing this for a while), so we recommend searching the IETF RFC archive and going over the vl MIBs before implementing them, as newer SMIv2 versions of the MIB module (or the portions you are interested in implementing) may exist.

7.6.5 SNMP Application Components

The Simple Network Management Protocol is the protocol that is used to send management information as is defined in MIB modules. This information is exchanged between SNMP entities. SNMP entities are traditionally referred to as SNMP *managers* and SNMP *agents*. However, in the current IETF SNMP architecture as defined in RFC 3411, managers and agents have been generalized into SNMP entities. The architecture of an SNMP entity is shown in Figure 7.9.

All entities are comprised of an engine and applications. An SNMP engine provides services for sending and receiving messages (dispatcher and message processing system), authenticating and encrypting messages (security subsystem), and controlling access to managed objects (access control subsystem). There is a

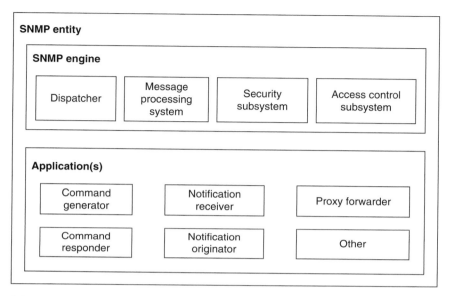

SNMP application components.

Table 7.5 SNMP Application Components	
SNMP Application	**Description**
Command generator	Typically resides in an NMS or similar device.
Command responder	Typically resides in a managed device such as a router.
Notification originator	Typically resides in a managed device such as a router.
Notification receiver	Typically resides in an NMS or similar device.
Proxy forwarder	Translates between various SNMP versions.
Other	Other application types defined in the future.

one-to-one association between an SNMP engine and the SNMP entity that contains it. All SNMP entities also contain SNMP applications. There are several types of SNMP applications, enumerated in Table 7.5.

Previous versions of SNMP did not allow a command generator to reside within a managed device. Similarly, notification originators were not allowed to reside within a management station. However, the new architecture as defined in RFC 3411 does not make that distinction and instead only refers to an SNMP entity.

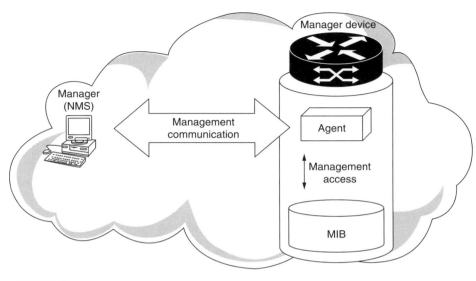

FIGURE 7.10

SNMP manager and agent entities conversing using SNMP. The agent maintains a database of managed information that a manager accesses to manage the device on which the agent resides.

This obviates the need for referring to the different components as an SNMP manager, agent, or a dual-role entity.

In Figure 7.10 an agent and a manager are shown conversing using SNMP. The agent maintains a database of managed objects in its MIB. When the agent accepts a request from the manager, it processes the requests using its security and access control systems. If all tests performed by these systems are successful, then the request is made to its database of managed objects to access the information specified in the request. Once the information is retrieved, it is encoded in a response message that is returned to the manager entity.

Dual-Role Entity

Until now, we have discussed the interaction between the manager and the agent as one of a manager requesting objects or modifying their values by sending protocol operations to an agent. However, a variation of this model of interaction is possible that will allow an entity to act as a translator between SNMP and another protocol, including a different version of SNMP. Recall the scenario previously in the CORBA section (see Section 7.3.1) that explained how SNMP messages could be translated between SNMP and CORBA. This not only included protocol retrieval or modification messages, but also included SNMP notification conversion. For this configuration to work correctly, the entity responsible for translating between CORBA and SNMP needs to be implemented as an entity with a proxy-forwarder application. Such an entity is commonly referred to as a *dual-role entity* or a *midlevel manager.*

7.6.6 **SNMP Notifications**

Network devices often maintain system software that is capable of operating in an asynchronous manner. Node software can sometimes be programmed to raise asynchronous alarms that are intended to alert the system's operator of some interesting condition or event. SNMP provides a means by which agents are able to issue asynchronous messages to managers (or midlevel managers). These messages are called *SNMP notifications.* SNMP notifications are defined in a MIB module with the NOTIFICATION TYPE macro. Notifications can be sent from a notification originator to a notification receiver using one of two mechanisms: either a TRAP (a TRAPv1 or a TRAPv2, depending on the version of the protocol operations being used), or an INFORM (only available with version 2 of the protocol operations).

The notification message contains one or more pairs of oids and values. Each pair consists of an oid and a corresponding value that is informative for the notification the object is contained in. The TRAP version of a notification message is sent either in a reliable (INFORM) or unreliable (TRAPv2) manner. Therefore, reception of a notification is not always guaranteed. SNMPv2 added a reliable notification called an INFORM. An INFORM notification contains similar semantics to the notification except that the agent continues to attempt delivery of the INFORM message until it receives an acknowledgment from the manager that it has received it (or it times out). The TRAP or INFORM destinations are specified either directly on a device via its CLI, or using SNMP's RFC 2573 MIB module. Retry counts and timeouts for INFORMs are specified in those MIB modules.

Special care should be taken when using TRAPs to ensure that a manager is generally capable of both catching them and then reacting in a reasonable amount of time to those messages if necessary. The transmission of notifications in large amounts can actually exacerbate a failure condition by either overloading the network between the device entity and the manager entity, or overloading the manager entity such that it cannot take appropriate corrective action because it is busy processing notifications.

7.6.7 **SNMP Security**

SNMP provides varying degrees of security and security features depending largely on the version of SNMP used. SNMPv1 provides a very weak form of security called the *community-based security model.* In this model, a clear-text phrase is associated with certain access privileges. Unfortunately, this level of security has proven to be very weak because most implementations use the same phrases for access (e.g., public is used for read-only access, while private is often used for write access). When the IETF redesigned SNMPv1, one of the major hurdles to the new version being standardized was a new model of security.

Unfortunately, a compromise could not be reached, so several versions of SNMP were released. At this time, VACM offered a stronger means of configuring access control than the community-based model of SNMPv1. VACM allows for more constrained access to objects by allowing the per-object access policy to be configured. However, since this mechanism still used the community-based pass phrase token for authentication, it could still be easily compromised. When SNMPv3 was standardized, one of the most significant new features it provided was a very robust and comprehensive security model. SNMPv3 security provides approaches for encrypting the SNMP message, replay detection/protection, and antispoofing mechanisms. These, coupled with VACM, provide a very comprehensive security model that can be used as an effective means by which operators can allow full write access to their systems with the confidence that they are secure.

7.6.8 SNMP Transport Protocols

It is mandatory that an SNMP entity supports and implements SNMP over UDP/IP. However, SNMP can certainly be run over a variety of other network transport protocols. SNMP has been successfully run over IP/TCP, XML/HTTP, and IPX. It is difficult to say specifically whether one network transport is necessarily better than another, but it is clear that SNMP over UDP/IP is the most prevalent mode of operation, due to it being mandatory for compliance to the standard. We suggest that you determine what network and operational requirements exist and choose a transport protocol that best suits these requirements. From our experience, however, we have seen that although a small and dwindling number of vendors may implement some of the non-IP/UDP transports above for SNMP, the trend today is to use IP/UDP or IP/TCP for those requiring reliable transport services.

7.6.9 Protocol Operations

SNMP defines a simple protocol that is used to carry out the interaction between the manager and agent. We will now discuss three of the most widely used operations, although please keep in mind that others such as GetBulk exist and can be quite useful. These operations are used to access or modify the objects maintained by the agent. We will discuss the Get, GetNext, and Set operations. We should first note that it is not possible to obtain or modify the value of anything other than an instance of an object; thus the Get and Set operations must include the oid of a valid object instance. However, the GetNext operation may act on an invalid oid, as the agent will always attempt to find an object instance whose oid is lexically greater than the one specified.

The Get operation is issued by the manager entity when it wishes to know the value of a specific instance of a managed object. To do so, the manager entity inserts the oid of a specific object instance into an SNMP PDU and sends it to an agent entity. If the agent entity accepts the request, it will fill in the value portion

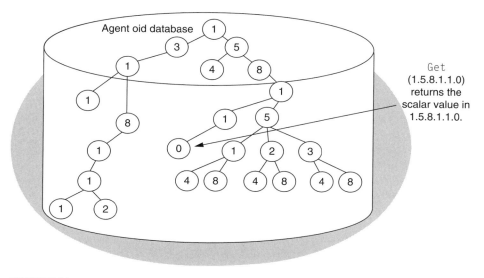

Get
(1.5.8.1.1.0)
returns the
scalar value in
1.5.8.1.1.0.

FIGURE 7.11

Example of an SNMP Get operation.

of the request with the value of the object instance and return it to the manager entity. This operation is very straightforward for scalar object instances. However, it is slightly more complicated for tabular object instances. To retrieve the value of an object instance that resides within a table, it is necessary to specify the index of that object instance in such a way as to precisely reference it within the table. Recall that conceptual tables represent rows and columns. The columns in the table represent objects and are specified with one or more indexes.

It is generally not possible to directly retrieve or modify indexes of a table using the Get, Set, or GetNext operations. Columnar indexes defined in MIB modules are required to define their indexes as having a MAX-ACCESS of not accessible, therefore an agent entity that receives a request for such an object will return an error. This restriction exists because it is not necessary to access the indexes of a table directly. This is because the indexes of a table must be specified in order to specify a unique object instance in the table.

The Get operation is demonstrated in Figure 7.11. The figure shows a simulated oid tree rooted somewhere under the enterprise oid. After a manager issues a Get operation using the oid 1.5.8.1.1.0, the agent accepts the request, queries its object database, and returns the value of this scalar object. All scalar objects have associated instances that are conventionally identified with instance 0. In this case, the .0 at the end of the 1.5.8.1.1.0 oid specifies the instance of object 1.5.8.1.1. Notice that when the manager issues a Get operation containing the oid 1.5.8.1.5.3, the agent returns an error because 1.5.8.1.5.3 does not represent an

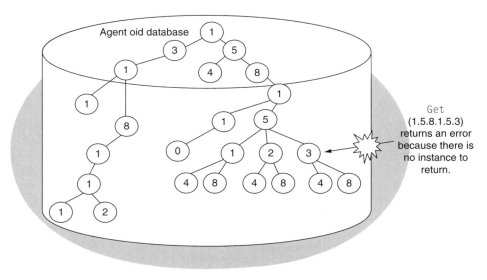

Get
(1.5.8.1.5.3)
returns an error
because there is
no instance to
return.

FIGURE 7.12

Example of invalid Get operation.

instance of any object; it instead represents an actual object. This is demonstrated in Figure 7.12.

The second protocol operation defined is called the Set operation. Set represents the analog to the Get operation: It is used to modify the value of an object instance versus simply retrieving it. To this end, a Set operation must specify both an object instance *and* a value to assign to that instance. When an agent receives a Set request, it first checks the access specifics for that object. If the object is specified with a MAX-ACCESS of read-write (or read-create), the agent will modify the value of that object with the one specified in the request. If, however, write access to the object specified is not allowed, the agent will return an error informing the manager that the requested modification has not taken place.

The last operation we will cover is GetNext. This operation is used to retrieve the value of the next *lexically* greater *object instance* in the oid database. Remember, the GetNext operation must still retrieve the value of the next lexically greater oid, so it must end up executing a Get operation on a valid object instance. By "lexically greater," it is meant that the object with the next largest oid should be retrieved. To find the next largest value, the agent traverses the oid tree from the point specified in the request using a depth-first search and will return either the next scalar object or instance of a tabular column. For example, using the oid tree shown in Figure 7.13, the object 1.3.1.8.1.1.2 is lexically greater than 1.3.1.8.1.1. Let us examine why. Begin at the root of the oid tree and traverse down it using a depth-first traversal, stopping when you arrive at the second-to-last node in the

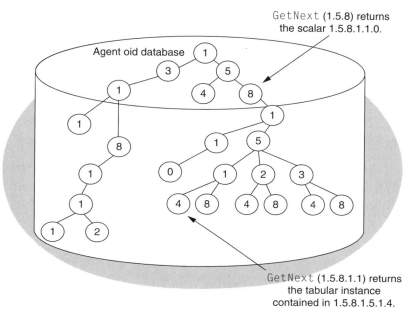

GetNext (1.5.8) returns
the scalar 1.5.8.1.1.0.

GetNext (1.5.8.1.1) returns
the tabular instance
contained in 1.5.8.1.5.1.4.

FIGURE 7.13

Examples of the GetNext operation on both tabular and scalar objects.

oid tree. If we do this, we arrive at the .1 node on the far bottom left of the figure (just above the 1 and 2 terminal nodes).

At this point, we now need to find the oid of an object instance that is lexically greater than 1.3.1.8.1.1. What this means is that either we need to find the oid of an object instance that has the last number in its oid greater than 1.3.1.8.1.1, or we need to find the first oid with one more part to its oid (i.e., the oid is longer than the one we are using by at least one dotted decimal). In this case, since 1.3.1.8.1.1 possesses six parts to its oid, and since we have exhausted all of the available oids at this ply in the oid tree, we need one with seven. Since no other nodes exist at this level, we will not be able to find an oid with a prefix of 1.3.1.8.1 that has six parts to its oid. Therefore, we must descend one more ply in the oid tree. If we do this, we find that the next level down contains two leaf nodes: 1 and 2. Appending either to the prefix of 1.3.1.8.1.1 will result in a lexically larger oid; however, the *next* lexically greater oid only results if we pick the first oid available—1. If we then choose this node and attach it to the current prefix of 1.3.1.8.1.1, we correctly arrive at the next lexically larger oid of 1.3.1.8.1.1.1.

Let's investigate a slightly more difficult oid. Let's examine how we discover the next lexically larger object instance oid to oid 1.5.4. If we begin with the depth-first search algorithm starting at node 1 in Figure 7.13 and traverse the tree down to node 1.5.4, we will first notice that we have run out of levels in the oid tree below this point. When this happens, we must use the same steps that the depth-first search algorithm would use. In this case, the algorithm would back up the tree until it found a place where it could descend down again. When the algorithm backs up one level in the tree, it will then try to descend down to a terminal leaf node. Since leaf nodes in the oid tree always represent object instances, the algorithm will correctly discover the next lexically greater instance.

To continue with the example, after we back up one level in the tree, we will continue down to .8.1.1.0 using the rules just described. We have arrived at a terminal leaf node. Examining the complete oid of the path just traversed reveals that we have found an oid for an object instance (actually a scalar object instance) of 1.5.8.1.1.0. If we compare this oid to the original one of 1.5.4, we find that we have satisfied all of the criteria of the next lexically greater oid. Eureka!

This GetNext operation is useful for several tasks. In general, a manager will often use the GetNext operation repeatedly by feeding in the oid that is returned by the operation into a subsequent call to "walk" some subset of the oid tree, or even the entire tree. The walk operation might be terminated when an object instance is encountered whose oid length exceeds the one used to start the operation. It might also be terminated when the oid of a valid object instance whose last dotted decimal that is greater than the one given is found. Some commercial SNMP toolkits provide tools with "walk" as part of their name, and they behave this way. Using these tools, several operations are available to the operator. First, it is possible to walk the entire oid tree contained in an agent by specifying 1.1 as the point of the walk. Second, it is possible for a manager to specify the "top" oid of a table and use this to walk all columnar instances, or even all rows and columnar instances within a table. This is often useful if either the manager does not know the indexes of the instances within a particular table, or the snapshot stored by the manager has grown stale.

In addition to the examples just shown for GetNext, two examples of the GetNext operation are illustrated in Figure 7.13. In the first example, the GetNext operation is executed on oid 1.5.8. Using the algorithm we described earlier for locating the next lexically greater object instance reveals that this oid is 1.5.8.1.1.0. The value returned for this object is the value of the scalar object represented by the object instance. The type of this object is specified by the object 1.5.8.1.1. The second example attempts a GetNext operation on oid 1.5.8.1.1. Using the algorithm described earlier again, we arrive at the oid 1.5.8.1.5.1.4. This oid represents an instance of a tabular object. The type of the value returned depends on the type of the columnar object.

Protocol Operation Versions

At the protocol level, SNMP has been specified as two versions. That is, two protocol specifications exist for the protocol data units (PDUs) that are transported within SNMP messages. Version 1 of the protocol operations as specified in RFC 1157 specifies the version 1 protocol operations (PDU types) that can be used.

These operations include Get, GetNext, GetResponse, Set, and TRAPv1. It also specifies the remaining parts of the format of a PDU such as the request-id, the error-status and error-index, and the variable-bindings.

Version 2 of the protocol operations is specified in RFC 1905. This document is currently a draft standard, but a revision has been approved as full standard. This document specifies the version 2 protocol operations (PDU types) that can be used. These operations include Get, GetNext, GetResponse, GetBulkSet, INFORM, TRAPv2, and Report. It also specifies the remainder of the PDU format of a PDU that includes things such as the request-id, the errorstatus and error-index, and the variable-bindings. It is important to note that as of the second version of the protocol operations, the TRAPv1 no longer exists. The GetBulk, INFORM, TRAPv2, and Report that are introduced in the specification as new PDU types represent what are essentially new SNMP protocol operations. The error-status value that is contained in the new message format has a much more detailed list of possible errors, which can be used to further isolate errors or recover from them. Lastly, the variable-bindings can now contain special values to indicate exceptions such as noSuchObject, noSuchInstance, and endOf-MibView, which further enhance the functionality of SNMP.

7.6.10 SNMPv1, SNMPv2c, and SNMPv3

Several versions of SNMP have existed since the protocol's inception in the late 1980s. The original SNMPv1 was used until it was realized that it had many SNMP message header SNMP PDU shortcomings. In particular, additional protocol operations were necessary as well as additional security features. It was at that time that work on SNMPv2 began. During that time, there were various iterations of SNMPv2. All but one of these intermediate versions has failed. The IETF has declared (or soon will) these versions as historic standards. The only version that is still used in the field is SNMPv2c as defined in RFC 1901. This version is an experimental protocol as far as the IETF is concerned, and it too will soon be reclassified as historic. Since then, SNMPv3 has been approved as a full IETF standard.

When management applications and managed devices exchange management information, they do so by exchanging SNMP messages. The basic format of an SNMP message is shown in Figure 7.14. This basic format consists of an SNMP message header and an SNMP PDU.

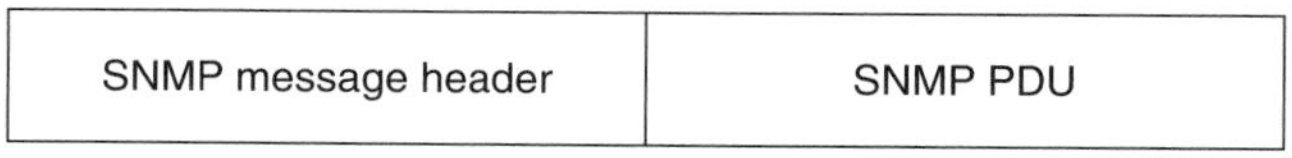

SNMP message header	SNMP PDU

FIGURE 7.14

Basic SNMP message format.

Since three versions of the SNMP protocol exist, three versions of SNMP messages are also possible. The format of the SNMPvl message version is described in the now full standard RFC 1157. An SNMPvl message is composed of an SNMPvl message header that includes a field to indicate it is an SNMPvl message, a community string (a clear-text password that is included in the message), and the version 1 protocol operation (PDU type), which can only contain SMIvl data types in the `variable-bindings`.

The format of the SNMPv2c message is described in RFC 1901. An SNMPv2c message is composed of an SNMPv2 message header (very similar to an SNMPvl message header) that includes a field that indicates it is an SNMPv2c message, a community string, and a version 2 protocol operation (PDU type), which can only contain SMIv2 data types in the `variable-bindings`, plus three exceptions: `noSuchObject`, `noSuchInstance`, and `endOfMibView`. It is important to note that SNMPv2c messages have a very similar header as SNMPvl messages, and as such, they are as (in)secure as SNMPvl messages. The big difference is that an SNMPv2c message must carry a version 2 PDU and thus the data in such PDUs must be one of the SMIv2 data types.

The format of the SNMPv3 message is described in RFC 2572. This RFC is a draft standard, but a revision has been approved as a full standard. An SNMPv3 message is composed of an SNMPv3 message header. This message header is much more extensive than the message headers defined in the earlier versions of the protocol, but does still carry a version 2 PDU, which implies that these PDUs can only contain SMIv2 data types. The SNMPv3 message header contains several new message fields. Specifically, the new header includes a field that indicates it is an SNMPv3 message (instead of SNMPvl or SNMPv2c), a message ID, the maximum message size, and other message flags. The header also contains a field indicating the security model in use. This field contains additional security-related fields that depend on the security model specified therein. For instance, if the user-based security model (USM) is specified, then the authoritative `engineID`, `engineBoots`, `engineTime`, `username`, `authenticationParameters` (MAC code), and `privacyParameters` are also included. This added header information provides for a high level of security for SNMPv3 messages.

To summarize, the difference between SNMPvl and SNMPv2c message types is that the SNMPvl message carries version 1 PDUs and thus SMIvl data types, and an SNMPv2c message carries version 2 PDUs that use SMIv2 data types. SNMPvl and SNMPv2c are similar in that they both use community-based security (i.e., plain-text passwords/pass phrases) and so both are equally insecure. The message formats of SNMPv2c and SNMPv3 differ in that SNMPv3 messages allow secure SNMP message exchanges, while SNMPv2 messages do not. SNMPv2c and SNMPv3 both carry version 2 PDUs that use SMIv2 data types. For the reader who wishes to pursue this topic further, we suggest reading RFC 2576. RFC 2576 explains the coexistence of the different SNMP versions and how to map from one to the other.

This documentation is quite useful for those wishing to migrate from one version to the other.

7.7 SUMMARY

This chapter introduced the concept of management interfaces. Management interfaces are useful because they provide a well-known and well-understood method of both modeling managed objects within a device, as well as a protocol for accessing these managed objects. The differences between many of the management interfaces we discussed are largely a matter of object definition completeness using data modeling language used for that management interface. Other differences exist, however, such as security, efficiency under certain circumstances, and portability. Of course, with any technology that is deployed in the marketplace, the most important differences between it and its competitors are the *perceived* ones. These perceptions are largely related to cost and performance effectiveness of the interface. Unfortunately, in many cases, these perceptions are not grounded in technical reasoning, but rather on the marketing literature from one corporation or another.

The chapter began with a general introduction to management interfaces and what the advantages are to standards-based and proprietary versions. The discussion then focused on specific approaches to management interfaces. The first management interface discussed was the ever-ubiquitous command-line interface. We investigated how CLIs could be managed using various scripting languages, and how this was preferable to an operator accessing each device personally. We also discussed how this interface was the most pervasive in the industry today despite its shortcomings. We explained how the widespread use of the CLI, as the preferred management interface from device vendors, was not such a great achievement from the perspective of the network operators who operate a heterogeneous network. Having to manage multiple CLI languages and perhaps different data models for each type of device in a network is expensive and wasteful of resources.

Next, we investigated the Common Object Request Broker Architecture. We gave an overview of the CORBA technology and then discussed how CORBA could be used to build management applications as well as agents in managed devices using CORBA ORBs. We investigated how you might translate between CORBA and another management interface. In particular, we showed how a CORBA translator could act as an SNMP mid-level manager and translate SNMP requests and notifications to and from CORBA, and how this would be advantageous for existing CORBA management systems that might be in use today without native SNMP support.

We then delved into a discussion of the eXtensible Markup Language. We first investigated the basic definitions and properties of XML, in particular, how XML describes a class of data objects called *XML documents* and specifies the behavior of applications that are used to process these documents. We showed how data are embedded within XML documents as strings of text and are surrounded by special markers that describe the data so that they can be parsed and displayed, and how these delineated strings were called *XML elements.* One of the greatest advantages of XML documents is that the markup used in an XML document not only describes the document's structure, but also allows you to determine which elements are associated with one another. Furthermore, XML documents are written using plain ASCII text that can be read and written by a wide variety of word processors. We showed how XML could be used as a general RPC mechanism, and potentially as a management protocol by building features on top of it. We then investigated how XML could be used as a general encapsulation of managed data stored natively in a variety of formats and, specifically, how CLI text could be encapsulated in XML for easy parsing and display by management stations. In addition, XML can be used to delineate SNMP data, both using HTTP as a transport and within bulk file transports.

Next, we discussed many forms of bulk file transfer. Bulk file transfer is a popular mechanism for offloading large volumes of data from managed devices. Once transferred to a management station, data can be processed offline at the manager's convenience. This is important for management applications such as offline TE calculations that require large volumes of data with a high degree of integrity. That is, if the same offline TE application had fetched the same managed objects over the network as the data were available, it might have missed some of the data either due to network conditions causing the responses to be lost, or because the counters on the device changed too quickly. We also discussed the issues surrounding the format of these files, and how it could make a difference for an operator with a heterogeneous network.

Finally, we discussed the Simple Network Management Protocol, the basic components of the SMI, MIB modules, and the protocol operations. We first investigated the details of the SMI and why it is so important to the definition of a MIB module. We also explained the differences and similarities between the various versions of the SMI. We then defined a MIB module as containing object definitions using the SMI. MIB modules were collectively part of the larger MIB that constituted a data model for a device. The key elements of MIBs were discussed, including objects, object instances, tables, and tabular indexing. Next, we introduced and later demonstrated the various key protocol operations provided by SNMP. Specifically, we gave an example of how some of the protocol operations could be used to retrieve instances of managed objects from an entity's MIB. In particular, we gave detailed examples of how the `Get`, `Set`, and `GetNext` operations would function under certain circumstances. We ended the section with an overview of the various versions of SNMP.

It is clear that management interfaces play an important part in the overall management of any network. Given this, you must weigh the relative benefits and weaknesses of each approach within the context of your network deployment to determine which interface or interfaces to deploy. We hope that our introduction has given you an even-handed look at many of the options for management interfaces. In many cases, one or more of the interfaces introduced in this chapter can be applied to an MPLS-enabled network. If you are a network operator, the question is how much work do you want to do to use a management interface? What are the benefits given your specific style of network operations management? If you are a device vendor, you must cater to the needs of your customers, who are in large part network operators if you are selling MPLS-enabled equipment. This probably means that you must implement at least two of the management interfaces described in this chapter—and sometimes more.

Optical Networks: Control and Management

Network management is an important part of any network. However attractive a specific technology might be, it can be deployed in a network only if it can be managed and interoperates with existing management systems. The cost of operating and managing a large network is a recurring cost and in many cases dominates the cost of the equipment deployed in the network. As a result, carriers are now paying a lot of attention to minimizing *life cycle* costs, as opposed to worrying just about upfront equipment costs.

This chapter is from *Optical Networks 2e* by Ramaswami and Sivarajan, Chapter 9; it starts with a brief introduction to network management concepts in general and how they apply to managing optical networks. This is followed with a discussion of optical layer services and how the different aspects of the optical network are managed.

8.1 NETWORK MANAGEMENT FUNCTIONS

Classically, network management consists of several functions, all of which are important to the operation of the network:

Performance management deals with monitoring and managing the various parameters that measure the performance of the network. Performance management is an essential function that enables a service provider to provide quality-of-service guarantees to their clients and to ensure that clients comply with the requirements imposed by the service provider. It is also needed to provide input to other network management functions, in particular, fault management, when anomalous conditions are detected in the network. This function is discussed further in Section 8.5.

Fault management is the function responsible for detecting failures when they happen and isolating the failed component. The network also needs to restore traffic that may be disrupted due to the failure, but this is usually considered a separate function. We will study fault management in Section 8.5.

Configuration management deals with the set of functions associated with managing orderly changes in a network. The basic function of managing the equipment in the network belongs to this category. This includes tracking the equipment in the network and managing the addition/removal of equipment, including any rerouting of traffic this may involve and the management of software versions on the equipment.

Connection management is an aspect of configuration management that deals with setting up, taking down, and keeping track of connections in a network. This function can be performed by a centralized management system. Alternatively, it can also be performed by a distributed *network control* entity. Distributed network control becomes necessary when connection setup/takedown events occur very frequently or when the network is very large and complex.

Adaptation management, also an aspect of configuration management, is applied when the network needs to convert external client signals entering the optical layer into appropriate signals inside the optical layer. We will study this and the other configuration management functions in Section 8.6.

Security management includes administrative functions such as authentication of users and setting attributes such as read and write permissions on a per-user basis. From a security perspective, the network is usually partitioned into domains, both horizontally and vertically. Vertical partitioning implies that some users may be allowed to access only certain network elements and not other network elements. For example, a local craftsperson may be allowed to access only the network elements he or she is responsible for and not other network elements. Horizontal partitioning implies that some users may be allowed to access some parameters associated with all the network elements across the network. For example, a user leasing a light path may be provided access to all the performance parameters associated with that light path across all the nodes that the light path traverses.

Data protection is a part of security that involves protecting data belonging to network users from being tapped or corrupted by unauthorized entities. This part of the problem needs to be handled by encrypting the data before its transmission and by providing the decrypting capability to legitimate users.

Accounting management is the function responsible for billing and for developing lifetime histories of the network components. This function doesn't appear to be much different for optical networks, compared to other networks, and we will not be discussing this topic further.

Safety management is an additional consideration for optical networks, needed to ensure that optical radiation conforms to limits imposed for ensuring eye safety. This subject is discussed in Section 8.7.

8.1.1 Management Framework

Most functions of network management are implemented in a centralized manner by a hierarchy of management systems. However, this method of implementation is rather slow, and it can take several hundreds of milliseconds to seconds to communicate between the management system and the different parts of the network because of the large software path overheads usually involved in this process. Decentralized methods are usually much faster than centralized methods, even in small networks with only a few nodes. Therefore, certain management functions that require rapid action may have to be decentralized, such as responding to failures and setting up and taking down connections if these must be done rapidly. For example, a SONET ring can restore failures within 60 ms, and this is possible only because this process is completely decentralized. For this reason, restoration is viewed as more of an autonomous control function rather than an integrated part of network management.

Another reason for decentralizing some of the functions arises when the network becomes very large. In this case, it becomes difficult for a single central manager to manage the entire network. Further, networks could include multiple domains administered by different managers. The managers of each domain will need to communicate with managers of other domains to perform certain functions in a coordinated manner.

Figure 8.1 provides an overview of how network management functions are implemented on a typical network. Management is performed in a hierarchical manner, involving multiple management systems in many cases. The individual components to be managed are called *network elements.* Network elements include optical line terminals (OLTs), optical add/drop multiplexers (OADMs), optical amplifiers, and optical cross-connects (OXCs). Each element is managed by its *element management system* (EMS). The element itself has a built-in *agent,* which communicates with its EMS. The agent is implemented in software, usually in a microprocessor in the network element.

The EMS is usually connected to one or more of the network elements and communicates with the other network elements in the network using a *data communication network* (DCN). In addition to the DCN, a fast *signaling channel* is also required between network elements to exchange real-time control information to manage protection switching and other functions. The DCN and signaling channel can be realized in many different ways, as will be discussed in Section 8.5.5. One example is the *optical supervisory channel* (OSC), shown in Figure 8.1, a separate wavelength dedicated to performing control and management functions, particularly for line systems with optical amplifiers.

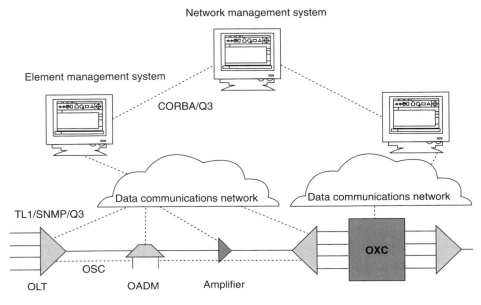

FIGURE 8.1

Overview of network management in a typical optical network, showing the network elements (OLTs, OADMs, OXCs, amplifiers), the management systems, and the associated interfaces.

Multiple EMSs may be used to manage the overall network. Typically each EMS manages a single vendor's network elements. For example, a carrier using wavelength division multiplexing (WDM) line systems from vendor A and cross-connects from vendor B will likely use two EMSs, one for managing the line systems and the other for managing the cross-connects, as shown in Figure 8.1.

The EMS itself typically has a view of one network element at a time and may not have a comprehensive view of the entire network, and also of other types of network elements that it cannot manage. Therefore, the EMSs in turn communicate with a *network management system* (NMS) or an operations support system (OSS) through a management network. The NMS has a network-wide view and is capable of managing different types of network elements from possibly different vendors.

In some cases, it is possible to have a multitiered hierarchy of management systems. Multiple OSSs may be used to perform different functions. For example, the regional Bell operating companies (RBOCs) in the United States—Verizon, Southwestern Bell, Bellsouth, and U.S. West (now part of Qwest)—use a set of OSSs from Telcordia Technologies: network monitoring and analysis (NMA) for fault management, trunk inventory and recordkeeping system (TIRKS) for inventorying the equipment in the network, and transport element management system (TEMS) for provisioning circuits. These systems date back a few decades, and introducing new network elements into these networks is often gated by the time taken to modify these systems to support the new elements.

In addition to the EMSs, a simplified local management system is usually provided to enable craftspeople and other service personnel to configure and manage individual network elements. This system is usually made available on a laptop or on a simple text-based terminal that can be plugged into individual elements to configure and provision them.

8.1.2 Information Model

The information to be managed for each network element is represented in the form of an *information model* (IM). The information model is typically an object-oriented representation that specifies the attributes of the system and the external behavior of the network element with respect to how it is managed. It is implemented in software inside the network element as well as in the element and network management systems used to manage the network element, usually in an object-oriented programming language.

An object provides an abstract way to model the parts of a system. It has certain attributes and functions associated with it. The functions describe the behavior of the object or describe operations that can be performed on the object. For example, the simplest function is to create a new object of a particular type. There may be many types, or *classes,* of objects representing different parts of a system. An important concept in object-oriented modeling is *inheritance.* One object class can be inherited from another parent object class if it has all the attributes and behaviors of the parent class but adds additional attributes and behaviors. To provide a concrete example in our context, an OLT typically consists of one or more racks of equipment. Each rack consists of multiple shelves and multiple types of shelves. Each shelf has several slots into which line cards can be plugged.

Many different types of line cards exist, such as transponders, amplifiers, multiplexers, and so on. With respect to this, there may be an object class called *rack,* which has as one of its attributes another object class called *shelf.* Multiple types of shelves may be represented in the form of inherited object classes from the parent object *shelf.* For example, there may be a common equipment shelf and a transponder shelf, which are inherited from the generic shelf object.

A shelf object has as one of its attributes another object called *slot.* Each line card object is associated with a slot. Multiple types of line cards may be represented in the form of inherited object classes from the parent object *line card.* For example, the transponder shelf may house multiple transponder types (say, one to handle SONET signals and another to handle Gigabit Ethernet signals). The common equipment shelf may house multiple types of cards, such as amplifier cards, processor cards, and power supply cards.

Each object has a variety of attributes associated with it, including the set of parameters that can be set by the management system and the set of parameters that can be monitored by the management system. As an example, each line card object normally has a state attribute associated with it, which is one of *in service, out of service,* or *fault,* and there are detailed behaviors governing transitions between these states.

Another example that is part of a typical information model is the concept of *connection trails,* which are used to model light paths. Again multiple types of trails may be defined, and each trail has a variety of associated attributes, including ones that can be configured as well as others that can be used to monitor the trail's performance.

8.1.3 Management Protocols

Most network management systems use a master–slave sort of relationship between a manager and the agents managed by the manager. The manager queries the agent to obtain the status of parameters in the network element (called the Get operation). For example, the manager may query the agent periodically for performance-monitoring information. The manager can also change the values of variables in the network element (called the Set operation) and uses this method to effect changes within the network element. For example, the manager may use this method to change the configuration of the switches inside a network element such as an OXC.

In addition to these methods, it is necessary for the agent sometimes to initiate a message to its manager. This is essential if the agent detects problems in the network element and wants to alert its manager. The agent then sends a *notification* message to its manager. Notifications also take the form of *alarms* if the condition is serious and are sometimes called *traps.*

There are multiple standards relating to network management and perhaps thousands of acronyms describing them. Here is a brief summary. In most cases, the physical management interface to the network element is through an Ethernet or RS-232 serial interface.

The Internet world uses a management framework based on the *Simple Network Management Protocol* (SNMP). SNMP is an application protocol that runs over a standard Internet Protocol (IP) stack. The manager communicates with the agents using SNMP. The information model in SNMP is called a *management information base* (MIB).

In North America, the carrier world has been using for a few decades a simple textual (or ASCII) command and control language called *Transaction Language-1* (TL1). TL1 was invented in the days when the primary means of managing network elements was through a simple terminal interface using textual command sets. However, it is still widely used today and will probably remain for a while, as many of the existing legacy management systems still mainly support only TL1.

Over the past decade, there has been a huge effort to standardize a management framework for the carrier world called the *telecommunications manage-*

ment network (TMN). TMN defined a hierarchy of management systems and object-oriented ways to model the information to be managed, and also specified protocols for communicating between managers and their agents. The protocol is called the *common management information protocol* (CMIP), which usually runs over an *open systems interconnection* (OSI) protocol stack; the associated management interface is called a *Q3* interface. Adaptations have also been defined for running CMIP over the more commonly used TCP/IP protocol stack. The specific object model is based on a standard called *guidelines for description of managed objects* (GDMO). The first two concepts of TMN, namely, the hierarchical management view and the object-oriented way of modeling information, are widely used, but the specific protocols, interfaces, and object models defined in TMN have not yet been widely adopted, mostly because of the perceived complexity of the entire system.

There is currently a significant effort under way to migrate toward a model where network elements from different vendors come with their own element management systems, and a common interface is specified between these element management systems and a centralized network management system. This interface is based on the *Common Object Request Broker Architecture* (CORBA) model. CORBA is a software industry standard developed to allow diverse systems to exchange and jointly process information and communicate with each other.

8.2 OPTICAL LAYER SERVICES AND INTERFACING

The optical layer provides light paths to other layers such as the SONET, IP, or ATM layers. In this context, the optical layer can be viewed as a *server* layer, and the higher layer that makes use of the services provided by the optical layer is the *client* layer. From this perspective, we need to specify clearly the service interface between the optical layer and its client layers. The key attributes of such a managed light path service are the following:

- Light paths need to be set up and taken down as required by the client layer and as required for network maintenance.

- Light path bandwidths need to be negotiated between the client layer and the optical layer. Typically the client layer specifies the amount of bandwidth needed on the light path.

- An adaptation function may be required at the input and output of the optical network to convert client signals to signals that are compatible with the optical layer. This function is typically provided by transponders. The specific range of signal types, including bit rates and protocols supported, need to be established between the client and the optical layer.

- Light paths need to provide a guaranteed level of performance, typically specified by the bit error rate (typical requirements are 10^{-12} or less). Adequate performance management needs to be in place inside the network to ensure this.

- Multiple levels of protection may need to be supported, for example, protected, unprotected, and protect on a best-effort basis, in addition to being able to carry low-priority data on the protection bandwidth in the network. In addition, restoration time requirements may also vary by application.

- Light paths may be unidirectional or bidirectional. Almost all light paths today are bidirectional. However, if more bandwidth is desired in one direction compared to the other, it may be desirable to support unidirectional light paths.

- A multicasting, or a *drop-and-continue,* function may need to be supported. Multicasting is useful to support distribution of video or conferencing information. In a drop-and-continue situation, a signal passing through a node is dropped locally, but a copy of it is also transmitted downstream to the next node. The drop-and-continue function is particularly useful for network survivability when multiple rings are interconnected.

- Jitter requirements exist, particularly for SONET/SDH connections. In order to meet these requirements, 3R regeneration may be needed in the network. Using 2R regeneration in the network increases the jitter, which may not be acceptable for some signals.

- There may be requirements on the maximum delay for some types of traffic, notably ESCON. In ESCON, the throughput of the protocol goes down as the propagation delay increases. This causes ESCON devices to place restrictions on the maximum allowed propagation delay (or equivalent link length) between them. This will need to be accounted for while designing the light paths.

- Extensive fault management needs to be supported so that root-cause alarms can be reported and adequate isolation of faults can be performed in the network. This is important because a single failure can trigger multiple alarms. The root-cause alarm reports the actual failure, and we need to suppress the remaining alarms. Not only are they undesirable from a management perspective, but they may also result in multiple entities in the network reacting to a single failure, which cannot be allowed. We will look at examples of this later.

Enabling the delivery of these services requires a control and management interface between the optical layer and the client layer. This interface allows the client to specify the set of light paths that are to be set up or taken down and to set service parameters associated with those light paths, and enables the optical layer to provide performance and fault management information to the client layer. This interface can take on one of two facets. The simple interface used today is through the management system. A separate management system communicates with the optical-layer EMS, and the EMS in turn then manages the optical layer.

The present method of operation works fine as long as light paths are set up fairly infrequently and remain nailed down for long periods of time. It is quite possible that, in the future, light paths are provisioned and taken down more dynamically in large networks. In such a scenario, it would make sense to specify a *signaling* interface between the optical layer and the client layer. For instance, an IP router could signal to an associated optical cross-connect to set up and take down light paths and specify their levels of protection through such an interface.

Different philosophies exist as to whether such an interface is desirable or not. Some carriers are of the opinion that they should decouple optical layer management from its client layers and plan and operate the optical network separately. This approach makes sense if the optical layer is to serve multiple types of client layers, and allows its management to be decoupled from a specific client layer. Others would like tight coupling between the client and optical layers. This makes sense if the optical layer primarily serves a single client layer, and also if there is a need to set up and take down connections rapidly as we previously discussed. We will discuss this issue further in Section 8.6.

8.3 LAYERS WITHIN THE OPTICAL LAYER

The optical layer is a complicated entity performing several functions, such as multiplexing wavelengths, switching and routing wavelengths, and monitoring network performance at various levels in the network. In order to help delineate management functions and in order to provide suitable boundaries between different equipment types, it is useful to further subdivide the optical layer into several sublayers. The International Telecommunications Union (ITU) has identified three such layers within the optical layer, as shown in Figure 8.2. At the top is the *optical channel* (OCh) layer. This layer takes care of end-to-end routing of the light paths.

We have been using the term *light path* to denote an optical connection. More precisely, a light path is an optical channel trail between two nodes that carries

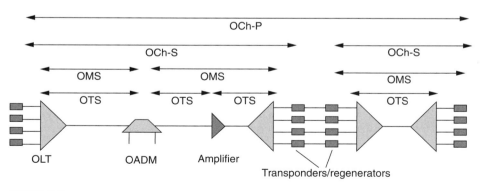

FIGURE 8.2

Layers within the optical layer, showing OCh-P, OCh-S, OMS, and OTS layers.

an entire wavelength's worth of traffic. A light path traverses many links in the network, wherein it is multiplexed with many other wavelengths carrying other light paths. It may also get regenerated along the way. Note that we do not include any electronic time-division multiplexing functions in the optical layer. This is a higher-layer (e.g., SONET/SDH) function. So a 10 Gbps connection between two nodes that is carried through without any electronic multiplexing/demultiplexing would be considered a light path.

Each link between OLTs or OADMs represents an *optical multiplex section* (OMS) carrying multiple wavelengths. Each OMS in turn consists of several link segments, each segment being the portion of the link between two optical amplifier stages. Each of these portions is an *optical transmission section* (OTS). The OTS consists of the OMS along with an additional OSC, which we will discuss further in Section 8.5.7.

The optical channel layer itself is further subdivided into multiple sublayers. ITU G.709 describes these sublayers. To keep the discussion simple, we will use some terms that differ slightly from the ITU definitions. An *optical channel–transparent section* (OCh-TS) represents the section of a light path within an all-optical subnetwork. Within this section, a light path is carried optically without any conversion into the electrical domain. At the boundary of an OCh-TS, a light path is regenerated. Just above the OCh-TS is the *optical channel–section* (OCh-S). This layer adds some overheads to the light path, such as forward error correction (FEC), to condition the signal for transport over an all-optical subnet. Finally, the *optical channel–path* (OCh-P) represents the end-to-end transport of a light path across multiple regenerators in the path.

In principle, once the interfaces between the different layers are defined, it is possible for vendors to provide standardized equipment ranging from just optical amplifiers to WDM links to entire WDM networks. Equally important, the layers help us break down the management functions necessary in the network, as we will see later in this chapter. For example, dropping and adding wavelengths is a function performed at the optical channel layer. Monitoring optical power on each wavelength also belongs to this layer, but monitoring total power belongs either to the OTS layer or OMS layer, depending on whether the optical supervisory channel is included or not.

The preceding definition of an optical layer does not include optical networks that may be able to provide more sophisticated packet-switched services, such as virtual circuits or datagrams. Photonic packet-switched networks can potentially provide such services; however, these types of networks are several years away from commercial realization.

8.4 MULTIVENDOR INTEROPERABILITY

Service providers like to deploy equipment from multiple vendors that operate together in a single network. This is desirable to reduce the dependence on any single vendor as well as to drive down costs, and is one of the driving factors behind network standards. For instance, without standards, we would have to have special interoperability between every pair of vendors, rather than having to deal with a single standardized interface to which all vendors conform. Another important effect of standards is that they allow operations personnel to get trained on a single type of equipment and then become capable of managing that type of equipment from a variety of vendors, in contrast to being trained separately to deal with each vendor's equipment.

However, interoperability between WDM equipment from different vendors is easier said than done. The SONET standards were established in the late 1980s, and only recently have we been able to achieve interoperability between equipment from different vendors. In the case of WDM, achieving interoperability at the optical level is made particularly difficult by the fact that the interface is a fairly complex analog interface, rather than a simple digital interface. The set of parameters that we would need to standardize to achieve interoperability include optical wavelength; optical power; signal-to-noise ratio; bit rate; and the supervisory channel wavelength, bit rate, and its contents.

Different vendors use significantly different parameters in their link design and make different compromises among the various impairments. For example, vendor A might choose to use directly modulated lasers and dispersion compensation inside the network to eliminate dispersion. Vendor B instead might choose to use externally modulated lasers and avoid dispersion compensation inside the network. This would make it difficult to have vendor A's equipment and vendor B's equipment on opposite sides of the same WDM link. Even if some interoperability can be achieved, it is quite difficult to locate and isolate faults in such an environment.

Rather than trying to solve this complex problem, the practical solution toward interoperability is to use regenerators or transponders to interconnect disparate all-optical subnetworks, as shown in Figure 8.3. While this approach may result

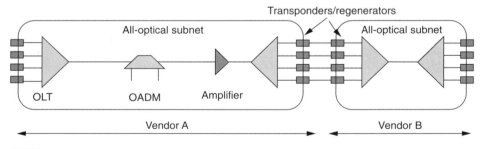

FIGURE 8.3

Interoperability between WDM systems from different vendors, showing all-optical subnets from different vendors interconnected through transponders/regenerators.

in higher equipment costs, it provides clear-cut boundaries between all-optical subnets, making it easier to locate and identify faults. Each all-optical subnet would include equipment from a single vendor. For example, a subnet could simply be a WDM link with some intermediate add/drops. So a service provider could deploy vendor A's equipment on one link and vendor B's equipment on another link and have them interoperate through transponders. The interface between the transponders would be either SONET/SDH or the digital wrapper, which we will discuss in Section 8.5.7. Using the digital wrapper allows the service provider to manage the entire network effectively.

The standards bodies initially started with the goal of establishing optical interoperability and are still pursuing this (ITU G.959, Telcordia GR-2918), although it will be a while before this comes to fruition in a practical network. Meanwhile there is a consensus building around the digital wrapper standard (ITU G.709).

In addition to accomplishing interoperability at the data level, we also need to have interoperability as far as the control and signaling protocols are concerned, particularly if we are using the distributed methods discussed in Section 8.6.2. This is a goal that appears to be accomplishable, given that similar functions have been standardized for other networks in the past.

8.5 PERFORMANCE AND FAULT MANAGEMENT

As we stated earlier, the goal of performance management is to enable service providers to provide guaranteed quality of service to the users of their network. This usually requires monitoring of the performance parameters for all the connections supported in the network and taking any actions necessary to ensure that the desired performance goals are met.

Performance management is closely tied in to fault management. Fault management involves detecting problems in the network and alerting the management systems appropriately through alarms. If a certain parameter is being monitored and its value falls outside its preset range, the network equipment generates an alarm. For example, we may monitor the power levels of an incoming signal and declare a loss-of-signal (LOS) alarm if we see the power level drop below a certain threshold. In other cases, alarms could be triggered by outright failures, such as the failure of a line card or other components in the system.

Fault management also includes restoring service in the event of failures. This function is considered an autonomous network control function because it is typically a distributed application without network management intervention (except for configuring various protection parameters up front, reporting events, and performing maintenance operations).

8.5.1 The Impact of Transparency

The light paths provided by the optical layer need to be managed just like SONET and SDH connections are managed. To a large extent how much management can be provided depends on the level of transparency provided by the optical layer. Different levels of transparency are possible, based on the range of signals, bit rates, and protocols that can be carried on a light path.

In a purely transparent network, a light path will be capable of carrying analog and digital signals with arbitrary bit rates and protocol formats. This is the utopian vision of optical networking and would allow service providers to offer a range of services without any constraints and provide future-proofing in case the service mix changes over time or when new services are added. However, such a network is very difficult to engineer and manage. It is difficult to engineer because the various physical layer impairments that must be taken into account in the network design are critically dependent on the type of signal (analog versus digital) and the bit rate. It is difficult to manage because the management system may have no prior knowledge of the protocols or bit rates being used in the network. Therefore, it is not possible to access overhead bits in the transmitted data to obtain performance-related measures. This makes it difficult to monitor the bit error rate.

Other parameters such as optical power levels and optical signal-to-noise ratios can be measured. Most systems today only measure optical power levels. However, small, portable optical spectrum analyzers are now becoming available to measure the signal-to-noise ratio, making it practical to incorporate this measurement in newer systems. However, the acceptable values for these parameters depend on the type of signal. Unless the management system is told what type of signal is being carried on a light path, it will not be able to determine whether the measured power levels and signal-to-noise ratios fall within acceptable limits.

At the other extreme, we could design a network that carries data at a fixed bit rate (say, 2.5 Gbps or 10 Gbps) and of a particular format (say, SONET/SDH only). Such a network would be very cost effective to build and manage. However, it does not offer service providers the flexibility they need to deliver a wide variety of services using a single network infrastructure, and it is not future-proof at all.

Most optical networks deployed today fall somewhere in between these two extremes. The network is designed to handle digital data at arbitrary bit rates up to a certain specified maximum (say, 10 Gbps) and a variety of protocol formats such as SONET/SDH, IP, ATM, Gigabit Ethernet, and ESCON. These networks make use of a number of unique techniques to provide management functions, as we will see next.

8.5.2 **BER Measurement**

The bit error rate (BER) is the key performance attribute associated with a light path. The BER can be detected only when the signal is available in the electrical domain, typically at regenerator or transponder locations. Framing protocols used in SONET and SDH include overhead bytes. Part of this overhead consists of parity check bytes by which the BER can be computed. This provides a direct measure of the BER. Similarly, the digital wrapper overhead developed specifically for the optical layer also allows the BER to be measured. We will discuss the digital wrapper in Section 8.5.7. As long as the client signal data are encapsulated using the SONET/SDH or digital wrapper overhead, we can measure the BER and guarantee the performance within the optical layer.

Given the complexity of optical physical layer designs, it is difficult to estimate the BER accurately based on indirect measurements of parameters such as the optical signal power or the optical signal-to-noise ratio. These parameters may be used to provide some measure of signal quality and may be used as triggers for events such as maintenance or possibly protection switching (which could be based, for example, on loss of power and signal detection) but not to measure BER.

8.5.3 Optical Trace

Light paths pass through multiple nodes and through multiple cards within the equipment deployed at each node. It is desirable to have a unique identifier associated with each light path. For example, this identifier may include the IP address of the originating network element along with the actual identity of the transponder card within that network element where the light path terminates. This identifier is called an *optical path trace*. The trace enables the management system to identify, verify, and manage the connectivity of a light path. In addition it provides the ability to perform fault isolation in the event that incorrect connections are made.

A trace can be used in different layers within the optical layer. For instance, a light path passes through multiple nodes and potentially gets regenerated along the way. We can verify the end-to-end connectivity of a light path using an *optical channel-path trace*. This trace is inserted at the beginning of the light path and monitored at various locations along its path. In order to localize and verify connectivity between regenerator locations, we make use of an additional identifier called the *optical channel-section trace,* which is associated between each adjacent pair of regeneration points of the light path. Within an all-optical subnet, we can use an *optical channel-transparent section trace*. The last two traces are inserted and removed at regenerator locations in the network. We will look at different ways of carrying the trace information in Section 8.5.7.

8.5.4 Alarm Management

In a network, a single failure event may cause multiple alarms to be generated all over the network and incorrect actions to be taken in response to the failed condition. Consider, in particular, a simple example. When a link fails, all light paths on that link fail. This could be detected at the nodes at the end of the failed link, which would then issue alarms for each individual light path as well as report an entire link failure. In addition, all the nodes through which these light paths traverse could detect the failure of these light paths and issue alarms. For example, in a network with 32 light paths on a given link, each traversing through two

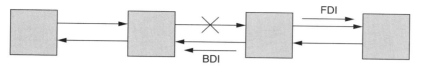

FIGURE 8.4

Forward and backward defect indicator signals and their use in a network.

intermediate nodes, the failure of a single link could trigger a total of 129 alarms (1 for the link failure and 4 for each light path at each of the nodes associated with the light path). It is clearly the management system's job to report the single root-cause alarm in this case, namely, the failure of the link, and suppress the remaining 128 alarms.

Alarm suppression is accomplished by using a set of special signals, called the *forward defect indicator* (FDI) and the *backward defect indicator* (BDI). Figure 8.4 shows the operation of the FDI and BDI signals. When a link fails, the node downstream of the failed link detects it and generates a *defect condition.* For instance, a defect condition could be generated because of a high BER on the incoming signal or an outright loss of light on the incoming signal. If the defect persists for a certain time period (typically a few seconds), the node generates an alarm.

Immediately on detecting a defect, the node inserts an FDI signal downstream to the next node. The FDI signal propagates rapidly and nodes further downstream receive the FDI and suppress their alarms. The FDI signal is also sometimes referred to as the *alarm indication signal* (AIS). A node detecting a defect also sends a BDI signal upstream to the previous node, to notify that node of the failure. If this previous node didn't send out an FDI, it then knows that the link to the next node downstream has failed.

Note further that separate FDI and BDI signals are needed for different sub-layers within the optical layer, for example, to distinguish between link failures and failures of individual light paths, or to distinguish between the failure of a section of the link between amplifier locations and that of the entire link. The exact types and behavior of defect indicators for the optical layer are being standardized currently (ITU G.709). Figure 8.5 illustrates one possible use of these different indicator signals in a network. Suppose there is a link cut between OLT A and amplifier B as shown in the figure. Amplifier B detects the cut. It immediately inserts an OMS-FDI signal downstream indicating that all channels in the multiplexed group have failed and also an OTS-BDI signal upstream to OLT A. The OMS-FDI is transmitted as part of the overhead associated with the OMS layer, and the OTS-BDI is transmitted as part of the overhead associated with the OTS layer.

Note that an OMS-FDI is transmitted downstream and not an OTS-FDI. This is because the defect information needs to be propagated all the way downstream to the network element where the OMS layer is terminated, which, in this case,

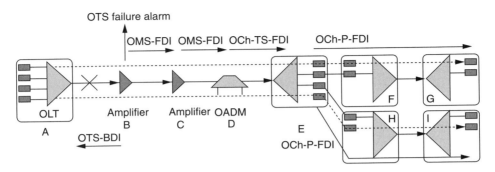

FIGURE 8.5

Using hierarchical defect indicator signals in a network. Defect indicators are used at the OTS, OMS, and the various OCh sublayers.

is OADM D. Amplifier C downstream receives the OMS-FDI and passes it on. OADM D, which is the next node downstream, receives the OMS-FDI and determines that all the light paths on the incoming link have failed. Some of these light paths are dropped locally and others are passed through.

For each light path passed through, the OADM generates the OCh-TS-FDIs and sends them downstream. The OCh-TS-FDIs are transmitted as part of the OCh-TS overhead. At the end of the all-optical subnet, at OLT E, the wavelengths are demultiplexed and terminated in transponders/regenerators. Therefore, the OCh-TS layer is terminated here. OLT E receives the OCh-TS-FDIs. It then generates OCh-P-FDI indicators for each failed light path and sends that downstream to the ultimate destination of each light path as part of the OCh-P overhead. Finally, the only node that issues an alarm is node B.

Another major reason for using the defect indicator signals is that defects are used to trigger protection switching. For example, nodes adjacent to a failure detect the failure and may trigger a protection-switching event to reroute traffic around the failure. At the same time, nodes further downstream and upstream of the failure may think that other links have failed and decide to reroute traffic as well. A node receiving an FDI knows whether it should or shouldn't initiate protection switching. For example, if the protection-switching method requires the nodes immediately adjacent to the failure to reroute traffic, other nodes receiving the FDI signal will not invoke protection switching. On the other hand, if protection switching is done by the nodes at the end of a light path, then a node receiving an FDI initiates protection switching if it is the end point of the associated light path.

8.5.5 Data Communication Network and Signaling

The element management system communicates with the different network elements through the data communication network. This DCN is usually a standard

TCP/IP or OSI network. If the DCN is sufficiently well connected (2-connected, to be more precise), then the DCN can stay up even if there is a failure in the network. The DCN can be transported in several ways:

1. Through a separate out-of-band network outside the optical layer. Carriers can make use of their existing TCP/IP or OSI networks for this purpose. If such a network is not available, dedicated leased lines could be used for this purpose. This option is viable for network elements that are located in big central offices where such connectivity is easily available, but not viable for network elements such as optical amplifiers that are located in remote huts in the field.

2. Through the OSC on a separate wavelength (see Section 8.5.7). This option is available for WDM line equipment that processes the optical transmission section and multiplex section layers, where the optical supervisory channel is made available. For example, optical amplifiers are managed using this approach. However, this option is not available to equipment that only looks at the optical channel layer, such as optical cross-connects.

3. Through the rate-preserving or digital wrapper in-band optical channel layer overhead techniques, described in Section 8.5.7. This option is useful for equipment that only looks at the optical channel layer and does not process the multiplex and transmission section layers, such as optical cross-connects. Also, it is available only at locations where the light path is processed in the electrical domain, that is, at regenerator or transponder locations.

Table 8.1 summarizes the applicability of different DCN options available for each type of network element. We assume that OADMs are part of the line system that includes OLTs and amplifiers. Access to the optical supervisory channel is typically restricted to elements within a line system due to the proprietary nature of the OSC.

Table 8.1 Methods for Realizing the DCN for Different Network Elements

Network Element	Out-of-Band	OSC	Rate-Preserving Overhead or Digital Wrapper
OLT with transponders	Yes	Yes	Yes
OADM	Yes	Yes	Yes (for dropped channels)
Amplifier	No	Yes	No
OXC with regenerators	Yes	No	Yes
All-optical OXC (no regenerators)	Yes	No	No

Note: *The OADM is assumed to have transponders for channels that are dropped and added, but not for channels that are passed through.*

In addition to the DCN, in many cases, a fast signaling network is needed between network elements. This allows the network elements to exchange critical information between them in real time. For instance, the FDI and BDI signals need to be propagated quickly to the nodes along a light path. Other such signals include information needed to implement fast protection switching in the network. Just as with the DCN, the signaling network can be implemented using dedicated out-of-band connections, the optical supervisory channel, or through one of the overhead techniques.

8.5.6 Policing

One function of the management system is to monitor the wavelength and power levels of signals being input to the network to ensure that they meet the requirements imposed by the network. As we previously discussed, the acceptable power levels will depend on the signal types and bit rates. The types and bit rates are specified by the user, and the network can then set thresholds for the parameters as appropriate for each signal type and monitor them accordingly. This includes threshold values for the parameters at which alarms must be set off. The thresholds depend on the data rate, wavelength, and specific location along the path of the light path, and degradations may be measured relative to their original values.

Another more important function is to monitor the actual service being utilized by the user. For example, the service provider may choose to provide two services, say, an ESCON service and an OC-3 service, by leasing a transparent light path to the user. The two services may be tariffed differently. With a purely transparent network, it is difficult to prevent a user who opts for the ESCON service from sending OC-3 traffic. What this implies is that services based on leasing wavelengths will likely be tariffed based on a specified maximum bit rate, with the user being allowed to send any signal up to the specified maximum bit rate.

8.5.7 Optical Layer Overhead

Supporting the optical path trace, defect indicators, and BER measurement requires the use of some sort of overhead in the optical layer. We have alluded indirectly to some of these overheads earlier, for example, the use of the SONET/SDH overhead to measure the BER and the use of the optical supervisory channel to carry some of the defect indicator signals. In this section, we describe four different methods for carrying the optical layer overhead. These methods are illustrated in Figure 8.6 and compared in Table 8.2.

The pilot tone approach and the optical supervisory channel are useful to carry overhead information within an all-optical subnetwork. At the boundaries of each subnetwork, the signal is regenerated (3R) by converting into the electrical domain and back. The rate-preserving overhead and the digital wrapper can be used to carry overhead information across an entire optical network through multiple all-optical subnetworks.

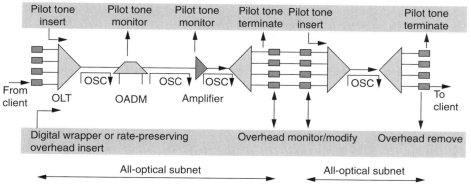

◼ Transponders/regenerators

FIGURE 8.6

Types of optical-layer overhead techniques. The OSC is used hop by hop. The pilot tone is inserted by a transmitter and can be monitored at elements in an all-optical subnet until it is terminated at a receiver. The digital wrapper or rate-preserving overhead is used end to end across multiple subnets through intermediate regenerators.

Table 8.2 Applications of Different Optical-Layer Overhead Techniques

	All-Optical Subnet		End to End	
Application	**OSC**	**Pilot Tone**	**Rate Preserving**	**Digital Wrapper**
Trace	OTS	OCh-TS	OCh-P, OCh-S	OCh-P, OCh-S
DIs	OTS, OMS, OCh-TS	None	OCh-P	OCh-P
Performance monitoring	None	Optical power	BER	BER
Client signal compatibility	Any	Any	SONET/SDH	Any

Note: *The different techniques apply to different sublayers within the optical layer—namely, OTS, OMS, OCh-S, or OCh layers. The trace and DI signals are defined at multiple sublayers.*

Pilot Tone or Subcarrier Modulated Overhead

Here, the overhead is realized by modulating the optical carrier (wavelength) of a light path with an additional subcarrier signal. This signal is also sometimes called a *pilot tone*. As long as the modulation depth of this signal is kept small compared to the data, typically between 5–10 percent, and the subcarrier frequency is chosen carefully, the data are relatively unaffected as a result. The pilot tone itself may be amplitude or frequency modulated at a low rate, say, a few kilobits per second, to carry additional overhead information.

At intermediate locations, a small fraction of the optical power can be tapped off and the pilot tones extracted without receiving and retransmitting the entire signal. Note that the pilot tones on each wavelength can be extracted from the composite WDM signal carrying all the wavelengths without requiring each wavelength to be demultiplexed.

The pilot tone frequency needs to be chosen carefully. First, it should have minimal overlap with the data bandwidth. For instance, a light path carrying SONET data at 2.5 Gbps has relatively little spectral content below 2 MHz, and a pilot tone in the 1- to 2-MHz range can be added with minimal impact to the data. The pilot tone frequency also needs to lie above the gain modulation cutoff of the erbium-doped optical amplifiers, which is typically around 100 kHz. Tones below this frequency will cause the amplifier gain to vary with the pilot tone amplitude, causing this modulation to be imposed on other channels as undesirable "ghost" tones or crosstalk. The pilot tone frequency can also be chosen to lie above the data band, in this example, say, above 2.5 GHz, but it is relatively more expensive to process signals at higher frequencies than at lower frequencies.

The advantages of the pilot tone approach are that it is relatively inexpensive and that it allows monitoring of the overhead in transparent networks without requiring knowledge of the actual protocol or bit rate of the signal.

The disadvantages of this approach are that it cannot be used to monitor the BER, and the pilot tone can be modified only at the transmitter or at a regenerator and not at the intermediate nodes. Thus, it can be used for the OCh-TS trace function inside a transparent subnetwork between regenerator points, but cannot be used to insert FDI and BDI signals at intermediate nodes without a regenerator. The trace function can be accomplished using pilot tones in several possible ways. For example, each light path could have a unique pilot tone frequency, which by itself serves as the trace. Alternatively, we could have a unique pilot tone frequency for each wavelength, and the pilot tone can be modulated with a digital signal containing a unique light path identifier.

Optical Supervisory Channel

In systems with line amplifiers, a separate OSC is used to convey information associated with monitoring the state of the amplifiers along the link, particularly if these amplifiers are in remote locations where other direct access is not possible. The OSC is also used to control the line amplifiers, for example, turning them on or off for test purposes. It can also be used to carry the DCN, as well as some of the overhead information.

The OSC is carried on a wavelength different from the wavelengths used for carrying traffic. It is separated from the other wavelengths at each amplifier stage and received, processed, and retransmitted, as shown in Figure 8.7.

The choice of the exact wavelength for the OSC involves a number of trade-offs. Figure 8.8 shows the usage of various wavelength bands in the network for

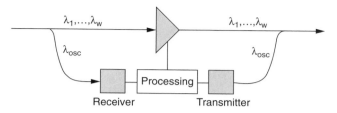

FIGURE 8.7

The optical supervisory channel, which is terminated at each amplifier location.

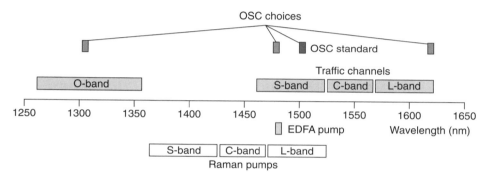

FIGURE 8.8

Usage of wavelengths in the network. Traffic is carried on the O (original), S (short), C (conventional), or L (long) wavelength bands. Raman pumps, if used, are located about 80–100 nm below the signal.

carrying traffic, for pumping the erbium or Raman amplifiers, and for the OSC. The OSC could be located within the same band as the traffic-bearing channels, or in a separate band located away from the traffic-bearing channels. In the latter situation, it is easier to filter out and reinsert the OSC at each amplifier location. However, we need to locate the OSC away from the Raman pumps if they are used in the system.

Perhaps the only advantage of locating the OSC in the same band as the traffic-bearing channels is a slight reduction in amplifier noise. For instance, if a two-stage amplifier design is used, the in-band OSC can be filtered out after the first stage along with the amplifier noise that is present at this wavelength.

For WDM systems operating in the C-band, the popular choices for the OSC wavelength include 1310 nm, 1480 nm, 1510 nm, or 1620 nm. Using the 1310-nm band for the OSC precludes the use of this band for carrying traffic. The 1480-nm wavelength was considered only because of the easy availability of lasers at that wavelength—it happens to be one of the wavelengths used to pump an erbium-doped fiber amplifier (EDFA). For the same reason, however, there can be some undesirable interactions between the OSC laser and the EDFA pump, so this is not a popular choice.

After going through some of these trade-offs, the ITU has adopted the 1510-nm wavelength as the preferred choice. This wavelength is outside the EDFA pass-band, does not coincide with an EDFA pump wavelength, and lies outside the C-band and L-band. Note, however, that this wavelength falls in the S-band and may also overlap with Raman pumps for the L-band.

Yet another choice used by some vendors is the 1620-nm wavelength, on the outer edge of the L-band. This choice avoids most of the preceding problems, except that we have to be careful about separating this channel from a traffic-bearing channel toward the edge of the L-band.

The OSC can be used to carry OTS traces and defect indicators, as well as OMS and OCh-TS defect indicators.

Rate-Preserving Overhead

The idea here is to make use of the existing SONET/SDH overhead that is used with most of the signals entering the optical layer. This overhead includes several bytes that are currently unused. Some of these bytes can be used by the optical layer. These bytes can also be used to add forward error correction (FEC), which improves the optical-layer link budget. This technique can be used only at locations where the signal is available in electrical form, that is, at regenerator locations or at the edges of the network. Unlike the pilot tone method, it cannot be used inside a transparent optical subnetwork.

The advantages of this method are the following: First, it can be used with the existing equipment in the network. For example, a new network element with this capability can communicate with other network elements of the same type through intermediate WDM and SONET equipment that is already present in the network. Second, it retains the existing hierarchy of bit rates in the SONET/SDH standards, without the need for creating a new hierarchy of rates that would be needed with the digital wrapper technique to be discussed next. This allows existing SONET/SDH chipsets, such as clock-recovery circuits, receivers, modulators, and overhead processing chips, to be used without requiring the development of a new set of components to support the new rates.

The disadvantages of this method are the following: First, the number of unused bytes available is limited and may not offer sufficient bandwidth to carry all the optical-layer overhead and FEC. Second, while the SONET/SDH standards specify the set of unused bytes, several vendors have already made use of some of these bytes for their own proprietary reasons, which makes it difficult to determine which set of bytes are truly unused! Third, it does not work with signals that don't use SONET/SDH framing, such as Fibre Channel or Gigabit Ethernet.

Digital Wrapper Overhead

Here, a new set of overhead bytes is added to the signal as it enters the optical layer and removed when the signal is handed back to the client layer. This scheme offers essentially the same capabilities as the rate-preserving overhead discussed previously. The digital wrapper defines a new set of overheads associated with the optical layer and can be used instead of the SONET/SDH overhead. It is being standardized in the ITU.

The advantages of this method are the following: First, sufficient overhead bytes can be added so as to provide adequate FEC and support the DCN as well as to allow for future needs. Second, a new standard based on this technique would allow better interoperability among multiple vendors through regenerators. Third, the technique is not limited to SONET/SDH signals. The wrapper can be used to encapsulate a variety of different signals, such as Fibre Channel and Gigabit Ethernet.

The main disadvantages of the digital wrapper approach are that it is not suitable for use with legacy equipment, and that it requires the development of a new set of components to support the new hierarchy of bit rates. However, new components have already been developed to support the wrapper, and it is now available on many WDM products.

The digital wrapper is ideally suited to carrying OCh-section and path layer traces and defect indicators, as well as providing other overheads for management, such as those used by an automatic protection-switching (APS) protocol for signaling between network elements during failures.

8.6 CONFIGURATION MANAGEMENT

We can break down configuration management functions into three parts: managing the equipment in the network, managing the connections in the network, and managing the adaptation of client signals into the optical layer.

8.6.1 Equipment Management

In general, the principles of managing optical networking equipment are no different from those of managing other high-speed networking equipment. We must be able to keep track of the actual equipment in the system (e.g., number and location of optical-line amplifiers) as well as the equipment in each network element and its capabilities. For example, in a terminal of a point-to-point WDM system, we may want to keep track of the maximum number of wavelengths and the number of wavelengths currently equipped, whether there are optical pre-amplifiers and power amplifiers or not, and so forth.

Among the considerations in designing network equipment is that we should be able to add to existing equipment in a modular fashion. For instance, we should be able to add additional wavelengths (up to a designed maximum number) without disrupting the operation of the existing wavelengths. Also, ideally the failure of one channel shouldn't affect other channels, and the failed channel should be capable of being serviced without affecting the other channels.

An issue that comes up in this regard is the use of arrayed multiwavelength components versus separate components for individual wavelengths, such as multiwavelength laser arrays instead of individual lasers for each wavelength. Using arrayed components can reduce the cost and footprint of the equipment. However, if one element in the array fails, the entire array will have to be replaced. This reduces the system availability, as replacing the array will involve disrupting the operation of multiple channels, and not just a single channel. Using arrays also increases the replacement cost of the module. Therefore, there is always a trade-off between obtaining reduced cost and footprint on one front against system availability and replacement cost on the other front.

We may also want to start out by deploying the equipment in the form of a point-to-point link and later upgrade it to handle ring or other network configurations. And we may desire flexibility in associating specific port cards in the equipment with specific wavelengths. For example, it is better to have a system where we can choose the wavelength transmitted out of a port card independently of what slot it is located in.

Another problem in WDM systems is the need to maintain an inventory of wavelength-specific spare cards. For example, each channel may be realized by using a card with a wavelength-specific laser in it. Thus, you would need to stock spare cards for each wavelength. This can be avoided by using a wavelength-selectable (or tunable) laser on each card instead of a wavelength-specific laser; such devices are only now becoming commercially available at reasonable cost.

8.6.2 Connection Management

The optical network provides light paths, or more generally, circuit-switched connections, to its user. Connection management deals with setting up connections, keeping track of them, and taking them down when they are not needed anymore.

The traditional telecommunications way of providing this function is through a centralized management system, or rather a set of systems. However, this process has been extremely cumbersome and slow. The process usually involves configuring equipment from a variety of vendors, each with its own management system, and usually one network element at a time. Moreover, interoperability between management systems, while clearly feasible, has been difficult to achieve in practice. Finally, service providers in many cases deploy equipment only when needed. The net result of this process is that it can take months for a service provider to turn up a new connection in response to a user request. Given this fact, it is not surprising that once a connection is set up, it remains in effect for a fairly significant period of time, ranging from several months to years!

As optical networks evolve, connections are getting more dynamic and networks are becoming bigger and more complex. Service providers would like to provide connections to their customers rapidly, ideally in seconds to minutes, and not impose long-term holding time commitments on these connections. In other words, users would *dial up* bandwidth as needed.

Supporting all this requires carriers to predeploy equipment (and bandwidth) ahead of time in the network and having methods in place to be able to turn on the service rapidly when needed. This is becoming a significant competitive issue in differentiating one carrier from another. This method of operation also stimulates what is called *bandwidth trading,* where carriers trade their unused bandwidth with other carriers for increasingly shorter durations to improve the utilization of their networks and maximize their revenue.

Due to the preceding reasons, we are seeing a trend toward a more distributed form of control for connection management. Distributed control protocols have been used in IP and ATM networks. They have also had a fair degree of success with respect to standardization and accomplishing interoperability across vendor boundaries. We can make use of similar protocols for performing these functions in the optical layer.

Distributed connection control has several components to it:

Topology management: Each node in the network maintains a database of the network topology and the current set of resources available as well as the resources used to support traffic. In the event of any changes in the network, for example, a link capacity change, the updated topology information needs to be propagated to all the network nodes. We can use the same techniques used in IP networks for this purpose. Nodes periodically, or in the event of changes, *flood* the updated information to all the network nodes. We can use an Internet routing and topology management protocol such as OSPF or IS-IS, with suitable modifications to represent optical-layer topology information, and update it automatically.

At the time the network is brought up, or whenever there is a topology change (link/node addition or removal), nodes will need to automatically discover the network topology. This is done typically by having adjacent nodes exchange information to determine their local connectivity (to their neighbors) and then broadcasting this information to all the network nodes using the same procedure used to convey topology changes.

Route computation: When a connection is requested from the network, the network needs to find a route and obtain resources along the route to support this connection. This can be done by applying a routing algorithm on the topology database of the network. The routing algorithm needs to take into account the various constraints imposed by the network, such as wavelength conversion ability, and the capacity available on each link of the network. In addition to computing routes for carrying the *working* traffic, the algorithm may also have to compute *protection* routes for the connection, which are used in the event of failures.

Signaling protocol: Once routes are computed, the connection needs to be set up. This process involves reserving the resources required for the connection and setting the actual switches inside the network to set up the connection. The process requires nodes to exchange messages with other nodes. Typically, the destination or source of the connection signals to each of the nodes along the connection path to perform this function. Protocols based on MPLS Internet signaling protocols such as RSVP-TE can be used for this purpose. The same protocols can also be used to take down connections when they are no longer needed.

The process of setting up or taking down a connection must be executed carefully. For example, if the connection is simply taken down by the source and destination, then the intermediate nodes may sense the loss of light on the connection as a failure condition and trigger unwanted alarms and protection switching. This can be avoided by suitable coordination among the nodes along the route of the light path.

Signaling network: Nodes need a signaling channel to exchange control information with other nodes. We described the many options available to attain this in Section 8.5.5.

Interaction with Other Layers

One important aspect of the connection management protocols is in how they interact with the client layers of the optical layer. With IP routers emerging as the dominant clients of the optical layer, and because the optical layer control protocols are based on Internet protocols, the issue of how these protocols interact in particular with the IP layer becomes a crucial issue.

Different types of interactions are likely needed for different scenarios, such as metro versus long-haul networks, incumbent versus new service providers, multiservice versus IP service-centric providers, and facility ownership versus leasing providers.

There are many schools of thought with respect to this interaction, ranging from the so-called overlay model to a peer model. Figure 8.9 shows a variety of models being considered today.

Figure 8.9(a) shows the *overlay model.* In this model, the optical layer has its own control plane, and the higher layers have their own independent control planes. The optical layer provides a *user network interface* (UNI), through which higher (client) layers can request connections from the optical layer. Within the optical layer, different subnetworks can interoperate through a standardized *network-to-network interface* (NNI). This approach allows the connection control software for the optical layer to be tailored specifically to the optical layer without having to worry about developing a single unified piece of control software. It also allows the optical layer and client layers to scale and evolve independently.

Details of the optical network topology can be hidden from the client layer through the UNI. We can use this model to interconnect a variety of clients,

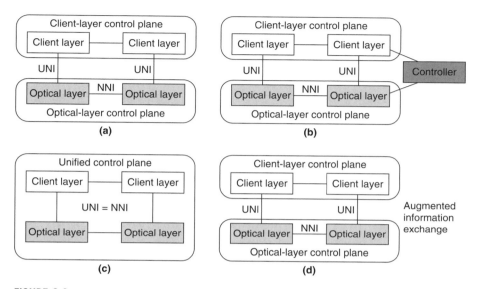

FIGURE 8.9

Different control plane models for interconnecting client layers with the optical layer: (a) overlay model, (b) overlay-plus model, (c) peer model, and (d) augmented model.

including IP, ATM, Ethernet, and SONET/SDH clients, with the optical layer. The model is also appropriate for supporting private-line light path service, transport bandwidth brokering, carrier's carrier trunking, and optical virtual private networks. Finally, this model can be applied to incumbent or new multiservice carriers who either own or lease their transport facilities.

An enhanced version of the overlay model is the *overlay-plus model,* shown in Figure 8.9(b), which allows closer interaction between the layers. In this case, there is a trusted intermediate intelligent controller between the two layers that has available to it a suitably abstracted version of specific client and optical-layer topology and status information. The controller can use this information to request and release light paths based on specific policies, such as specific service level agreements made between the client and optical layers. These requests can be rapidly invoked to avoid network abnormalities such as congestion and failures, increase infrastructure utilization, coordinate protection and restoration options, and automate engineering by rebalancing the network and forecasting needed resource (such as node and link capacity) upgrades for both the IP and optical layers.

Figure 8.9(c) shows the *peer model,* where IP routers and optical-layer elements, such as OXCs and OADMs, run the same control plane software. This would allow routers to look at OXCs as if they were routers, effectively treating the IP layer and optical layer as peers. An OXC would simply be a special type of router, analogous to a label-switched router (LSR). Routers would have full topology awareness of the optical layer and could therefore control optical-layer connections directly. While this is an elegant approach, it is made complicated by the fact that optical-layer elements impose significantly different constraints with respect to routing and protection of connections, compared to the IP layer. In this case, we need to find a way to suitably abstract optical-layer routing constraints into a form that can be used by route computation engines residing on IP routers.

Figure 8.9(d) shows another enhanced version of the overlay model, called an *augmented model,* where the IP layer has access to summarized routing, addressing, and topology information of the optical layer, but still operates as a separate control plane from the optical layer.

The models in Figures 8.9(c) and (d) tend to apply mainly to new IP-centric providers or IP-centric business units within established carriers who own their transport facilities. These models allow (or require) significantly more trust and closer coupling between the IP and optical layers, compared to the overlay models of Figures 8.9(a) and (b). All these models are being pursued today, but the overlay approach is likely to be the first one implemented. It has also been adopted for standardization by the ITU.

8.6.3 Adaptation Management

Adaptation management is the function of taking the client signals and converting them to a form that can be used inside the optical layer. This function includes the following:

- Converting the signal to the appropriate wavelength, optical power level, and other optical parameters associated with the optical layer. This is done through the use of transponders, which convert the signal to electrical form and retransmit the signal using a WDM-specific laser. In the other direction, the WDM signal is received and converted into a standardized signal, such as a short-reach SONET signal.

- Adding and removing appropriate overheads to enable the signal to be managed inside the optical layer. This could include one or more of the overhead techniques that we discussed in Section 8.5.7.

- Policing the client signal to make sure that the client signal stays within boundaries that have been agreed on as part of the service agreement. We discussed this in Section 8.5.

The WDM network must support several types of interfaces to accommodate a variety of users requiring different functions. Figure 8.10 shows the different possible adaptation interfaces.

Compliant wavelength interface: One interface might be to allow the client to send in light at a wavelength that is supported in the network. In this case, the user would be expected to comply with a variety of criteria set by

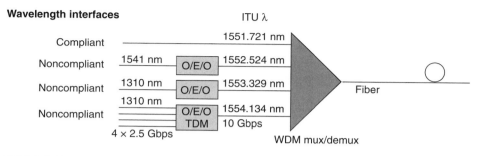

FIGURE 8.10

Different types of interfaces between a WDM optical network and its clients.

the network, such as the signal wavelength, power, modulation type, and so on. These wavelengths may be regarded as *compliant* wavelengths. In this case, the interface might be purely optical, with no optoelectronic conversions required (a significant cost savings). For example, you might envision that SONET or IP equipment must incorporate WDM-capable lasers at wavelengths suitable for the WDM network. Likewise, it would be possible to directly send a wavelength from the WDM network into SONET equipment. Here the user complies to the requirements imposed by the network.

Noncompliant wavelength interface: This is the most common interface and encompasses a variety of different types of attached client equipment that use optical transmitters and/or receivers not compatible with the signals used inside the WDM network. For example, this would include SONET equipment using 1.3-μm lasers. Here, until all-optical wavelength conversion (and perhaps all-optical regeneration) becomes feasible, optoelectronic conversion must be used, along with possibly regeneration, to convert the signal to a form suitable for the WDM network. This is likely to be the interface as well when we need to interconnect WDM equipment from different vendors adhering to different specifications, as we discussed in Section 8.4.

Subrate multiplexing: Additional adaptation functions include time-division multiplexing of lower-speed streams into a higher-speed stream within the WDM equipment prior to transmission. For example, the WDM equipment could include multiplexing of SONET OC-48 streams into OC-192 streams. This could reduce costs by eliminating the separate equipment that would normally be needed to perform this function.

The level of transparency offered by the network also affects the type of adaptation performed at the edges of the network. The network needs to be capable of transporting multiple bit rates. In general, the optical path can be engineered to support signals up to a specified maximum bit rate.

The adaptation devices and regenerators used within the network need to be capable of supporting a variety of bit rates as well. An important enabler for this purpose is a programmable clock data-recovery chip that can be set to work at a variety of bit rates. The chips available today are capable of handling integral multiples of bit rates (e.g., 155 Mbps, 622 Mbps, 1.25 Gbps, and 2.5 Gbps). They are also capable of handling a narrow range of bit rates around a mean value. For example, a single chip could deal with SONET OC-24 signals or with Gigabit Ethernet signals, which are both around 1.25 Gbps, but not exactly at the same rate. Finally, using a digital wrapper to encapsulate the client signal allows the network to transport multiple data rates and protocol formats in a supervised way.

8.7 OPTICAL SAFETY

The semiconductor lasers used in optical communication systems are relatively low-power devices; nevertheless, their emissions can cause serious damage to the human eye, including permanent blindness and burns. The closer the laser wavelength is to the visible range, the more damage it can do, since the cornea is more transparent to these wavelengths. For this reason, systems with lasers must obey certain safety standards. Systems with lasers are classified according to their emission levels, and the relevant classes for communication systems are described next. These safety issues in some cases can limit the allowable optical power used in the system.

A *Class I* system cannot emit damaging radiation. The laser itself may be a high-power laser, but it is prevented from causing damage by enclosing it in a suitably interlocking enclosure. The maximum power limit in a fiber for a Class I system is about 10 mW (10 dBm) at 1.55 µm and 1 mW (0 dBm) at 1.3 µm. Moreover, the power must not exceed this level even under a single failure condition within the equipment. A typical home CD player, for example, is a Class I system.

A *Class IIIa* system allows higher emission powers—up to 17 dB in the 1.55-µm wavelength range—but access must be restricted to trained service personnel. Class IIIa laser emissions are generally safe unless the laser beam is collected or focused onto the human eye. A *Class IIIb* system permits even higher emission powers, and the radiation can cause eye damage even if not focused or collected.

Under normal operation, optical communication systems are completely "enclosed" systems—laser radiation is confined to within the system and not seen outside. The problem arises during servicing or installation, or when there is a fiber cut, in which case the system is no longer completely enclosed and emission powers must be kept below the levels recommended for that particular system class. Communication systems deployed in the enterprise world must generally conform to Class I standards since untrained users are likely to be using them. Systems deployed within carrier networks, on the other hand, may likely be Class

IIIa systems, since access to these systems is typically restricted to trained service personnel.

The safety issue thus limits the maximum power that can be launched into a fiber. For single-channel systems without optical power amplifiers using semiconductor lasers, the emission levels are small enough (-3 to 0 dBm typically) that we do not have to worry much about laser safety. However, with WDM systems, or with systems using optical power amplifiers, we must be careful to regulate the total power into the fiber at all times.

Simple safety mechanisms use shuttered optical connectors on the network equipment. This takes care of regulating emissions if a connector is removed from the equipment, but cannot prevent emissions on a cut fiber further away from the equipment. This is taken care of by a variety of automatic shutdown mechanisms that are designed into the network equipment. These mechanisms detect open connections and turn off lasers and/or optical amplifiers (the spontaneous emission from amplifiers may itself be large enough to cause damage).

Several techniques are used to perform this function. If an amplifier senses a loss of signal at its input, it turns off its pump lasers to prevent any output downstream. There is some handshaking needed between the two ends of a failed link to handle unidirectional cuts. If one end senses a loss of signal, it turns off its transmitter or amplifier in the other direction. This in turn allows the other end to detect a loss of signal and turn off its transmitter or amplifier. Another technique is to look at the back-reflected light. In the event of a fiber cut, the back-reflection increases and can be used to trigger a shutdown mechanism.

After the failure is repaired, the system can be brought up manually. More sophisticated *open fiber control* mechanisms allow the link to be brought back up automatically once the failure is repaired. These mechanisms typically pulse the link periodically to determine if the link has been repaired. The pulse power is maintained below the levels specified for the safety class. Here, we describe a particular protocol that has been chosen for the Fibre Channel standard.

8.7.1 Open Fiber Control Protocol

Figure 8.11 shows a block diagram of a system with two nodes A and B using the OFC protocol. Figure 8.12 shows the finite-state machine of the protocol. The protocol works as follows:

1. Under normal operating conditions, A and B are in the ACTIVE state. If the link from A to B fails, receiver B detects a loss of light (LOL) and turns off laser B, and B enters the DISCONNECT state. Receiver A subsequently detects a LOL and turns off its laser and also enters the DISCONNECT state. Similarly, if the link from B to A fails, or if both links fail simultaneously, A and B both enter the DISCONNECT state.

2. In the DISCONNECT state, A transmits a pulse of duration τ every T seconds; B does the same. If A detects light while it is transmitting a pulse, it enters the

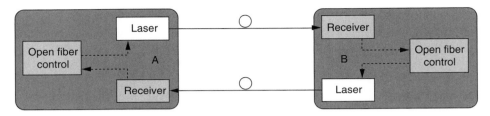

FIGURE 8.11

Open fiber control protocol in the Fibre Channel standard.

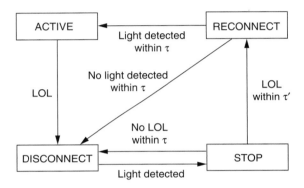

FIGURE 8.12

State machine run by each node for the open fiber control protocol in the Fibre Channel standard.

STOP state and is called the *master*. If A detects light while it is not transmitting a pulse, it transmits a pulse for τ seconds and then enters the STOP state and is called the *slave*; likewise for B.

3. Upon entering the STOP state, the node turns off its laser for a period of τ' seconds. It remains in this state until a LOL condition is detected on the incoming link. If this happens within the τ' seconds, it moves into the RECONNECT state. Otherwise, it moves back into the DISCONNECT state.

4. Upon entering the RECONNECT state, if the node is the master, it sends out a pulse of duration τ. If light is detected on the incoming link within this time period, the node enters the ACTIVE state. Otherwise, it shuts off its transmitter and enters the DISCONNECT state. If the node is the slave, it monitors the link for a period of τ seconds, and if light is detected on the incoming link within this period, it turns on its laser and enters the ACTIVE state. Otherwise, it goes back to the DISCONNECT state.

This is a fairly complex protocol. A simpler version of this protocol would not have the STOP and RECONNECT states. Instead, the nodes would directly enter the ACTIVE state from the DISCONNECT state upon detecting light. The reason for having the other states is to try to ensure that both nodes have functioning safety circuitry. If one of the nodes does not turn off its laser during the STOP period, it is assumed that the safety circuitry is not working and the other node goes back to the DISCONNECT state.

In order for the protocol to work, τ, τ', and T must be chosen carefully. In the DISCONNECT state, the average power transmitted is $\tau P/T$, where P is the transmitted power when the laser is turned on. This must be less than the allowed emission limits for the safety class. The values chosen for τ and τ' depend on the link propagation delay.

Since the Class I safety standard also specifies that emission limits must be maintained during single fault conditions, the open fiber control circuitry at each node is duplicated for redundancy.

8.8 SUMMARY

Network management is essential to operate and maintain any network. Operating costs dominate equipment costs for most telecom networks, making good network management imperative in ensuring the smooth operation of the network. The main functions of network management include configuration (of equipment and connections in the network), performance monitoring, and fault management. In addition, security and accounting are also management functions. Most functions of management are performed through a hierarchy of centralized management systems, but certain functions, such as restoration against failures, or the use of defect indicators to suppress alarms, are done in a distributed fashion. Several management protocols exist, the main ones being TL1, SNMP, and CMIP.

It is useful to break down the optical layer into three sublayers: the optical channel layer, which deals with individual connections or light paths and is end to end across the network; the optical multiplex section layer, which deals with multiplexed wavelengths on a point-to-point link basis; and the optical transmission section layer, which deals with multiplexed wavelengths and the optical supervisory channel between adjacent amplifiers.

Interoperability between equipment from different vendors is a major issue facing the industry today. Initially the focus was on trying to get interoperability between vendors at the WDM level, but that has been recognized now as being very complex. Today the focus is on establishing interoperability by defining standard port-side single-wavelength interfaces at regenerator (or transponder) locations. There is also significant work under way to define optical-layer overheads and their functions, as well as to establish signaling and control protocol standards for controlling connections in the optical layer.

The level of transparency offered by the optical network affects the amount of management that can be performed. Key performance parameters such as the bit error rate can only be monitored in the electrical domain. Fast signaling methods need to be in place between network elements to perform some key management functions. These include the use of defect indicator signals to prevent the generation of unwanted alarms and protection-switching action, and other signaling bytes to control rapid protection switching. Optical path trace is another indicator that can be used to verify and manage connectivity in the network. Several methods exist for exchanging management information between nodes, including the optical supervisory channel, pilot tones, the use of certain overhead bytes in the SONET/SDH overhead, and the new digital wrapper overhead defined specifically for the optical layer.

Connection management in the optical network is slowly migrating from a centralized management plane-based approach to a more distributed connection control plane approach using protocols similar to those used in IP and ATM networks. Eye safety considerations are a unique feature of optical fiber communication systems. These considerations set an upper limit on the power that can be emitted from an open fiber, and these limits make it harder to design WDM systems, since they apply to the total power and not to the power per channel. Safety is maintained by using automated shutdown mechanisms in the network that detect failures and turn off lasers and amplifiers to prevent any laser radiation from exiting the system.

GMPLS Provisioning and Management

This chapter, based on Chapters 14 and 15 of *GMPLS: Architecture and Applications* by Farrel and Bryskin, introduces some of the ways Generalized Multi-Protocol Label Switching (GMPLS) networks and devices can be provisioned and managed.

9.1 PROVISIONING AND MANAGEMENT SYSTEMS

GMPLS reduces the management burden in transport networks by offloading functions from the operator and management plane to the control plane. For example, the collection and correlation of information about the status and capabilities of the links are automatically handled and kept up to date by the GMPLS routing protocols. Similarly, the GMPLS signaling protocols make it possible to provision new label switched paths (LSPs) and manage existing LSPs with only a small number of management plane interactions.

From the perspective of an operator at their console in the network operations center, there may be very little visible difference between the tools used to manage a traditional transport network and a GMPLS-enabled network, but it would be a mistake to assume that the efficiency or mode of operation of the underlying transport plane is unchanged. The GMPLS control plane makes sure that the operator is always working with the most up-to-date information and also makes sure that the services are managed efficiently by the management plane.

Nevertheless, the management plane is an essential component of the GMPLS-enabled network. The first and most important question is the structure that is applied to the management framework for the network: How does the operator coordinate the many devices that make up the network and are physically remote and supplied by different vendors? Next we look at how management networks are physically provided and what network resources are needed so that the network itself can be managed. We then discuss proprietary management interfaces and describe some of the more common standardized techniques used to manage network devices. There is then a brief discussion of alarms and asynchronous events.

9.1.1 The Structure of Management

A transport network is typically constructed from equipment supplied by several different vendors. Despite the long-term goal of complete and free interchangeability of devices from different vendors, operators usually build clusters of devices from the same vendor and manage them as separate administrative domains. There are several benefits to this approach, not the least of which is a reduction in the number of points within the network where genuine interoperability is occurring. (This is a good thing, because these are the points where most protocol and hardware problems are likely to be seen.)

Devices from different vendors have different management characteristics even though they perform very similar network functions. As we will see later in this chapter, there is a wide variety of proprietary interfaces and standardized protocols that could be used to manage a transport network device. This means that the operator will need to use many different applications or at least remember several different command syntaxes to control the entire network. In this situation it makes good sense to collect the devices with the same management characteristics into separate administrative domains—a different operator can be given control of each domain and they need only be familiar with the management techniques for the devices within their domain. Although interactions between operators will be needed for services that span domains, these interactions can be managed at a more abstract level and will not require a deep understanding of the configuration techniques of the other domains.

Another fact that influences the distribution of vendors' equipment within networks is network mergers. Small networks are typically resourced from one or at most two vendors. This naturally forms clusters of network nodes of a similar type. However, the trend is to increase the size of networks by connecting together smaller networks within a single company, through corporate acquisitions or through cooperative agreements between service providers. The result naturally produces islands or administrative domains of devices from the same vendor.

9.1.2 Management Tools

The four major management system components are shown in Figure 9.1.

User interfaces: Most devices have some way for the operator to connect directly so that he or she can configure and control the local resources. A device may have a dedicated terminal, may support the attachment of a terminal emulator (perhaps through a serial port), and usually also supports remote access through

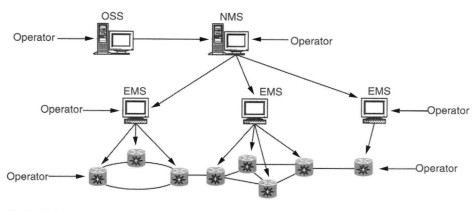

FIGURE 9.1

The structure of a management network.

an application such as Telnet. All of these mechanisms give the operator the ability to connect to individual network nodes as separate entities rather than as part of the whole network.

The element management system (EMS): EMS is an application or workstation dedicated to the management of one or more network elements. Typically, an EMS application is specific to a single vendor's equipment, but can manage multiple nodes of the same type. An EMS workstation may run several EMS applications (for different equipment) and may be where the operator sits to use the remote user interfaces of various network devices. It is important to note that the EMS does not manage the network, but manages individual network nodes.

The network management system (NMS): NMS is a central management station or application that has a view of the whole network and can control and configure all of the devices in the network. The NMS operator does not want to handle multiple applications to control the network, so the NMS provides a single application that presents a common interface to all of the subnetworks, administrative domains, and individual network elements. In practice, the NMS is sometimes bundled with one or more EMSs so that it can talk to network devices directly, but more often the NMS speaks a standardized management protocol to a group of EMS workstations that manage the devices.

The operations support system (OSS): OSS is also a central management system, but it has a less hands-on interaction with the network. The OSS is where planning and service installation are managed. The operations at the OSS may be asynchronous and disjointed in time from the day-to-day management of the network. Nevertheless, the OSS needs to issue management requests to provision and control services in the network (or networks) for which it is responsible. It does this by issuing commands (usually through a standardized protocol) to the NMS.

Additionally, one may consider a fifth component that passively collects information from network devices rather than exerting control over the resources. Management events, such as alarms, are usually fed back up the management tree so that the various components of the management system are fully aware of them. But other operational information, such as statistics and event logs, are normally collected through separate distributed utilities that are responsible for collating and aggregating the information before passing it back to a centralized server. The devices that provide support for statistics gathering and processing may be coincident with the EMS, NMS, and OSS nodes, or may be completely separate workstations.

9.1.3 Management Networks

Figure 9.1 shows the logical connectivity for control of a network, but it would not be practicable to physically connect the EMSs and network elements in the manner shown—that would require far too many point-to-point connections. In practice, the management plane must achieve the same level of connectivity as the control plane so that the EMSs can send management commands to any network element. Unlike the control plane, the emphasis is not on hop-by-hop connectivity to parallel the data plane; the management plane needs connectivity from the EMSs to network elements.

This connectivity is usually provided by an IP management network. It may be that each network element is connected directly to the management network, but where there is in-band or in-fiber control plane communication between the network elements, the management messages may be carried that way (see Figure 9.2).

9.1.4 Proprietary Management Interfaces

As previously described, most network devices are supplied equipped with one or more proprietary interface. The most common format is the command-line interface (CLI). Here an operator can issue a series of text commands to manage the device. The CLI may be run through a directly attached terminal or over a remote-access protocol such as Telnet. CLIs are usually the most powerful management tools available for any vendor's equipment: They give access to the entire function of the device and allow a very fine level of control. For this reason, however, a CLI can also be very hard to use; it has a great number of commands, each with many parameters, and a complex syntax based on keywords, which sometimes have obscure meanings and are hard to remember. The CLI is really a tool for developers, support engineers, or the well-trained operator.

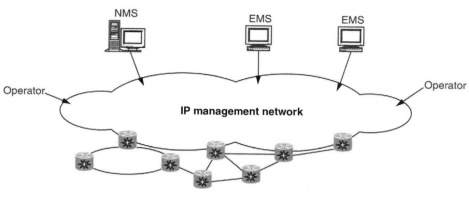

FIGURE 9.2

The management network may partially coincide with the transport network.

Some vendors also develop their own graphical user interfaces (GUIs) to help users manage their devices. There is really no big distinction between a GUI and an EMS in this context, because it is very unusual for a network device to support a GUI through a directly attached terminal; the GUI is usually an application that runs on a separate workstation. A well-organized GUI provides a hierarchical view of the configurable and manageable components of each network device, allows point-and-click navigation, hides complex functions behind an "Advanced" button, and supplies well-thought-out defaults for most parameters. Although there are great similarities between the configurable components and commodities from one network device to another, the GUIs often only bear comparison at the highest level.

9.1.5 Standardized Management Protocols

Proprietary management interfaces are fine up to a point, but as a service provider attempts to add equipment from different vendors to their network it becomes a major problem. Operators are either required to learn the user interfaces, programming languages, and GUI layouts of each new piece of equipment, or some form of homologation is needed to map from the operator's favorite set of commands to the instructions understood by each device. This latter choice makes life considerably easier for the operator, but is only achieved at great expense and effort by the service provider.

Many attempts have been made to standardize the way in which management workstations communicate with network devices. The aim in all cases is to produce a single management protocol that will be understood by all equipment in the network and can be spoken by the management station to control the network.

Unfortunately, the standardization process has led not to a single protocol but to a whole set of different solutions. Each has its advantages and disadvantages, and each its proponents and detractors. A few of the more common protocols are described in the following paragraphs.

The Simple Network Management Protocol (SNMP) is IETF's management protocol of choice. It has a checkered past, with version 1 regarded as unscalable, and version 2, insecure. Version 3 has recently been stabilized and claims to address all issues in previous versions. However, the time that it has taken to evolve, combined with a widespread belief that SNMP is in no way "simple," means that many vendors are reluctant to offer SNMP management of their devices, and where they do, the take-up in live networks (especially core, transport networks) is very poor and the protocol is used for monitoring rather than for control.

Nevertheless, because SNMP is actively promoted by the IETF, it is a significant configuration protocol. In SNMP, data are encoded in Abstract Syntax Notation One (ASN.1). It has two formats, one for carrying data on the wire (within protocol messages) and one for representation in text documents. The total set of data managed in SNMP is known as the management information base (MIB), and each new protocol developed within the IETF is required to have a MIB module defined. The MIB modules for GMPLS are discussed in a later section of this chapter.

The eXtensible Markup Language (XML) is a text-formatting language that is a subset of the Standard Generalized Markup Language (SGML) specified in the International Standards ISO 8879. XML documents look very much like those written in the Hypertext Markup Language (HTML) used to encode Web pages. However, XML includes the ability to characterize data fields giving their data types and encodings as well as their values.

XML is a somewhat verbose way of encoding data. The management data for a device are presented as a document with tags that give meaning and format to each field. The tags are usually descriptive, so several text words may be used to encapsulate a single piece of data. This is a great strength because the format and meaning are encoded in XML in a way that can be simply parsed by the recipient, but it also imposes an overhead compared with a binary encoding of a known structure. XML documents are exchanged using the Simple Object Access Protocol (SOAP), a lightweight, transaction-oriented protocol that utilizes an underlying transport protocol.

The Common Object Request Broker Architecture (CORBA) takes an object-oriented approach to management through a distributed management architecture. CORBA specifications include the definition of the managed objects; the rules for communication between management applications and the managed objects; and the requests, access control, security, and relationships between the objects.

In CORBA, data are encoded using Interface Definition Language (IDL), which extends a subset of the C++ programming language by adding constructs to support the type of object management that is needed in the context of network management. Data sets are constructed as objects and are exchanged using the General Inter-ORB Protocol (GIOP), a message-based transaction protocol. When

GIOP is adapted to use TCP/IP as its transport, it is known as the Internet Inter-ORB Protocol (IIOP).

Transaction Language-1 (TL1) is a standardized, transaction-based ASCII scripting language that is very popular in management systems. It grew out of the Man Machine Language (MML) specified by Bellcore as a standard language for controlling network elements within the Regional Bell Operating Companies (RBOCs).

TL1 is certainly the most common management protocol in transport networks. It owes this position partly to the fact that it is a man–machine language—a language that is understood both by users and by the devices it controls. However, its success must also be attributed to the fact that around 80 percent of the devices in telecommunication networks in the United States utilize OSS software from Telcordia: Telcordia compatibility certification (through OSMINE) is therefore a crucial (and expensive) requirement for vendors in this market, and because Telcordia uses TL1, most vendors support TL1 either directly to their network devices or as a management interface to their EMSs.

The Lightweight Directory Access Protocol (LDAP) is a set of protocols for sharing and accessing information in distributed directories. When you look at the requirements for controlling and managing the equipment within a network, you discover that it is not far removed from a distributed directory with some portions of the data held on the network devices, and a central directory held on the EMS or NMS.

LDAP has grown out of the X.500 set of directory standards, and the data are encoded in ASN.1. But unlike X.500, LDAP operates over TCP/IP, making it available within the Internet and across an Internet Protocol (IP) management network. Although not currently very popular as a management tool, LDAP is increasingly used as an automated inventory mechanism. In this mode, network elements can report the components and cards that they have installed (and the status of those components) to the EMS.

As can be seen from the previous descriptions, the common standardized management protocol solutions do not just use different message exchanges, they also have entirely different ways of representing and encoding the configuration data for the managed devices. Far from making things easier, the array of choices tends to reduce the take-up of interoperable solutions by vendors who, unable to decide which standard solution to offer, simply stick with their own proprietary solution.

Some multivendor interoperability consortia under pressure from service providers are now beginning to develop and agree on common approaches (e.g., the TeleManagement Forum and the Multiservice Switching Forum). These are tending to converge on CORBA and TL1, with XML still making a strong showing, resulting in the model shown in Figure 9.3.

9.1.6 Web Management

There is nothing very special about Web management of network devices, although it is hyped somewhat by equipment vendors. The chief advantage for operators

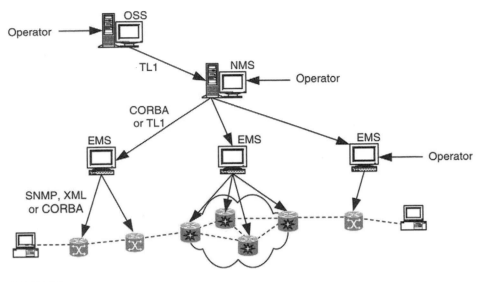

FIGURE 9.3

Common network management usage is assigning specific roles to the different network management protocols within the management network.

is that they are able to use a GUI to control and configure their network without actually having to run a specific application (such as an EMS) on their own work-station. All that an operator needs is a Web browser and connectivity (usually across the IP management network) to the server that runs the management application. The management application generates control panels as forms that the operator can complete.

The most common implementation of Web management simply provides a remote GUI to a vendor-specific EMS. The facilities of HTML mean that this sort of management tool can be made to look very sexy and can perform all sorts of clever point-and-click operations.

In some extreme cases, network devices may be capable of running Web servers to allow browsers to connect to them directly and send configuration commands. This, however, is very rare because the primary purpose of a network device is not to host HTTP sessions, and it is unusual for there to be space to put this kind of software support on a switch or router.

9.1.7 Alarms and Events

The collection, correlation, and servicing of alarms or events raised by network elements is an important feature of network management systems. Although some alarms may be handled by the network elements, possibly in conjunction with the control plane, to minimize the impact on services, it is crucial that the alarms are passed on to the management system so that the operator (or some automatic trouble-ticketing system) can take remedial actions to protect existing services and to repair the fault.

To ensure that the operator or his or her applications are fully informed of their status, the network elements report (raise) alarms and other key events to their EMS. The EMS passes the fault notifications on to the NMS, and the NMS may even tell the OSS, so that planning and procurement actions can be taken. Although any layer in this model may take remedial action, the notifications are still sent so that the higher layers can make their own judgments.

Note, however, that a network device may raise many alarms in response to a single fault. For example, if a fiber is cut, the associated line card may raise a "loss of light" alarm, but other components of the device such as the cross-connect and the downstream transmitter may also suffer from the error and raise corresponding "loss of signal" alarms. These alarms can be correlated vertically; that is, the alarms can be seen to all correspond to the same event and are in some sense a chain reaction. In other circumstances a single failure, such as of a whole line card, may cause multiple parallel alarms to be raised; for example, an "interface down" alarm for each port on the line card. These alarms can be correlated horizontally.

If each device passed all alarms to its EMS, and each EMS passed all alarms to the NMS, the NMS could be seriously overloaded. To prevent this from happening, two features are configurable within the network. The first assigns priorities or severities to each alarm or event and allows control of which faults are reported and which are silently ignored or just logged. The second feature allows levels within the management network to correlate alarms and only report the issue to which all other alarms can be traced (and from which all other alarms can be deduced).

Alarm and event reporting mechanisms typically utilize the same protocols that are used for management control. Thus, SNMP has the concept of a `Trap` or `Notification` that allows a device to pass unsolicited information to its management station. Similarly, CORBA and TL1 all allow a lower management level to report an event to a higher level.

Other asynchronous event protocols such as `Syslog` can also be used to collect alarm and event notifications from network elements, but these are typically used for historic archival and are examined by operators and field engineers who want to understand what has been happening in the network.

9.2 GMPLS MIB MODULES

SNMP is the management protocol of choice within the IETF. This does not mean that GMPLS-conformant devices are restricted to SNMP or are forced to implement SNMP. Indeed, most GMPLS-capable network elements have a variety of management interfaces as described in the previous sections.

However, it is an IETF requirement that all IETF protocols have MIB modules defined to allow implementations to be modeled and managed. The MIB is the global distributed database for management and control of SNMP-capable devices, and a MIB module is a collection of individual objects and tables of objects, each of which contains a value that describes the configuration or status of a manageable entity or logical entity of the same type.

This section briefly describes the MIB modules that exist for MPLS traffic engineering (TE) and then describes how those modules are extended for GMPLS.

9.2.1 MPLS TE MIB Management

Three MIB modules are of particular relevance to the management of devices in an MPLS TE network: the MPLS textual conventions (TC) MIB module, the MPLS label switching router (LSR) MIB module, and the MPLS TE MIB module.

The MPLS TC MIB module (MPLS-TC-STD-MIB) contains an assortment of general definitions for use in other MIB modules. In a sense it is a little like a header file that defines types and structures for use in other files. It includes definitions of things like bit rates, but more important, it defines textual conventions (that is, types) for use when representing tunnel IDs, extended tunnel IDs, label switched path (LSP) IDs, and MPLS labels.

The MPLS LSR MIB module (MPLS-LSR-STD-MIB) is used to model and control an individual MPLS label switching router. This MIB module concerns itself with the core function of an LSR (that is, forwarding of labeled packets), so it is as applicable to Label Distribution Protocol (LDP) as it is to RSVP-TE. In fact, the LSR MIB module could be used in the absence of any signaling protocol to manually configure LSPs through the LSR.

There are four basic units to the LSR MIB module. There is a table of MPLS-capable interfaces on which labeled packets can be sent and received. There is a table of in-segments corresponding to labels received on interfaces or upstream legs of LSPs. There is a table of out-segments modeling downstream legs of LSPs identified with a stack of one or more labels to be pushed onto a packet and indicating the interface out of which to send the packet. The fourth unit is a table of cross-connects that shows the relationships (which may be more complex than one-to-one) between in-segments and out-segments.

A third MIB module, the MPLS TE MIB module (MPLS-TE-STD-MIB), is used to model and control MPLS TE LSPs. The primary purpose of the module is to allow an operator to configure and activate a TE LSP at an ingress LSR, but the module is equally valid for examining the LSP at any LSR along its path.

The MPLS TE MIB module contains tables to configure multiple instances of an LSP tunnel for simultaneous activation (such as for load-sharing or protection) or for sequential activation (such as for recovery). Thus, a tunnel, which is an end-to-end traffic trunk or service, has a common root in the `mplsTunnelTable` and may be supported by one or more LSPs either at the same time or at different times. Each LSP is represented in the `mplsTunnelTable` as an "instance" of the tunnel.

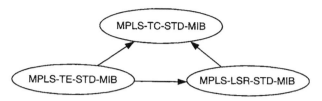

FIGURE 9.4

The relationship between the MPLS TE MIB modules.

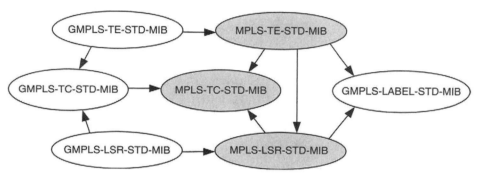

FIGURE 9.5

The relationship between the GMPLS MIB modules.

Other tables allow the configuration and inspection of resource usage for the LSP, and the requested, computed, and actual routes of the LSP.

The dependencies between the MPLS TE MIB modules can be seen in Figure 9.4. The arrows indicate the relationship depends on.

9.2.2 GMPLS MIB Modules

GMPLS MIB management is built on MPLS TE management. Nearly every aspect of the MPLS TE MIB modules is reused, but a fair amount of new objects are needed to handle the extra complexity and function of a GMPLS system.

Figure 9.5 shows the new MIB modules (in white) and their relationship to the MPLS TE MIB modules (in gray). As can be seen, there are four new modules for GMPLS. The GMPLS-TC-STD-MIB provides some additional textual conventions specific to GMPLS. The GMPLS-LSR-STD-MIB and the GMPLS-TE-STD-MIB are mainly used to "extend" tables in the MPLS TE MIB modules; that is, they effectively provide additional objects for inclusion in the tables defined in the MPLS TE MIB modules.

The GMPLS label management MIB module (GMPLS-LABEL-STD-MIB) is a new module designed to handle the fact that GMPLS labels may be considerably more complex than the 20-bit numbers used as labels in MPLS. It contains a table of labels that have simple indexes, but may have complex forms, and that may be referenced from the other MIB modules.

9.2.3 GMPLS Label Switching Router Management

The GMPLS LSR is managed using all of the tables in the MPLS LSR MIB with extensions to handle the additional function for GMPLS.

The table of MPLS-capable interfaces (`mplsInterfaceTable`) is extended by the `gmplsInterfaceTable`. An entry in the former means that the interface uses RSVP-TE for MPLS unless there is also an entry in the GMPLS table. In this case, there is an object in the `gmplsInterfaceTable` that defines the GMPLS signaling protocol in use, and another that defines the signaling `Hello` period to use on the interface.

The performance of label switching on the interface is recorded in the `mplsInterfacePerfTable`, and no extensions are made for GMPLS. In fact, two of the counters are specific to packet processing and are consequently only valid when GMPLS is used in a packet-capable environment.

Inward segments in MPLS are tracked in the `mplsInSegmentTable`. For GMPLS, where bidirectional LSPs are permitted, this might appear confusing; however, the table is well named and the entries refer to the direction of data flow and have no bearing on the signaling used to establish the LSP. Thus, a bidirectional LSP would have one in-segment on the upstream interface (for the forward direction) and one in-segment on the downstream interface (for the reverse direction). The in-segment table is extended for GMPLS by the `gmplsInSegmentTable`, which tells us whether the segment is used on the forward or reverse direction of a bidirectional LSP, and provides a pointer to an external table (perhaps of a proprietary MIB module) that can contain additional parameters to support technology-specific transports (e.g., SONET resource usage). The `mplsInSegmentTable` may contain a pointer into the `gmplsLabelTable` to handle the encoding of complex labels.

The performance of in-segments is tracked in the `mplsInSegmentPerfTable`. Most of the objects in this table are specific to bytes and packets and would only be used when GMPLS is running in a packet-capable environment.

The `mplsInSegmentMapTable` allows an operator to make a reverse lookup from {`interface`, `label`} to find the relevant in-segment in the `mplsInSegment-Table`. This useful function is preserved for GMPLS, but is slightly complicated by the fact that the label may be found by an indirection to the `gmplsLabelTable`.

Similar extensions are made for the `mplsOutSegmentTable` that contains the details of LSP legs that carry data out of the device. Through indirection, the top label to impose on the outgoing traffic may now be found in the `gmplsLabelTable`. The `gmplsOutSegmentTable` extends the MPLS table to say whether the segment is in use on the forward or reverse path of the LSP. There is also a pointer to an external table to encode additional parameters if appropriate. Finally, the gmplsOutSegmentTable contains an object to specify by how much to decrement the time-to-live (TTL) of any payload packets forwarded on the segment if per-hop decrementing is done; this is clearly also only relevant in packet-switching environments.

The performance of out-segments is tracked in the mplsOutSegmentPerfTable. In the same way as for in-segments, most of the objects in this table are specific to bytes and packets and would only be used when GMPLS is running in a packet-capable environment.

The mplsLabelStackTable is preserved for GMPLS, but also only applies in packet environments because this is the only time that label stacking is relevant. This table lists the additional label stack to be applied to outgoing packets beneath the topmost label. These labels may also be found through indirection to the gmplsLabelTable (although this particular usage is unlikely because the stack will be made up from simple 23-bit labels).

Both the in-segment and out-segment tables may contain pointers to an external table that contains parameters that describe the traffic on this LSP. The pointer may indicate an entry in the mplsTunnelResourceTable in the MPLS TE MIB module, or it may point to an entry in a proprietary MIB module. This leaves just the mplsXCTable, which is unchanged in usage from MPLS. That is, it ties together in-segments and out-segments to provide LSPs through the device.

Figure 9.6 shows all of the MIB tables used for managing a GMPLS LSR with their relationships indicated by arrows. Gray boxes denote tables in the MPLS LSR MIB module, ovals are tables in external MIB modules, and white boxes are tables in the GMPLS LSR MIB module.

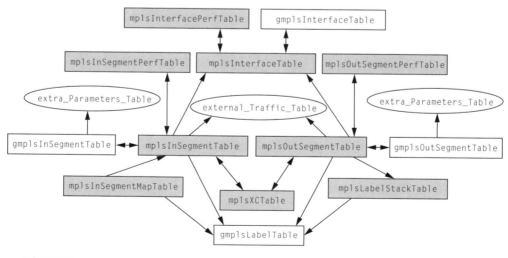

FIGURE 9.6

The relationship between MIB tables in GMPLS LSR management.

9.2.4 **GMPLS TE LSP Management**

Management of individual TE LSPs is slightly simpler and requires fewer tables than the management of the label-switching router described earlier. The basis of the management is the `mplsTunnelTable`, which contains active and configured LSP tunnels that start, end, or transit the device. Entries in the tunnel table are not indexed by the five-tuple that defines the LSP, as might seem natural, but by a slightly different set of parameters. That is, the normal group of identifiers of the LSP {`source`, `destination`, `tunnel ID`, `extended tunnel ID`, `LSP ID`} is replaced in this MIB table by {`tunnel index`, `tunnel instance`, `ingress LSR ID`, `egress LSR ID`}. The tunnel index maps to the tunnel ID that is signaled, while the tunnel instance disambiguates distinct LSPs that support the tunnel (either simultaneously or over time) and thus may be safely mapped to the LSP ID that is signaled. The MIB module assumes that the source and destination of the LSP will be expressed as LSR IDs (which might not be the case) and makes the false assumption that the extended tunnel ID will always be set equal to the ingress LSR ID and thus does not need to be configured. Having said this, the indexing scheme is actually quite acceptable for nonpacket systems and, because it is now used for MPLS packet systems, it is clearly extensible for GMPLS packet LSPs.

The purpose of the GMPLS TE MIB module is both to allow LSPs to be configured and managed at their ingresses and to allow the LSPs to be inspected at any point within the network. To configure an LSP it must be possible to select parameters for any constraint or option that can be signaled. The core set of objects for this are found in the `mplsTunnelTable`, and `gmplsTunnelTable` extends it to support the following additional features:

- Presentation of this tunnel within the LSR as an unnumbered interface.
- Selection of label recording.
- The encoding type requested for the LSP.
- The switching type requested for the LSP.
- The link protection requested for the LSP.
- The payload (G-PID) carried by the LSP.
- Whether the LSP is a secondary (that is, backup) LSP.
- Whether the LSP is unidirectional or bidirectional.
- The control of alarms and other LSP attributes.
- What manner of path computation the ingress LSR is required to perform.

Some of these attributes are useful in MPLS as well as GMPLS and can be used by picking up the `gmplsTunnelTable` and setting the encoding type to zero to indicate an MPLS LSP. All of the objects listed before are also used when an LSP is examined at a transit or egress LSR. Additionally, it is possible to see the Notify recipients for forward and backward notification and the Admin Status flags. A pointer from the `gmplsTunnelTable` can be used to reference an additional external table (perhaps of a proprietary MIB module) that can contain additional parameters to support technology-specific transports (e.g., SONET resource usage).

The MPLS TE MIB module contains the `mplsTunnelPerfTable` to record the performance of the LSP. However, because the MPLS tunnels are unidirectional, the GMPLS TE MIB module introduces the `gmplsTunnelReversePerfTable` to record the performance in the opposite direction. Both performance tables are primarily concerned with packets and bytes and may be largely inappropriate in nonpacket environments.

The resource requirements and usage of each LSP are recorded in the `mplsTunnelResourceTable`. No changes are needed to this table for GMPLS.

A significant part of TE LSP management relates to the specification, computation, and recording of the path taken by the LSP. The MPLS TE MIB module provides three tables for this function: the `mplsTunnelHopTable`, the `mplsTunnelCHopTable`, and they are the `mplsTunnelARHopTable`, respectively. GMPLS increases the level of control that may be specified in a configured and signaled route (e.g., by adding explicit control of labels) and also allows for this information to be recorded. Thus, it is necessary to extend all three of the tables within the GMPLS TE MIB module. Further, because labels are now involved, the new tables include pointers into the `gmplsLabelTable`.

The final extension in the GMPLS TE MIB is the `gmplsTunnelErrorTable`. This table is not really specific to GMPLS because it records errors that occur when trying to establish an LSP or when the LSP fails at some later stage. Because it extends the `mplsTunnelTable` it may be used equally in MPLS and GMPLS systems.

Figure 9.7 shows all of the MIB tables used for managing GMPLS TE LSPs with their relationships indicated by arrows. Gray boxes denote tables in the MPLS TE MIB module, ovals are tables in external MIB modules, and white boxes are tables in the GMPLS TE MIB module.

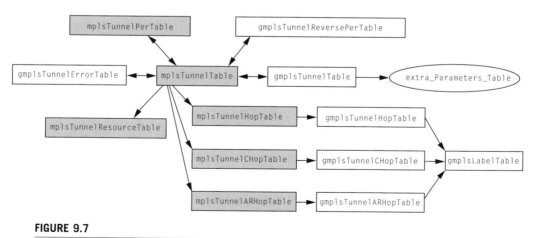

FIGURE 9.7

The relationship between MIB tables in GMPLS TE management.

9.2.5 Traffic Engineering Link MIB Module

The TE link MIB module is equally applicable to MPLS and GMPLS systems. It allows TE links to be configured and managed to help an operator set up and use link bundles. Configuring a bundled link involves defining the bundled link and the TE links, assigning shared risk link groups (SRLGs) to the TE link, configuring the component links to their bandwidth parameters, associating the component links with the appropriate TE link, and associating the TE links with the appropriate bundled link. To this end, the TE link MIB module includes seven tables:

- Entries in the `teLinkTable` represent the TE links, including bundled links, and their generic TE parameters.
- The `teLinkDescriptorTable` contains the TE link interface switching capabilities.
- The `teLinkSrlgTable` lists the SRLGs that may be associated with the TE links.
- Priority-based bandwidth TE parameters for association with the TE links are placed in the `teLinkBandwidthTable`.
- Entries in the `componentLinkTable` represent the component links and show their generic TE parameters.
- The `componentLinkDescriptorTable` holds the switching capability descriptors for each component link.
- Priority-based bandwidth TE parameters for association with each component link are placed in the `componentLinkBandwidthTable`.

This MIB module contains the basic necessities for managing TE links but is somewhat short of configurable constraints for links in optical networks. Further developments and extensions to this MIB are likely as traffic engineering becomes more established in photonic networks.

9.2.6 Link Management Protocol MIB Module

The TE link MIB module allows an operator to configure and manage data links so that they can be bundled and advertised as TE links. But what is also needed is a way to manage the use of the Link Management Protocol (LMP) on links between GMPLS devices. This can be found in the LMP MIB module (LMP-STD-MIB).

The first requirement to run LMP is to configure the neighbors with which a label switching router will exchange LMP messages. The Link Management Protocol does not have a neighbor discovery mechanism, so each would-be peer must be configured in the `lmpNbrTable`. The operator must configure the node ID of each partner and can also provide values for the retransmission interval and limit for each message that is sent.

Once we know about neighbors, we need control channels to be configured. Although control channel activation involves a degree of negotiation, it is nevertheless underpinned by configuration, and the `lmpControlChannelTable` is used to enable LMP exchanges on a per-interface basis. The addresses for the control channel messages and the options, including the `Hello` and `Dead Interval` timers, can be configured.

The behavior of the control channel can be monitored through the `lmpControlChannelPerfTable`. Unlike the management of the signaling protocols where the performance tables show the characteristics of data traffic, this table strictly monitors the LMP traffic, indicating the number of bytes sent and received, recording the number of errors, and counting the number of each message type used on the control channel.

At this point, the protocol can be run and monitored, and the remainder of the MIB module is concerned with the TE links that will be reported and monitored by LMP. The `lmpTeLinkTable` is used to specify those TE links for which LMP exchanges information, and contains some basic LMP parameters. The information that can be configured includes the LMP neighbor to which the link connects, and whether the optional procedures (link verification, fault management, and LMP-WDM) are supported.

If link verification is used, the verification parameters are configured through the `lmpLinkVerificationTable` for each TE link. As well as configuring the timer values for the verification process, the MIB table includes an object to select the transport verification mechanisms to use on the associated data links.

LMP discovery procedure results are recorded in the `lmpDataLinkTable`. An entry is created in this table for each data link, and the relevant local information (interface address and encoding type) is configured. As LMP discovers the remote configuration information, it updates the table with the remote interface address and interface index. This information can then be utilized by GMPLS signaling to ensure that adjacent nodes have the same understanding of which data link is being referred to.

The performance of LMP in relation to a given TE link is recorded in the `lmpTeLinkPerfTable`. The objects count the same events that are found in the `lmpControlChannelPerfTable` (protocol messages), but in this case only the messages specifically related to the TE link are recorded. In the case where there is only one control channel between a pair of LMP peers, the numbers in this table are a subset of those in the `lmpControlChannelPerfTable`, but where more than one control channel is used the relationship is not so simple.

The performance of the data link is still related to the exchange of protocol messages, but because the only messages sent on the data link are Test messages (and even those might not be sent on the data link), `lmpDataLinkPerfTable` records the performance of the link verification process for each data link.

9.2.7 The Interfaces MIB Module

The interfaces MIB module defines generic managed objects for managing interfaces. An interface in this context is the end of a logical connection through which an application can send or receive data. This concept used to be limited to physical connections but has been extended to include logical connections (such as LSPs) that are carried by physical connections. In the context of GMPLS, this meaning of interface is synonymous with the term *data link end*. The GMPLS and MPLS MIB modules make references to interfaces so that it can be clearly determined where the procedures managed by the MIB modules should be performed and, specifically, to manage those interfaces.

Additionally, modules utilize interface stacking when there is a hierarchical relationship between interfaces on a device. Such interface stacking is primarily used for logical interfaces, although the bottom element in any stack is a physical interface. Note that this hierarchical relationship is not the hierarchy of LSPs, but a familiar concept from the interfaces MIB that allows a subdivision of a physical interface (a logical interface) to be presented to an application for its use as though it was a dedicated physical interface.

The TE MIB modules based on MPLS-TE-STD-MIB allow TE LSPs to be managed as logical interfaces. The interfaces MIB module contains a table (the interfaces table—ifTable) that includes information on each interface, and is constructed so that each sublayer below the internetwork layer of a network interface is considered an interface in its own right. Thus, a TE LSP managed as an interface is represented as an entry in the ifTable.

The interrelation of entries in the ifTable is defined as interface stacking. When TE LSPs are managed as interfaces, the interface stack might appear as in Figure 9.8. In the figure, the "underlying layer" refers to the ifIndex of any interface type for which (G)MPLS internetworking has been defined. Thus, two distinct TE LSPs may be presented as separate interfaces to their applications, but may actually be carried over a single, (G)MPLS-enabled physical interface. GMPLS inherits the terminology of the MPLS usage so that interfaces that are realized through TE LSPs are known as TE LSP tunnel interfaces, and physical interfaces that are MPLS- or GMPLS-enabled are called MPLS interfaces.

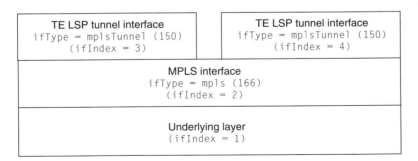

FIGURE 9.8

Two TE LSPs managed as interfaces over a single MPLS-capable interface.

```
+-----------------------------------------------------------------+
|                        MPLS interface                           |
|                     ifType = mpls (166)                         |
|                       (ifIndex = 6)                             |
+-----------------------------------------------------------------+
|                    TE link (bundledlink)                        |
|                    ifType = teLink (200)                        |
|                       (ifIndex = 5)                             |
+------------------------------+----------------------------------+
|          TE link             |             TE link              |
|    ifType = teLink (200)     |      ifType = teLink (200)       |
|       (ifIndex = 3)          |         (ifIndex = 4)            |
+------------------------------+----------------------------------+
|        Component link        |          Component link          |
| ifType = opticalTransport(196)|  ifType = opticalTransport(196) |
|       (ifIndex = 1)          |         (ifIndex = 2)            |
+------------------------------+----------------------------------+
```

FIGURE 9.9

Two physical component links managed as separate TE links and then bundled.

Interface stacking is also used in the TE link MIB module to manage TE links as logical interfaces. The TE link interface is represented as an entry in the ifTable and stacking may be carried out as before. When using TE link interfaces, the interface stack table might appear as is shown in Figure 9.9. In the figure, opticalTransport is an example of an underlying physical interface. Both TE link management and link bundling can be seen in the figure. Two TE links are defined, each managing an optical transport link; these two TE links are combined into a single bundle that is managed as a single TE link interface that supports MPLS and is presented as an MPLS interface.

The Foundation of Policy Management

10

This chapter, Chapter 1 from *Policy-Based Network Management* by Strassner, will first provide a brief retrospective of how policy-based network management (PBNM) has been conceived in the past. This will be used to point out two fundamental problems of previous solutions—the lack of use of an information model, and the inability to use business rules to drive configuration of devices, services, and networks. A path forward, and benefits resulting from this improved approach, are described.

10.1 INTRODUCTION—A RETROSPECTIVE

Policy management means many things to many people. As Michael Jude writes:

> When first conceived in the late 1990s, PBNM promised enterprise information technology shops the ability to control the quality of service (QoS) experienced by networked applications and users. . . . In fact, the hype went further than that: Vendors promised that CIOs or CEOs would soon be able to control policies through a simple graphical interface on their desk. Behind the scenes, those instructions would translate into specific traffic management adjustments, bypassing traditional network operations.

QoS means many things to many people. Contrary to popular belief, QoS does not mean "just" an increase or decrease in bandwidth speed. Rather, it means differentiated treatment of one or more metrics. These metrics are completely dependent on the type of application(s) that the QoS is being designed for. Thus, QoS for a voice application is usually different than QoS for a mission-critical data application, because the characteristics of each application are different. This causes the specific QoS mechanisms to be made different.

One favorite definition of QoS is "managed unfairness." This describes the differences in how network elements are programmed to provide different QoS mechanisms to treat various application traffic streams differently. Clearly, this is complex to perform for the same type of devices; the complexity of this configuration increases dramatically if different devices with different capabilities and commands are used in the same network.

Differentiated QoS, which is the ability to provide different configurations of QoS for different types of applications, is the key to opening up new avenues of revenue. Because providing QoS is currently very difficult, the application of policy to provide differentiated QoS is one of the primary drivers for implementing PBNM solutions.

The emphasis on managing and implementing QoS describes some of the buildup and excitement that followed the dawn of PBNM. The reason, of course, is because networks are complex, and running different services, each of which have different requirements on the same network, is very difficult. People who were looking for a "quick fix" to their network problems were disappointed; PBNM was found to be time intensive, complex, and expensive. There were several reasons for this:

- Most early PBNM solutions were single-vendor approaches and could only manage some of the devices on the network. As a result, multiple incompatible PBNM solutions had to be introduced to manage the entire network, which caused hard-to-solve integration problems.

- PBNM solutions were focused on particular technologies and devices. For example, a QoS policy server might be able to control most (but probably not all) of the QoS functions of a particular vendor's device or device families. However, it probably could not control other types of technologies, such as security and Internet Protocol (IP) address management.

- PBNM solutions focused on the IP world. This caused disruption in organizations that have different technologies present in their networks.

- PBNM solutions were misunderstood.

- PBNM solutions rushed forth without a solid set of standards in place.

Although the first three problems are important, the last two are fundamental problems that prevented the first wave of PBNM solutions from realizing their goals.

In addition, two other problems prevented wide adoption. First, the solutions initially available were not very scalable, and hence could not easily be used in large service provider networks despite the fact that they provided some attractive technology (e.g., configuring QoS functions).

Second, network monitoring technology lagged behind the new provisioning technology promoted by PBNM solutions to control the network. As a result, there was no easy way to monitor whether the PBNM solutions were actually working.

10.1.1 **Early PBNM Solutions Missed the Point**

In its early days, PBNM was characterized (and unfortunately, this characterization continues somewhat today) as a sophisticated way to manipulate different types of QoS. The motivation for this was to avoid overprovisioning the network, (i.e., enough resources are present for the network to respond to any anticipated need). The problem with this approach is that it is static and cannot adjust to the changing environment. Thus, if the network is provisioned according to the maximum expected load, resources will be wasted most of the time. Furthermore, if that load is exceeded for some reason (e.g., a heavy day of stock trading), then the network will still be unable to perform.

PBNM was used to set the QoS levels based on inspecting different fields in the header of traffic that was being sent. People then reasoned that PBNM could also be used for other applications (such as ensuring that high-priority traffic was delivered ahead of less important traffic and that different services received the level of service that they were contracted for) and for different types of security applications (such as refusing traffic from an unknown source to enter the network or starting an accounting application when a connection was completed).

The common theme to each of these (and other) applications is the desire to link the way the business runs to the services that the network provides. Regardless of application, PBNM was defined as reacting to a particular condition and then taking an appropriate action. The missing point is that some centralized authority has to decide which users and applications get priority over other users and applications.

Business rules are defined as the set of rules, regulations, and practices for operating a business. They often define and sometimes constrain business processes. Business processes are defined as the means by which one or more activities are accomplished in operating business practices. They take the form of an interconnected set of business functions (perhaps constrained by various business rules) to obtain a specific set of business goals.

Recently, the focus has turned to integrating business rules and processes with PBNM solutions. This focus makes intuitive sense, as it is certainly natural to want the network to provide services according to business contracts. However, the relationship can be, and should be, deeper than that. Business rules and processes govern how a system is run. They are responsible for the many decisions that must be made for every action performed by the system.

If policies are the reasons for doing something and business rules and processes are the means for doing it, why not connect them together? Although this seems obvious in retrospect, precious few information models have been constructed with this direction and capability. An important corollary of this decision is as follows:

> PBNM solutions require information models that contain business and system entities that can be easily implemented.

This chapter describes a unique object-oriented information model, called DEN-ng (Directory Enabled Networks—new generation). It is being developed in the TeleManagement Forum. The development is led by this author, and many different companies are involved. The author's company, Intelliden, is also actively involved in implementing DEN-ng and has incorporated it into the latest release of its product. Other companies, such as British Telecom, Telecom Italia, Telstra, MetaSolv, Hewlett Packard, and Agilent, have participated in reviews of DEN-ng.

An object-oriented information model is a means to represent various entities in a managed environment. An entity can be a person, a computer, a router, or even a protocol message—anything that needs a uniform and consistent representation for configuration and management is a possibility for definition and representation in DEN-ng.

An object-oriented information model provides a common language in which different types of management entities can be represented. This common language is of the utmost importance. Operational support systems (OSSs) are large, complex sets of applications that are composed of best-of-breed applications. This tendency to use best-of-breed applications encourages the use of "stovepipe" applications, which are applications that maintain their own definition of data. Much of the data used by each stovepipe application should be shared with other stovepipe applications. Unfortunately, this simply cannot be accomplished unless a common language exists to represent these common data.

One difficulty in building an OSS lies in the large variety of different management objects that must be harmonized and shared among the different management applications being used. Further exacerbating this problem is the fact that different types of management data have different characteristics. For example, very volatile data, such as statistical interface measurements, change much too fast to be placed in a directory. Other data are very appropriate to put into a directory. Thus, an OSS needs to use multiple repositories to accommodate the different characteristics and uses of different management information.

An object-oriented information model, such as DEN-ng, is independent of any specific type of repository, software usage, or access protocol. Therefore, DEN-ng can be used as a single authoritative means for describing how different management information are related to each other.

To put this into perspective, Figure 10.1 shows five exemplary management applications that comprise an OSS. Notice that for two of these applications, the same data appear. For the `Username` attribute, two different names are given. This makes it very difficult for applications to realize that these two different names actually refer to the same attribute of the same object. Furthermore, both applications define the same `Employee` attribute. However, the data types are different. This can cause problems in trying to write a single query to gather data based on this and other attributes across these two repositories.

Thus, unless there is a way to relate different information that are implemented using different data models to each other, it will be impossible to share and reuse management information. This raises the cost of the OSS and increases the prob-

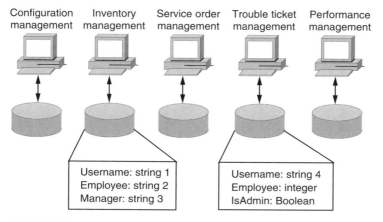

FIGURE 10.1

Problems in not using a single information model.

ability that errors (resulting from the inability to share and reuse management data) will be embedded in the system. Furthermore, it means that entire processes will be repeated to derive and/or retrieve the same data (because the data cannot be shared). Instead, what is desired is a single, unified information model that relates the differences in data model implementations to each other.

DEN-ng is unique because it contains business and system entities that can be used to build management representations and solutions. In fact, in the Intelliden implementation, the DEN-ng information models are translated to two types of data models (Java and directory models). Specifically, business and system entities are represented in generic form in the information model and are then translated to platform-specific implementations. The Intelliden product uses these models to define business rules to activate network services. Other companies, such as MetaSolv (in their case, primarily a database), are using different repositories to implement DEN-ng and the shared information and data (SID).

10.1.2 Early PBNM Solutions Were Ahead of the Standards

The Internet Engineering Task Force (IETF) took the DEN policy model and, in August 1998, formed a working group to start modeling policy. This working group was originally cochaired by myself and was based on using the DEN policy model. This model concentrated on the generic representation of policy and chose QoS as a representative application that would be modeled as a separate set of extensions of the generic representation of policy. This is shown in Figure 10.2.

The policy core information model defined a framework of classes and relationships that could represent the *structure* of policy of any discipline. This is an important point. The use case in 1998 is still the same as it is now—to build a single PBNM solution that can be used to manage different types of policies

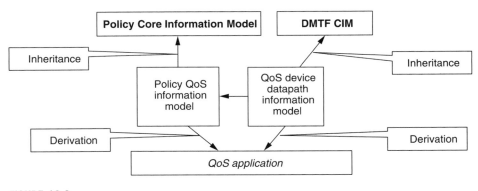

FIGURE 10.2

The structure of the IETF information models.

required by different applications. For example, QoS for voice applications is fundamentally different than QoS for data applications. As such, the target of the Policy Core Information Model (PCIM) was to be able to represent how a policy was defined—it was not targeted at defining the *content* of the policy.

The policy QoS information model refined this framework and added semantics to represent policies that could be used to control QoS mechanisms. The QoS device data-path information model was derived from the Distributed Management Task Force's (DMTF) common information model and represented much of the original DEN network model. The QoS device data-path information model was used to represent the various mechanisms that the policy QoS information model would be used to manage. Both information models were designed to provide *content* within a common overall *representational structure*.

The DMTF's Common Information Model (CIM) was proposed as a way to provide a high-level representation of network elements. Thus, the policies could be "grounded" and applied to a network device. For example, a policy could describe a change in a function of a device; the content of this change could be represented by the policy QoS information model, and the structure of the policy could be represented in PCIM.

Unfortunately, the CIM model was too high-level and confused many people in how policy would be applied. For example, the CIM had no representation of either a physical port or a logical device interface (and this is true even today). This made it very difficult for people to picture how policies were going to be applied and built. Furthermore, the DMTF CIM was not really an information model—it was more of a data model. An information model is supposed to be independent of platform and technology.

The DMTF CIM is based on the use of "keys"—special attributes that are used to name and uniquely identify a particular object. Keys are really a database construct, and their use must be carefully considered or else mapping to other types of data models that do not use keys (or have different keys than those of a database) will be much harder. This is why specific constructs used in one type of data model should not be part of a more general information model. In contrast, DEN-ng is a true information model in that it does not contain keys or other technology-specific concepts and terms. It instead concentrates on defining managed objects and their interrelationships. This is also true of the TeleManagement Forum's (TMF) SID, of which the DEN-ng information model is one component.

The approach shown in Figure 10.2 was good. It took a very long time, however, to get the participants in the IETF to agree to these models. The PCIM was not published as an RFC until February 2001. Although the policy QoS information model was ready, it was not published as RFC 3644 until November 2003. The QoS device data-path information model is further behind.

There were many reasons for the holdup. This was the first time that the IETF was working with information models. Second, policy models of this depth had not been done before in the industry. The main holdup was the fact that the IETF is composed of many different people; each of whom are there primarily to represent the companies that they work for. Each network vendor had by then launched its own set of policy applications. No one wanted a standard to come out that would brand their products as noncompliant! Thus, the standards were worked on, and watered down, and watered down some more, until they represented something that everyone could agree on. The delay in issuing standards is due to these reasons plus the delay in getting different companies (through their IETF members) to announce consensus. Members are always fearful that a last-minute change in the standard will adversely impact their companies' products, and so consensus building is a relatively long process.

However, there was another, more serious, problem. The above models focused "just" on network devices. Although the PCIM was generic in nature, it was also limited. For example, there was no model of how a policy rule would be evaluated. More important, there were no business entities in these models and very few non-network entities. Thus, there was no formal way to define how business rules could use policy to control network services. The primary motivation for building the DEN-ng model was to address these problems.

10.2 WHERE WE ARE

Work has proceeded in various standards bodies and forums to rectify problems. Prominent among these is the work of the TMF. Two examples of this work are in the new-generation operational systems and software (NGOSS) architecture and the TMF's SID model.

10.2.1 NGOSS Architecture

The NGOSS architecture is characterized by the separation of the expression and execution of business processes and services from the software that implements these business processes and services. Fundamentally, NGOSS is concerned with defining an architecture that automates business processes.

For example, policies can be used to choose which set of processes are used to perform a function. Feedback from executing processes can then be used to change which policies are in force (or even applicable) at any given time. Thus, although either policy management or process management can be used by itself to manage an NGOSS system, to do so is to fail to realize the greater potential afforded by using both to manage the same system.

The NGOSS behavior and control specification defines in high-level terms the architectural ramifications of using policy management. The NGOSS policy specification defines in high-level terms the definition of a policy model that includes business, system, and implementation viewpoints. This is based on work from ISO and on a Unified Modeling Language (UML).

Although these are evolving specifications, credit should be given to the TMF for having the vision to try and specify these important concepts and also to develop them for all to use. Good examples of this are the catalyst programs of the TMF. These team demonstrations are usually led by a service provider or independent software vendor (ISV) and are designed to demonstrate one or more concepts of the NGOSS architecture. This work is important because it defines architectural and implementation ramifications of using PBNM solutions. This is one of the few forums in the world where this is being studied in depth by commercial, academic, and industrial players.

One of the prominent differences between the design of DEN-ng and the design of other information models is that DEN-ng was built to support the needs of the NGOSS architecture. All other information models that the author is familiar with were *not* built to support any particular architecture.

The TMF approach is inherently better suited to produce useful standards faster. First, it is centered on real-world work that is proven to be implementable through its catalyst programs. Second, the TMF has as one of its goals the production of a shared information model. While the IETF emphasizes protocol development, the TMF emphasizes architecture and information modeling. Finally, because the different vendors are all united in achieving common goals (architecture and information modeling), it is easier for them to come to agreement than in the IETF.

10.2.2 **TMF Shared Information and Data Model**

TMF's shared information and data model is a federated model, which means that it is composed of different "submodels," which have either been contributed by companies, mined from other standards, or developed within the TMF.

The communications industry is seeking technological advances that will improve time to market for new products and services. Service providers and enterprises like to use best-of-breed software. However, this software is hard to integrate with other software products constructed in a similar manner. Furthermore, each software product that is produced in a "vacuum" more than likely redefines concepts that are used by other applications.

To achieve true interoperability (where data from different components can be shared and reused), a common language needs to be developed and agreed on. This goal is even more important in an NGOSS system, because one of its key architectural principles is to use component-based software, interacting through contracts. Therefore, the TMF embarked on building a shared information model that could be used as a single source for defining common data.

The SID consists of inputs from Intelliden, MetaSolv, British Telecom, Telstra, Vodaphone, Motorola, Agilent, AT&T, and others. Material donated includes DEN-ng and several models and model snippets from many of these companies. The objective of the SID is to provide the industry with a common language, defined using UML, for common shared data. By agreeing on a common set of information/data definitions and relationships, the team sets forth a common language used in the definition of NGOSS architectures.

Another important feature of the SID is that it contains multiple models that concentrate on different disciplines. Most other information models concentrate on a single subject, such as networking. In contrast, the charter of the SID is to define business and system concepts for a variety of different domains. These domains characterize how network elements and services are represented, used, and managed in business and system environments.

10.2.3 **The Ingredients in a Compelling PBNM Solution**

The industry is now starting to appreciate the complexity of PBNM solutions. PBNM is more than writing a policy rule and building elaborate UML models; it is about a paradigm shift.

Historically, network management has focused on setting parameters of individual interfaces of a device one at a time. Recent innovations of policy management, ranging from new protocols to the use of information models to represent policy rules, have helped simplify this daunting task. However, in and of themselves these are insufficient to develop PBNM solutions that will solve network configuration problems and help make network services profitable once again.

We need a more extensible, more robust solution. The key to implementing this solution is to think more holistically about policy management. Most people consider policy to be a set of rules that express a set of conditions to be monitored and, if those conditions are met, one or more actions will be executed. This definition fails to take into account two key issues: users and process.

First, different types of people use policy. Business people do not want to express their policies in networking terminology, and networking people do not want policies written using business concepts. However, business and network personnel must work together to ensure that network services are managed according to the business goals of the organization. A new form of policy is needed that can translate business needs into device configuration.

However, this by itself is not enough. The second missing feature is process. No matter how simple or sophisticated, every configuration change has an underlying set of business rules that govern its deployment. Business procedures will define who checks the change for correctness (sometimes from a technical and a business point of view). They identify who must approve the change and who must implement the change. They also describe how to verify that the change has been properly implemented and what to do if a problem is discovered.

Policies define how the shared resources of the organization are accessed and allocated. Different users and services have different needs, and policy is the tool that enables the appropriate process to be applied as a function of business priority. This enables network services to be adjusted in response to the changing environment (e.g., new users logging on, different application usage, and so forth) by providing dynamic and automatic (re)configuration of the appropriate network devices according to the business rules of the organization.

The realization that business rules and processes, device configuration, and service activation are all tightly bound together provides the clue to our answer. We need a robust, extensible information model that can represent the managed environment as a set of entities. If policies are also entities that exist in this information model, then we can be assured that policies are represented using the same tools, and therefore can be applied to users, applications, device interfaces, services, and other managed objects. The information model provides a set of formalisms through which we can build a robust system.

10.3 DEFINITION OF POLICY MANAGEMENT

Policy is typically defined as a set of rules. Each policy rule consists of a condition clause and an action clause. If the condition clause is `true`, then the actions in the action clause are allowed to execute. Therefore, our first definition of policy management is:

> Policy management is the usage of rules to accomplish decisions.

Policy is usually represented as a set of classes and relationships that define the semantics of the building blocks of representing policy. These building blocks usually consist of a minimum of a policy rule, a policy condition, and a policy action. They are represented in Figure 10.3 as classes. This simple UML model

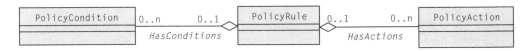

FIGURE 10.3

A simplistic policy model.

shows the relationships between these three classes. Attributes and methods have not been shown to keep the discussion simple.

Figure 10.3 shows that a `PolicyRule` contains a set of conditions and a set of actions. These are represented by the `hasConditions` and `hasActions` aggregations, respectively (an aggregation is a special type of relationship that is used to represent whole-part dependencies).

PBNM solutions usually use an information model to represent policy. Some of the better ones also use an information model to represent the subject and target of the policy. DEN-ng is unique, in that it does this for business, system, and implementation viewpoints. By representing what you want the policy to do and how you want it to act, you can use the power of an information model to represent how different entities relate to each other. For example, two different users can be logged on to the same system but receive different classes of service, which dictate how the applications that each operate are handled in the network.

An information model is a means for defining common representation of information. This enables management data to be shared, reused, and altered by multiple applications. The DEN-ng policy model is different to other policy models in the industry. However, three differences are important to discuss now. The first is the use of an event model to trigger the evaluation of the policy condition clause. This changes Figure 10.3 to what is shown in Figure 10.4.

Figure 10.4 can be read as follows:

> On receipt of an event, evaluate the `PolicyCondition` of a `PolicyRule`. If it evaluates to `true`, then execute the set of `PolicyActions` that are associated with this `PolicyRule`.

The second difference is the use of constraints to better define (through restriction and more granular specification) what the model represents. For example, it makes no sense to define a `PolicyRule` that does not have any conditions.

This is allowed in the simplistic model of Figure 10.3, because the cardinality on each end of the `hasConditions` aggregation is 0. However, this is not the case

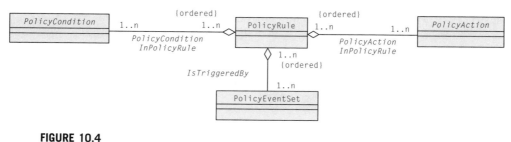

FIGURE 10.4

A simplistic view of the DEN-ng policy model.

in Figure 10.4, as the cardinality is `1..n` on each side of the `PolicyCondition InPolicyRule` aggregation. Another example is the Object Constraint Language (OCL) expression `{ordered}`. This expression requires that the `PolicyEvents`, `PolicyConditions`, and `PolicyActions` are each ordered when aggregated in the `PolicyRule`.

The third difference is that DEN-ng uses a finite-state machine to represent the state of a managed entity. Most current information models, such as those from the DMTF, IETF, and International Telecommunications Union (ITU), are *current state* models (i.e., they define a managed entity to represent a state of an object). Although important, that does not make a closed-loop system. In particular, it does not enable the life cycle of the managed object to be represented.

Therefore, DEN-ng defines a finite-state machine and instantiates multiple current state models to represent the different states that a managed object can take. This enables behavior of an individual or a group of managed objects to be represented. More important, the behavior of an object or set of objects can be related to the value of one or more attributes that are used to represent the current state of the attribute. This helps simplify the design of closed-loop PBNM solutions. For example, suppose that a particular state transition sets the attribute of an entity to a particular value and that this represents a bad or failed state. The changing of this attribute value is in fact an *event*, which can be used to trigger the evaluation of a `PolicyRule`. The `PolicyRule` can cause a state transition back to a valid state, which is checked by ensuring that the value of the attribute is changed to an acceptable value.

> Without events or a state machine, such closed-loop control is not possible. More important, policy is represented as a means to control when a managed object transitions to a new state.

This notion is simple, yet powerful. It succinctly captures the connotation of "control" that policy has and shows how policy can be used to govern the behavior of a managed object throughout its life cycle. Furthermore, it provides a means to control the behavior of a managed system in a predictable and consistent fashion. Events represent external stimuli that correspond to changes in state. If policies are used to control state transitions, then policies can be defined that govern each state of the managed object—from creation, to deployment, to destruction. This guarantees that the correct state of the managed object is achieved in response to a given event, in a simple and consistent manner.

10.4 INTRODUCTION TO AND MOTIVATION FOR POLICY MANAGEMENT

The promises of policy management are varied, powerful, and are often conceptualized as a single, simple means to control the network, as illustrated in Figure 10.5.

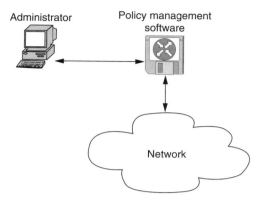

FIGURE 10.5

The promise of policy management.

The simplicity of the components shown in Figure 10.5 is part of the appeal of policy management. In particular, the ability to hide vendor-specific interfaces behind a uniform information model is very important. Without this ability, a common interface to programming the same function in different network devices cannot be accomplished. This is one of the toughest problems a network manager needs to deal with—how to string a network of multivendor equipment together to provide a seamless set of customer-facing services. Furthermore, the growth of large ISP networks that seek to provide multiple specialized services exacerbates this problem.

This drive for simplicity has led to six commonly heard value propositions for policy management that position policy management as a means of:

- Providing better than best-effort service to certain users.
- Simplifying device, network, and service management.
- Requiring less engineers to configure the network.
- Defining the behavior of a network or distributed system.
- Managing the increasing complexity of programming devices.
- Using business requirements and procedures to drive the configuration of the network.

These six points are discussed in more detail in the following subsections.

10.4.1 Providing Different Services to Different Users

The Internet was built to handle traffic on a best-effort basis. Clearly, people will not be satisfied with best-effort service. People want *predictable* services— services that they can rely on for providing information and functionality that they desire (whether the Internet is being used or not). This is the fundamental motivation for QoS.

When I worked at Cisco, we used to describe QoS as "managed unfairness." This complements the above desire for information and functionality that meet a specific set of needs. QoS is not just about providing faster downloads or more bandwidth. Rather, it is about providing the right set of functionality to provide a user with the service(s) that the user is requesting. Although this may mean faster downloads or more bandwidth, the point is that such metrics in and of themselves are not a good definition of QoS.

QoS is harder to provision and manage than it may first appear because of two factors:

1. Complexity of implementing QoS.
2. Variety of services that can use QoS.

The complexity of implementing QoS is caused by two main factors: (1) network vendors continue to add additional types of mechanisms that can be used (by themselves or with other mechanisms) to implement QoS, and (2) different devices have different QoS mechanisms. This makes it hard to ensure that the same relative levels of service are implemented by different devices that use different mechanisms.

Another problem is the lack of specificity in standards. For example, the IETF has completed a set of RFCs that specify different approaches for implementing differentiated services (e.g., the Differentiated Services RFCs). However, these RFCs by themselves are not sufficient to build an interoperable network because they concentrate on specifying behavior without specifying how to implement that behavior. For example, none of the RFCs specify what type of queuing and drop algorithms to use to implement a particular type of behavior. This is in recognition of the IETF—this is in fact in recognition of the fact that network vendors have designed a vast arsenal of different mechanisms to condition traffic as well as recognizing that different services uses different QoS mechanisms.

Thus, we have the first motivation for policy management—the promise of using a set of standard declarations for managing the different QoS mechanisms required to implement a service. This desire is amplified by the fact that multiple users want different services. Clearly, a service provider or enterprise cannot provide tens or hundreds of different services because of the complexity of managing these different services coupled with the fact that most approaches (such as DiffServ) define far less than these. DiffServ, for example, provides a set of 64 total code points, but these are divided into 32 standard and 32 experimental code points. Most service providers offer between three and ten different services. This provides the second motivation for policy management—the promise of providing a small set of standard rules that can be used to manage the set of services provided to multiple customers.

10.4.2 Simplifying Device, Network, and Service Management

PBNM was conceptualized as a set of mechanisms that can be used to "fine-tune" different network services. Similarly to how a stereo equalizer gives the user control over the response of the stereo to different frequencies, a PBNM-based system provides a set of mechanisms that can be used to condition traffic flowing through the network. PBNM systems also have the ability to define a complex set of mechanisms that can be used to implement a predefined service. This is a particularly attractive characteristic—choosing a single command to implement what previously consisted of a set of commands.

In addition, the real power of PBNM systems is through abstraction. Imagine a network where a switch feeds a router. The switch uses the IEEE 802.1q specification for delivering QoS, while the router uses DiffServ. This causes a problem, because there is not a defined set of standards for relating an 802.1q marking to a DiffServ code point (DSCP). Now, assume that the switch is programmed using Simple Network Management Protocol (SNMP) set commands, while the router is programmed using command-line interface (CLI) commands. The network administrator is now forced to learn two different ways to program a single network connection.

The motivation for PBNM is one of simplification through abstraction. By providing an intermediate layer of policy rules, PBNM users can concentrate on the task at hand, rather than the myriad programming models and traffic-conditioning mechanisms used to program a device.

However, an equally powerful motivation exists—recovery from changes and failures. Networks present an ever-changing infrastructure for providing services. The day-to-day management of this infrastructure includes making subtle changes to how different components are configured. Sometimes, these changes can adversely affect network services. These changes are hard to find, because most of the time, the change being made is not obviously related to the service that was being changed. In addition, networks can develop faults that impair the ability for the network to provide services that people and applications depend on. When this happens, administrators tend to fix the fault by changing the configuration of the device.

These and other factors culminate in a set of changes that, over time, impact the ability of the device to support one or more of its services. When this happens, PBNM systems can be used to restore the configurations of devices to their original state. Thus, PBNM provides a means to fix the fault and to also keep track of the state of various network devices. This requirement for tracking state is one of the reasons why DEN as well as DEN-ng both use finite-state machine models.

10.4.3 Requiring Fewer Engineers to Configure the Network

There is an acute shortage of engineers who understand new technologies and mechanisms implemented by network vendors. There are even less engineers who understand these technologies and are able to deploy and manage them on a network. In addition, the cost of using an emerging technology is very high, interactions with other legacy technologies are not completely known, and management costs associated with initially deploying the technology often outweigh the advantage provided by that technology.

Many network operators, for example, choose to overengineer their networks to address any performance concerns rather than deploy QoS techniques. This is because the cost associated with learning the new technologies (and the tools used to deploy them) and managing them is much higher than the savings in bandwidth-related costs that would result from deploying these technologies. Another factor is the previous lack of specificity mentioned—if different technologies are being used, then they can only interoperate if their functionality is specified at a sufficiently detailed level. For example, there is no standard that defines how to map ATM's concept of QoS to the different DSCP values that are present in an IP network.

The theory behind being able to use fewer personnel to run a network is based on distributing intelligence to managed devices and applications that manage devices so that dynamically changing environments can be more easily managed and controlled. Although the number of skilled individuals may be reduced, it is wrong to think that PBNM applications will eliminate the need for specialized network engineers. Skilled personnel will always be needed to build and operate systems.

However, PBNM systems provide two important benefits. First, the majority of network configuration tasks are simple in nature and do not require a specialist. Many of these are also repetitive. If the PBNM system can be programmed to deal with these mundane changes, then they enable more highly skilled engineers to be used on other, more strategic problems. Second, PBNM systems enforce process. Figure 10.6 illustrates this.

PBNM can be used to define processes, such as:

- Which personnel are qualified to build a configuration change.
- Which personnel must approve a configuration change.
- Which personnel must install a configuration change.
- Which personnel must validate a configuration change.

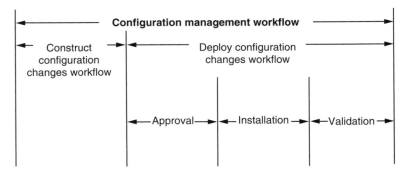

FIGURE 10.6

Processes used in configuration management.

The preceding four processes are meant to be exemplary in nature and should not be construed as being the "only" processes that are involved in device configuration.

The strength of PBNM is that these four processes (and others) can be enforced by a PBNM system independent of whether it is used to implement a configuration change or not. For some reason, this message has not been emphasized by most vendors. Even some researchers tend to ignore it, concentrating instead on the representation of policy. Two counterexamples to this trend are Intelliden and MetaSolv, both of which are building software to help in this area.

PBNM systems also offer the ability to ensure that the same approved processes are used to consistently implement specific types of configuration changes. The Intelliden product is a good example of offering these benefits.

10.4.4 Defining the Behavior of a Network or Distributed System

Networks are growing in complexity because of several factors, including an increasing number of people using networks, a growing number of different applications used, and an increase in the number of different services required by network users.

These factors all help to create an ever-growing overhead of operating and administrating networks. As a result, it is very difficult to build management systems that can cope with growing network size, complexity, and multiservice operation requirements. There is also a need to be able to dynamically change the behavior of the system to support modified or additional functionality after it has been deployed.

A single network device can have thousands of interfaces or subinterfaces. Clearly, if an administrator has to manually configure each of these, the network cannot scale. For example, assume each device interface takes 10 minutes to configure and that there are 10,000 total interfaces. This works out to requiring 69.44 days, or 9.92 weeks, to program this set of interfaces. Without software, this is simply not possible. In addition, the chances of making an error without automation software are enormous.

PBNM software can help in several ways. First, it can be used to define policy rules once and mass deploy them. For example, the Intelliden product has a concept called "command sets" that enable sets of configuration changes (which are controlled by policy) to be deployed to multiple devices concurrently. Second, policy rules can be used in either an ad hoc or reusable fashion. Although ad hoc policy rules are intended to be used once, reusable policy rules (or even policy components) are designed to be used multiple times by different applications.

This concept can be used to help simplify the arduous process of configuring different interfaces. For example, an access control list can be defined that filters on certain fields in the IP header and then performs a set of actions if those fields matched or not. This is a fundamental building block that can be used for many different types of policies. Third, large systems will execute many different policies. PBNM systems should enable different sets of policies to be analyzed to ensure that they do not result in conflicting actions.

However, most important, PBNM software can be used to capture business logic that is associated with certain conditions that occur in the network. Although centralizing the development and management of this business logic is important, coordinating its proper application is mandatory for large systems. This last point raises four important questions readers should ask when evaluating PBNM systems:

- How many physical devices is the PBNM software capable of managing?
- How many logical components (e.g., subinterfaces) is the PBNM software capable of managing?
- How many changes per time period (e.g., minute or hour) can the PBNM software execute?
- How does the PBNM solution handle errors?

Each of these points is important. The third point is especially important, because most organizations operate using a "time window" in which changes must occur. The point, then, is how many changes can your PBNM software physically perform during that time window? The reader will find that this is often the limiting factor in choosing a PBNM system. The fourth point is also critical, because one of the reasons for deploying a PBNM solution is to automate complex tasks. The form of this question is different than a simple "can it scale" question. Vendors will all claim that their solutions scale. Thus, a much easier way to be sure of what you are buying is if it can provide a common error-handling methodology for large deployments. This is a simpler and better test of what you are buying.

10.4.5 Managing the Increasing Complexity of Programming Devices

Present-day IP networks are large, complex systems that consist of many different types of devices. Different devices are chosen for cost and functionality. However, from the end user's point of view, it is imperative that the end user not have to be explicitly aware of these differences. In other words, the network should appear as a single homogenous entity that provides services for the end user.

Therefore, when most services are defined, they are characterized as having a set of properties that exist from one end of the network to the other. For example, think of a service level agreement (SLA) that specifies availability (which in this example is defined as remote access accessibility without busy signals). While the service provider will likely specify different times for different networks (e.g., a connection to a U.S. network versus a connection to a European network), it certainly will not specify availability between different parts of the network. Not only is this too hard to do (and very costly for the service provider), it doesn't really matter, because the service is specified as an end-to-end service. The end user does not care what devices or QoS mechanisms are used or what the latency or drop rate is along an intermediate path in the network as long as the service that was contracted for is successfully delivered.

Network engineers do not have this luxury. In fact, ensuring that all of the different devices that comprise a network interoperate smoothly is far from a trivial task. This is because different devices have different functionality, represented as different commands that are available to the network developer. The problem is that these different network devices are each responsible for doing their best in providing *consistent* treatment of the traffic. Clearly, if the two devices have different commands, then this is harder to achieve, because a mapping needs to be defined to map the different commands to each other.

For example, consider two Cisco devices, one running a pre-12.x release of IOS (a common operating system used by Cisco routers and other types of devices) and another running a 12.x release of IOS. Suppose that the task is to provide QoS for traffic that contains voice, video, and data. Both devices can do this. However, the actual commands that are used are very different. As an example, the design for the 12.x device is likely to use low-latency queuing, which is not available in pre-12.x IOS releases. Thus, someone (or something) has to provide a mapping between the set of commands used in each version of an operating system.

Clearly, if different devices are using different operating systems, this mapping becomes both harder and more important. Mapping the commands is a good start, but even that is not sufficient. Other factors must also be taken into account. Two important ones are side effects and dependencies in executing each command.

Sometimes, when a command is executed, effects occur that cause other entities to be affected besides the ones that are targeted by the command. These are called side effects, because though these changes were not intended, they nevertheless happened. If these commands have any side effects, then they must be noted, and if the side effects affect the traffic, then they must be emulated for each device.

Exacerbating this situation is the notion of hardware and software dependencies. For example, a device that uses an older processor may be unable to perform the same functions as a device that uses a newer processor past a certain line rate. This is a hardware dependency and must be accounted for to ensure that each device performs traffic conditioning in a consistent manner. Similarly, software dependencies exist; if they affect the flow of the traffic, then their effect must be emulated in devices that do not have these same software dependencies.

If that is not bad enough, new technologies have emerged or will continue to emerge to either address current limitations or to perform a task better. Thus, the PBNM system must be capable of addressing new commands and features of the devices that it supports. This is best done using an information model to abstract the different functionality that is present in multiple devices. For example, Figure 10.7 shows a simplified approximation of the DEN-ng QoS model, which is an information model designed to represent QoS.

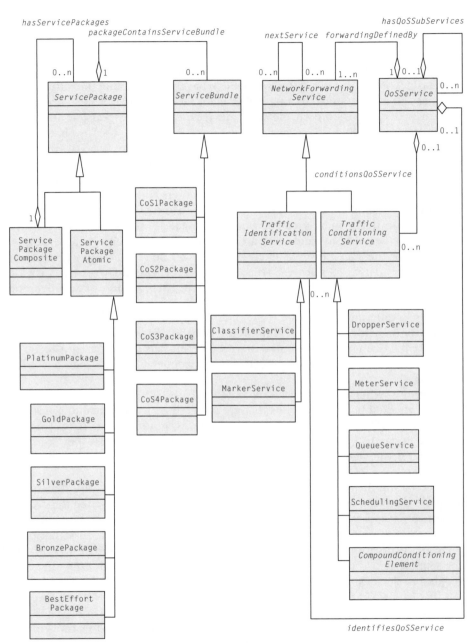

(Remember that a line with an arrowhead denotes inheritance in UML. Thus, GoldPackage is a subclass of ServiceBundle, which is a subclass of CustomerFacingService, which is a subclass of Service.)

FIGURE 10.7

Simplified DEN-ng QoS model.

In DEN-ng, there are two types of services: CustomerFacingServices and ResourceFacingServices. This is modeled as two separate subclasses that inherit from the Service superclass.

CustomerFacingServices are services that a customer is directly aware of. For example, a virtual private network (VPN) is a service that a customer can purchase. ResourceFacingServices are network services that are required to support the functionality of a CustomerFacingService, but which the customer cannot (and should not!) know about. For example, a service provider doesn't sell Border Gateway Protocol (BGP, a means of advertising routes between networks) services to a customer. Yet, BGP is required for different types of CustomerFacingServices to operate correctly. Thus, BGP is an example of a ResourceFacingService.

A ServicePackage is an abstraction that enables the packaging of different CustomerFacingServices together as a group. Thus, a GoldService user may access high-quality voice, video, and data, whereas a SilverService user may be unable to use voice.

Several types of ResourceFacingServices are shown in the preceding figure. QoSService is an abstraction that relates the particular networking architecture to its ability to provide QoS. For example, ToSService uses the 3-bit type-of-service (ToS) bits in IPv4 to define the QoS that can be given, whereas DiffServService uses the 6-bit code point to define much more granular QoS for IPv4. Because a given network may have both DiffServ-compliant and DiffServ-unaware devices, the information model provides a formal way to synchronize their configurations, so that a given ToS setting provides the same QoS as a particular DiffServ setting.

Finally, NetworkForwardingService defines how traffic is conditioned and has two types of subservices: the ability to identify traffic and the ability to affect the order in which packets are transmitted from the device. Again, because these are distinct concepts, two distinct subclasses are used to represent them: TrafficIdentificationService and TrafficConditioningService, respectively. As for TrafficIdentificationServices, ClassifierService performs the separation of traffic into distinct flows that each receive their own quality of service, whereas MarkerService represents the ability of a device to mark or remark the ToS or DiffServ bits. This marking tells the other devices what type of QoS that flow should receive. With respect to TrafficConditioningServices:

- DropperService drops packets according to a particular algorithm, which has the effect of telling certain types of sending applications to slow their transmission.
- MeterService limits the transmission of packets.
- QueueService delays the transmission of packets.
- SchedulingService defines which queue (of multiple output queues) should send packets.

■ `CompoundConditioningService` models advanced features, which are combinations of the above basic services.

The objective in such a model is to describe a particular feature (such as metering) and how that feature relates to other features (e.g., classification and dropping) in a particular function (e.g., traffic conditioning) using classes and relationships. The idea is that if the abstractions are defined properly they can be used to model the types of functions that are present in different vendor devices and accommodate new functionality.

Put another way, the model can be used as a design template for constructing commands that are to be applied to a device or set of devices. The advantage of such a model is that the model can be used to represent the functionality desired and can hide the intricacies of translating to different implementations from the user. In fact, this is one of the principles on which the Intelliden R-Series was founded.

Sometimes, such models are all that are needed, and enable vendor-specific programs that are derived directly from these models to be used. Often, however, additional information is required. In the DEN-ng information model, this will take the form of subclasses that are used to model vendor-specific differences from the model.

10.4.6 Using Business Rules to Drive Network Configuration

The thesis of *A New Paradigm for Network Management* is that existing network management architectures prevent business processes from being used to drive the configuration and management of the network. In essence, this paper states that businesses must define and implement network services according to their own business processes and policies. Although this is true for all businesses, it is even more true for the so-called "next-generation network" initiatives and corporations that are striving to become more profitable by changing the network services that they provide.

Business driven device management (BDDM) is one example of using business rules to drive network configuration. As defined by the author, BDDM is a new paradigm that enables business rules to be used to manage the construction and deployment of network configuration changes. The difference is that BDDM controls both the construction and the deployment of configuration changes using a combination of policies and processes.

Most of the current research in PBNM systems revolves around the definition of policy class hierarchies that can be used to represent functionality of a network device. BDDM leverages this work, but combines it with policies and processes that define how configuration changes are created, deployed, and modified in a scalable and consistent manner. Part of the desire to use business rules to drive the configuration of a device is because business rules provide a higher-level view of what needs to be accomplished. This is necessary to ensure that those changes will not disrupt the operation of the device or the network. This, in turn, requires other entities besides devices and services (such as users and their various different roles) to be modeled.

Although abstractions that are used to represent business entities can still be modeled in UML, their content and detail is significantly different than that used for device and service entities. The administrator does not have to understand the low-level details of the technology used to support a particular business need to direct its usage. For example, suppose that a network operator needs to define three levels (gold, silver, and bronze) of customers. An administrator can easily assign each customer to a particular level based on their contract.

A variety of techniques can be used to implement these three services in the network; one such example is to use DiffServ. However, there is a difference between the business person, whose job is to assign a particular service level to a customer, and a network administrator, who is responsible for implementing commands that will enable the network to recognize and enforce these three network service levels.

Both the business person and the network administrator can use policies. For example, a business person may need to write policies for handling service outages or interruptions, whereas a network administrator will be more interested in writing policies that control how the configuration of a device is changed. This difference is fundamental to how policies for each are used and expressed, and mandates that different representations of policy should be used for the business person and the network administrator.

If business rules and processes are not used to manage changes made to the configuration of network devices, the device's configuration is reduced to changing lines in a file. This doesn't reflect how the business operates! Even worse, this means that the network is probably not reflecting the proper set of services that the organization needs to run its business. The semantics of what to change, when to change it, and who can change it are all captured using business rules and processes. These semantics must be used to drive how the configuration is constructed and deployed.

However, the problem is more complex than "just" modeling QoS commands or defining which user can make a configuration change. Fundamentally, different types of people—having different responsibilities and different functions in the organization—use policy for different reasons. Business people do not want to express their policies in networking terminology, because network terminology is not needed to express their requirements. Similarly, networking people do not want policies written using business concepts, because these concepts are usually not precise enough to enable them to program the devices that they are managing. However, both business and network personnel must work together to ensure that network services are managed according to the business goals of the organization. A set of policies that supports the translation between one type of policy and another is therefore needed.

This translation between different types of policies is called the *policy continuum*. Each level in the policy continuum addresses a specific type of user who

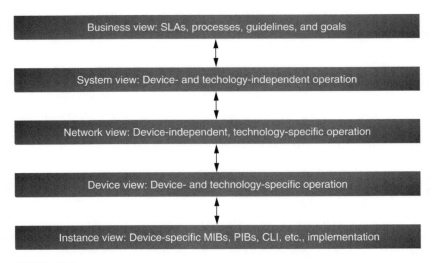

FIGURE 10.8

The policy continuum as defined in DEN-ng.

has a very specific understanding of the managed entities operating at that particular level of abstraction. The policy continuum is shown in Figure 10.8. The PBNM system must translate these entities and concepts between layers of the policy continuum. The DEN-ng model is the only information model that uses the concept of a policy continuum.

This chapter and the next use the new DEN-ng information model to represent managed entities, people, and applications that use those managed and policy entities. The advantage of using a single information model that has multiple domains is that it is easier to relate different elements in each domain to other elements in other domains.

10.4.7 Summary of the Benefits of PBNM

PBNM's traditional promise is that people will be able to deploy more complex services across a wider array of devices with fewer highly skilled individuals. This will in turn simplify network and service management. This is augmented by newer promises, such as those envisioned by BDDM, that use business requirements to drive the network's configuration. This forms a tight closed-loop system in which decisions governing the behavior of the network and the services it provides are driven by business rules. The results of these promises are compelling: increased revenue, faster time to activate services, and decreased expenses.

The next two sections will focus on two key themes:

- The need for and use of a shared information model.
- The benefits of using PBNM.

10.5 THE NEED FOR A NEW SHARED INFORMATION MODEL

The two big issues that face us today concerning network devices and network management are:

1. Lack of a consistent product model prevents predictable behavior.
2. No standard for shared data.

10.5.1 Lack of a Consistent Product Model

The lack of a consistent product model means that, despite all the standards that you hear about, different vendors build devices with different hardware and software. One router can have vastly different characteristics and functionality than another router. This situation is exacerbated when mergers, acquisitions, and divestitures occur, as the customer ends up buying completely different devices that happen to have the same logo and vendor name on them. Therefore, when different devices are used in the same network, predictable behavior cannot be obtained.

Standards help define invariant parts of the programming model. However, they are usually not explicit enough to guarantee interoperability. For example, RFC 2474 defines the structure of a DSCP, which is used to indicate how to condition traffic. The invariant portion of this RFC includes the fact that a DSCP is 6 bits long, and certain bit patterns are already defined. However, this RFC does not define which dropping and queuing algorithms to use for different bit patterns. Thus, multiple vendors can be compliant with the differentiated service standard (of which this RFC is one element) without being able to interoperate.

This is also true, but to a lesser degree, of the emerging policy information model standards. RFC 3060 and RFC 3460 define a class hierarchy and relationships for representing generic policy elements, while further work in the IETF extends these to provide QoS models. There is even a Lightweight Directory Access Protocol (LDAP) mapping, and the beginnings of one for policy core extension LDAP schema. These classes and relationships help define how policy is used to control various QoS mechanisms. However, these models have very limited semantics and are subject to interpretation by different applications. For example, these networking concepts are not linked closely enough to network device and service entities to specify how policy could be used to program device features (let alone commands). As a simple example, because these models do not specify the concept of a device interface they cannot be used to specify how to program a device interface.

More important, these models do not contain any associations to business entities, such as `Product` and `Customer`. Thus, they cannot be used to define which `Services` from which `Products` are assigned to which `Customers`. This also contributes to the complexity of building a management system, because now additional components must be used if business rules and processes are used to drive the configuration of the network.

A networking model that is associated with other models that represent users and targets of networking services and a policy model that controls how networking services are implemented and provided to users are needed. This requires a layered, integrated information model.

10.5.2 Lack of a Standard for Representing Shared Data

Until the TMF launched its SID model effort, no standard existed for sharing and reusing data for network devices and services. The common information model (CIM) of the DMTF is rooted in instrumentation of desktop applications. Although the model has reached out over the last few years to encompass additional concepts, it still lacks many telecommunications concepts that enterprise and service provider networks need. For example, its physical device model has no physical port, and its logical model has no device interface. Without these, the model cannot be used in telecommunications applications. The CIM is not a bad model; it is simply not a self-contained model that can be used for telecommunications applications.

This is precisely why the DEN-ng and the SID efforts were started. The DEN-ng effort was designed to extend and enhance the original DEN effort to tie it more closely to the NGOSS effort of the TMF. The design of the DEN-ng model is unique, because one of its use cases is to support the NGOSS architecture specification.

The DEN-ng effort focuses on modeling network elements and services. However, it provides a business, system, and implementation viewpoint of these models. The focus of the SID is on the entire NGOSS environment. The SID uses many models, including DEN-ng, to provide comprehensive coverage of entities and concepts present in an NGOSS environment.

DEN-ng is being developed in the TMF because the TMF catalyst programs can be used to validate and spread the model across different service providers, vendors, and independent software vendors (ISVs). This distribution vehicle (which also provides detailed feedback) is lacking in other standards bodies and forums and is one of the main reasons why DEN-ng was developed in the TMF.

The DEN-ng policy model was developed using an iterative top-down, bottom-up approach. Business concerns were first considered, which provided a high-level structure for and helped define key concepts of the overall policy information model. This model was then augmented by adding detail necessary to build a system. This is currently where the public part of the DEN-ng set of specifications exists.

Intelliden's vision is to take this a step further in its product line. Once these business and system views were defined, a set of tools will be produced that will focus on translating the information model to two different data models: a directory data model and a Java model. This will enable the information model to be implemented in software. A second set of tools will be developed, which will focus on ease of implementation (Figure 10.9).

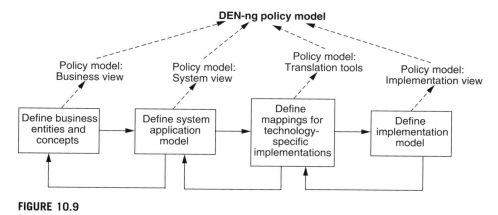

FIGURE 10.9

Design approach for building the DEN-ng policy model.

This brief description is meant to show the reader that information models can and should be used to drive software implementations. By embedding the information model in a product, that product is better able to adjust to changing features and functions. For example, in the Intelliden R-Series, the different functions of IOS are modeled using extensions of the DEN-ng logical model. When a new IOS train is released, Intelliden only has to update the model. Code is then generated that understands these features, and these features are updated as part of that release's product catalog. These features are assigned as capabilities to that particular IOS version.

This is a great example of building to accommodate the future. The information model provides a formal structure to represent different device capabilities. Software can then be written that uses this formal structure to represent these capabilities in the R-Series product. This enables the structure of the R-Series to be fixed; when new IOS releases are produced by Cisco, Intelliden updates the information model, new Java code is generated, and the *rest of the interface and APIs of the product stay the same*.

As another example, in the Intelliden implementation, the information model is used for the following tasks:

- Represent different functions that can be programmed using IOS software:
  - Routing and forwarding functions.
  - Peering with other hosts and devices.
  - Traffic classification and conditioning functions.
- Represent different commands and their structure as a function of a particular software release.
- Represent different hardware and software capabilities of a given device.

- Define business policies that control:
  - Who can perform what changes on which devices.
  - Who must approve a certain change (or category of changes).
  - When a change is deployed.
- Define system policies that control when certain actions happen (e.g., when a device is examined for changes to its configuration and/or to its physical composition).
- Define implementation policies that control how changes are made and how services are activated.

The information model serves as the centralized authority that links different parts of the managed environment to each other. As shown in the preceding example, the information model is used to define different types of policies that are used to control various types of behavior. Business, system, and implementation parts of the product are all seamlessly integrated using the DEN-ng information model.

10.5.3 Why an Information Model Is Important

An information model is more than just a representation of a set of objects. The most important feature of an information model is its ability to describe relationships between managed objects. From this, other types of models and diagrams, such as defining how data flow within the system, can be defined.

The information model serves as a normalization layer. By concentrating on invariant aspects of an object (e.g., a device has physical ports over which information flows), a framework can be defined that can represent the different features and functions of heterogeneous devices. Device-specific differences can then be modeled by extending the common framework to accommodate the features and functions of these different devices. Without a common framework, different device features and functions cannot be easily accommodated because there is no common set of objects that can be used to build them from.

In other words, to accommodate ten new features, a system that does not have a common information modeling framework must define ten new sets of objects (and more if interactions between these objects are to be modeled). If it is desired to interoperate between these ten new features, then in the worst case, all of the permutations of each new object operating with not just the other objects, but existing objects, must be defined.

Compare this to a system that uses a common framework. Adding ten new features means that the framework itself will be expanded to accommodate as many of these as extensions (i.e., subclasses) as possible. Furthermore, by developing these new features as extensions, interoperability with existing concepts and information is guaranteed.

It is not feasible to have a single information model that can represent the full diversity of management information that is needed. This is because the charac-

DEN-ng common framework model						
SID business interaction model	SID party model	SID product model	SID location model	DEN-ng and SID policy framework model	DEN-ng and SID service framework model	DEN-ng and SID resource framework model
	DEN-ng party model (subclass of SID model)	DEN-ng product model (subclass of SID model)	DEN-ng location model (subclass of SID model)	DEN-ng business policy model DEN-ng application policy model	DEN-ng MPLS VPN model DEN-ng IPsec model	DEN-ng physical resource model DEN-ng logical resource model

	Representative of other models	Representative of other models	Representative of other models

FIGURE 10.10

A simplified view of the DEN-ng layered information model.

teristics of managed data are very different and require many different subject matter experts. DEN-ng solved this problem by defining a layered information model that used patterns and roles.

A layered information model is one in which a common framework is built that supports different domain models. A simplified view of the DEN-ng layered information model is shown in Figure 10.10.

The DEN-ng common framework model consists of a set of classes and relationships that enable the different lower-level models to be associated with each other. Because DEN-ng and SID are complementary, the DEN-ng model takes the work of the SID team and either uses it in an unaltered state (as shown by the business interaction model) or makes minor modifications to it (as is done in the party, product, and location models). Note that for the party, product, and location models, DEN-ng takes the SID models and defines new subclasses wherever possible.

This means that the DEN-ng versions are more granular versions of the SID models. If DEN-ng needs to change something in the SID, then it is submitted as a change for review by the SID team. In addition, many parts of the DEN-ng model are in the process of being contributed to the SID team, as is shown in the policy, service, and resource models. Each of these is in reality another framework model, which additional submodels "plug into." For example, the DEN-ng policy model provides a generalized framework into which business policy, application use of policy, and other policy models can each plug into.

To provide as extensible a framework as possible, DEN-ng uses patterns and roles to model common concepts in as generic a way as possible. This differentiates DEN-ng from most other models (e.g., DMTF, IETF, and ITU), as they do not use roles and patterns.

Modeling objects describe entities in a system, their interrelationships and behavior, and how data flow within the system. This provides the ability to represent and understand the programming model of the device. Three examples are CLI, SNMP, and Transaction Language-1 (TL1). TL1 is a set of ASCII instructions that an OSS uses to manage a network element—usually an optical device.

More important, modeling provides the ability to understand dependencies between hardware and software. For example, a router may have a line card that has a main CPU and memory that are dedicated to performing traffic-conditioning functions. This may work fine at low speeds (e.g., a fractionalized T1). However, at high speeds, such as OC-48, suppose that this particular type of CPU cannot keep up. Or even if it could, suppose that there was not enough memory.

This is an example of a dependency that most current PBNM systems will not catch. That is, the card has the correct operating system version, and the operating system says that it can perform this type of function. However, the physical media are simply too fast for this card to perform this type of function. The reason that most PBNM systems will not catch this dependency is because there is no convenient way to represent it. In contrast, any PBNM system that uses an information model, such as DEN-ng, will be able to model this and other dependencies naturally.

Information modeling provides a common language to represent the features and functions of different devices. DEN-ng uses the concepts of *capabilities* to represent functions of an entity and *constraints* as restrictions on those functions. Think of the information model as defining a common language that enables the different capabilities of each device to be represented in a common way. This enables them to be programmed together to deliver a common service. But sometimes, a particular environment might restrict the use of certain commands. For example, export control laws might restrict different encryption or other features from being used. These are modeled as constraints.

> The combination of capabilities and constraints form a set of powerful abstractions that can be used to model current and future devices and services.

10.5.4 Linking Business, System, and Implementation Views

Most information models have focused on policy as a domain that is isolated from the rest of the managed environment. Here, domain is used to signify a set of related information and concepts. In contrast, the main use case for the DEN-ng policy model is to define a policy model that is closely integrated with the rest of the managed environment. The DEN-ng policy model is best thought of as an information model that defines how policy interacts with the rest of the managed environment (which is also represented as an information model). This has three important consequences.

First, it was apparent that building a policy information model in isolation of other information models was not going to work. The original DEN specification, as well as CIM, had many different domains in addition to policy. However, little effort was made to associate policy in detail with these other domains. In addition, the original DEN and CIM models did not specify in enough detail how policy could be applied to a managed object. The DEN-ng model takes a different approach. It builds out the policy model as one of the last domain models and then concentrates on associating appropriate parts of the policy model with appropriate parts of other domain models.

Second, the existing models concentrated on representing policy. They either did not address or addressed in a very superficial manner how policy affected other managed entities. The difference here is subtle but important. Current policy models concentrate on defining the structure of a policy rule, what its condition terms are, and so forth. Although there was a lot of talk about policy changing a value in a device configuration file, the details of *how* that was accomplished were left unspecified.

For example, the IETF and DMTF models do not specify the concept of a device interface or physical port. If the device uses CLI to change its configuration, how then can policy be used if these fundamental concepts are not modeled? The DEN-ng policy model fixes this unfortunate situation by developing other domain models alongside the policy model and ensuring that appropriate elements in the policy model can be associated with appropriate elements in other models. The goal of DEN-ng is the ability to translate policy expressions *directly* to running code—something that cannot be done with existing models.

Third, the original models (and almost all current additions to those models) are still thinking of policy in a very static way (i.e., they use policies to express the static configuration of target devices). Most models concentrate solely on the network layer and do not provide an information model for representing business entities and how they affect target devices. In fact, there is very little literature on detailed information models that are designed with business views in mind, and even less literature describing how business information models can be linked to information models of other domains.

For example, how does a changed SLA affect device configuration files? Clearly, the SLA defines how traffic should be treated, but when it is changed, the policy of treating that traffic is changed—how is that accomplished? Or how does a customer, who has just bought a new product with a higher class of service, get that service installed and running? These are two simple examples of linking the business world, with its set of entities and concepts, to the system and networking worlds, which have different expressions for those concepts. Although policy is required, unless the representations are equated, the business, system, and networking domains will always remain disconnected. This adversely affects service activation and deployment.

Both the IETF and DMTF approaches do not attempt to represent business entities and objectives. Although a few other approaches do, none have addressed building a set of models that are designed to support business, system, implementation, and runtime views that are closely tied to an overall architecture.

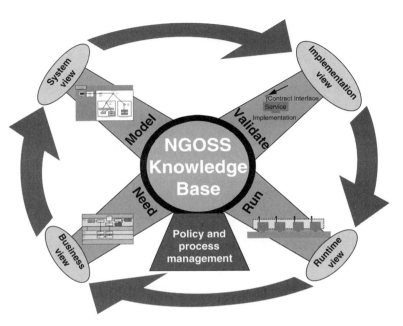

FIGURE 10.11

The TMF NGOSS architecture.

Figure 10.11 shows a conceptual view of the NGOSS architecture. The NGOSS knowledge base is a collection of information and data models, specifications, contracts, code, and supporting documentation that collectively and cooperatively describe how to build an NGOSS system. The four quadrants represent the business, system, implementation, and runtime views. The overall behavior of the system is driven by the holistic combination of policy and process management functions.

The TMF has developed a set of principles and procedures to coordinate each of these four processes. This takes the form of the various architectural specifications (e.g., TMF053 series), the TMF documents, the contract work, and other elements, which together form the NGOSS knowledge base. Each of the DEN-ng domain models were built to fit into this approach.

A key objective of the NGOSS methodology is the development of models that focus on particular characteristics and procedures in an NGOSS system. These are characterized by the four viewpoints shown in Figure 10.11. The viewpoints are in turn tied together through the use of common shared information and a common means to exchange that information—contracts. The combination of the SID and contracts allow interoperability to be realized.

The SID (as well as DEN-ng) was built to provide a set of entities that model business, system, implementation, and runtime concepts. Put another way, the

SID (and DEN-ng) were built to help realize the NGOSS architecture shown in Figure 10.11 by providing a common language to represent the transition of a concept from the business through the runtime views.

One main goal of the DEN-ng policy model was to accommodate the NGOSS architecture as shown in Figure 10.11. The DEN-ng policy model accomplishes this goal in two ways. First, it uses the different layers of the policy continuum to define different abstractions that must be modeled. This enables the different users of policy to work with and express concepts in their own terminology, rather than having the terminology and concepts of a static model given to them, never to be changed. Second, the different viewpoints are each supported by different views of the DEN-ng information model. This is realized by focusing on different entities for each of the DEN-ng domain models.

10.6 THE BENEFITS OF PBNM

There are many benefits to PBNM solutions. Some of the original drivers were listed at the beginning of this chapter. This section describes some of the more popular current benefits.

10.6.1 An Intelligent Alternative to Overprovisioning the Network

The economic downturn has forced companies to stop overprovisioning their networks and instead look to more intelligent means of delivering needed network services.

Overprovisioning may be done for several reasons. An organization may be running several mission-critical applications that must run in a timely, noninterrupted fashion. Or, it may use overprovisioning to achieve the desired levels of application delivery, such as QoS, which its users require. However, the real reason that most networks have been overprovisioned is that it is supposedly easier and cheaper than its alternative—classifying, prioritizing, and conditioning the different types of traffic that exist in the network.

In truth, although overprovisioning can deliver on some of its promises, it cannot really solve QoS, and it is very expensive. With respect to QoS, overprovisioning attempts to solve the problem by making it go away. That is, its approach is to provide more resources than will be needed. However, QoS is all about *levels*. For example, although the following mechanisms all take a different approach to QoS, they all use a particular level on which to act:

- Congestion management methods, which essentially are different ways to sort and schedule traffic.
- Congestion-avoidance methods, which use various techniques to avoid congestion from occurring.
- Policing and shaping enable the input and output rates of traffic to be controlled.

Part of managing different types of traffic is planning on which types of traffic need which resources and trying to ensure that those resources exist. The problem with overprovisioning is that it never establishes a minimum level of performance. In addition, you must be careful what you overprovision. For example, providing extra bandwidth for certain types of applications, such as Systems Network Architecture (SNA) and voice, does nothing; these applications need strict requirements on jitter, latency, and delay.

Of course, other problems exist with overprovisioning. The most important of these is that your network is being severely underutilized most of the time. Overprovisioning means that you will provision the network for a particular capacity. The longer you run at less than that capacity, the less your valuable (and expensive!) equipment is used.

PBNM solutions can be used to intelligently allocate resources. There is no free lunch here, however. A lot of work must be done, and the amount of work is arguably more than simply throwing equipment at the problem, as is done in overprovisioning. This is because what is important is ensuring that different applications having different needs of the network can peacefully coexist. This is more difficult than simply adding more bandwith. However, the benefits are a more efficient, cost-effective, streamlined operation. Plus, as PBNM is implemented to classify traffic, it can also be used for a variety of other tasks (such as providing better security) at the same time.

10.6.2 Providing Better Security

As the number of users and applications proliferate, networks get more complex, and with complexity comes risk. One important form of risk is resource abuse.

The benign form of resource abuse is when authorized users misuse their network privileges (e.g., downloading large music or video files when the network is congested, playing network games, and other acts). Users often do not realize what an adverse effect such acts can have on a network. PBNM solutions can help by simplifying the enforcement of policies that clamp down on these abuses and prevent them from happening.

The worrisome form of resource abuse is when unauthorized users attempt to gain access to corporate information. A variant of this is when malicious users attempt to disrupt the operation of the network by either a denial-of-service attack or by sending a worm or virus into the network. PBNM can help categorize traffic into expected and unexpected types and assign rules to deal with each. For example, if a Web-based virus is detected, a PBNM product can easily shut down the ability for routers to forward Web traffic. This helps contain the problem while it is being diagnosed.

The dangerous form of resource abuse is when an employee or similarly trusted user decides to willfully misuse his or her privileges and violate a company's intellectual property rights. Studies show that the greatest threats to intellectual property come from within a company. PBNM lets administrators restrict users to only those applications and information sources that they need during their current session.

Any one of these forms can stop unauthorized applications from using shared resources that they should not have access to. For example, if the goal is to meet a particular SLA that has availability levels specified, the seemingly innocent use of the network to download research information may cause periods of congestion that cause the SLA to fail. An SLA is a business concept. Therefore, it makes sense to let the business and IT personnel define which users can use which shared resources. This allows the company to define its network utilization based on the real requirements of the business contract. PBNM solutions are a good match for business policies that seek to optimize the performance of the network—the PBNM tools can be used to catch such unwanted occurrences and help ensure that the SLA is met. PBNM solutions can also be used to reveal traffic usage patterns, so that policies can be fine-tuned on an ongoing basis.

The common thread in all of these examples is that PBNM tools operate by first classifying traffic. Just as classification is used to decide which type of traffic conditioning to give to a particular flow, it can also be used to determine whether a particular user can access a resource or not. Depending on the capabilities of the PBNM tool, it may be able to do even more. For example, some PBNM tools can perform "deep packet inspection" and examine the contents of URLs. Security improvements can be done if the PBNM tool enables administrators to write policies to perform these checks and actions.

10.6.3 Managing Device Complexity

Network devices can be classified along several different dimensions. Some of the more important ways of classifying network devices are:

- What is the role of this device? For example, will it be on the edge or in the core? Is it a border router?
- What is the physical capacity of this device? For example, how much of a particular resource (e.g., number of ports) does a device have?
- What is the logical capacity of this device? For example, how many VPNs can a particular device support?
- What is the programming model (e.g., CLI, SNMP, TL1, etc.) used to program the device?
- What is the programming model used to monitor the device?
- Which version of the operating system is this device going to use?
- What are the critical features (i.e., commands) that this device must support?
- Which types of cards are available for this device?
- Is the configuration small enough to fit in flash memory, or does it require RAM?
- Which types of services are planned to be activated on this device?

This is a very short list of many of the different factors that need to be considered. An information model is well suited for managing this complexity, as it is able to represent these different device characteristics and relate them to each other. For example, the simplified DEN-ng model shown in Figure 10.10 provides separate physical and logical resource models. Associations and constraints can be defined that relate different logical features to different physical features, thereby building up a more complete picture of the device.

Similarly, policy can be applied to control which combinations of features can be used in a given situation. Separating the different domain models (e.g., physical resource from logical resource in the preceding example) enables each domain model to change without adversely impacting the other domain models. All that needs to be updated are the relationships between the different domain models. Furthermore, the ability to work on each domain model in parallel enables the information model to be more rapidly updated to accommodate new devices.

The benefit of using an information model to model device features and functionality is that this method is robust enough to justify the investment in understanding the capabilities of the information model. It provides a robust starting point for managing device and service complexity and offers an extensible and scalable platform to accommodate the future requirements of new devices and services.

10.6.4 Managing Complex Traffic and Services

The world has changed. Today, more types of applications are available that generate more types of traffic than ever before. Some sophisticated applications generate several types of traffic of different types (e.g., H.323 traffic, which generates both UDP and TCP flows). Other applications provide unpredictable behavior (e.g., they open random ports for communication).

In addition, networks have increased in complexity. Security is more important than ever, because a network can carry many types of different traffic. Many of the individual flows representing this traffic load have different requirements. In the typical converged network (i.e., a network that carries data, voice, and video application traffic), some of the flows are sensitive to delay and jitter, whereas others are not. Thus, different flows require different types of traffic conditioning. For example, using any of the weighted fair-queuing approaches will adversely affect voice traffic. Instead, voice traffic demands priority queuing so that jitter, latency, and delay can be controlled. However, if priority queuing is used for data traffic, relatively unimportant flows can swamp the priority queue and effectively starve other types of traffic. As another example, some traffic is classified as mission critical. If this traffic is to share the same network resources, then it demands completely different treatment to avoid compromising its usage.

Therefore, simply throwing bandwidth at network traffic is no longer the answer (not that it ever was for certain types of flows, such as Systems Network

Architecture traffic, but people keep stubbornly associating PBNM with bandwidth). The real problem that network administrators face today is how to enable multiple applications that each demand slightly different resources from the network to not just peacefully coexist, but to work and consume shared resources according to their importance.

PBNM solutions are natural choices for these types of applications. PBNM solutions are predicated on analyzing traffic and classifying it into one of several predefined categories. Each category will correspond to preprovisioned traffic conditioning that is suited to the type of traffic that is being carried by that application. Advanced network technologies, such as Multi-Protocol Label Switching (MPLS) or DiffServ (or even both), can be used to mark this traffic so that appropriate traffic conditioning is applied.

10.6.5 Handling Traffic More Intelligently

Because PBNM solutions rely on classification, they provide the opportunity to make other more intelligent decisions regarding how to handle all types of traffic. In addition to deciding how the flow is to be conditioned, the classification decision itself can be used to help direct different types of traffic. For example:

- Nonauthorized users, as well as other forms of unwanted traffic, can be denied access to network resources. This is not to say that firewalls or VPNs are no longer needed; rather, it means that an additional measure of security is present and available.

- Business-critical applications can be identified immediately and transported using special mechanisms, such as policy-based routing (i.e., based on a classification decision, traffic can be instructed to use a special path that normal traffic is not allowed to use).

Many more examples could be given. PBNM solutions provide the inherent intelligence to be used to accomplish more tasks than those that were originally intended.

10.6.6 Performing Time-Critical Functions

PBNM solutions can simplify and better implement two basic types of time-critical network functions:

1. Change device configurations within a specific time window.
2. Perform scheduled provisioning functions.

The first point reflects the need to address common maintenance functions. Most organizations perform maintenance operations on their network at night or during other nonbusiness hours to avoid any inadvertent adverse effects on the operation of network services. The second point addresses small, simple changes for a specific customer or set of customers. This is the "network equivalent" of setting up a conference call.

Part of the allure of PBNM solutions is that they can address both of these functions.

10.7 SUMMARY

This chapter provided a quick retrospective on how PBNM was designed. Despite many of its early limitations, such as having single-vendor approaches and being focused on a particular technology, great promise was envisioned for PBNM solutions. Accordingly, vendors poured resources into making various types of policy solutions, and the press hyped these new solutions.

Unfortunately, these early solutions were misunderstood and were quickly developed without supporting technology and, most important, standards. Interoperability was destroyed, and PBNM started to get a bad reputation.

Fortunately, the TMF rejuvenated this effort. It brought a completely different approach—one predicated on tying policy to an architecture that used a shared information model—to the forefront. The TMF's NGOSS architecture emphasized the importance of business rules and processes, which was something that was lacking in previous efforts. Furthermore, it resurrected early work done using viewpoints to help provide an integrated, multifaceted approach for defining policy. This was picked up by the TMF's SID effort. The SID is a federated approach that incorporates DEN-ng and other models and information definitions. *The result is that policy has reemerged as a new approach that is tightly integrated with other domain models.*

The DEN-ng effort was based on this premise. It added additional insight, such as the use of a policy continuum and a finite-state machine, to transform it to a *collected set of models, each of which represented a state of a managed object. Policy, then, was redefined as the means to control when a managed object transitioned to a new state.*

With this introduction in place, the motivation for PBNM was examined in more detail. Part of the allure of PBNM was its simplicity. Other benefits were also its ability to provide different services to different users; its promise of simplifying device, network, and service management; and its promise of requiring less engineers to do the work. Newer promises, such as helping to define the behavior of a system and managing the ever-increasing complexity of devices and services, were added.

However, the true breakthrough was when PBNM was defined as a means for business rules to drive the configuration of the network. This brought forth the promise of changing the network from a cost center to a profit center. Although the other benefits are very important, they only incrementally affect profitability. Transforming the network into a profit center is very compelling, as it affects the bottom line of the entire organization.

To complete this transformation, two key ingredients were needed. The first was the establishment of a shared information model. This was needed for many reasons, but one of the most important ones was interoperability. Modern-day OSSs are not purchased from a single vendor, as they are too complex. Instead, they are built from best-of-breed applications. For these applications to scale, they should be constructed as components. For the components to share and reuse data, they need to use the same data, defined in a "universal language" that any OSS component that needs to share data can use. This universal language takes the form of a layered information model. DEN-ng and the SID are part of that solution.

The second ingredient is a revolution in how management applications are built. Management applications should be constructed using models to define their data and architecture. This revolutionary idea is epitomized by the NGOSS architecture. Its design process uses four viewpoints—business, system, implementation, and runtime—to define the functionality and processes of the architecture. Interoperability is achieved using the SID and contracts, which define how data are communicated.

Finally, five new benefits of PBNM solutions were provided. Two of these focused on providing more intelligence to routing and managing traffic. Instead of overprovisioning the network and wasting valuable resources, PBNM can be used to intelligently assign different traffic to preprovisioned paths that already have the appropriate traffic conditioning in place. In addition, managing complex traffic and services, where different types of traffic having different needs compete for the same shared resources, can be efficiently managed using PBNM solutions.

Additional benefits were provided by realizing that the classification portion of PBNM solutions can be used for providing better security, accommodating the needs of confidential and mission-critical traffic, and others.

Finally, PBNM can be used to manage device complexity. Combined with an information model, a system can be built that can accommodate new types of devices that have new types of functionality by changing the information model and ensuring that software can be used to translate changes in the information model to code. In other words, the structure, graphical user interface, and application programming interfaces of the application remain constant; only the internals (which are governed by the information model) change. An example of this new avant-garde application is the Intelliden R-Series.

Policy-Based Network Management Fundamentals

This chapter, taken from Chapter 2 of *Policy-Based Network Management* by Strassner, introduces basic terms and definitions that are used in the study of policy management, as well as a simplified conceptual model of policy. This will be followed by describing the high-level system requirements of a policy-based network management system. Key among these is the notion of business rules driving the construction and deployment of device and network configuration. This new approach enables the network to be operated as a profit center instead of a cost center.

11.1 INTRODUCTION

This chapter describes where policy-based management (PBM) systems fit in the overall scheme of management systems and provides an introduction to their operating context. As such, it will answer three fundamental questions:

- What is policy-based management?
- Why is it important?
- How is it used?

Policy-based management was briefly defined in Chapter 10. This is a very active research area, with entire conferences and parts of prestigious conferences covering various aspects of policy. However, to understand policy, we need to define some common terms. Therefore, this chapter begins by defining those terms. Next, a simple conceptual model of policy will be built to provide brief answers to the three questions—what, why, and how. Subsequent sections of this chapter will then examine each question in detail.

Terminology is very important. The third section of this chapter reviews and summarizes current accepted terminology and provides some additional terms to help explain how PBM systems are implemented and used. This is important because words, such as "policy" and "goal," have many levels of meaning and understanding. Next, common requirements of PBM systems will be discussed. This section builds on Section 10.6, The Benefits of PBNM, in Chapter 10 by defining the common features needed to realize these benefits. Finally, the notion of a workflow-based process for implementing policy is introduced. This process is essential to enabling policy-based network management (PBNM) systems to integrate the needs of the business world with the services that the network can provide.

11.2 THE NEED FOR OOA, DESIGN, AND MODELING IN PBNM SYSTEMS

This section will describe the need for object-oriented analysis (OOA), object-oriented design (OOD), and object-oriented information modeling (OOIM) for PBNM systems. First, important concepts of object orientation will be defined. Second, OOA and OOD will be briefly explained, along with a description of their essential benefits. Finally, a brief description of why OOIM is important will be provided. A familiarity with object-oriented concepts will help the reader.

11.2.1 A Guide to Object-Oriented Concepts for PBNM Systems

Object-oriented technology models the real world in terms of *objects*. This important point is often overlooked. Many people are intimidated by the set of formalisms used by object-oriented technology. However, this intimidation is unfounded. The basic object-oriented paradigm uses human description of the environment to create software models. In other words, object-oriented tools seek to represent what already exists in the real world in a consistent format.

An *object* is an abstraction of something that consists of a collection of characteristics and behavior. This collection is treated by the system as a named entity that has state and a unique identity. We define objects to represent system entities that can be managed, configured, and reported on, as well as objects to represent things, places, and concepts. Objects promote understanding of the system components, the interaction between these components, and the overall system. They are, in effect, a set of building blocks that can be used to describe the entity or concept in a reusable manner. In addition, they provide an extensible basis for implementation of a system.

For our purposes, an object has four fundamental parts: attributes, methods, relationships, and constraints.

Attributes

An *attribute* (also called a *property*) represents data that define fundamental characteristics of a particular object. The data can be defined using a simple data type (e.g., integer), a complex data type that is composed of simple data types (e.g., a `TimePeriod`, which is made up of two `Date` attributes), or as a reference to another object whose semantics are used to define the attribute (e.g., `Authen-ticationMethod`). Not all attributes that are defined in a class have to be created; some are mandatory and some are optional.

Two criteria are used to decide whether an attribute should be created or not. The first criterion is imposed by the model. This criterion defines whether an attribute is required or not as a function of the integrity of the model. For example, a salary attribute of an employee will probably be designated as a required attribute because it represents common information that is present in all employees and because it also models a key aspect of what makes an employee an employee. Conversely, including the middle name of the employee might be nice, but not required, because some people do not have a middle name, whereas others have several. The second criterion is common sense: If that attribute describes a key characteristic of what is being modeled, then it should be created; otherwise, it is extraneous and does not need to be created (as long as the model does not declare it to be required, of course).

Methods

A *method* is a function or procedure that represents some behavior that is characteristic of the class. This behavior can be simple and fundamental to using the object or can be more complex. For example, the accessing and storing of its attributes (e.g., via "getter" and "setter" methods) enable the object's data to be *encapsulated* and not manipulated directly. This fundamental tenet of object-oriented systems ensures that the *specification* of what an object can do is kept separate from its *implementation*. As another example, methods could be defined that enable the transformation and/or sharing of that attribute with other objects, perhaps by performing a computation using one attribute and writing the result into another attribute.

Complex operations may also have side effects, which may also be modeled. We assume that all attributes of a class are read, written, and edited using the methods of the class (direct manipulation of attributes without using methods violates the principles of object orientation, which are discussed later in this section). Methods may therefore be viewed as performing a transformation, or mapping, of the attribute(s).

Relationships

A *relationship* is a construct that defines how two or more objects are related to each other. The nature of the relationship defines how the objects are semantically related to each other. Four types of relationships are used here: generalization, associations, aggregations, and compositions. The following definitions are based on the Unified Modeling Language (UML)—the de facto standard for defining and implementing information models.

A *generalization* defines how more generic objects (i.e., superclasses or "parent" classes) are used to define more specific objects (i.e., subclasses or "child" classes). Generalization enables separate concepts that are common to many objects to be used by each of those objects through *inheritance* (i.e., if an attribute is defined once in a superclass, that same attribute is inherited by all of its subclasses).

An *association* is a semantic relationship (e.g., "depends on," "requires") between two or more classifiers. A *classifier* is a mechanism that describes behavioral and structural features of interest, such as classes and data types. An association can be thought of as a way to "connect" two or more objects and is therefore the "glue" that is used in an object model to connect different objects together to describe a concept. *Without associations, the object model is nothing more than a set of disparate classes that are unrelated to each other.*

An *aggregation* is a special form of association that specifies a whole–part relationship between the aggregate (whole) and a component part. Thus, if an object "depends on" or "requires" a set of other objects to exist, then it is an aggregation.

A *composition* is a strong form of aggregation that requires that a part instance be included in at most one composite at a time and that the composite object is responsible for the creation and destruction of the parts. It is this propagation of operations from the composite to the constituent parts of the composite that differentiates a composition from an aggregation. Composition may be recursive. Compositions are used for many things, but one of their essential uses is to represent containment.

Constraints

Finally, a *constraint* is a semantic condition (often in the form of a *restriction*) that in UML is represented as a Boolean expression using the Object Constraint Language (OCL). Constraints are used to represent global properties, conditions, or restrictions that apply to an object. For example, a constraint may be defined to say that an object can be created only after some operation to one or more other objects has been successfully completed.

Additional Object Parts

Two additional constructs deserve mention. The first is the notion of a class, and the second is an introduction to abstraction. The structure and behavior of similar objects is defined by their common object *class*. A *class* is a description of one or more objects that have a uniform set of data (called *attributes*) and functions that manipulate and operate on the data (called *methods*). *Concrete* classes can be instantiated, whereas *abstract* classes cannot be instantiated. Abstract and concrete classes are used to organize and classify information in a class *hierarchy*, which is a set of classes that is used to organize information about a management domain. For example, Figure 11.1 defines the high-level construct of a Network Device. Although a Router, Switch, or Firewall is each a different type of

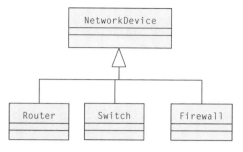

FIGURE 11.1

Different types of `NetworkDevice`.

`NetworkDevice`, all have a set of attributes and concepts in common. Thus, these different objects are grouped together in a hierarchy of related classes.

11.2.2 Introduction to Object-Oriented Modeling by Way of Example

As a brief introduction to object-oriented modeling, we will take the preceding model and improve and enhance it.

The model shown in Figure 11.1 has several inherent problems. The most basic problem is that it defines each of the three subclasses to be a "fixed" concept. To illustrate this point, consider a switch. A switch is traditionally classified as a "layer-2" device, meaning that it operates at the data link layer (below the network layer and above the physical layer).

Layers 3 and 4 are two of the seven layers defined in the International Standards Organization (ISO) open systems interconnect (OSI) model. This model is used to describe defined layers in a network operating system. The layers provide clearly defined functions that can better enable different devices from different manufacturers to interoperate. Each layer has a standard defined input and output.

Many manufacturers advertise traditional switches and so-called "layer-3 switches" and "layer-4 switches." One possible solution that accommodates these additional types of switches is shown in Figure 11.2.

The problem with the approach in Figure 11.2 is that it misses the point of why these devices are called `Layer3Switch` and `Layer4Switch`. A `Layer2Switch` forwards packets based on the unique address of each device connected to the network. Layer 3 is traditionally used to partition subnetworks. Layer 4 is known as the transport layer and is the communications path between end user devices and the network infrastructure. Thus, layer 4 is associated with a "higher intelligence."

`Layer3Switch` and `Layer4Switch` add intelligence to the switching function by switching traffic at higher network layers. Thus, subclassing a `Layer3Switch` or a `Layer3Switch` from a `Layer2Switch` is wrong, because the behavior defined

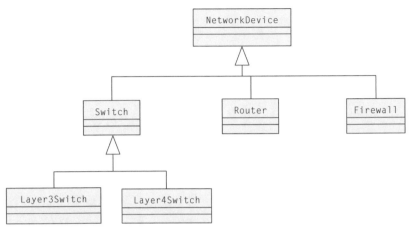

FIGURE 11.2

Trying to model layer-3 and layer-4 switches—a bad approach.

for switching functions in each of these different layers is at different levels of abstraction.

A similar problem arises if a manufacturer makes a router that also has some firewall capabilities; this is shown in Figure 11.3.

This example tries to define a new class by using multiple inheritance (i.e., the new RouterWithFirewall class is derived from both the Router class and the Firewall class). Although this makes intuitive sense, the problem is that many systems cannot support multiple inheritance. The model is useless if it cannot be implemented!

A better approach is to use the concept of roles. *Roles* define different concepts an object can play with in the context of its related objects. The key to unraveling this puzzle is to think differently. Instead of conceptualizing a Router, a Switch, and a Firewall each as an atomic device, separate the device from its functionality. Then, abstract the different functionality defined and associate each bit of functionality back to a device. Thus, instead of embedding functionality into a device, the role approach used by Directory Enabled Networks–new generation (DEN-ng) defines roles to represent different functions and then enables a device to aggregate one or more roles. This provides a much more extensible approach to defining functionality.

In the approaches illustrated in Figures 11.2 and 11.3, if a new function is added, an entire new subclass must be built. In the DEN-ng approach, a new role is created and then it can be decided if it should be associated with a particular device or not. The DEN-ng role-based approach for solving this problem is shown in Figure 11.4.

The following simplified DEN-ng role model enables a LogicalDevice to take on zero or more roles. (In DEN-ng, a device, such as a router, is divided into a

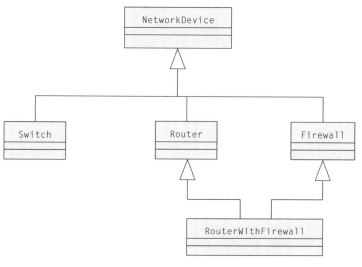

FIGURE 11.3

Trying to model a router with firewall capabilities—a bad approach.

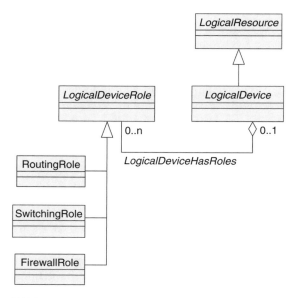

FIGURE 11.4

Using roles in DEN-ng to model device functionality.

`PhysicalDevice` and a `LogicalDevice`; `PhysicalDevice` models physical aspects of the device, such as cards and power supplies, whereas the `LogicalDevice` models logical aspects such as routing and switching traffic.) Different functionality is now abstracted as a `LogicalDeviceRole`, and new roles, such as `Layer3SwitchingRole`, can be added without affecting the definition of the `LogicalDevice`.

DEN-ng also defines various physical roles. Roles will be discussed later in this chapter.

11.2.3 What Are OOA and OOD?

Object-oriented analysis is the process of understanding a problem domain, determining what the responsibilities of the various components of the system(s) and participants using the system are, and developing a specification of how the objects of that domain function are related to each other. Implicit in this definition is the use of abstraction (i.e., the principle of ignoring certain aspects of a subject that are not relevant to the current purpose, so that the aspects of a subject that are relevant can be focused on exclusively). This is in effect a "divide-and-conquer" strategy, where a difficult problem is divided into smaller parts to better understand each part. Thus, by understanding each constituent part, a better and more thorough understanding of the whole problem can be achieved.

Object-oriented design is the process of taking a specification produced by OOA and adding enough detail to enable it to be implemented. The implementation is developed using the object-oriented principles defined earlier.

Traditionally, OOA and OOD have been defined and used as separate disciplines. However, most methodologies suggest or implement a "blurring" between the hard lines of OOA and OOD. This important principle deserves further elaboration. In traditional approaches, the strict definitions of OOA and OOD defined a set of differences that required different languages and notations. There are two obvious problems with this approach. First, if different notations and languages are used, how can all of the appropriate concepts, principles, and objects from OOA be represented in OOD? A good analogy is in the problems encountered when a literal translation between dissimilar human languages is attempted. Literal word-for-word translation and replacement of these words often forms gibberish or meaningless phrases. The second problem is that if the representation cannot be guaranteed, how can it be implemented correctly?

Instead, it should be realized that, fundamentally, both OOA and OOD are based on object-oriented principles. Therefore, the opportunity is to bridge these traditionally separate disciplines and concentrate on the unified representation of objects and concepts. After all, the basic object-oriented paradigm uses fundamental human linguistic and cognitive mechanisms to create software models. Why, then, cannot this same paradigm be used to analyze, design, and implement PBNM systems? We argue here that it can and should be used.

11.2.4 **Benefits of OOA and OOD**

When blended together, OOA and OOD provide several compelling benefits over alternative methods that do not use object-oriented concepts. The most important of these are as follows:

- Provide a consistent underlying representation for representing the information being analyzed and modeled.
- Improve the ability for analyst, subject matter experts (i.e., theorists), and implementation personnel to interact.
- Improve the ability to cope with the complexity of a distributed system.
- Improve the ability to better recognize common concepts and behavior within a system and to realize them as objects that can be shared and/or reused by other system components.
- Build specifications that are robust and resilient to change (a key feature of the DEN-ng and SID object-oriented information models).

Providing a Consistent Frame of Reference

OOA is concerned with understanding a given problem domain. It aids this process by bringing a set of formal methods and procedures to help understand the problem. One key advantage of this approach is that it is resistant to redefining the same concepts. Rather, an initial concept will instead become more detailed as additional analysis and design is performed.

For example, Figure 11.5 shows a simple UML model of an `Individual` suitable for business analysts. This figure is taken from the DEN-ng specification, which is

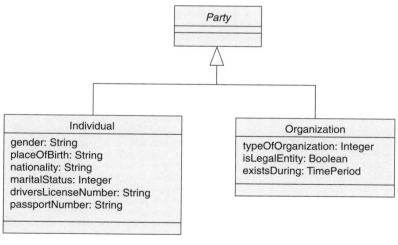

FIGURE 11.5

Simple business model of a `Party`.

a system view of the higher-level (as in more abstract) business view of the TeleManagement Forum's shared information and data (SID) model common business entity definition party specification. This figure shows that two common concepts—Individual and Organization—are *generalized* into a new concept called Party. This abstraction makes it easier to represent behavior where an individual, a group of individuals, or an entire organization can be the subject and/or target of *policy* (policy subject and target are defined later in this chapter).

Although useful for a variety of uses, Figure 11.5 is not very extensible. Consider, for example, the simple case where an employee can play several roles in an organization. If the approach of Figure 11.5 is used, many different subclasses of Individual and Organization will have to be created, and a complex set of associations linking them will also have to be defined. This is because individuals and organizations exhibit complex behavior that can change over time. Subclasses can only represent a single particular *fixed* concept. Thus, if a Party has to play more than one role at any given point in time, multiple subclasses with a complicated set of associations must be used.

Figure 11.6 shows an improved model, where the concept of a PartyRole is introduced (attributes have been suppressed to make the figure simpler). It uses the role object pattern to simplify this problem. By separating the information held about any Individual and Organization from the roles that they perform, this model enables any Party to aggregate one or more PartyRole. Note that the Party model has been significantly enhanced by building on existing simpler concepts. In fact, the DEN-ng specification, and each addendum of the SID, is written to lead the reader through a progressively more complex representation of an entity. This approach enables different abstractions of the same concepts to be used by different types of users.

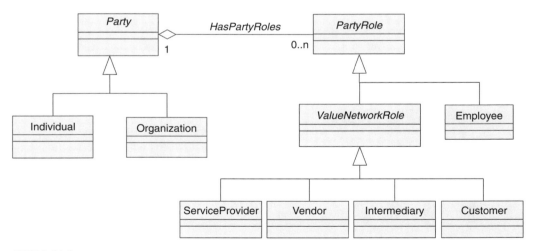

FIGURE 11.6

Improved business model of a Party, using the role object pattern.

This use of roles is very similar to the previous use of roles to abstract device functionality. In fact, both DEN-ng and SID use roles throughout the information model to make each part of the information model inherently extensible.

Another important point in Figure 11.6 is how easily varying amounts of detail can be accommodated using OOIMs. The amount of detail shown on any given OOIM is determined by the use of that model and the needs of the users of that model. This enables a single "infrastructure" to be built, whose details are shown and hidden to suit the needs of the users.

Details of each class (e.g., attributes and methods) and constraints and relationships can be shown or hidden to suit the needs of the users and/or applications that are using the OOIM. Additional subclasses and components of those classes can be defined where needed and can be used to define additional functionality. For example, the full SID model has a flexible and robust set of mechanisms for dealing with how different instances of `Party` and `PartyRole` are used. For example, different individuals and organizations can be referred to by different names. Consequently, the full SID model has a robust naming model that satisfies this need. This advanced functionality is rarely needed and was hidden (along with other features of the `Party` model) in Figure 11.6 because it was not needed.

Enable Different Types of Users to Interact Better

Complex systems require a variety of different users, ranging from business analysts, to system designers, to implementation specialists, to work together to build a working system. OOA and OOD both rely heavily on classification, which is a formal way to organize the knowledge represented by an information model. This enables different people with different responsibilities to better add their knowledge to the collective whole without having to understand every detail of every part of the design. By merging the OOA and OOD disciplines, specific knowledge can be applied to a consistent underlying representation. In effect, a continuum of knowledge is built—some of the continuum is applicable at the analysis stage, some at the design stage, and some at the implementation stage.

Complexity in PBNM Systems

One reason that policy is needed in network management is to cope with the inherent complexity of networks. OOA and OOD provide formal, yet intuitive, methods for tackling the complexity of network management systems. Various forms of abstraction, which are represented naturally using OOA and OOD methods, can be used to reduce system complexity. Three examples are procedural, data, and entity abstraction:

Procedural abstraction enables any operation that provides a well-defined result to be treated by its users as a single process, even though the operation may in fact have been realized through a sequence of lower-level operations. This also enables the various entities that participate in this set of operations to be similarly abstracted.

Data abstraction enables a data type to be defined in terms of the operations that are applied to objects of that type. This enables complex data types to be designed and used by many different objects. For example, DEN-ng defines a `TimePeriod` complex data type that can be used to define the starting and ending points of a period of time. It is an object because it contains many different features that enable the starting and ending points of the time period to be specified. Because it is an object, it can be used by any other DEN-ng object that supports the concept of a time period. As we will see, this is an important concept in representing policy rules.

Entity abstraction: To describe this principle, for example, consider a router. The *wrong* way of modeling a router is as a single class with a large number of attributes because such a model is not reusable. When one aspect of the router changes, the entire router model has to change.

Abstraction enables us to separate distinct aspects and functions of the router, as shown in Figure 11.7. This is a simplified and abstracted view of six types of different aspects of a managed device, as modeled in DEN-ng and the SID.

This fundamental abstraction is the DEN-ng definition of a managed device, which is also used in the SID. This abstraction enables each of these different aspects of a device to be defined in its own submodel. Development of each submodel can then proceed in parallel. More important, each of these different models can be reused by other types of devices. For example, the concepts of

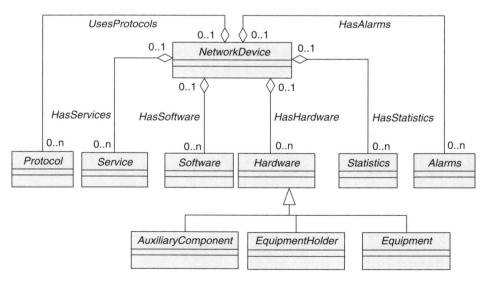

FIGURE 11.7

Using abstraction to define different aspects of a device.

Statistics and Alarms are applicable not only to Routers, but also to many other types of NetworkDevice. A Router is defined as a type of NetworkDevice (see Figure 11.3). Similarly, in Figure 11.4, the function of routing is defined as a type of LogicalDeviceRole. Therefore, both Statistics and Alarms can be applied to various types of NetworkDevice and to roles that network devices play.

This design also provides inherent flexibility. For example, if the Statistics of one type of device differ from those of a different type of NetworkDevice, then this difference can be accommodated by defining different subclasses of the Statistics class. Because the overall model still relates Statistics to Network-Device, the new subclasses of Statistics will also be "automagically" related to network devices.

Improvements in Reusing and Sharing Objects

OOA uses inheritance to identify common objects and concepts that can be shared and reused by different components. When combined with OOIM, a set of powerful class hierarchies—one for each different concept—can be defined. Furthermore, if both OOA and OOD are merged, then a common language and representation enables the best of OOA (representing what is to be built) and OOD (describing how to build the components identified in the OOA stage) to be holistically merged. This combination establishes a continuum for the objects being defined and specifies how knowledge can be systematically expanded and applied to different applications.

The previous example of defining new types of Statistics classes is a good example of this point. The model shown in Figure 11.7 captures the fundamental relationship of a device aggregating a set of Statistics. Because a subclass inherits the relationships defined by its superclasses, new types of Statistics classes can be defined whenever needed. This provides an inherent robust extensibility to the model. Furthermore, because NetworkDevice can be subclassed as well, different NetworkDevice uses can have different Statistics classes. Thus, by taking care and building a rich infrastructure, different instances of NetworkDevice having different statistical capabilities can be easily accommodated, and new classes can be reused by other classes.

Building Robust, Resilient Object Specifications

OOA and OOD (as well as OOIM) mechanisms use classification to organize information. This has the wonderful side effect of limiting changes to objects to a particular portion of the model. DEN-ng and the SID take this concept a step further by defining the concept of a Specification class (Figure 11.8).

DEN-ng and the SID represent different types of managed objects using different types of patterns. *Patterns* can be thought of as specifying a repeatable way to represent and/or implement a concept. This particular pattern is called the Entity-EntitySpecification pattern and features prominently in DEN-ng, SID, and OSS/J (the OSS for Java effort). It is used to define how a managed object is represented. The idea is for the invariant (i.e., nonchanging) characteristics and

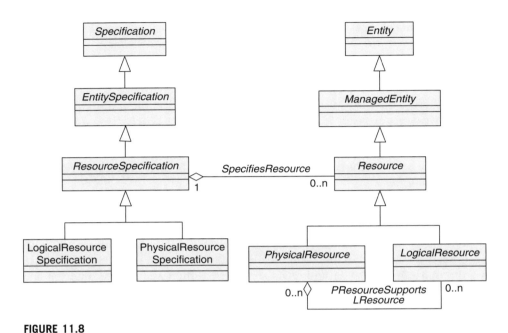

FIGURE 11.8

The use of a `Specification` class in the DEN-ng model.

behavior of a `ManagedEntity` to be represented by an `EntitySpecification` (or an appropriate subclass). This enables different `ManagedEntities` to specify the changeable characteristics and behavior of the managed object being modeled.

Put another way, the `EntitySpecification` defines characteristics and behavior that different `Entities` have, and each of the `Entities` can then define its own unique characteristics and behavior that can be used to differentiate its instance from other instances. For example, suppose we want to model a phone. The `EntitySpecification` for the phone is used to define common things that all phones share. Differences in individual phone capabilities, such as whether it is a single, dual-band, or tri-band phone, can be captured in the specific phone `Entity`. Continuing the example, if there are multiple types of tri-band phones, then a subclass of the more general `EntitySpecification` can be created to model this capability.

The `SpecifiesResource` aggregation defines which `ManagedEntities` are related to which `ResourceSpecification`. For example, a vendor could make a `Layer2Switch` and a `Layer3Switch`; the difference is that the `Layer3Switch` also has some simple routing capabilities. If the only difference is additional software capabilities, then a `ResourceSpecification` could be defined for both the `Layer2Switch` and the `Layer3Switch`, and the differences between the two switches captured with two different `ResourceRole` classes.

In Figure 11.8, a `Specification` is an object that represents the invariant (i.e., nonchanging) characteristics and behavior of an object that it is associated with. The `EntitySpecification` class is the particular class (along with the `ManagedEntity` class) that establishes the `Entity-EntitySpecification` pattern. The `ResourceSpecification` class is one of several subclasses of the more generic `EntitySpecification` class, just as `Resource` is one of the more specific sub-classes of `ManagedEntity`. `ResourceSpecification` is an abstract base class used to define the invariant characteristics (attributes, methods, relationships, and constraints) of a `Resource`. Other examples include `ProductSpecification` and `ServiceSpecification`.

An `Entity` represents the base class of all discrete devices in the managed environment. Its subclass, `ManagedEntity`, represents all devices that can be managed. This is an important distinction. An `Entity` is not manageable, however, even if the `Entity` is not manageable, it may still provide an important function that needs to be represented. A good example is a legacy hub, which provides connectivity. Thus, DEN-ng and the SID are capable of representing all entities in the environment.

A `Resource` is the abstract base class for all entities that are inherently manageable and comprise a `Product` (note that `ManagedEntities` are not necessarily tied to `Products`). Because `ResourceSpecification` is related to `Resource` through the `SpecifiesResource` association, more specific subclasses of `Resource` and `ResourceSpecification` are also related. Thus, the subclasses `PhysicalResource` and `LogicalResource`, which represent the physical and the logical aspects of a `Resource` (such as a `NetworkDevice`), are related to the sub-classes `PhysicalResourceSpecification` and `LogicalResourceSpecification`, respectively.

This pattern is a robust and extensible way to model managed objects of different types. Although Figure 11.8 shows this pattern applied to `Resources`, it is also used for `Products`, `Services`, and many other DEN-ng objects.

11.2.5 Why Object-Oriented Information Modeling Is So Important to PBNM Systems

Object-oriented modeling is a design methodology that applies OOA and design techniques to describe a system. A complete object-oriented model will describe both the physical and the logical aspects of the system. To do this, object-oriented terminology is introduced.

Basic Terminology

Objects that are grouped into the same class can also share similar relationships between other objects as well as share common semantics. Through *inheritance*, a subclass (child) of a superclass (parent) automatically has the same attributes, methods, constraints, and relationships defined as its superclass does. Therefore, a class can be thought of as a template that defines attributes, methods, constraints, and relationships that describe the class in a uniform way.

An *instance* refers to an actual object that belongs to a particular class. Each instance of a class can potentially have the same attributes and methods. However, it can contain different values for its attributes. It also does not need to instantiate all of the possible attributes that are defined by its class. The class defines the attributes, methods, and relationships that the instance can possess, and the instance defines and differentiates objects that belong to the same class.

Object-Oriented Thinking

Object oriented implies a particular way of organizing and using information to build software and systems. Specifically, it means that a system is thought of as composed of a set of objects, each of which encapsulates data and behavior. Six fundamental axioms are required by this type of thinking:

1. *Identity:* The ability to distinguish each object within a system; this implies that two instances of the same class can be identified even if they have the exact same attribute values.

2. *Abstraction:* The process of focusing on a subset of essential characteristics of an object, even if other characteristics of that object must be ignored.

3. *Classification:* The process of grouping objects that have the same characteristics and behavior (e.g., attributes, methods, and relationships) into the same class. Classification further implies that there is a structured hierarchy for organizing all classes in a system.

4. *Encapsulation:* The process of separating the external characteristics and behavior of an object from its internal implementation. Other objects in the system can then depend on those characteristics and behavior without having to know how the object is implemented. Encapsulation conceals the structure and implementation of an object, and instead focuses on its externally visible characteristics and behavior. This enables the implementation of an object to change without drastically affecting other objects in the system.

5. *Inheritance:* A mechanism for expressing that two classes are related to each other. Specifically, a *subclass* inherits all of the attributes, methods, and relationships of its *superclass*. Thus, common characteristics and behavior are expressed once in a superclass, enabling subclasses to represent specific refined behavior of the superclass.

6. *Polymorphism:* A mechanism that enables several classes to share the same basic type of functionality, but to implement the same operation differently in each class. For example, a draw function that is used by two different shapes (a line and a circle) renders each shape in slightly different ways. Furthermore, each function may have different prerequisites and side effects.

11.3 CONCEPTUAL POLICY MODEL

It will be easier to understand what PBM is all about if we first start by understanding one of its fundamental building blocks: the *policy rule*.

The underlying model of a policy rule, `PolicyRule`, is deceptively simple and is illustrated in Figure 11.9 using UML notation. The lines with the diamonds at the end are aggregations, with the diamond denoting the aggregate part of the relationship. In this model, a `PolicyRule` is a container that aggregates a set of `PolicyConditions` and a set of `PolicyActions`. The cardinalities of these two aggregations are defined so that at least one condition and at least one action must be defined as part of the `PolicyRule`.

Note that the Internet Engineering Task Force (IETF) and Distributed Management Task Force (DMTF) made these two cardinalities zero-or-more to zero-or-more. This was to allow for policies that are in an incomplete state. However, this is wrong, because this mixes the state of constructing a `PolicyRule` with the state of an already constructed `PolicyRule`. If the PBM system is supposed to manage the construction of a `PolicyRule`, then as a minimum, the process of constructing a `PolicyRule`, including its life cycle aspects, must be modeled. This results in a set of interrelated models that work together to model various aspects of the life cycle of a `PolicyRule`. The simplified model shown in Figure 11.9 is just one portion of this set of models and is used to model the current state of a `PolicyRule`.

Directory-enabled networks (DEN) and DEN-ng both model the process of constructing and deploying a `PolicyRule` using a finite-state machine. Figure 11.10 shows the other major processes needed to model the life cycle of a `PolicyRule`.

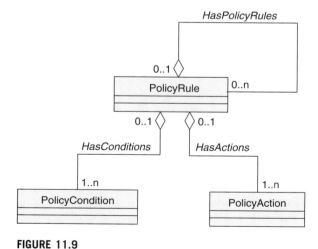

FIGURE 11.9

Simplified conceptual model of a `PolicyRule`.

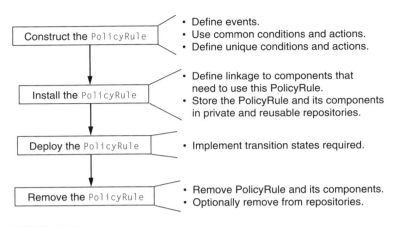

FIGURE 11.10

Simplified life cycle model of a `PolicyRule`.

(Note that conflict detection and resolution, as well as the basic notion of editing a `PolicyRule`, are not specifically included in this figure. This is because they need more description, as each is a potentially complicated operation.)

The semantics of this simple `PolicyRule` are as follows. The `PolicyRule` is itself a container that consists of three things:

1. Metadata, which defines the overall behavior and function of the `PolicyRule`.
2. Boolean condition clause.
3. Action clause.

Although the Boolean `PolicyCondition` clause may be composed of a set of `PolicyCondition` clauses, the end result is a single result that says whether or not the `PolicyCondition` is satisfied. If the `PolicyCondition` is satisfied, then the actions aggregated by this `PolicyRule` may be evaluated. In theory, one could define action clauses that define what should happen if the `PolicyCondition` clause is not satisfied. Practice has shown, however, that the (dramatic) increase in complexity of doing this results in little practical return. The increase in complexity results from many factors, such as the interaction of a `PolicyRule` with another `PolicyRule`, as well as the side effects that can result from the execution of a `PolicyRule`. In addition, this greatly complicates the policy conflict detection and resolution process.

Similarly, the `PolicyAction` clause is composed of one or more `PolicyAction`. `PolicyAction` can be optionally prioritized. This prioritization, along with what we refer to as an "execution strategy," enables a set of common semantics to be applied that govern how these `PolicyActions` execute with respect to each other. For example, one `PolicyAction` could have an execution strategy of execute and exit (i.e., prevent further processing of the actions), whereas another could have the semantics of execute and continue (i.e., try and execute the next action).

This structure and more advanced policy structures could be examined in more detail. For now, it is sufficient to note that this simple definition will be expanded in three important ways:

1. Concept of nested (as in hierarchical) `PolicyRules` and `PolicySubRules` will be added (true of the IETF, DMTF, and DEN-ng approaches).
2. Concept of rule-specific versus reusable policy components will be added to enhance the (simplistic) definitions of conditions and actions in the `PolicyRule` (true of the IETF, DMTF, and DEN-ng approaches, although the DEN-ng approach enhances this beyond the IETF and DMTF approaches).
3. The concept of events that trigger the evaluation of the conditions in the `PolicyRule` will be added (true *only* of the DEN-ng approach).

The IETF (and DMTF) have defined the first and second of these additional concepts, but not the third. This is important, because events can be used as a mechanism to explicitly indicate how a `PolicyCondition` is evaluated. Without this triggering mechanism, there is no way to indicate when a `PolicyCondition` is going to be evaluated. This is why DEN-ng expands this model to an event-condition-action triplet (as shown in Figure 11.11).

The preceding model of a DEN-ng `PolicyRule` has three important differences (even at this simplified level) compared with the IETF and DMTF approaches, as shown in Figure 11.12.

These differences exist for the following three reasons. First, if the triggering mechanism for evaluating a `PolicyCondition` is not specified, then it is impossible to guarantee interoperability between different implementations of PBNM systems. Second, it is important for the model to be precise. Specifying a cardinality of 1..n prevents degenerate structures (e.g., a `PolicyRule` with no

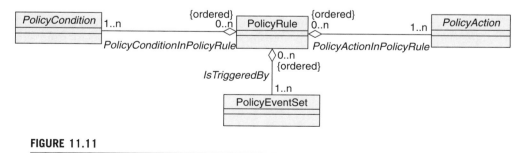

FIGURE 11.11

Simplified DEN-ng model of a `PolicyRule`.

Functionality	IETF/DMTF Approach	DEN-ng Approach
Triggering evaluation of a policy condition	Not specified	Specified using a set of events
Cardinality of aggregations	`0..n` to `0..n` for all	`0..n` to `1..n` for all
Use of OCL	None	Specified in each aggregation

FIGURE 11.12

High-level comparison between the IETF/DMTF and DEN-ng `PolicyRule` models.

`PolicyAction`) and enables a higher degree of interoperability. Finally, the use of OCL enables rule-specific semantics to be specified in a simple way.

11.4 DEFINITION OF A PBM SYSTEM

We can now provide a more formal definition of a PBM system: *Policy-based management is defined as the usage of policy rules to manage the configuration and behavior of one or more entities.*

This definition implies the use of an object model that expresses the `PolicyRule` as an instance of a class hierarchy, along with the use of a management method (i.e., a finite-state machine). This last point is critical. Most models are "open-loop" systems (i.e., they represent just the state of a set of managed entities). DEN and DEN-ng, as well as the emerging policy work in the TMF, all use a finite-state machine to model the various states that a managed entity can have in its life cycle and the operations required to transition a managed entity to a new state (or to keep it in a current state). This enables models to be built to represent the entire life cycle of the managed system.

Given these definitions, we can now answer the three questions posed at the beginning of this chapter. Note that the IETF and DMTF approaches do not specify any type of management method and hence are current state models.

Simply stated, PBM is a methodology for managing systems. It does this by modeling the different entities in the environment to be managed as a set of objects. However, it does not stop here—it also models the various relationships between objects and constraints placed on those objects. For example, two different users can be logged on to the same system but receive different classes of service, which dictate how the applications that each operate are handled in the network.

The models used by PBM provide a common representation of information that different system components and applications can use to build more intelligent, easier-to-manage systems. A common representation of information enables management data to be shared, reused, and altered by multiple applications. This common representation has as one of its foundations the principle of abstraction, which enables us to construct class and relationship hierarchies that model different aspects of managed objects.

For example, instead of having one class to model a router, with many (i.e., unmanageable) attributes, we can instead focus on different aspects of the router—for example, its physical composition, the protocols it runs, the management information bases (MIBs; a body of knowledge that defines characteristics about an aspect or function of a network device) it supports, the traffic it filters, and so forth—and develop classes to represent each of these aspects. This enables us to reuse valuable concepts (e.g., a card that contains memory is not specific to a router and can be used to add memory to a wide variety of objects) and apply them to different objects. This in turn enables consistent representation of these same concepts.

PBM is a methodology that describes one or more applications that manage one or more systems according to a set of rules. These rules take the form of policies that are applied to components of the system to better and more efficiently manage those components. The application of the rules is governed by the finite-state machine that describes how to manage the system. In this way, we can achieve true end-to-end control, as opposed to having just device- or element-level control without PBM control because the behavior of each component is captured by the states defined in the finite-state machine.

PBM differs from other approaches in its use of policies to control the behavior of managed entities. As stated previously, implicit in our definition of a PBM system is the use of a management methodology—in our case, a finite-state machine—to manage the life cycle aspects of entities.

PBM uses policies to control the behavior of a managed system in a predictable and consistent fashion. To do this, the characteristics of the system that is being managed must be represented in as much detail as required. Then, policies can be defined that govern each state of the managed object—from creation, to deployment, to destruction. Without policies, there is no way to coordinate the behavior (e.g., the state and state transitions) of the objects being managed, and there is no way to guarantee consistent behavior and reaction to events.

How PBM uses policies is critical to the implementation of a PBM system. Many current PBM systems are focused on a particular component in a system, or a set of features, that must be controlled. For example, many quality-of-service (QoS) PBM systems are designed to control a small subset of the features of a device, such as a router. The worry, of course, is the interaction between the QoS features and other features of the router: What if the QoS PBM system makes an adjustment that adversely affects the delivery of some other service or feature that the router is supporting? The answer, of course, is for a PBM system to holistically manage the different components in a system and the different services that each device supports.

11.5 POLICY TERMINOLOGY—AN APPROACH

Now that we understand what a PBM system is, we can identify the essential terminology needed to study PBM. These terms provide a basic overview of the key components comprising a policy system and give insight into how PBM systems are implemented and used.

The motivation for a consistent set of policy terminology is that without common terminology, interoperable PBM systems will be impossible to describe, let alone implement and use. However, until relatively recently, no document defining a policy terminology existed.

In November 2001, RFC 3198, an informational RFC that took the first step to formally define terminology for PBM systems, was released. This delay wasn't for lack of effort. Rather, the problem was one of getting agreement from the major vendors who were implementing PBM systems. To understand this, realize that virtually all of the major network vendors have at least one, and usually multiple, PBM systems. Therein lies the problem—no vendor wants their *deployed* product branded as "nonstandard." Furthermore, because the IETF operates by consensus, until there is a majority consensus, a specification of the IETF will not be advanced regardless of how seminal the work is. Even then, the process of advancing an Internet draft can be delayed based on the review of one or more respected people. Given these considerations, the fact that this RFC was produced is indeed a positive step forward.

One may ask why such specifications are required, given that vendors are already producing products. The answer is to promote interoperability. Sometimes, one can buy a policy server to control all of the functions of a device. However, the usual case is that a policy server is built to have a purposely narrow scope. For example, vendors will build a QoS policy server that controls *some* of the QoS functions for a set of different devices. Most policy servers that control a particular function, such as QoS, do not control *all* of the different commands of a given device corresponding to that particular function, let alone control all of the commands for other functions. Furthermore, if a network vendor builds a policy server, then that policy server will almost certainly be limited to supporting devices from that vendor. Thus, people need to integrate different policy servers, so that either the appropriate functionality and/or necessary vendor devices are managed.

RFC 3198 is important because it is the first specification that seeks to formally define policy terminology from the IETF. However, because the information model that this RFC was describing was not completely defined and because this was arguably the first information model that the IETF had dealt with, there are several errors in this document. The author's name is on the document because more good would come out of a partially correct document than not having a document be released at all and because the author was at that time still actively involved in the IETF. Because that is no longer the case (the author having shifted most of his "standards" time to other forums), the following section contains *just* the essential policy terminology, with due accreditation, that the author uses. The advanced practitioner can refer to RFC 3198 for other terms.

11.6 ESSENTIAL TERMINOLOGY FOR PBM SYSTEMS

This section will summarize only those terms that are relevant to generic PBM system design. There are in general two sources for these terms:

- RFC 3198.
- From the author, who is part of the ongoing DEN-ng specification work.

RFC 3198 is focused on policy-based network management, and in particular is strongly influenced by current IETF work in the areas of differentiated services, policy representation, and security. As such, it is not generic to PBM, but rather is specific to policy-based network management.

Some of these definitions will be changed, based on implementation experience of the author. In other cases, the definitions of RFC 3198 will be modified to make these terms more generic to PBM systems (i.e., when a single definition is overloaded with conflicting meanings resulting from different uses that are forced into a single definition). In every case, the RFC definition will first be analyzed to explain why it needs modification and then a new definition will be provided.

This RFC is a perfect example of how the standards process works in real life. The reader will notice that I am a coauthor of this RFC, yet I do not agree with all of its definitions. This is because the IETF standards process is driven by consensus. Coauthors can influence the content of the draft, but at the end of the day, the working group chairs need to go for consensus. Plus, vendors will often become more involved as the Internet draft nears completion, to avoid the stigma of having their product labeled as "nonconforming" with the standard.

The pertinent definitions from RFC 3198 now follow in alphabetical order, except when terms are dependent on each other. Each definition is given in its own section, and comments (where appropriate) are provided immediately below each one.

11.6.1 Terms Relating to the Object-Oriented Foundations of PBM

This initial set of terms are formal definitions for terms used by PBM. They are either conceptual or architectural in nature, and although they don't define directly what a PBM term is, they do define needed concepts for PBM.

Data Model (defined in RFC 3198; modified by DEN-ng)
RFC 3198 defines a data model as:

> A mapping of the contents of an information model into a form that is specific to a particular type of data store or repository. A "data model" is basically the

rendering of an information model according to a specific set of mechanisms for representing, organizing, storing, and handling data.

The problem with the preceding definition is that it is not so much a *mapping* as it is the definition of an *implementation* (which requires not just a mapping, but other factors, such as implementing for ease of querying or performance). A better definition is as follows:

> A data model is a concrete implementation of an information model in terms appropriate to a specific type of repository that uses a specific access protocol or protocols. It includes data structures, operations, and rules that define how the data are stored, accessed, and manipulated.

Information Model (defined in RFC 3198; modified by DEN-ng)

RFC 3198 defines an information model as:

> An abstraction and representation of the entities in a managed environment. This includes definition of their properties, attributes and operations, and the way that they relate to each other. It is independent of any specific repository, software usage, protocol, or platform.

This definition is workable, although there are some small problems with it: (1) What is the difference between a property and an attribute (they are actually synonyms)? (2) "The way they relate to each other" lacks the formalism to mandate the use of object-oriented relationships, such as associations, aggregations, and compositions. (3) Platform doesn't have any effect on the structure or implementation of an information model. Therefore, this definition is modified as follows:

> An information model is an abstraction and representation of the entities in a managed environment. This includes definition of their attributes, operations, constraints, and relationships. It is independent of any specific type of repository, software usage, or access protocol.

An information model can be thought of as the defining document that is used to model all of the different managed objects in a managed environment.

Figure 11.13 illustrates the relationship between an information model and a data model in DEN-ng.

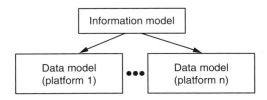

FIGURE 11.13

Relationship between an information model and a data model.

DEN-ng specifies that a single information model is to be used. Multiple data models must be used, because management information is diverse and requires different types of repositories to facilitate the storage, querying, and editing of these data. This single information model will thus serve as the basis for all data models that are used. This helps ensure that different data models that represent parts of the same object will be able to interoperate.

Model Mapping (from DEN-ng)

RFC 3198 does not define the term *model mapping*. It defines the term *policy translation*; however, this isn't quite the same thing, as this relates just to policies, not to entire models. Policy translation is covered later in this section.

Model mapping is used to enable different types of models to be related to each other. It is defined here so that other definitions in this section can use the term.

> A model mapping is a translation from one type of model to another type of model. Model mapping changes the representation and/or level of abstraction used in one model to another representation and/or level of abstraction in another model.

The most common form of model mapping is from an information model to a data model; another important form is from a vendor-neutral data model to a vendor-specific data model. Another important form of model mapping is being done in the SID modeling working group of the TMF, where different types of models (e.g., business domain models and system analysis models) are being integrated to form a common continuum of shared data.

Figure 11.14 shows one form of model mapping. In this figure, a particular data model (e.g., a directory) is mapped from an information model. This mapping produces a directory implementation that conforms with the appropriate

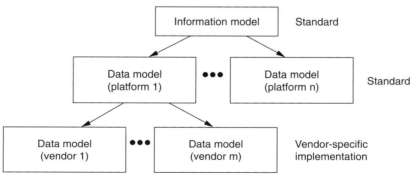

FIGURE 11.14

The concept of model mapping.

standards (e.g., LDAP or X.500). The second tier of mapping accounts for the fact that different vendors provide varying degrees of compliance with the standard. In addition, some vendors provide features that are not yet standardized. This second tier of mapping enables these differences to be normalized, so that different implementations of the same data model can better interoperate. Thus, our hierarchy shows an information model standard being mapped to the appropriate data model standard, from which various vendor-specific implementations are built.

DEN (defined in RFC 3198; modified by DEN-ng)

RFC 3198 defines DEN as:

> A data model that is the LDAP mapping of the Common Information Model (CIM). Its goals are to enable the deployment and use of policy by starting with common service and user concepts (defined in the information model), specifying their mapping and storage in an LDAP-based repository, and using these concepts in vendor- and device-independent policy rules.

This definition is wrong and misleading; the DEN specification was defined as two things:

- An information model (as defined earlier).
- A mapping to a specific data model that used the directory access protocol (DAP; part of the ITU X.500 suite) or lightweight DAP (LDAP; defined by the IETF) to access data stored in a directory.

Thus, we see that DEN is not just an LDAP mapping, and it is not solely a mapping of CIM. CIM is not a pure information model by the preceding definition because it contains elements of data models (e.g., keys and weak references, which are both database concepts) that cause problems when mapping to various types of data models. The correct definition of DEN is as follows:

> DEN is two things. First, it is a specification of an object-oriented information model describing the elements and entities in a managed environment and how they are related to each other. Second, it also specifies a model mapping to a format that can be stored in a directory that uses (L)DAP as its access protocol.

DEN-ng (defined in DEN-ng)

DEN-ng is the next version of the DEN standard. It is being constructed in the TeleManagement Forum, not the DMTF, because it is very strongly tied to the NGOSS architecture effort. In addition, DEN-ng, like DEN, is UML compliant. The DMTF CIM is not UML compliant. Thus, it is easier to develop DEN-ng outside of the DMTF DEN effort. The definition of DEN-ng is as follows:

> DEN-ng is an object-oriented information model that describes the business and system views of managed entities and their relationships. This definition is done using UML and is strongly tied to the definition of new-generation operational systems and software (NGOSS).

Because there was confusion regarding DEN being both a specification for building an information model and a data model, these efforts have been split apart in DEN-ng. Thus, there is a DEN-ng information model and a set of DEN-ng data models.

11.6.2 Main Worker Terms of Policy

This section contains a set of formal definitions for the policy-specific terms *policy*, *policy rule*, *policy group*, *policy condition*, and *policy action*.

Policy (defined in RFC 3198; modified by DEN-ng)

RFC 3198 defines policy in a very generic fashion as follows:

Policy can be defined from two perspectives:

■ A definite goal, course, or method of action to guide and determine present and future decisions. "Policies" are implemented or executed within a particular context (such as policies defined within a business unit).
■ Policies as a set of rules to administer, manage, and control access to network resources as described in RFC 3060.

Both perspectives of this definition are too generic to be useful. This definition fails to account for the differences among business, system, and network policies. For example, no difference is offered between a low-level queuing policy (to control how network traffic is conditioned) versus a high-level policy governing what resources can be accessed as a function of how the user is logged on (e.g., intranet versus public Internet), time of day, and other factors.

There are more problems with this definition. Looking at the first perspective, it specifically avoids the use of the word "rule." This means that no definitive mechanism exists to define, implement, and use policy. More important, the "context" referred to in the first perspective is not present in RFC 3060. Therefore, it conflicts with the RFC that defines the policy information model in the first place. (Note that policy core information model extensions defined in RFC 3460 make mention of defining a "context" by using a role. I think that this is a misuse of roles as defined in RFC 3060.)

A policy can be defined as follows:

A policy is a rule that can be used to change the behavior of a system.

The only thing lacking from this definition is that it is specific to changing behavior. Let's instead use the following definition:

Policy is a set of rules that are used to manage and control the changing and/or maintaining of the state of one or more managed objects.

In this definition, "behavior" is replaced with "changing and/or maintaining of the state." This emphasizes the relation of policy to a management methodology; in our case, a finite-state machine. The changing and/or maintaining of the state could indeed denote a behavioral change, but it does not have to. Hence, the preceding definition is more flexible.

The definition is influenced by the design of DEN and DEN-ng, which both use a finite-state machine model. This is fundamental to the design of DEN-ng, which consists of three sets of classes: to model the state, the changing of the state, and policies to control when the state is being changed.

Policy Rule (defined in RFC 3198; modified by DEN-ng)

RFC 3198 defines a policy rule as:

> [A] basic building block of a policy-based system. It is the binding of a set of actions to a set of conditions—where the conditions are evaluated to determine whether the actions are performed.

This definition is somewhat obtuse. Furthermore, this definition is not accurate enough for our purposes, because the actions are not bound to the conditions (as implemented in RFC 3060, which is quoted in the definition). Rather, the actions and conditions are both aggregated by the policy rule, and the actions are enabled by the condition being satisfied. This was shown in Figure 11.11.

Furthermore, metadata contained in the policy rule itself defines how the different actions will be executed (e.g., in which specific order) and whether execution should continue if a problem is encountered. In other words, the policy rule is an intelligent container that plays a vital role in determining how the events, conditions, and actions all work together. This leads to the following revised definition for a policy rule:

> A policy rule is an intelligent container. It contains data that define how the policy rule is used in a managed environment as well as a specification of behavior that dictates how the managed entities that it applies to will interact. The contained data are of four types: (1) data and metadata that define the semantics and behavior of the policy rule and the behavior that it imposes on the rest of the system, (2) a set of events that can be used to trigger the evaluation of the condition clause of a policy rule, (3) an aggregated set of policy conditions, and (4) an aggregated set of policy actions.

In our usage, the conditions and actions each form clauses, and the action clause is only executed if the condition clause is satisfied. Although many conditions can exist in a condition clause, the end result of all such policy conditions is to determine whether this policy rule is applicable. If applicable, then additional logic residing in the policy rule container is used to determine which policy actions are executed and how they are executed.

One or more events, or a combination of events, can be used to trigger the evaluation of the policy condition. Similarly, many actions may exist in a condition clause, and one or more of them will execute as a function of the logic contained in the policy rule.

A simplified picture of the DEN-ng `PolicyRule` has already been shown in Figure 11.11.

Policy Group (defined in RFC 3198; modified by DEN-ng)

RFC 3198 defines a policy group as:

> [A]n abstraction in the Policy Core Information Model. It is a class representing a container, aggregating either policy rules or other policy groups. It allows the grouping of rules into a Policy, and the refinement of high-level Policies to lower-level or different (i.e., converted or translated) peer groups.

This definition should not be restricted to RFC 3060. Otherwise, interoperability is impaired. In addition, the last part of the last sentence is wrong. `PolicyGroup` classes do not cause *refinement* or *translation* of policy abstraction levels; they are used simply to coordinate the actions of separate policy rules. This results in the following modified definition of policy group:

> A policy group is a container that can aggregate `PolicyRule` and/or `Policy-Group` objects.

In DEN-ng and policy core information model extensions (PCIMe), a superclass of `PolicyGroup`, called `PolicySet`, is defined. By defining a recursive aggregation on `PolicySet`, both `PolicyRule` and `PolicyGroup` can inherit this relationship. This also enables us to define compound policy rules. Thus, a simplified picture of the DEN-ng `PolicyGroup` is shown in Figure 11.15.

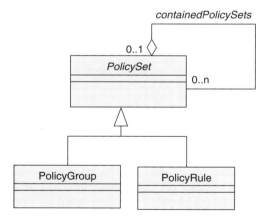

FIGURE 11.15

The DEN-ng simplified view of `PolicyRule` and `PolicyGroup`.

Policy Condition (defined in RFC 3198; modified by DEN-ng)

RFC 3198 defines a policy condition as:

> [A] representation of the necessary state and/or prerequisites that define whether a policy rule's actions should be performed. This representation need not be completely specified, but may be implicitly provided in an implementation or protocol. When the policy condition(s) associated with a policy rule evaluate to `true`, then (subject to other considerations such as rule priorities and decision strategies) the rule should be enforced.

The problem with this definition is its insistence that "this representation need not be completely specified." The original thinking in the RFC was that part of the representation would serve as a guide for implementation. However, this makes interoperability impossible, as there is no single standard to tie together different implementations. Another problem in the preceding definition is its lack of specificity.

The final problem with this definition is that it does not say what happens when multiple policy conditions are present. Although a simple policy rule may only require a single policy condition, most policy rules need a set of policy conditions that must be evaluated together. This is called a `PolicyCondition` *clause* in DEN-ng.

Experience has shown that implementing the `PolicyCondition` clause as a Boolean expression clause is simple and flexible enough to handle most PBM implementations. In this context, the task is to evaluate a Boolean expression to see if the policy actions of the policy rule should be executed or not. As with the nested rules, there can be complex conditions, which are conditions that are composed of many individual condition clauses that are bound together. In such cases, one policy condition in a `PolicyCondition` clause may need evaluation first for efficiency reasons (i.e., if it fails, then there is no need to evaluate the other condition clauses). The formal definition of a `PolicyCondition` clause is as follows:

> A `PolicyCondition` clause is an aggregation of individual policy conditions and is treated as an atomic object that is aggregated by a `PolicyRule`. It is represented as a Boolean expression and defines the necessary state and/or prerequisites that define whether the actions aggregated by that same `PolicyRule` should be performed. This is signified when the `PolicyCondition` clause associated with a `PolicyRule` evaluates to `true`.

A policy condition is typically associated with the occurrence of an event (i.e., something significant that has happened). The PBM system itself will define what events are of interest. Common examples include a user logging onto the system, a link failing, and someone logging on to a router to change its configuration.

A policy condition is usually represented by an expression that typically consists of three elements: a variable, an operator, and another variable or constant.

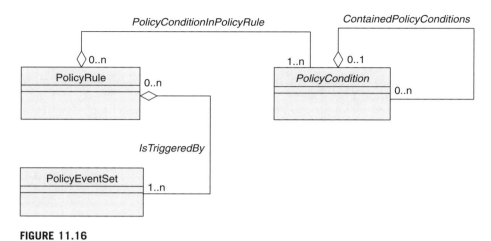

FIGURE 11.16

The DEN-ng simplified view of a `PolicyCondition`.

A simplified view of the DEN-ng `PolicyCondition` class is shown in Figure 11.16. OCL expressions (such as the ordering of the `PolicyConditions`) have been omitted for simplicity and so as to emphasize the three fundamental relationships that affect `PolicyConditions`.

The recursive aggregation `ContainedPolicyConditions` will be used to build compound `PolicyConditions`. The aggregation `IsTriggeredBy` defines the set of `PolicyEvents` that can trigger the evaluation of the `PolicyCondition`. This is associated to the `PolicyRule` using the `PolicyConditionInPolicyRule` aggregation.

Policy Action (defined in RFC 3198; modified by DEN-ng)

RFC 3198 defines a policy action as:

> [A] definition of what is to be done to enforce a policy rule, when the conditions of the rule are met. Policy actions may result in the execution of one or more operations to affect and/or configure network traffic and network resources.

The problem with the preceding definition is its use of the word "enforce." Because a policy rule is an aggregation of policy conditions and policy actions, what exactly is being enforced?

Although some representations implicitly define this, it is incorrect to abstract *all* definitions of policy actions to have this form. For example, consider the simple `PolicyRule`: "If traffic originated from this range of IP addresses, mark it with this DSCP." It's easy to see that "enforcing" this `PolicyRule` means that anytime packets are detected with a particular range of source IP addresses, they should be marked a special way (e.g., certain bits in the IP header should be changed to a special value).

Consider a policy that says: "Only relegate 30 percent of my core bandwidth to streaming video applications." How do you enforce this policy as it is currently written? First, you have to define what network elements are in the "core" of your network, and then you have to define which traffic corresponds to "video streaming" traffic. But what happens when there is no video traffic—does 30 percent of your network remain idle?

The other problem with this definition is that the representation of policy in RFC 3060 lacks the semantics and metadata required to enforce anything because there is no specification of what is to be enforced. (As a side note, we could not get agreement in the working group about how to include a specification of what to enforce, which is why it is lacking. Vendor implementations played a large part in removing semantics and metadata from the definition.)

The final problem with this definition is that it does not say what happens when multiple policy actions are present. Although a simple policy rule may only define a single policy action, most policy rules need a set of policy actions that must be executed together. In DEN-ng, this is called a `PolicyAction` *clause*.

The formal definition of a `PolicyAction` clause is as follows:

A `PolicyAction` clause is an aggregation of individual policy actions and is treated as an atomic object that is aggregated by a `PolicyRule`. It represents the necessary actions that should be performed if the `PolicyCondition` clause evaluates to `true`. These actions are applied to a set of managed objects and have the effect of either maintaining an existing state, or transitioning to a new state, of those managed objects.

Note that DEN-ng differentiates between executing a `PolicyAction` and enforcing the results of that `PolicyAction`. This concept is missing in the IETF and DMTF approaches.

A simplified view of the DEN-ng `PolicyAction` class is shown in Figure 11.17. OCL expressions (such as the ordering of the `PolicyActions`) have been omitted for simplicity and to emphasize the two fundamental relationships that affect `PolicyActions`.

The `ContainedPolicyActions` aggregation is used for defining nested `PolicyActions`. The `PolicyActionInPolicyRule` aggregation is used to associate a set of `PolicyActions` with a particular `PolicyRule`.

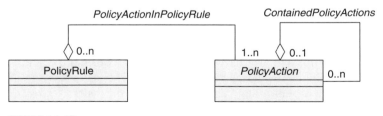

FIGURE 11.17

The DEN-ng simplified view of a `PolicyAction`.

11.6.3 **Terms for Controlling Policy**

This section contains a set of formal definitions for the policy-specific terms *policy conflict, policy decision, policy server, PDP*, and *PEP*.

Policy Conflict (defined in RFC 3198; modified by DEN-ng)

RFC 3198 states that a policy conflict,

> . . . occurs when the actions of two rules (that are both satisfied simultaneously) contradict each other.

Although correct, this definition is terse. The following expands on this definition, making its purpose clearer:

> A policy conflict occurs when the conditions of two or more policy rules that apply to the same set of managed objects are simultaneously satisfied, but the actions of two or more of these policy rules conflict with each other.

Actions can conflict with each other in several ways. For example, two actions may generate two different values for an object. In general, conflicting actions will cause conflicting states to be specified for the same managed object.

Policy Decision (defined in RFC 3198; modified by DEN-ng)

RFC 3198 defines a policy decision as follows:

> [T]wo perspectives of "policy decision" exist:
> - A "process" perspective that deals with the evaluation of a policy rule's conditions.
> - A "result" perspective that deals with the actions for enforcement, when the conditions of a policy rule are true.

The problem with the preceding definition is that it is overloading a single definition with two different meanings that arise from two different uses. Each of these different meanings should be given its own definition, as follows:

> A policy evaluation is the set of computations necessary to determine if the PolicyCondition clause is satisfied.
>
> A policy decision is the determination that one or more policy actions that are aggregated by a policy rule should be applied to a set of managed objects. These policy actions correspond to either maintaining the current state or transitioning to a new state of each of the managed objects that they are affecting.

Policy Server (defined in RFC 3198; modified by DEN-ng)

RFC 3198 defines a policy server as:

> [A] marketing term whose definition is imprecise. Originally, RFC 2573 that defined a framework for policy-based admission control referenced a "policy server." As the RFC evolved, this term became more precise and known as the

policy decision point (PDP). Today, the term is used in marketing and other literature to refer specifically to a PDP or for any entity that uses/services policy.

This definition needs further clarification. Although it is an imprecise marketing term, it should not be perceived as just a PDP. A "server" connotes more than just requesting and providing decisions; it also implies a broader interaction with the rest of the system.

As a bare minimum, the definition should be enhanced to include a PDP and a PEP. (By the way, this was not agreed to in the IETF because of differing vendor implementations, as some products were just PDPs and others combined the notion of a PDP with a PEP, and *both* wanted to call their products a policy server.)

This thinking is predicated on the IETF decision to define a simple policy system, as illustrated in Figure 11.18. The DMTF also uses this definition; however, the TMF and DEN-ng do not for reasons that will soon become apparent.

There is more to a functioning PBM system than just these simple components. Two examples include the tasks of detecting (let alone resolving) policy conflicts and of translating policies to legacy entities that are not aware of policy. These require functionality that is not present in a PDP or PEP. This is because, in the most general case, conflict detection between different technologies, such as QoS and security, requires the PDP or PEP to be knowledgeable in each of those domains. When you add to this the needs of different devices having different programming models, a monolithic solution to conflict detection and resolution quickly becomes nonimplementable.

Therefore, a policy server needs to include these additional entities as a minimum. This is clearly a much longer discussion and is covered in detail in the Strassner book, *Policy-Based Network Management*. However, it is instructive to

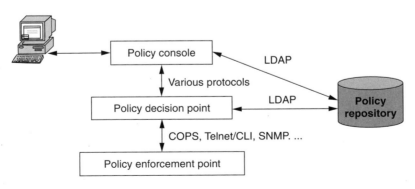

FIGURE 11.18

The IETF/DMTF conceptual model of a policy-based system.

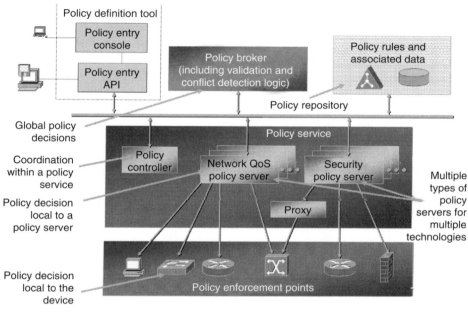

FIGURE 11.19

The IETF/DMTF conceptual model of a policy-based system.

see the differences between what I think is a minimal specification of a realistic PBM system and the conceptual model shown in Figure 11.18. Therefore, Figure 11.19 shows my definition of a realistic PBM system.

Several important differences exist between Figures 11.18 and 11.19. The main points of this architecture are as follows. First, this architecture defines PBM systems as distributed systems, which means that all of the components of a PBM system must communicate with each other. This can be accomplished in a variety of ways. The figure uses a message bus; however, other methods, such as distributed communication using Jini, are also possible. Second, this architecture provides for three different types of conflict detection: global, neighborhood (inter-PDP), and local (intra-PDP). Global detection catches conflicts that are technology independent; inter-PDP detection catches conflicts between different technologies and/or vendors; and intra-PDP detection catches conflicts within a particular device or family of devices (or, depending on the complexity of the implementation, conflicts within particular functions of a device or device family).

Furthermore, legacy devices may be unable to communicate with the PBM system; they may use different protocols and/or object models and/or programming mechanisms and may not have the ability to translate policy rules into their own configuration commands. (By the way, this gives rise to the definition of a *policy-unaware entity* in the following section.) Therefore, a policy proxy is used to translate PBM policy rules into legacy configuration commands, such as command-line interface (CLI).

Policy Decision Point (defined in RFC 3198; modified by DEN-ng)

RFC 3198 defines a PDP as:

> [A] logical entity that makes policy decisions for itself or for other network elements that request such decisions.

The obvious problem with this definition is the explicit reference to a network element. In addition, it does not define what a "decision" is. This latter problem is solved by the previous definition of a policy decision. Our definition of a PDP is as:

> An entity that makes policy decisions for itself or for other entities that request such decisions.

Policy Execution Point (defined in RFC 3198; modified by DEN-ng)

RFC 3198 defines PEP as:

> A logical entity that enforces policy decisions.

This definition is terse and does not define what is meant by "enforcement." Our definition of a PEP is as follows:

> An entity that is used to verify that a prescribed set of policy actions have been successfully executed on a set of policy targets. Note that DEN-ng differentiates between enforcement and execution.

11.6.4 Policy Container Terms

This section contains a set of formal definitions for the policy-specific terms *policy domain* and *policy repository*.

Policy Domain (defined in RFC 3198; modified by DEN-ng)

RFC 3198 defines a policy domain as:

> [A] collection of elements and services, and/or a portion of an Internet over which a common and consistent set of policies are administered in a coordinated fashion. This definition of a policy domain does not preclude multiple sources of policy creation within an organization, but does require that the resultant policies be coordinated.

To be honest, I've never understood this definition.

RFC 2474 defines the DiffServ fields for use in IPv4 and IPv6 headers and doesn't even contain the term *policy domain*. Second, a domain is used to contain

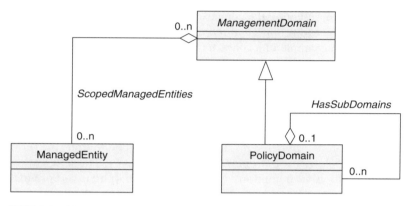

FIGURE 11.20

The DEN-ng simplified view of a `PolicyDomain`.

things, so that common operations can be executed against a group of the contained entities. The preceding IETF definition mentions "coordinated fashion," but this isn't necessarily true—domains are more about *who* than *how*. Third, elements and services are limiting—what about managing the allocation of common IP addresses, which are neither elements nor services?

The key to fixing this definition is as follows:

- A *managed entity* is what we want to collect in a domain—a managed entity can be a network device, a network service, an IP address, a route, or anything else that we need to manage in a common way.
- The purpose of defining a *domain* is to define a set of managed entities that are all operated on in the same way. Although administration is important, it is only one of a set of operations that are targeted on entities in a domain.

Thus, the following definition of a policy domain is used instead:

A policy domain is a collection of managed entities that are operated on using a set of policies. The policies are used to administer and control the set of characteristics and behavior of these managed entities.

A simplified diagram of the DEN-ng `PolicyDomain` is shown in Figure 11.20.

Policy Repository (defined in RFC 3198; modified by DEN-ng)
RFC 3198 defines a policy repository from three perspectives:

- A specific data store that holds policy rules, their conditions and actions, and related policy data. A database or directory would be an example of a store.

- A logical container representing the administrative scope and naming of policy rules, their conditions and actions, and related policy data. A QoS policy domain would be an example of a container.
- In RFC 3060, a more restrictive definition than the prior one exists. A policy repository is a model abstraction representing an administratively defined, logical container for reusable policy elements.

Again, the preceding definitions suffer from overloading different meanings into a single definition.

The original definition of a policy repository was the third definition (the term "model abstraction" should really be replaced by "object class"). The text stating that it was "a more restrictive definition" was added to signify that the original purpose of the policy repository was just for reusable elements. Vendors with existing implementations, however, were using repositories for rule-specific elements, and therefore the attempt to make a "better" (as in more flexible) first definition. (Basically, a rule-specific component is one that conceptually is "attached" to a particular policy and is not usable by other policy rules; a reusable component is one that can be used by multiple rules.)

The problem with the first definition is that it loses the essential semantic of being an administratively defined container (as opposed to an entire data store, as the RFC 3198 definition states). The second definition arose from some vendors who believed that their implementations were providing extra semantics. That is, a policy repository was more than just a container; it was a container that had a specific purpose.

In real-life implementations, there is no reason that the second and third definitions cannot be combined. There is also no reason that a policy repository be restricted to a particular type of object (reusable or rule specific). This allows us to ignore the first definition, because it now represents a subset of the second and third definitions. This leads to the following definition:

> A policy repository is an administratively defined logical container that is used to hold policy information.

For the purposes of this definition:

- "Administratively defined" means that it resides in a single policy domain.
- "Logical container" means that it may be implemented as either a separate data store or a special area of a data store that is used expressly to contain policy information.
- "Policy information" means policy rules and groups, their constituent elements, and related data that may be used in the evaluation and/or execution of policy conditions and actions.

A simplified view of a DEN-ng `PolicyRepository` is shown in Figure 11.21.

A `PolicyRepository` is subclassed from `Collection` because a `Collection` provides the necessary semantics to iterate over, group, and select sets of entities

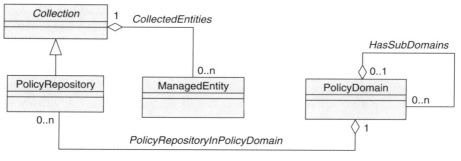

FIGURE 11.21

The DEN-ng simplified view of a `PolicyRepository`.

that are residing in the `PolicyRepository`. In Figure 11.21, the `Collected Entities` aggregation enables different types of `ManagedEntities` to be placed in a `PolicyRepository`. Sets of `PolicyRepositories` can be defined as being contained in a particular `PolicyDomain` using the `PolicyRepositoryInPolicy Domain` aggregation. This enables different policies to be applied to a particular `PolicyRepository`.

11.6.5 Terms Defining Roles, Policy Subjects, and Policy Targets

This section contains a set of formal definitions for the terms *role* and *role combination*, as well as *policy subject* and *policy target*.

Role (defined in RFC 3198; modified by DEN-ng)

This is a difficult concept. The Policy Framework working group wanted to constrain the concept of a role to an attribute, per the following definition from RFC 3198:

> Role is defined from three perspectives:
> - A business position or function, to which people and logical entities are assigned.
> - The labeled endpoints of a Unified Modeling Language association. . .
> - An administratively specified characteristic of a managed element (e.g., an interface). It is a selector for policy rules and Provisioning Classes (PRCs) to determine the applicability of the rule/PRC to a particular managed element.

Only the third definition (roles as selectors of policy) is directly related to the management of network policy. However, the first definition (roles as business positions and functions) may be referenced in policy conditions and actions.

This definition is confusing, because it overloads different meanings and uses into one word. Furthermore, it completely ignores the existence of the role object pattern. This design pattern is used in DEN-ng and in the TMF SID modeling group. Thus, this definition needs clarification.

Looking at the third definition from RFC 3198, we see that a role as far as the IETF and DMTF are concerned is nothing more than an attribute. Thus, we need to differentiate between the use of the role object *pattern* and the role *attribute*. The role object pattern is used when different abstractions of the same entity (e.g., two different types of people) are required. Rather than having one large "bloated" class that contains different attributes, methods, and relationships corresponding to the different abstractions, the role object pattern defines an aggregate object that consists of a "core" object to which separate "role" objects are dynamically attached and removed from as needed (Figure 11.22).

An important benefit of this pattern is that different roles can be defined to suit different clients' needs. Object interfaces are kept pure and simple because

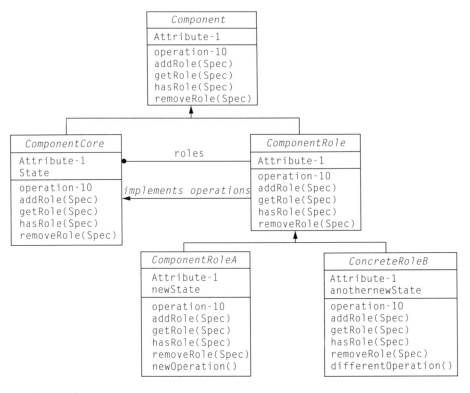

FIGURE 11.22

The structure of the role object pattern.

each interface can be optimized to serve the needs of particular clients. The use of the role object pattern in DEN-ng and in the TMF SID group is explained in more detail in *Policy-Based Network Management* by Strassner.

One obvious way to differentiate between the role object pattern and the role attribute is to qualify their usage with different names and to avoid using the term *role* unless its meaning is unambiguous. Therefore, the following terms and definitions are proposed:

- A *role attribute* is a fundamental characteristic of an object that is used to define the purpose or function of that object.
- A *role object pattern* is as an aggregate set of objects that enable a component object to be adapted to different needs through transparently attached role objects.
- A *role object* is an object that is not meant to stand on its own; rather, it is meant to supply a combination of common and unique functionality that can augment the basic definition of another object. The unique functionality may be supplied in the form of additional attributes, methods, and/or relationships (note that this is a characteristic of DEN-ng and the work in the SID).

In terms of quantifying the semantics of roles, the following definitions are used:

- A *role selector* is a means of grouping together a set of objects, so that a set of policies can be applied to them.
- A *role behavior* is a means of explicitly defining behavior that is expected of one or more objects.

Finally, we have teased apart the essence of using a role as an attribute—sometimes it is used to group objects together for operating on them, and sometimes it is used for specifying behavior. Note that DEN-ng uses role in this object pattern sense by default, since this provides the greatest flexibility and extensibility.

Role Combination (defined in RFC 3198; modified by DEN-ng)

RFC 3198 defines a role combination as:

> [A] lexicographically ordered set of roles that characterize managed elements and indicate the applicability of policy rules. . . . A policy system uses the set of roles reported by the managed element to determine the correct rules . . . to be sent for enforcement. That determination may examine all applicable policy rules identified by the role combination, its sub-combinations, and the individual roles in the combination. The final set of rules . . . for enforcement are defined by the policy system, as appropriate for the specified role combination of the managed element.

There is little use in addressing this definition in detail, as we have already decided not to use "role" without a qualifier and because we have changed the semantics of roles as defined in RFC 3198.

The essence of this definition, however, is the ability to combine roles in some meaningful way. For example, we might have the roles "edge interface," "core interface," "Ethernet interface," and "OC-48 interface." It would be beneficial to be able to differentiate between ports on a router in the core of the network that carry Ethernet traffic and ports on that same router that carry OC-48 traffic. By allowing a role selector to contain more than one attribute value, we achieve this. (The same beneficial effect can be achieved for allowing a role behavior to specify more than one type of behavior, but that gets more complicated.)

However, the "devil is in the details." In the preceding example, what objects get selected by the combination of the "core interface" and "OC-48" roles—only those objects that contain both roles or all objects that contain either one (or both) of the roles? The IETF decided that (quoting from RFC 3060), "the selection process for a role combination chooses policies associated with the combination itself, policies associated with each of its sub-combinations, and policies associated with each of the individual roles in the role combination." In other words, the "kitchen sink."

This is simply too general to be useful. If the purpose of the role selector is to indeed select objects, then it stands to reason that fewer is better. This yields the following slight modification to the definition of role selector:

> A role selector is a means of grouping together a set of objects, so that a set of policies can be applied to them. Multiple role selectors can be combined to select a set of objects, in which case only those objects that contain all attributes specified by the role selector will be selected.

However, the preceding changes should *not* be applied to the definition of role behavior, because the crispness of the role behavior specification will then be lost. Practice has shown that combining multiple behavioral specifications into a single specification makes implementation very difficult, if not impossible.

The definitions of role selector and role behavior give rise to the definitions of policy subject and policy target.

Policy Subject (defined in RFC 3198; modified by DEN-ng)

Policy subject is defined in RFC 3198 as:

> [A]n entity, or collection of entities, which originates a request, and is verified as authorized/not authorized to perform that request.

There are several problems with this definition.

Although originating a policy information (or decision) request is certainly interesting, the subject of a policy is the identification of the theme, or focus, of the policy. Therefore, the subject of a policy will do more than simply request information. Furthermore, whether or not a subject is authorized to perform an operation (such as requesting information) is completely separate from the act of performing the operation. Therefore, we'll use the following definition instead:

A policy subject is a set of entities that is the focus of the policy. The subject can make policy decision and information requests, and it can direct policies to be enforced at a set of policy targets.

Policy Target (defined in RFC 3198; modified by DEN-ng)

Policy target is defined in RFC 3198 is defined as:

> [A]n entity, or collection of entities, which is affected by a policy. For example, the "targets" of a policy to reconfigure a network device are the individual services that are updated and configured.

There are also several problems with this definition.

First, the term *target* implies an object that a set of operations is being directed at, which is lacking in the preceding definition. Second, the example is confusing at best. To reconfigure a network device, its configuration must change, which means that one or more interfaces on the device will be changed. Services may be changed, but this is a second-order effect that is a direct function of the changing of the configuration of the device interfaces. In other words, in the preceding example, the "target" should be the configuration that is applied to the set of interfaces over which the services run. Therefore, we will use the following definition instead:

> A policy target is a set of entities that a set of policies will be applied to. The objective of applying policy is to either maintain the current state of the policy target or to transition the policy target to a new state.

With respect to the preceding example on reconfiguration, a policy target could be a device (e.g., power it on), a device interface (e.g., check if it is up or down), or a device configuration (as in the preceding example). The new definition is able to link in the notion of using a finite-state machine to control the behavior of the policy target—this is one of the foundations of PBM.

11.7 NEW TERMINOLOGY NOT COVERED IN RFC 3198

This section will define additional terminology that is not covered in RFC 3198, but which is important for a clear understanding of the design and implementation of PBM systems.

11.7.1 Capabilities

One difficulty in providing an end-to-end service is that the path that traffic will take usually traverses different devices. These devices often use different means to provide a common function, such as the mechanisms used to condition traffic (e.g., classification, dropping, queuing, and so forth). Unless these mechanisms are abstracted into a common layer, they cannot be controlled in a unified manner. DEN-ng uses the term *capabilities* to describe this abstraction:

The capabilities of a device represent the set of features that the device supports that can be harnessed to perform a service. This set of capabilities is independent of any particular protocol, repository, or programming mechanism, and enables different devices having different implementation mechanisms to coordinate their features to apply the equivalent function.

An example will help clarify this concept. Imagine a scenario that defines three different classes of service (CoS). Traffic is flowing through two routers made by two different vendors. Each router uses different mechanisms to implement various traffic-conditioning functions, such as dropping and queuing, which are required by each CoS. The notion of capabilities enables the different high-level features of each device to be abstracted from their low-level implementations. This in turn allows the high-level abstraction of CoS to be understood by each router.

Furthermore, each router is free to use different low-level mechanisms to do its part in conditioning the traffic in accordance with the high-level CoS. The end result is consistent traffic conditioning according to the capabilities of each device, even though different commands and mechanisms are being used. This powerful concept is crucial to providing end-to-end service in heterogeneous environments.

11.7.2 Constraints

Another important concept is constraints, which DEN-ng defines as follows:

> Constraints represent invariant conditions that must hold for the system being modeled. These conditions do not have side effects and can not alter the state of the system that they are applied to. Rather, they represent limitations and/or restrictions on using certain aspects of the system.

Although constraints are *not* policies, there are many similarities between them. Figure 11.23 illustrates these differences.

The difference is subtle, yet important. Constraints represent predefined system restrictions or limitations that *do not change over time*. Constraints are expressions

Functionality	Policy	Constraint
Predefined	Almost always is	Can be
Triggering mechanism	`PolicyEvent`	`PolicyEvent` or statically defined
Invariance	Different policies apply at different times	Constraint applies once
Object	Yes	No

FIGURE 11.23

High-level comparison between DEN-ng policy and constraint functionality.

(usually Boolean) that restrict or limit the operation or behavior of the managed entity that they apply to. Because constraints are expressions, they can be triggered statically or dynamically. In contrast, policies are objects that are evaluated, which can give different results at different times in response to different conditions. Policies can use constraints, but constraints normally do not use policies.

11.7.3 Policy-Aware Entity

It is important to be able to distinguish between entities that can operate using policies versus those that do not. That represents one of the first design decisions in a PBM system: Will policy be used to control all, or just some, of the objects in the system? The definition of a policy-aware entity is as follows:

> A policy-aware entity is one that can understand and use policies to make present and future decisions. These decisions are used to manage and control the changing and/or maintaining of the state of one or more managed objects that are the targets of the policy.

11.7.4 Policy-Unaware Entity

The definition of a policy-unaware entity is as follows:

> A policy-unaware entity is one that can neither understand nor use policies to make present and future decisions. A policy-unaware entity cannot use policies to manage and control the changing and/or maintaining of the state of one or more managed objects.

11.7.5 Policy-Enabled System

Similarly, it is important to be able to distinguish between systems that can operate using policies versus those that do not. The definition of a policy-enabled system is:

> A policy-enabled system is one that can operate using policies to make present and future decisions. These decisions are used to manage and control the changing and/or maintaining of the state of one or more managed objects that are the targets of the policy.

A policy-enabled system can be explicitly disabled from processing policies.

11.7.6 Reusable and Rule-Specific Policy Components

Policy rules may consist of several components, not just conditions and actions. Reusable policy components are defined as follows:

> A reusable policy component is one that can be associated with multiple policy rules. This implies that reusable policy components are stored in a different location than the policy rules that are using them.

Similarly, the components of a policy rule that are designed to be used by just a single policy rule are called rule-specific policy components and are defined as follows:

A rule-specific policy component is one that is only associated with a single policy rule.

The difference between a rule-specific policy component and a reusable one is based solely on the intent of the policy *administrator*, not on how many policy rules are using a policy component. This means two things:

1. There is no limitation in functionality between what a reusable policy component and a rule-specific policy component can be used to represent.
2. A policy component that a policy administrator has created to be reusable may at some point in time be associated with exactly one policy rule, without thereby becoming a rule-specific policy component.

Figure 11.24 provides a simple example of the difference between reusable and rule-specific policy rules.

In DEN-ng, many different types of `ManagedEntities` can be placed in a `PolicyRepository`. This enables these entities to be used by multiple containing entities. In Figure 11.24, both `PolicyRuleA` and `PolicyRuleB` are reusable policy

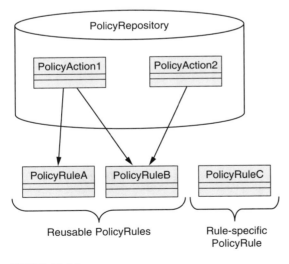

FIGURE 11.24

Conceptual difference between reusable and rule-specific policies.

rules, because they both reuse at least one reusable `PolicyRepository` entity. `PolicyRuleC` is a rule-specific policy rule because it does not use any reusable entities.

A rule-specific policy rule can be thought of as an object that has embedded in it all of the information (e.g., the `PolicyCondition` and `PolicyAction` clauses) that it needs to be used. Although this clearly makes it nonreusable, it just as clearly enables it to be accessed more efficiently (because it is in effect a single object). In contrast, a reusable policy rule requires a set of access operations (one for the policy rule itself and one for each reusable component). However, the components are all able to be used by other entities.

11.8 DEFINITION OF POLICY-BASED MANAGEMENT

PBM controls the state of the system and objects within the system using policies. Control is implemented using a management model, such as a finite-state machine. It includes installing and deleting policy rules as well as monitoring system performance to ensure that the installed policies are working correctly. PBM is concerned with the overall behavior of the system and adjusts the policies that are in effect based on how well the system is achieving its policy goals.

11.9 DEFINITION OF POLICY-BASED NETWORK MANAGEMENT

Policy-based network management is an area of network management that treats the system being managed as a policy-enabled system. As in a PBM system, policies are used to control the state of objects within a network (such as the ports on a router). This includes installing and deleting policy rules in network devices and monitoring network performance related to the installed policy. PBNM is specifically concerned with the overall behavior of the network (e.g., the end-to-end or edge-to-edge services provided by the network) and uses policy to provide consistent and predictable network services across the entire network, not just on a device-by-device basis. As such, PBNM treats the network as a provider of intelligent services and assigns these services based on the needs of clients using the network.

11.10 HIGH-LEVEL REQUIREMENTS OF A PBNM SYSTEM

IT administrators are searching for tools to better manage their service offerings. PBNM systems offer the promise of being able to better manage large and dynamic environments. The basic approaches to building such tools form the basic requirements for a PBNM system and are discussed in this section.

11.10.1 Controlling Access to Shared Resources

Data traffic continues to grow, and the number of users keeps on increasing. Furthermore, applications are also increasing in complexity, and they demand different services from the network. The issue is no longer bandwidth; rather, the real issue is which applications get priority usage of shared system resources. For example, imagine three classes of service (CoS) that govern, at a high level, which applications get preferred access to network resources. Different applications are assigned to each CoS, as shown in Figure 11.25.

Each CoS (Gold, Silver, and Bronze) has its own set of services. Some of the services represent new functionality that is only available at that (and higher) levels of service (e.g., ERP and SAP applications). Other services, such as Data and Web, are available at all levels—the difference is quality. For example, in a TCP-based environment, the lowest CoS would have the highest probability of dropping packets, which signals some types of sending applications to slow down their transmission rates; similarly, the highest CoS would have the lowest-drop probability. These drop probabilities work together to tell the router to drop traffic belonging to a lower CoS when there is congestion.

Sharing the definition of CoS and the specifications that govern router behavior (e.g., through DiffServ), enables these relationships to be more easily implemented in a consistent fashion. Abstracting the capabilities of each router enables these definitions to be built in a vendor- and technology-independent fashion. The set of model mappings that transform these vendor- and technology-independent

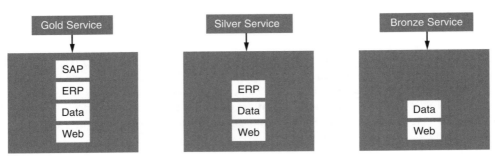

There are three differences between Gold, Silver, and Bronze Service:

> ➤ Functionality
> ➤ Quality
> ➤ Gold Services are treated better collectively than Silver Services, which are treated better collectively than Bronze Services

FIGURE 11.25

Different classes of service for prioritizing application traffic.

specifications to (ultimately) a set of device-specific configuration commands can then be done in a structured fashion using different model mappings (as will be shown later in Figure 11.30).

Another advantage in this grouping is that all of the applications in Gold service will receive "better" service than similar applications in Silver and Bronze services. "Better" takes many forms, such as more bandwidth, less jitter, and optimized costs. Each metric requires preferential access to different types of shared resources in the network. Without the ability to abstract different services into different CoSs, this becomes much more difficult to implement consistently. Thus, the requirement is for a set of abstractions, structured as a set of models, to represent the translation of business goals to device configurations.

11.10.2 Integrating the Business and Networking Worlds

One current problem with network management is that it is not linked to the business processes that run the network. For example, people should not be allowed to Telnet into a router and start changing its configuration! This violates fundamental business processes and makes it very difficult for the overall state of the network to be tracked and updated. For every configuration, regardless of how large or how small, defined processes govern how a configuration file is built, who must approve it, when it can be scheduled for installation, and what to do if something goes wrong. *Ultimately, the business and operational policies that govern the construction and deployment of configuration changes are more important than the configuration changes themselves!*

Process is everything. The network is not a "fat, dumb pipe" that is composed of individual interfaces; businesses do not operate or sell interfaces! Businesses operate and manage services according to the priority and contractual obligations that the business enters into. This mandates intelligent processes that can manage the rich functionality of your network and ensure that changes to your network devices follow approved processes.

This philosophy can be recursively applied to different types of services. Specifically, many processes are associated with the management of a service. In the DEN-ng model, there is a difference between a *customer-facing* service and a *resource-facing* service. A good example of a *customer-facing* service is an RFC 4364 (i.e., RFC 2547-bis) VPN, which is a type of virtual private network (VPN). A VPN is a private network (e.g., a network that ensures confidential communications) that is constructed within a larger public network, where "virtual" means that the private network has no physical counterpart and is in reality a virtual connection.

This service is termed a *customer-facing* service in DEN-ng because *the customer is explicitly aware of and can purchase such a service.* In contrast, a *resource-facing* service is one that the customer is *not* explicitly aware of (and hence cannot purchase), but nevertheless is required for the proper operation of the customer-facing service. Resource-facing services include protocols, such as

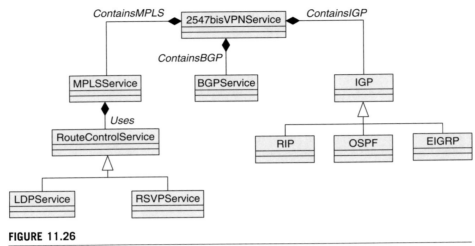

FIGURE 11.26

Different services in an RFC 4364 (RFC 2547-bis) VPN service hierarchy.

BGP or OSPF. Customers buy VPN services and are not interested in the *subservices* that are used to build up the customer-facing service. The informal model shown in Figure 11.26 reflects this.

The "simple things" that we often take for granted, such as corporate intranet connectivity using a VPN, can be quite complicated to manage. Furthermore, if business processes are used to manage complicated networking concepts, it is imperative that scalable, extensible, structured management approaches, such as PBNM, be used. The requirement—integrating the business and networking worlds—is achieved by using an information model to represent the entities to be managed and by using policy to control their management. Specifically, PBNM systems that use an information model with policy *enable the different business rules that govern how a configuration change is constructed, approved, installed, and verified to drive network and configuration management.* This enables business rules to drive service activation, making the network more responsive to business needs.

11.11 USING MODELING TO SOLVE INFORMATION OVERLOAD

Information overload comes in many forms. Two of them are the sheer increase in the number of entities to be managed, and the increase in the complexity of the solution to be managed. The solution to both of these problems is to use an information model to provide a set of abstractions to simplify the differences in the entities being managed.

11.11.1 **Managing an Increased Number of Devices**

The soaring demand for advanced IP services is leading service providers and enterprises to build IP backbones as fast as they can. Recent studies indicate that enterprise IP traffic (e.g., text, images, video, and audio) is doubling every year. In fact, at the time of this writing, more than 50,000 terabytes of IP traffic are created around the world every day, driving the demand for responsive data networks.

However, it is not just this sheer demand in moving data that is increasing the number of devices. Different data require very different types of traffic conditioning (i.e., behavior) in the network to provide appropriate quality, responsiveness, and other metrics that guarantee a good end-user experience. Figure 11.27 shows that different types of traffic require different types of conditioning. This is because they are sensitive to different characteristics in how data are transmitted.

Most companies built out separate networks to support these diverse needs. People then realized that all of the different costs in running separate networks outweighed the benefits of having separate networks. The lack of control means increased costs, because different networks require different protocols and management tools to configure devices. Reliability and availability suffered, because the overall reliability (and availability) of a system is the product of the reliability (and availability) of each of its individual components. Furthermore, it became increasingly problematic to find qualified people to run the different networks. Fundamentally, therefore, lack of control means lack of service.

Convergence is the coalescing of separate voice, data, and video networks onto a single (IP) network. Although the number of devices does not necessarily decrease, the number of management tools and protocols should decrease. This is in spite of the proliferation of different device-specific functions. For conver-

	Voice	FTP	ERP and mission critical
Bandwidth	Low to moderate	Moderate to high	Low
Random drop sensitive	Low	High	Moderate to high
Delay sensitive	High	Low	Low to moderate
Jitter sensitive	High	Low	Moderate

FIGURE 11.27

Traffic characteristics are not all the same.

gence to work, we must be able to abstract the differences among these different tools, protocols, and device functions and instead provide a unified method of provisioning and service activation. Thus, the requirement is for a *set of information models to abstract the differences in heterogeneous devices, so that their capabilities can be more easily harnessed to support different services.*

11.11.2 Managing the Proliferation of Device-Specific Functions

The combination of more users and more sophisticated applications necessitates more sophisticated handling of traffic in networks. Network vendors have responded with more features and functions, which have dramatically increased the complexity of managing and programming network devices. Device configurations used to be relatively straightforward and required hundreds of lines—now they are very complex and can be thousands of lines or much more.

From a modeling point of view, this can be characterized (and normalized) as increasing the number of capabilities that devices have. These increased capabilities are needed because of the integration of different applications and different users, each of which (in general) have different needs and therefore have spawned new services. These new network services cause a problem, because each new service has its own management approach, which usually requires new commands, new protocols, and new ways to program the service. This causes two immediate problems: (1) these new features and services must interoperate (or at the least, peacefully coexist) with existing features and services and (2) each of these new features and services are implemented in proprietary ways. Even if there is a standard that is produced to govern the service (e.g., RFC 4364, which specifies a particular type of VPN), most vendors support this new standard in either a proprietary (that is not necessarily interoperable) manner or by combining support for it with other new features.

This new service will require new management tools, which has placed a terrible burden on IT administrators who must learn each of these new tools and programming models to manage the environment. This causes the IT administrator to duplicate the actions used to configure and/or manage devices on a vendor-by-vendor basis, because these new services require new programming and management methods. Worse, when companies acquire or merge with other companies, the resulting products act differently and are often programmed differently, despite having the same vendor label. I have used networking as an exemplar—this problem exists not just for networking, but for just about anything an IT administrator may need to configure and manage.

The solution is to build a set of common information models that can represent the capabilities of different products of multiple vendors. We cannot stop vendors from implementing new functions in proprietary ways nor would we want to. We can model these new functions using a consistent representation. This enables different functions and different implementations of the same function to be categorized (i.e., placed in a class hierarchy), thereby facilitating their comparison and integration. This in turn lets us use the appropriate mechanism or feature from each device to build an end-to-end service.

For example, consider traffic flowing through two routers. One is "DiffServ-aware," which classifies traffic using different DSCPs. The other is not DiffServ-aware, and it classifies traffic using different settings of the ToS byte. These two different implementations of the same function—classification—use different mechanisms to communicate the result. End-to-end management is greatly facilitated by having a model that identifies these two different markings as two implementations of the same function. This enables a mapping to be defined between the values of the ToS byte and equivalent values in the DSCP. Once this mapping is defined, it is possible to build an end-to-end service that has common semantics supported by different mechanisms. Thus, the requirement is for a *set of device-specific functions to be modeled in a uniform manner, so that business rules can be used to define how each different device function can be used to provide the appropriate type and/or level of service.*

11.11.3 Using Models as Part of the PBNM Process

By itself, an information model is not enough to solve this problem. The information model will describe the characteristics and behavior of managed entities. However, this only defines the current state of an object. We need a finite-state machine that lets us model the system as a closed-loop system. Thus, we need classes to model the current state, classes to model the changing of the state, and classes to control when the state can be changed.

Policy is the mechanism to control when and how the state is changed. Policy will provide two essential benefits in the management of heterogeneous network devices:

1. Overall simplification of the management process through the use of a closed-loop system.
2. Automating what is currently done manually and improving consistency of configuration changes in the process.

The first benefit implies the use of a *layered* information model (i.e., a set of information models, each focused on a particular management domain, that work together to provide a single, unified, cohesive view of the managed environment). Examples of different layers are the business, administrative, system (device-independent), and other layers. This point addresses the holistic nature of management and recognizes the fact that managing a service is more than just taking fault or performance measurements.

The second benefit recognizes that to deploy a configuration change, multiple processes need to occur in a specific order. The notion of one or more *workflow processes* can be used to control the different processes of approving the configuration, installing it, and verifying that the installation was successful. This is made even more difficult by realizing that workflow processes can be

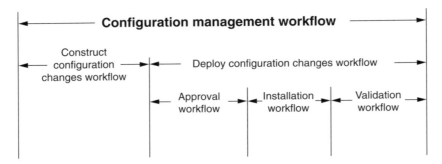

FIGURE 11.28

Workflows within workflows.

complicated. That is why two things are needed. First, a set of different models (e.g., information models, activity and sequence diagrams, and so forth) must be used to cooperatively specify what the workflow should do and how it should be managed. Second, we need the ability for workflows to contain workflows, so that different processes that have different execution patterns can have their own workflows, yet still be bound within a higher-level process (Figure 11.28).

This shows one master workflow, called *configuration management*, which has two subordinate workflows: construct configuration changes and deploy configuration changes. The former is an atomic workflow, whereas the latter is composed of three subordinate workflows. This flexibility is critical for modeling the different subprocesses involved in managing the configuration change process.

Policy controls the different management processes that are represented by workflows. The workflow encapsulates the set of managed entities that must be affected to accomplish a given task. The goal of automating configuration management cannot happen until these different subprocesses are also automated. Policy, therefore, gives us an extensible vehicle to control what happens when and how.

Thus, an information model should be used to represent not just entities, such as routers, services, and users, but also policies. If policies are an integral part of the information model, we can use them to control when and which managed entities are managed and how they are managed.

11.11.4 Sharing and Reuse of Data

Operational support systems (OSSs) are commonly built using best-of-breed products that provide solutions for different functions needed by the OSS. For example, an OSS may consist of one application for fault and performance measurement, another application for billing, and yet another application for configuration management and service activation.

Using a single common model provides two important benefits. First, it lets multiple applications share and reuse the same data. An example of this is using the output of a discovery application to feed an inventory application to dynamically catalog the devices that are currently operational. Second, it enables processes to be built to do a function once and to apply that function in different applications under different contexts. Continuing the preceding example, other applications (e.g., configuration and service activation) could also use the output of the discovery application as input for different processes. Thus, the requirement is for *a set of common information to be used to represent common functions, enabling different applications to share and reuse common information.*

11.11.5 Interfacing with Different Constituents

Most systems define a policy as a single entity; this is incorrect. For example, there are policies to represent business rules, and policies to represent configuring a feature of a device. There is little in common with these two ends of the policy continuum, because they use different grammars to express their function and because they are used by different constituencies. However, they are in reality different views of the same policy. This is shown in Figure 11.29.

Each view is optimized for a different type of user who needs and/or uses slightly different information. For example, the business user wants service level agreement (SLA) information and is not interested in the type of queuing that will be used. Conversely, the network administrator may want to develop CLI commands to program the device and may need to have a completely different representation of the policy to develop the queuing CLI commands. For now, it is sufficient to realize that this is indeed the case.

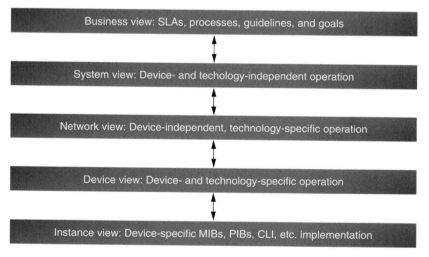

FIGURE 11.29

The policy continuum.

Thus, the requirement is for *policy to be treated as a continuum, where different policies take different forms and address the needs of different users.* Unless there is an information model that can be used to relate these different forms of policy to each other, it becomes difficult (if not impossible) to define a set of mappings that transform the data between each type of policy in the continuum. This is one of the cornerstones of the DEN-ng policy model. Specifically, it provides a layered set of policies with different levels of abstractions and model mappings to translate between them.

11.11.6 Interfacing with Devices and EMSs

Traditionally, device configurations were changed and managed using element management systems (EMSs). The conceptual model of the PBNM system shown in Figure 11.19 can either replace or augment this function.

This decision depends on how integral policy management is to your business and application. A gradual introduction of PBNM systems could be accomplished by having them control one or more aspects of device configuration management (e.g., control the configuring of DiffServ support) or perhaps define different IP address pools and enforce how IP addresses are allocated.

Although this simplifies integration (and possibly acceptance) of the new system, it does not offer the complete set of advantages that a true commitment to policy management provides. This latter puts the PBNM system in control of constructing, managing, and deploying device configurations, as well as other associated functions (e.g., user access rights, and permissions to access shared system resources). EMSs do not necessarily disappear in this approach; they are augmenting the function of "pushing the device configuration changes to the device" by wrapping that process in a higher-level workflow process that enables business policies to drive those changes. The main difference is that most EMSs do not use auditable workflows to manage the deployment of configuration changes.

Thus, a PBNM system must be able to interface with EMSs. Rather than being viewed as an alternative to an EMS, a PBNM system should instead be viewed as a higher-level process that guides the use of EMSs.

11.11.7 Interfacing with NMSs

The purpose of network management is to simplify the management and operation of large networks by maintaining network stability, tuning network performance, and troubleshooting problems that might arise. Network management also aids in strategic planning for network growth.

Network management architectures are implemented using a network management system (NMS) to manage a set of devices. Traditionally, managed devices contain software modules called agents that gather and store information about the managed device in a repository and provide this information (proactively or reactively) to the NMS. The NMS is a computer system that contains software processes that poll agents in managed devices (automatically or by user request) to check the management information that they contain. It also contains processes that react to alerts from managed devices by executing one or more actions, such as notifying the network administrator, performing event logging, shutting down a system, or attempting system repairs.

PBNM can augment NMSs by providing a framework in which to supply NMS components management information. This includes not just specific details on how a device is currently operating, but other important pieces of management information, such as when a configuration was changed, why it was changed, and who changed it. Thus, the requirement is:

> A PBNM system must be able to interface with NMSs. Rather than being viewed as an alternative to an NMS, a PBNM system should instead be viewed as a higher-level process that guides the use of NMSs and facilitates communication between the NMS and other systems in the OSS.

11.11.8 Interfacing with Other Portions of the OSS

The ITU-T's telecommunications management network (TMN) model attempted to provide a framework for telecommunications management. This framework provided for a large variety of functions that are commonly referred to as FCAPS (fault, configuration, accounting, performance, and security) management.

TMN is a collection of many standards that define three key areas of communications management:

- An architecture that views "management" as a set of layers and groups of functions. The architecture is recursive and can be used to model multiple operators who may be involved in the service delivery chain.
- A methodology for defining the management behavior of managed devices. This uses an object-oriented modeling methodology known as the "guidelines for the definition of managed objects."
- A set of protocols for management information to be passed between systems. These protocols define a standardized interface at all seven layers of the OSI model with options for wide-area and local area networking.

Theoretically, PBNM systems can, and should, interface with all of these different systems. As stated earlier, PBNM "treats the system being managed as a policy-enabled system." Thus, PBNM systems are not limited to just configuration management, but rather, are concerned with the overall behavior of the network. Managing this behavior requires PBNM systems to interface with other OSS components. Thus, a PBNM system must be able to interface with different components of the OSS. The PBNM system provides a common lingua franca for communicating between different OSS systems and enables different layers to more efficiently interface with each other.

A PBNM system spans multiple layers of the TMN model, which is in direct contrast to the association of an EMS with the element management layer (and to a lesser degree, the network element layer) of the TMN model. The relationship between a PBNM system and an NMS is less clear, because the definition of an NMS is not as straightforward. This is because most people have successfully disassociated the original meaning of an NMS, which had more to do with managing high-level features of the system, such as faults and alarms, with what they currently refer to as an NMS—a system that can perform higher-level network functions. However, PBNM systems include business functions, which are *not* included in the current (or original) definition of an NMS. Thus, PBNM systems are still fundamentally different than NMSs.

11.11.9 Communication with Policy-Unaware Elements

Many PBNM systems assume that they will use their protocols, object models, and programming methods to communicate with and configure devices that they manage. This assumes that the PBNM system is the "center of the universe." It is exactly this type of thinking that has created stovepipe applications! A common information model should instead be used to ensure that different PBNM systems can share and reuse management information from each other.

The question then is: How are policy-unaware entities controlled, and how do they communicate with and be managed by the PBNM system? This requires the use of a proxy (as was shown in Figure 11.19) or a mediation layer that performs a model mapping between the object model used in the PBNM system and the object model used in the policy-unaware entities (or their EMSs). Thus, the PBNM system must be able to interface with both policy-aware and policy-unaware entities.

11.12 POLICY USED TO EXPRESS BUSINESS REQUIREMENTS

Today, the network and the services that it provides exist as their own individual entities, divorced from the operation of the business. One goal of PBNM is to enable business requirements to drive the configuration and management of network services. Although PBNM can help express and integrate the different business, system, and implementation views of the system, the area that has been given the least attention is the link between PBNM and business requirements. This section will examine this link in more detail.

Given the policy continuum that was shown in Figure 11.29, we need a set of model mappings that will translate the purpose of each policy at its given level to a form that the policy at the next level can use. This can be better seen by revisiting the definition of policy:

> Policy is a set of rules that are used to manage and control the changing and/or maintaining of the state of one or more managed objects.

Therefore, a set of mappings is needed that define equivalent managed objects in each level. This is best explained by examining the example shown in Figure 11.30. This figure is by no means complete; its purpose is to provide a sample of how the mapping is done.

View	Sample objective	Sample objects
Business	*John gets Gold Service.*	Customer; GoldService; GoldApplications
System	*Define three Classes of Services.*	Set of customer-facing services: Gold, Silver, Bronze
Administrative	*Use DiffServ to define traffic conditioning for Gold, Silver, and Bronze; use RSVP to reserve bandwidth when required.*	Define mappings between devices that are DiffServ-aware and *not* DiffServ-aware.
Device	*Pick specific devices and software releases of their operating systems that support the above requirements.*	Define specific type of queuing objects used per device and map their functional differences.
Instance	*Write the appropriate CLI, and monitor using the appropriate MIBs.*	Define objects to represent CLI and MIBs and define mapping between them.

FIGURE 11.30

Mapping between different entities in the policy continuum.

Each view has its own particular grammar and type of objective, which means that the types of objects that are needed to support policies of one view are at a different level of abstraction than objects of a different view. What we have, therefore, is a set of two parallel mappings—one to translate between objectives and grammar, and one to translate between objects. This duality enables us to use business rules (which by definition do not use networking terms) to manage the construction and deployment of device and system configurations that by definition use very detailed networking terms. There are two fundamental principles of using business processes to drive configuration management: *individuality* and *process*.

11.12.1 Individuality

Individuality means that different types of configuration changes require different processes. For example, a huge difference exists between changing the SMTP server address of a device and changing how routes are distributed on that same device. Some of the differences include the technical complexity of each change (implying different proficiencies in the personnel who could be assigned to implement the change), different approval processes (because the *business impact* for each change is different), and different guidelines for installing the change. These differences mandate different, customized processes (i.e., workflows) for implementing these changes. The corollary—different configuration changes are not all the same—is significant and is a fundamental principle.

Because not every configuration task can be handled using the same "template," flexibility is needed to assign different processes to each task, but consistency is also needed to ensure that each task will be handled according to the proper procedure. This is the opportunity for a PBNM system.

11.12.2 Process versus Policy, or Process *and* Policy

Many people believe that process management and policy management should exist as separate management efforts and applications. One main point of this text is to define a richer, more holistic approach for PBNM systems where policy and process management can work together to better manage and control network elements and services.

Figure 11.28 showed a sample workflow for controlling different elements of configuring a change to a network device, and it is repeated for convenience here as Figure 11.31 with some embellishments.

As shown in Figure 11.31, policies can be used with processes to better control the different phases of the configuration process. Policies by themselves can define *what* to do, but not *how* to do it. Similarly, processes can define how to accomplish a particular task, but are not decision-making entities in and of themselves. This is because while policies take the form If <condition clause> is true then do <action clause> (or On <event clause> if <condition clause> is true then do <action clause> in DEN-ng), DEN-ng processes take the more restricted form On <event clause> do <action clause>. Thus, policies select which processes to use, and processes perform the requested task. Results of processes are then used to adjust which policies are currently active and enabled, forming a closed-loop management system.

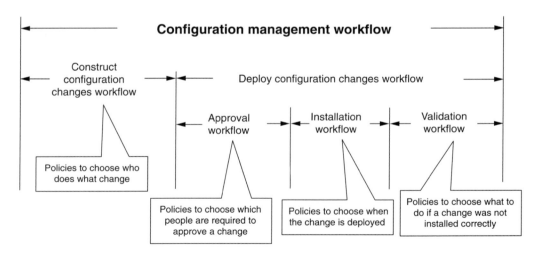

FIGURE 11.31

The interaction between policy and process management.

11.13 SUMMARY

This chapter has provided a foundation for understanding PBM. After a brief review of critical object-oriented terminology, a conceptual policy model was introduced to help define the key components of a PBNM system and enable us to focus on the specific terminology needed to better understand that system.

Policy terminology was then introduced and defined. Without a consistent set of terminology, we cannot describe (and certainly cannot build) interoperable policy systems. The terminology was compared against RFC 3198, an IETF document that defines several policy terms in the context of specific network management efforts in the IETF. This chapter's policy terminology section began with a detailed comparison of essential terms from RFC 3198 and provided enhanced definitions that made the terminology more generic, fixed definitions based on implementation experience, or disambiguated terms that were overloaded with multiple meanings. Then new terminology not covered by RFC 3198, but which is essential for understanding the design and implementation of PBNM systems, was discussed.

High-level requirements of a PBNM system were then discussed. The key requirements were:

- Use a set of layered information models to represent different objects at different abstraction layers.
- Build policy objects as part of the same information model that represents users, devices, and services.
- Form a closed-loop system by using a finite-state machine to model the allowable states and state transitions of managed objects and use policy to control when, where, why, and how managed objects change state.
- Use business rules to drive network configuration and management through the use of a common information model that includes policy as first-class objects.
- Use an information model to solve information overload of management data (both the number of devices and interfaces as well as the plethora of new, yet dissimilar, features of network devices).
- Use the notion of workflow and subworkflows to gather the different managed entities that need to be operated on to implement policy rules.
- Interface with all parts of the OSS in a uniform way using policy and a common information model.
- Ensure that PBNM systems can communicate with policy-aware and policy-unaware elements equally well.

One primary goal of PBNM systems is to enable the network to be operated as a profit center instead of as a cost center.

References and Further Reading

Requests for Comment

Many of the chapters in this book reference standardization efforts from the Internet Engineering Task Force (IETF). When this work is stable, it is published as a request for comment (RFC). The RFCs can be downloaded from IETF's web site at *www.ietf.org*. The RFCs referenced in this book are as follows:

RFC 1142—OSI IS–IS Intradomain Routing Protocol.

RFC 1155—Structure and Identification of Management Information for TCP/IP-Based Internets.

RFC 1157—Simple Network Management Protocol (SNMP).

RFC 1212—Concise MIB Definitions.

RFC 1213—Management Information Base for Network Management of TCP/IP-Based Internets: MIB-II.

RFC 1305—Network Time Protocol (Version 3) Specification, Implementation, and Analysis.

RFC 1901—Introduction to Community-Based SNMPv2.

RFC 1902—Structure of Management Information for Version 2 of the Simple Network Management Protocol (SNMPv2).

RFC 1903—Textual Conventions for Version 2 of the Simple Network Management Protocol (SNMPv2).

RFC 1904—Conformance Statements for Version 2 of the Simple Network Management Protocol (SNMPv2).

RFC 1905—Protocol Operations for Version 2 of the Simple Network Management Protocol (SNMPv2).

RFC 1906—Transport Mappings for Version 2 of the Simple Network Management Protocol (SNMPv2).

RFC 1907—Management Information Base for Version 2 of the Simple Network Management Protocol (SNMPv2).

RFC 2328—OSPF Version 2.

RFC 2474—Definition of the Differentiated Services Field (DS Field) in the IPv4 and IPv6 Headers.

RFC 2547—BGP/MPLS VPNs.

RFC 2572—Message Processing and Dispatching for the Simple Network Management Protocol (SNMP).

RFC 2573—SNMP Applications.

RFC 2574—User-Based Security Model (USM) for Version 3 of the Simple Network Management Protocol (SNMPv3).

RFC 2575—View-Based Access Control Model (VACM) for the Simple Network Management Protocol (SNMP).

RFC 2576—Coexistence between Version 1, Version 2, and Version 3 of the Internet-Standard Network Management Framework.

RFC 2578—Structure of Management Information Version 2 (SMIv2).

RFC 2579—Textual Conventions for SMIv2.

RFC 2580—Conformance Statements for SMIv2.

RFC 2679—A One-Way Delay Metric for IPPM.

RFC 2680—A One-Way Packet Loss Metric for IPPM.

RFC 2697—A Single-Rate, Three-Color Marker.

RFC 2698—A Two-Rate, Three-Color Marker.

RFC 2748—The COPS (Common Open Policy Service) Protocol.

RFC 2749—COPS usage for RSVP.

RFC 2753—A Framework for Policy-Based Admission Control.

RFC 2863—The Interfaces Group MIB.

RFC 3060—Policy Core Information Model—Version 1 Specification.

RFC 3076—Canonical XML Version 1.0.

RFC 3198—Terminology for Policy-Based Management.

RFC 3289—Management Information Base for the Differentiated Services Architecture.

RFC 3318—Framework Policy Information Base.

RFC 3357—One-Way Loss Pattern Sample Metrics.

RFC 3411—An Architecture for Describing Simple Network Management Protocol (SNMP) Management Frameworks.

RFC 3412—Message Processing and Dispatching for the Simple Network Management Protocol (SNMP).

RFC 3413—Simple Network Management Protocol (SNMP) Applications.

RFC 3414—User-Based Security Model (USM) for Version 3 of the Simple Network Management Protocol (SNMPv3).

RFC 3415—View-Based Access Control Model (VACM) for the Simple Network Management Protocol (SNMP).

RFC 3416—Version 2 of the Protocol Operations for the Simple Network Management Protocol (SNMP).

RFC 3417—Transport Mappings for the Simple Network Management Protocol (SNMP).

RFC 3418—Management Information Base (MIB) for the Simple Network Management Protocol (SNMP).

RFC 3432—Network Performance Measurement with Periodic Streams.

RFC 3460—Policy Core Information Model (PCIM) Extensions.

RFC 3470—Guidelines for the Use of Extensible Markup Language (XML) within IETF Protocols.

RFC 3512—Configuring Networks and Devices with Simple Network Management Protocol (SNMP).

RFC 3550—RTP: A Transport Protocol for Real-Time Applications.

RFC 3644—Policy Quality of Service (QoS) Information Model.

RFC 3811—Definitions of Textual Conventions (TCs) for Multiprotocol Label Switching (MPLS) Management.

RFC 3812—Multiprotocol Label-Switching (MPLS) Traffic Engineering (TE) Management Information Base (MIB).

RFC 3813—Multiprotocol Label-Switching (MPLS) Label-Switching Router (LSR) Management Information Base (MIB).

RFC 3814—Multiprotocol Label Switching (MPLS) Forwarding Equivalence Class to Next Hop Label Forwarding Entry (FEC-To-NHLFE) Management Information Base (MIB).

RFC 3815—Definitions of Managed Objects for the Multiprotocol Label Switching (MPLS), Label Distribution Protocol (LDP).

RFC 4265—Definition of Textual Conventions for Virtual Private Network (VPN) Management.

RFC 4364—BGP/MPLS IP Virtual Private Networks (VPNs).

RFC 4382—MPLS/BGP Layer 3 Virtual Private Network (VPN) Management Information Base.

RFC 4656—A One-Way Active Measurement Protocol (OWAMP).

RFC 4737—Packet Reordering Metrics.

RFC 4801—Definitions of Textual Conventions for Generalized Multiprotocol Label-Switching (GMPLS) Management.

RFC 4802—Generalized Multiprotocol Label Switching (GMPLS) Traffic Engineering Management Information Base.

RFC 4803—Generalized Multiprotocol Label-Switching (GMPLS) Label-Switching Router (LSR) Management Information Base.

Further Reading

Most of the chapters reproduced in this book also recommend further reading or reference other work. This section reproduces those references.

Chapter 1

Heiler, K. Eine Methodik zur Modellierung von Konfigurationsvorgängen für Szenarien im Net- und Systemmanagement. Dissertation. Technische Universität München, 1997.

Huntingdon-Lee, J. *Network Management Functions.* Data Pro Network Management 1510, January 1998.

Lariger, M., Loidl, B., and Nerb, M. Customer Service Management: A More Transparent View to Your Subscribed Services. *Proceedings of the Ninth IFIP/IEEE International Workshop on Distributed Systems: Operations and Management*, 1998.

McConnell, J. *Managing Client-Server Environments: Tools and Strategies for Building Solutions.* Prentice-Hall, 1996.

Terplan, K. *Communications Network Management,* 2nd Edition. Prentice-Hall, 1992.

Terplan, K. *Client/Server Management Datacom.* Buchverlag Bergheim, 1995.

Chapter 2

Abstract Syntax Notation One (ASN.1), International Standard ISO 8824.

The Basic Encoding Rules for ASN.1, International Standard ISO 8825.

Harold, E. R., and Means, S. *XML in a Nutshell.* O'Reilly, 2002.

Henning, M., and Vinoski, S. *Advanced CORBA Programming with C^{++}.* Addison-Wesley, 1999.

Hittersdorf, M. *CORBA/IIOP Clearly Explained.* AP Professional, 2000.

Nadeau, T. *MPLS Network Management: MIBs, Tools, and Techniques.* Morgan Kaufmann, 2003.

Mauro, D., and Schmidt, K. J. *Essential SNMP.* O'Reilly, 2001.

Perkins, D., and McGinnis, E. Understanding SNMP MIBs. Prentice-Hall, 1996.

Chapter 3

Abstract Syntax Notation One (ASN.1), "Constraint Specification," ITU-T Recommendation X.682 (1997) and ISO/IEC 8824-3, 1998.

Abstract Syntax Notation One (ASN.1), "Information Object Specification," ITU-T Recommendation X.681 (1997) and ISO/IEC 8824-2, 1998.

Abstract Syntax Notation One (ASN.1), "Parameterization of ASN.1 Specifications," ITU-T Recommendation X.683 (1997) and ISO/IEC 8824-4, 1998.

Abstract Syntax Notation One (ASN.1), "Specification of Basic Notation," ITU-T Recommendation X.680 (1997) and ISO/IEC 8824-1, 1998.

Downes, K., Ford, M., Lew H. K., Spanier, S., and Stevenson T. *Internetworking Technologies Handbook,* 2nd Edition. Macmillan Technical Publishing, 1998.

Stallings, W. *SNMP, SNMPv2, SNMPv3, and RMON 1 and 2,* Third Edition. Addison-Wesley Longman, 1998.

Chapter 4

Case, J. D., Fedor, M., Schoffstall, M. L., and Davin, C. Simple Network Management Protocol (SNMP), STD 0015, May 1990.

Perkins, D., McGinnis, E. *Understanding SNMP MIBs.* Prentice-Hall, 1996.

Stallings, W. *SNMP, SNMPv2, SNMPv3, and RMON 1 and 2,* Fourth Edition. Addison-Wesley, 1999.

Chapter 5

Hill, J. Assessing the Accuracy of Active Probes for Determining Network Delay, Jitter, and Loss. M.Sc. thesis, The University of Edinburgh, 2002.

Lima, S. R., Carvalho, P. M., and Freitas, V. L. Measuring QoS in Class-Based IP Networks Using Multipurpose Colored Probing Patterns. *Proceedings of SPIE,* vol. 5598:171–182, September 2004.

Tariq, M., Mukarram, B., et al. Poisson versus Periodic Path Probing (or, Does PASTA Matter?). *Proceedings of the Internet Measurement Conference*, October 2005, pp. 119–124.

Wolff, Ronald W. Poisson Arrivals See Time Averages. *Operations Research* 30(2), 1982.

Chapter 6

Davie, B. S., and Rekhter, Y. *MPLS: Technology and Applications.* Morgan Kaufmann, 2000.

Gray, E. W. *MPLS: Implementing the Technology.* Addison-Wesley Professional, 2001.

Chapter 7

Bray, T., Paoli, J., Sperberg-McQueen, C. M., and Maler, E. *Extensible Markup Language (XML) 1.0: W3C Recommendation*, Second Edition, 2000.

Chapter 8

Aidarus, S., and Plevyak, T. (eds.), *Telecommunications Network Management into the 21st Century.* IEEE Press, 1994.

American National Standards Institute. Z136.2, Safe Use of Optical Fiber Communication Systems Utilizing Laser Diodes and LED Sources, 1988.

ATM Forum. Private Network–Network Interface Specification, Version 1.0, 1996.

Awduche, D., and Rekhter, Y. Multiprotocol Lambda Switching: Combining MPLS Traffic Engineering Control with Optical Cross-Connects. *IEEE Communication Magazine* 39(4):111–116, 2001.

Black, U. *Network Management Standards.* McGraw-Hill, 1995.

Cidon, I., Gopal, I. S., and Segall, A. Connection Establishment in High-Speed Networks. *IEEE/ACM Transactions on Networking*, 1(4):469–482, 1993.

Epworth, R. E. Optical Transmission System. U.S. Patent 5463487, 1995.

Gruber, J., and Ramaswami, R. Towards Agile All-Optical Networks. *Lightwave*, December 2000.

Heismann, E., Fatehi, M. T., Korotky, S. K., and Veselka, J. J. Signal Tracking and Performance Monitoring in Multi-Wavelength Optical Networks. *Proceedings of European Conference on Optical Communication*, pp. 3.47–3.50, 1996.

Hill, G. R., et al. A Transport Network Layer Based on Optical Network Elements. *IEEE/OSA Journal on Lightwave Technology*, 11:667–679, 1993.

Hamazumi, Y., and Koga, M. Transmission Capacity of Optical Path Overhead Transfer Scheme Using Pilot Tone for Optical Path Networks. *IEEE/OSA Journal on Lightwave Technology*, 15(12):2197–2205, 1997.

International Electrotechnical Commission. 60825-1—Safety of Laser Products, Part 1: Equipment Classification, Requirements and User's Guide, 1993.

International Electrotechnical Commission. 60825-2—Safety of Laser Products, Part 2: Safety of Optical Fiber Communication Systems, 2000.

ITU-T SG15/WP 4. Rec. G.681: Functional Characteristics of Interoffice and Long-Haul Line Systems Using Optical Amplifiers, Including Optical Multiplexing, 1996.

ITU-T. Rec. G.664: Optical Safety Procedures and Requirements for Optical Transport Systems, 1999.

Maeda, M. Management and Control of Optical Networks. *IEEE Journal of Selected Areas in Communications*, 16(6):1008–1023, 1998.

McGuire, A. Management of Optical Transport Networks. *IEE Electronics and Communication Engineering Journal*, 11(3):155–163, 1999.

Ramaswami, R., and Segall, A. Distributed Network Control for Optical Networks. *IEEE/ACM Transactions on Networking*, December 1997.

Subramanian, M. *Network Management: Principles and Practice*. Addison-Wesley, 2000.

Udupa, D. K. *TMN Telecommunications Management Network*. McGraw-Hill, 1999.

U.S. Food and Drug Administration, Department of Radiological Health. Requirements of 21 CFR, Chapter J for Class I Laser Products, January 1986.

Wei, Y., et al. Connection Management for Multiwavelength Optical Networking. *IEEE Journal of Selected Areas in Communications*, 16(6):1097–1108.

Wilson, B. J., et al. Multiwavelength Optical Networking Management and Control. *IEEE/OSA Journal on Lightwave Technology*, 18(12):2038–2057, 2000.

Chapter 9

Farrel, A. *The Internet and Its Protocols: A Comparative Approach*. Morgan Kaufmann, 2004.

Harold, E. R., and Means, W. S. *XML in a Nutshell*. O'Reilly, 2002.

Hittersdorf, M. *CORBA/IIOP Clearly Explained*. AP Professional, 2000.

Mauro, D. R., and Schmidt, K. J. *Essential SNMP*. O'Reilly, 2001.

Nadeau, T. *MPLS Network Management: MIBs Tools and Techniques*. Morgan Kaufmann, 2003.

Perkins, D., and McGinnis, E. *Understanding SNMP MIBs*. Prentice-Hall, 1996.

Chapter 10

Alhir, S. *UML in a Nutshell—A Desktop Quick Reference*. O'Reilly, 1998.

Faurer, C., Fleck, J., Raymer, D., Reilly, J., Smith, A., and Strassner, J. NGOSS: Reducing the Interoperability Tax. TMW University Presentation, October 2002.

ISO. RM-ODP, Part 1: Overview and Rationale, ISO/IEC 10746-1:1998(E).

Jude, M. Policy-Based Management: Beyond the Hype. *Business Communications Review* March:52–56, 2001.

Low-Latency Queuing Combines Strict Priority Queuing with Class-Based Weighted Fair Queuing, article available at: *http://www.cisco.com/en/US/products/sw/iosswrel/ps1830/products_feature_guide09186a0080087b13.html*.

Rumbaugh, J., Jacobson, I., and Booch, G. *The Unified Modeling Language Reference Manual*. Addison-Wesley, 1999.

Strassner, J. *Directory Enabled Networks*, chapter 10. Macmillan Technical Publishing, 1999.

Strassner, J. A New Paradigm for Network Management: Business-Driven Network Management. Presented at the SSGRR Summer Conference, L'Aquila, Italy, July 2002.

Strassner, J. NGOSS Technology Overview. TMW Asia-Pacific Conference, August 2002.

TeleManagement Forum. GB921: eTOM—the Business Process Framework, version 2.6, March 2002 (TMF member document).

TeleManagement Forum. GB922: Shared Information/Data (SID) Model—Concepts, Principles, and Business Entities and Model Addenda, version 1.5, May 2002 (TMF member document).

TeleManagement Forum. GB922: Common Business Entity Definitions Addenda 1P, May 2002 (TMF member document).

TeleManagement Forum. TMF 053: The NGOSS™ Technology Neutral Architecture Specification, Annex C: Behavior and Control Specification, version 0.4, November 2002.

TeleManagement Forum, TMF 053: The NGOSS™ Technology Neutral Architecture Specification, version 3.0, April 2003.

TeleManagement Forum. TMF 053: The NGOSS™ Technology Neutral Architecture Specification, Annex P: Policy Specification, version 0.3 (work in progress).

UML 1.4 specification, available at: *http://www.rational.com/uml/resources/documentation/*.

Chapter 11

Baumer, D., Riehle, D., Siberski, W., Wulf, M. The Role Object Pattern. Available at: *http://www.riehle.org/papers/1997/plop-1997-roleobject.html*.

Booch, G. *Object-Oriented Analysis and Design with Applications*. Addison-Wesley, 1994.

Damianou, N., Dulay, N., Lupu, E., and Sloman, M. Ponder: A Language for Specifying Security and Management Policies for Distributed Systems—The Language Specification, version 2.3, October 2000.

Fowler, M. Role Patterns. *Proceedings from PLoP*, 1997.

International Standard 9594-1, ITU-T Recommendation X.500, Information Technology—Open Systems Interconnection—The Directory: Overview of Concepts, Models and Services.

ITU-T, *Principles for a Telecommunications Management Network*, Recommendation M.3010, May 1996.

Larman, C., *Applying UML and Patterns: An Introduction to Object-Oriented Analysis and Design*, Prentice-Hall, 1998.

LeRoux, J-L, et al. Evaluation of Existing GMPLS Protocols Against Multilayer and Multiregion Networks (MLN/MRN), 2008.

OMG. Unified Modeling Language Specification, version 1.4, September 2001.

Strassner, J. *Directory-Enabled Networks*. Macmillan Technical Publishing, 1999.

RFC 1633—Integrated Services in the Internet Architecture: An Overview, R. Braden, D. Clark, and S. Shenker, IETF, 1994.

RFC 1990—The PPP Multilink Protocol (MP), K. Sklower et al., IETF, 1996.

RFC 2098—Toshiba's Router Architecture Extensions for ATM: Overview, Y. Katsube et al., IETF, 1998.

RFC 2205—Resource ReSerVation Protocol (RSVP)—Version 1: Functional Specification, R. Braden et al., IETF, 1997.

RFC 2207—RSVP Extensions for IPSEC Data Flows, L. Berger and T. O'Malley, IETF, 1997.

RFC 2210—The Use of RSVP with IETF Integrated Services, J. Wroclawski, IETF, 1997.

RFC 2309—Recommendations on Queue Management and Congestion Avoidance in the Internet, R. Braden et al., IETF, 1998.

RFC 2328—OSPF Version 2, J. Moy, IETF, 1998.

RFC 2474—Definition of the Differentiated Services Field (DS Field) in the IPv4 and IPv6 Headers, K. Nichols et al., IETF, 1998.

RFC 2475—An Architecture for Differentiated Services, S. Blake et al., IETF, 1998.

RFC 2597—Assured Forwarding PHB Group, J. Heinanen et al., IETF, 1999.

RFC 2702—Requirements for Traffic Engineering over MPLS, D. Awduche et al., IETF, 1999.

RFC 2961—RSVP Refresh Overhead Reduction Extensions, L. Berger et al., IETF, 2001.

RFC 2998—A Framework for Integrated Services Operation over Diffserv Networks, Y. Bernet et al., IETF, 2000.

RFC 3031—Multiprotocol Label-Switching Architecture, E. Rosen et al., IETF, 2001.

RFC 3032—MPLS Label Stack Encoding, E. Rosen et al., IETF, 2001.

RFC 3175—Aggregation of RSVP for IPv4 and IPv6 Reservations, F. Baker et al., IETF, 2001.

RFC 3209—RSVP-TE: Extensions to RSVP for LSP Tunnels, D. Awduche et al., IETF, 2001.

RFC 3246—An Expedited Forwarding PHB (Per-Hop Behavior), B. Davie et al., IETF, 2002.

RFC 3270—Multi-Protocol Label-Switching (MPLS) Support of Differentiated Services, F. Le Faucheur et al., IETF, 2002.

RFC 3945—Generalized Multi-Protocol Label Switching (GMPLS) Architecture, E. Mannie et al., IETF, 2004.

RFC 4201—Link Bundling in MPLS Traffic Engineering (TE), K. Kompella, Y. Rekhter, and L. Berger, IETF, 2005.

RFC 4202—Routing Extensions in Support of Generalized Multi-Protocol Label Switching (GMPLS), K. Kompella and Y. Rekhter, IETF, 2005.

RFC 4364—BGP/MPLS IP Virtual Private Networks (VPNs), E. Rosen and Y. Rekhter, IETF, 2006.

RFC 4847—Framework and Requirements for Layer 1 Virtual Private Networks, T. Takeda et al., IETF, 2007.

RFC 5036—LDP Specification, L. Andersson et al., IETF, 2007.

RFC 5212—Requirements for GMPLS-Based Multi-Region and Multi-Layer Networks (MRN/MLN), K. Shiomoto et al., IETF, 2008.

TeleManagement Forum, SID Working Group. Mining Information from the DMTF CIM into the TMF SID, July 2002.

TeleManagement Forum. Shared Information/Data Model, Addendum 1P: Common Business Entity Definitions—Party, version 3.0, June 2003.

TeleManagement Forum. Shared Information/Data (SID) Model—Common Business Entity Definitions-Policy-Addenda 1-Pol, July 2003.

Index

Note: Page numbers followed by an italic *f* denote figures; those followed by *t* denote tables.